DEVELOPING A
SUCCESSFUL FOOTBALL PROGRAM
From A to Z and X's to O's

Mike Aruanno

©2003 Coaches Choice. All rights reserved. Printed in the United States.

No part of this book may be reproduced, stored in a retrieval system, or transmitted, in any form or by any means, electronic, mechanical, photocopying, recording, or otherwise, without the prior permission of Coaches Choice.

ISBN: 1-58518-852-2
Library of Congress Control Number: 2003102650
Book layout: Deborah Oldenburg
Cover design: Kerry Hartjen
Front cover photo: Tom Hauck/Allsport

Coaches Choice
P.O. Box 1828
Monterey, CA 93942
www.coacheschoice.com

DEDICATION

I dedicate this book to my family—my wife, Sue, my daughter, Shari, and my son, Mike, Jr. They have always given me their support.

My wife, Sue, has made most of this possible. She understands the importance of football and coaching in my life. She has always made every sacrifice in order for me to do the things that were important to me.

My son, Mike, whom I coached and mentored as a boy, is growing into a man. He was an assistant coach for me this past season, and I couldn't be prouder. It is another opportunity to share something we care about together.

My daughter, Shari, is serving our country in the Navy. Shari and her husband, Kevin, have recently given birth to Taylor, my first grandchild.

ACKNOWLEDGMENTS

The first person I must acknowledge is Tom Brown, the head coach at Washington Twp High School in Sewell, NJ, and his staff. Tom, Mark Wechter, and Gerry Taraschi were extremely helpful to me. These gentlemen opened their doors to a total stranger and opened a new world of football to me.

I was coaching youth football at the 13- to 14-year-old level in Washington Twp, NJ. I approached Tom Brown for some help. I thought it would be good way to draw a correlation between the high school and youth programs. He agreed and he made himself and his staff available to me at any time. I know that Tom could sense my enthusiasm for the game. Not only did he supply me with a wealth of information, he offered me a coaching opportunity at the high school level, knowing that I was taking the position to just be around the organization and learn all that I could.

After that season I made coaching football one of my life's priorities. I needed to know everything there was to know. My thirst for knowledge and my love of the game has never diminished.

I want to do what Tom Brown and his staff did for me. I want to share my knowledge of the game with anyone who it may help. To me, any coach that cares enough to seek help deserves all the help he can get. I will continue to seek the people and things that will help me learn more about coaching football.

You will see materials and influences of Tom and his staff throughout this book.

PREFACE

I truly believe that coaches are teachers first. We have a responsibility to not only teach the game of football, but also to develop quality young men. We are role models to the youth in our communities and should always conduct ourselves with that in mind.

We have an opportunity to teach children lessons that will help them the rest of their lives. Football can be a microcosm of society. Life can be very competitive and people sometimes need to pull together as a team to get things accomplished. We should be teaching them that "they are a part of something bigger than themselves." Not everyone is going to be a star, not everyone is going to go as far as they would like, but if they focus on a goal and work hard they will likely achieve great things.

Be demanding. Demand that they conduct themselves in a classy manner. Demand their best. Let them know that you won't settle for anything less than 100% effort and never give them anything less than 100% of your effort.

"If you were to ask me what I believe to be the most important element in my coaching, I would tell you it is 'love'. It is the 'love of the sport' that drives me, and it is the 'love of the kids' that fulfills me."

-Mike Aruanno

"All you need is love."

-The Beatles

CONTENTS

Dedication 3

Acknowledgments 4

Preface 5

Introduction 8

Chapter 1: Coaching 11

    The Five Aspects of Coaching   The New Coach

    Building a Coaching Staff

Chapter 2: Offense 20

    Offensive Glossary   Cadence

    Numbering Systems   Offensive Formations

    Line Splits   Motion

    Huddle Procedure

Chapter 3: Player Fundamentals—Offense 31

    Quarterbacks   Receiver Drills

    Quarterback Warm-Up Drills   Offensive Linemen

    Running Backs   Blocking Terminology and Techniques

    Running Back Drills   Linemen Drills

    Wide Receivers

Chapter 4: The Offensive Playbook 106

    Running Plays   Passing Plays

Chapter 5: Defense 130

    Gaps   Base Coverage Packages

    Defensive Techniques   Tackling

    Defensive Formations   Tackling Drills

Chapter 6: Player Fundamentals—Defense 159

    Defensive Line   Linebacker Drills

    Defensive Line Drills   Defensive Backs

    Linebackers   Defensive Back Drills

Chapter 7: The Defensive Playbook 228
      4-4 Defense   50 Defense
      4-5 Run Stopper Defense

Chapter 8: Special Teams 265
      Punting Team   Kickoffs
      Field Goals and Extra Point Kicks

Chapter 9: Practice 295
      Practice Schedule Overview   Positional Warm-Up Routines
      Practice Outline   Team Conditioning
      Parents Meeting   Practice Plan

Chapter 10: Game Preparation 312
      Scouting   Depth Charts
      Game Plan   Game Day
      Play Script/Chart

Chapter 11: Scouting Report 321

About the Author 336

INTRODUCTION

This coach's manual was originally written to aid the coaches of a youth football program that was growing by leaps and bounds. In a two-year span they had added six teams and finding good coaches was a huge challenge. One of the staffs that they had prior to this expansion was very inexperienced. During a discussion with one of those coaches I asked him if they would like some assistance. He welcomed it with open arms. Since I would be on the field with my team at the same time they would, I decided to write this manual as an outline of the fundamentals. Along with this manual I did a two-part coaching clinic for the new coaches who were coming into the program and anyone else who was interested.

Some interesting events took place during that time that inspired me to complete this manual and make it available to everyone. The first clinic I did was a three-and-a-half hour lecture in my basement. In attendance was a coach with 13 very successful years in the program. The coach who had asked me for help was the only coach from his staff that attended and there were a handful of new coaches who were coming aboard. I made it very clear that I was not telling them the only way to do things; these were simply the ways that had afforded me my success. Ego is one of the biggest obstacles to overcome when you are showing coaches a way of doing things. A lot of people believe they already know everything they need to know. Good coaches always want to know more.

It took some arm-twisting to convince one of the new coaches to attend. He had two years experience coaching 7- and 8-year-old boys. He said that he didn't need to come because he already had coaching experience and he expected to have a man on his staff with professional experience. I told him the story of how I coached with a man that played in the NFL for seven years; he was perhaps the worst head coach I had ever worked with. I convinced him

to come and listen. Not only did he attend, but he also, much to my surprise, began to take notes about 45 minutes into the clinic. Soon he was asking questions and participating intently. After the clinic was complete he asked me if I would go over his offense with him when he was finished with it. This coach has been an integral part of the program ever since. He continued to attend the clinics and apply some of the things he learned.

Perhaps the most inspiring event involved the veteran coach who was also the president of the organization. After attending the clinics he decided to use my manual as an outline for the structure of his practices. Keep in mind, this man had already enjoyed significant success in a program that I had only been a part of for two years. He saw things that he thought would improve his team and he took advantage of them. He didn't allow his ego to get in the way of his growth as a coach. He also displayed leadership by his actions.

The feedback that I was getting from the original version of this manual was tremendous. It inspired me to want to learn more. In these last two years I have spent an enormous amount of time trying to perfect my coaching ability. I will never stop trying to learn more. Everything I know, I have learned from someone else. I will continue to seek out those individuals who can help me. I am humbled by the amount of knowledge that is out there at everyone's disposal.

Sometimes coaches forget to do the little things that count. Hopefully, this manual will be a refresher and a reminder to pay attention to the basics. It has certainly highlighted areas that I had begun to gloss over. Everything begins with the fundamentals, regardless of the level you are coaching. You could win championships with only five plays in your entire offense. If your players are proficient in their fundamentals and your execution is flawless, I am confident that you will be successful.

If there is a secret to coaching it has to be organization. The most successful coaches I've ever met had two things in common: They were passionate about their sport, and they were extremely organized. Obviously, there are many other attributes that go into quality coaching, but they all come together when you are focused and prepared.

This manual will give you the basic information to coach at any level. It is by no means the only way to do things, nor is it necessarily the right way for everyone. It is intended as a guide to get you started. Remember, this manual only covers the basics. Much more exists that a coach will need to learn. If you truly want to coach, you should do everything you can to gain more knowledge.

> *"They call it coaching but it is teaching. You do not just tell them … You show them the reasons."*
>
> *-Vince Lombardi*

> *"Confidence comes from planning and practicing well. You get ready during the week and the confidence will be there on Sunday. This confidence is a difficult thing to explain. But you do get it and the team gets it if you have prepared properly."*
>
> *-Vince Lombardi*

How to Tell a Winner from a Loser

The following was passed on to me from Tom Brown, Washington Twp High School, Sewell, NJ. I pass it along to you, hoping you are a winner.

A WINNER credits his winning to "good luck" even though it wasn't–a LOSER blames his "bad luck" even though it wasn't.

A WINNER works harder than a LOSER and he has more time–a LOSER is "too busy."

A WINNER says, "Let's find out"–a LOSER says, "Nobody knows."

When a WINNER makes an error he says, "I was wrong"–when a LOSER makes an error he says, "It wasn't my fault."

A WINNER makes commitments–a LOSER makes excuses.

A WINNER knows what to fight for and what to compromise on–a LOSER compromises on what he shouldn't and fights for what is not worthwhile.

A WINNER says, "I'm not as good as I ought to be"–a LOSER says, "I'm not as bad as a lot of other guys."

A WINNER listens–a LOSER just waits until it's time to talk.

A WINNER would rather be admired than liked, although he would prefer both; a LOSER would rather be liked than admired, and is even willing to pay the price of contempt for it.

A WINNER respects those who are superior to him, and tries to learn from them; a LOSER resents those who are superior to him and tries to find chinks in their armor.

A WINNER feels responsible for more than his job–a LOSER says, "I only work here."

A WINNER says, "There ought to be a better way"–a LOSER says, "That's the way it's always been done."

-Author Unknown

CHAPTER 1

Coaching

The Five Aspects of Coaching

What does it take to be a good football coach? Obviously, this is an ambiguous question. To bring some clarity to this question this chapter presents the 'Five Aspects of Coaching'. These five categories outline what it takes to be a good coach. When you are building a coaching staff, these five categories should be used as a barometer for choosing coaches. Creating a quality staff is one of the most important parts of your program. If you and your staff are proficient in five these areas, you are sure to be successful.

All staffs start with the head coach. This person does not necessarily have to possess all of the skills mentioned. In fact, few head coaches are extremely strong in all five categories. However, the most important quality of a head coach is having strong organizational skills. He needs to be the leader of the staff, the one who puts it all together. An ability to see the shortcomings of others would certainly be a good quality. Head coaches need to find the right people to create a well-rounded staff.

The five aspects of coaching are just an outline of the skills required to be a successful coach. However, one other trait is necessary to truly become a great coach—a love for the game. Football is a way of life to great coaches. It is an institution that is looked at with dignity and respect. Great coaches have a value system that cannot be compromised. They do things the right way, not the easy way. They keep in perspective the fact that developing quality young men is as important as winning football games.

Knowledge

Knowledge will play a part in all aspects of football. The one quality that every coach must possess is a thorough knowledge of everything they are responsible for on the coaching staff. Knowledge is something that anyone can acquire. Therefore, a prospective coach should not be judged by his present level of knowledge, rather his desire to gain more knowledge.

It will take a few different coaches to cover all the knowledge needed to teach your team the fundamentals of the game. Even if a coach has great knowledge about different aspects of the game, he can only coach one part of your team. For instance, your backs coach and your line coach certainly have to be different people who are proficient in the area they are coaching.

It would also be advantageous to be able to break out your receivers and your quarterbacks. To do this you would need four coaches, and the linemen would need at least two coaches depending on the size of your team. On the other hand, a running back coach who also has quarterback expertise may be able to combine these two areas if needed. Keep in mind that every player needs to learn how to block and tackle. With this said, every offensive coach must know how to properly teach blocking no matter what position he coaches, and every defensive coach must be able to teach tackling. Like the saying goes, *'Football comes down to two things–blocking and tackling'*. If you out block and out tackle your opponent, you will surely come out victorious.

All staffs should have an offensive coordinator and a defensive coordinator. They are usually the coaches who call the plays during games. If you run a particular offense, your offensive coordinator needs to become an expert on that offense; he needs to know *every* nuance. That is the easy part. A great offensive coordinator should understand every potential defense you will face. The best offensive coordinators are the ones who can expose the weaknesses of a defense. They need to have a thorough knowledge of the inner workings of the opponent's defense to make the correct game-day calls. The same must be said for the defensive coordinator; to be truly successful he needs to have a great understanding of how specific offenses work.

Positional coaches need to gain technical knowledge about the fundamental skills needed to perform the duties required by the position they teach. This book will present ways to teach those skills. By no means will this be the only way; it happens to be the way I teach those positions. It will benefit coaches to learn different ways to teach these skills. Some ways work better with different players. Some coaches are more comfortable with a different style.

Many different ways exist to gain knowledge. Reading instructional books like this one or watching instructional videos will furnish technical knowledge.

Periodicals are available that are published specifically for football coaches. The Internet is also a good resource for knowledge.

Some of the best resources, however, are other coaches. Obviously, learning from great coaches is wise, but there is usually something to be learned from everybody. These other coaches may be on your staff or even your opponents'. Joining a coaching association can be beneficial if one is available. If one is not available, perhaps one could be started. Good judgment needs to be used when gleaning knowledge from other coaches. Not every coach does things the right way. You should learn from their shortcomings as well as their strengths. This is especially true when it comes to the more abstract aspects of coaching such as the manner in which you deal with your players. Learn from yourself as well. Never repeat your mistakes.

Another way of gaining knowledge is by attending coaching clinics. You should make an effort to attend as many clinics as possible. Be sure to take notes or bring a micro recorder with you so you don't forget the things you learn. This is also a great opportunity to meet other coaches who could potentially become a source of knowledge in the future. You will usually pick up different perspectives at these clinics that can expand your horizon.

If you are a youth football coach, spend time observing some high school practices. If you are a high school coach, spend time at some college practices. You will pick up some organizational skills and even some new drills to freshen up your practices.

Remember, you can't learn too much about anything. You should use every resource that is available to you, especially if you intend to change the way you teach something to your players. Make sure you completely understand the fundamentals of something before you try applying it to your team. Otherwise, instead of improving their skills, they may be learning an incorrect technique.

Knowledge is one of the most important of the five aspects of coaching. It is required in order to excel in the other four areas. The most important type of knowledge to gain is a complete understanding of the fundamentals. The three most important things in football are execution, execution, and execution. Execution could be defined as perfect fundamentals in action.

Organization

Knowledge without organization is significantly less effective, and organization without knowledge is futile. Everything you do on a football field should be thought out thoroughly beforehand. You can never be too organized.

Be extremely detail-oriented in everything from the way your team enters the field to the way they conduct themselves on the field. The way a team presents itself displays something about their character. And that presentation should be consistent. If your team is supposed to walk onto the field a certain way, be sure everyone walks that way every time. If players on the sideline are supposed to keep their helmets on, make sure every player keeps his helmet on *all the time*. Make your rules and be consistent with them.

Organization begins before the first practice of the year. You should make a practice plan for the entire preseason before the year begins. Detail when everything will be introduced to the team. If you plan on having 20 plays in by your first game, then you need a reasonable time frame set up to not only teach those plays but also perfect them. As you will hear again, don't run anything in a game that you haven't perfected in practice. Pre-plan when you will introduce your defense your special teams and so on.

If you have 18 practice days until your first game, then you should outline all 18 practices before the season begins. You can always adjust what you teach in practice but having a plan will help you accomplish your goals and make it less likely for you to overlook something. Therefore, everything about a practice should be organized right down to the minute. Make sure every coach is given a detailed agenda of every practice. Make every effort to stick with your plan without improvising too much. The more you find yourself having to improvise, the less organized you are.

Many coaches make the mistake of walking into practice without a written plan and therefore spend most of their practices scrimmaging. While you're scrimmaging it's typical to stop a play in order to show a player his mistake. During that time, most of the team ends up standing around doing nothing. If you calculate how often that happens during a scrimmage, you end up with a good chunk of time spent standing around that could have been used doing drills to hone fundamental skills. This is not to say that scrimmaging doesn't have its place, it just shouldn't be the most significant part of your practice regimen. We will get into great detail on organizing your practices later in this book.

You cannot hone the skills of a player without spending significant time drilling those skills. Time your drills and keep them moving. If you keep them short you will be able to perform many different drills. By keeping them short and varying them, practice will be more fun for the players and will move along quickly. Merely running a drill will not improve the skill of your player. Know the 'coaching point' to every drill and be sure they are being done correctly. This is where the little details really count. As someone once said, "Practice don't make perfect, perfect practice makes perfect!"

Be sure to set aside time in practice for every aspect of the game. Make sure there is time in every practice to work on offense, defense and the often-overlooked special teams. Special teams become more important, the higher the level you go. However, they can even be extremely important at the youth level where a kicked extra point is worth two points instead of one. Working on extra point attempts should be a significant part of a youth practice. It takes a team effort to kick an extra point. Don't neglect any part of your game. Passing should be perfected along with pass coverage. Punt coverage is equally as important as punt returning.

This brings up another sometimes-overlooked area. Most teams perform running repetitions during the course of their practice. The problem is that a lot of coaches don't take the time to teach their players how to run. Running is a skill that can easily be improved. Like any other drill, be sure your players are performing the fundamentals of their running drills correctly.

Game day organizational skills are just as important as planning efficient practices. Having a plan for every situation is the key. No situation should occur on the field that you haven't already considered an option for. This goes for strategic game situations as well as player personnel moves. You should have a situation chart that you can refer to at any time in the game. You should also have a depth chart that covers every position on the field. Every player should be aware of where they fall on the depth chart since injuries can happen any time. A lot of these issues will be dealt with in the Strategy aspect of this section.

Teaching

Transferring your knowledge to your players may sound fairly easy, but not every knowledgeable person has the ability to teach. Gaining knowledge is the easy part; effectively applying this knowledge is teaching. I have seen former professional football players who didn't have the ability to teach football to kids. On the other hand, brilliant teachers exist who have never played a down of high school football. Anyone can learn something, not everyone can teach it.

The person who has knowledge but lacks great teaching skills can still be an asset to your staff. Pair this 'knowledgeable' coach with a coach who is a great communicator, yet lacks his knowledge, and you will have a good coaching combination. However, the great teacher with less knowledge has much more potential to become a great coach because he can always gain the knowledge if he applies himself. The 'teacher' is one of the greatest assets to your staff. If your players don't learn the proper skills you will never succeed.

To be a good teacher you must demonstrate many qualities. They include the following:

- You will need to have good communication skills.
- Your players need to be able to clearly understand what you ask of them.
- You will need to gain the players respect so they will be more receptive of you.
- You must exude confidence in yourself and your system.
- You should have good organizational skills.
- Be patient.

Keeping things moving quickly and changing up your drills gives you the variety needed to make learning fun for your players and provides the pace to keep their attention. This is definitely a method of teaching that has been proven to be successful over the years. This theory of teaching works in every sport, in every classroom, and in every business.

Explain why you want your players to do something a certain way. I have watched coaches give instructions with no rhyme or reason and it is frustrating for the players and the coach. If you take the time to understand why you do something a certain way, you will be less likely to teach it incorrectly. You cannot give your players too much information when you are teaching them something.

Motivation

Good motivators are motivated themselves. Enthusiasm is contagious! Make sure there is a person on your staff who has the innate ability to 'fire-up' your team. This should be an intense person with a positive outlook. This is where positive reinforcement is so important. Take every opportunity to let a player know how well he did something. On game day encourage your team to point out the good things their teammates do during the game. Whether it is a good block, tackle, run or throw, they should let him know they appreciate his effort. A high five, chest bump or even a slap on the butt will go a long way to keep the emotional level high during a game. Positive reinforcement is always one of the best motivators, whether it comes from the coach or a teammate. This will also promote teamwork.

A good motivator can elevate the level of play. He can get the most out of a player, hence the most out of the team. I have seen average teams play great football. Usually this is attributed to the intensity that they play with throughout the entire game. Intensity is a byproduct of motivation.

Inspirational quotes are a great source of motivation. Get a book of motivational quotes and have a 'quote of the day' for your team. In the front of this book a page is dedicated to defining the difference between a winner and a loser. It was given to me by a man I considered my mentor, so I pass it along to other coaches whenever I can. I recently had a coach tell me that his team used those sayings for an entire season. Coaches and players alike would recognize certain behaviors and evaluate whether it was a winner or a loser who would display such behavior. If they felt it was a loser type behavior they would discuss how the winner would have conducted himself.

Emotion is a great motivator. Don't be afraid to show your emotions. Let your players know how much you care about them. Dick Vermiel, a man I have always admired, didn't hide his emotions. He was sometimes called the 'little dictator', yet he wouldn't hesitate to hug his players and let them know how much he loved them. He would tell players something like: "I love you, not like your mother or your sister loves you, but I love the way only a coach can love his players".

That sentiment rang so close to home because I get emotionally attached to my players. The day that I don't get attached to my players will be the day I stop coaching. In fact, I got a little choked up during a pre-game speech once before a championship game as I stated that this would be the last time I'd be on the field with that particular team so we should go out with a bang and leave it all on the field. Several players told me afterwards that they had almost started crying during my speech and my emotion got them so fired up that they wanted to win more than anything.

Share inspirational stories with your players. Talk about the things that have inspired you. In the preseason during your three-a-day practices, take an extended lunch and watch the movie *Rudy* with your players, or any other film you feel has an inspirational message. Take the time to bond on a human level. Don't be afraid to let them see the caring side of their coach. If you don't care, don't coach.

If you ever get the chance to attend a seminar performed by a motivational speaker, don't miss it. If nothing else it will re-energize you and get your football juices flowing. Better yet, try to get a motivational speaker to address your team.

We have all heard stories about the powers of 'adrenaline'. Adrenaline is a byproduct of emotion. If your emotions can create a chemical reaction to give your body a super rush of energy and power, can you imagine if you could channel that into a player's performance on the football field?

Motivation is not an easy thing to fake. This is why some people seem so natural at it. They're not faking. They are truly motivated themselves and they want to share their emotions with everyone. They are so excited that they get everyone around them excited. You need to find at least one individual like this for your coaching staff.

Strategy

Strategy is the proper use of knowledge and preparation on game day. Preparation is the key word. You need to be ready for any situation. For every plan you must have a contingency plan. Good coaches spend as much time, or more, on preparation as they do on the field.

The first thing you need is a game plan. You should develop your game plan based on the strengths and weakness not only of your opponent, but also of your own team. To do this, you will need a thorough understanding of your opponent. Hopefully, you will have scouted them at least once.

However, the best source of material you can get of your opponent would be videotapes of their games.

Film review is by far the most thorough means of scouting an opponent. Rewind and slow motion are your greatest tools. When you watch film of your opponent, the first thing you should do is chart all of their plays. Include information like down and distance on every play. Don't just chart the direction of the play; chart what all eleven players are doing on every play. Make sure you diagram every player's responsibility on that play. By doing this you will surely pick up on their tendencies. Player tendencies and team tendencies are equally important. Do they tend to lean toward a certain play or player in a particular situation? Do they have a lot of speed? Do they pass well? Does the quarterback have a favorite target? Although these questions are targeted mainly at opposing offenses, it is equally important to do the same charts for their defense. Be sure to watch every player on every play for tendencies. If you are diligent, you will find areas of weakness.

Now that you have developed a scouting report you should give a copy to every member of your team. Every player should get a detailed diagram of every play your opponent runs. They should also be given a tendency report. This will help them read certain keys during the game. Don't just tell your players what the other team does. Show them how to combat everything they do.

Make sure you have a written game plan before the practice week begins. In the back of this book are blank forms that will help you organize a game plan. The first thing you want to do is list the possible situations you will face. Don't forget to include field position in your scenarios. Then list three running plays and three pass plays that you would consider running for every situation. Remember to consider every conceivable situation you may find yourself in during the game. Consider using a script for the first 10 or 15 plays in the game. When you script plays you essentially list the 10 most important plays for that game. Make it a point to run every one of those in the beginning of the game. You don't have to run them in a certain order

but you must run them early in the game. This will help you to get a feel for what is and isn't going to work in a game.

Not every coach likes to call plays off a chart. They like to use their instincts during the game to call plays. However, creating the game plan will mentally prepare you for your opponent. The mere act of doing so will put things to the forefront of your mind when you need them. Keep in mind that the game plan was developed in a calm environment with no pressure or emotion, which doesn't accurately reflect the environment of a sideline during an intense football game.

Game plans will vary from opponent to opponent. Too many variables exist in football to create a 'cookie cutter' game plan. You may defend a similar offense differently depending on the types of players a team has. Make sure your game plan is level appropriate. Many things that are extremely effective at the youth level don't work at the high school level and vise versa.

During the game it is inevitable that you will have to make some adjustments. This is where your entire coaching staff comes into play. Each coach should have a different area to scout during the course of the game. You need to closely watch your opponent's players to figure out their game plan. Scout your own players too. Make sure they are following their assignments. You also want to listen to the players on the field. They may be able to give you insight on the tendency of an opposing player.

It is important to have a good offensive and defensive coordinator on your staff because there should be a good reason for every play called during a game. If you find yourself 'winging it' on game day, then you were ill prepared.

Building a Coaching Staff

Any coaching staff starts with a head coach. Contrary to popular belief, the head coach doesn't have to be the most knowledgeable person on the staff or even the best teacher. He simply needs to be a great leader and a great organizer. If he possesses those skills and chooses his staff wisely he will likely be successful.

When building a staff you need to make sure that you choose people who bring a positive addition to the team. They must be a team player that believes in you and your system. And you should make sure each person will fill a specific role such as linemen coach, backs coach, etc. Most coaches will coach an offensive and defensive position, which can help reduce the size of your staff. It is also helpful to have apprentice coaches around to hold bags and do other duties that can free you up to be more productive.

The offensive and defensive coordinators are extremely important to your staff. They should be given the freedom to make game day calls that fall within the game plan. They should also respect the head coaches' right to step in and adjust calls. On many staffs the head coach is also one of the coordinators. These two positions need to spend a lot of time working on films and giving input into the game plan.

The New Coach

Why do most people start coaching football? Obviously, a variety of answers exist for that question, and it really isn't that important why they start coaching, as long as they do the right things while they are coaching. By reading this book you are taking a step in the right direction. A desire to gain more knowledge is a characteristic of a good coach, no matter what level they are at.

Most people who start coaching at the youth level do so to be with their child. However, you should examine several possible pitfalls when considering coaching your own child. They include the following:

- Many fathers may be harder on their own son than they are on the rest of the team.
- Some coaches coddle their sons while being harder on the rest of the team.

- Some fathers try to relive their youth vicariously through their child.
- It is very hard to be as objective with your own child as you would be with someone else's child.
- It is a natural instinct for a parent to accentuate the positives and overlook the shortcomings of their own child.

Coaching your son's team can be a positive experience for both of you if you handle it the right way. The first thing you need to do is distance yourself from direct contact with your son as much as possible. Even if you have experience in the particular area your son is interested in, you and your son may prosper more if you coached a different position. If you truly want to learn how to coach, you need to be as well-rounded as possible. The things you learn about coaching an area you aren't as familiar with will expand your knowledge. You will still spend a lot of quality time with your son off the field. More than likely you will drive to and from practice together, which is a perfect time to share your experiences like only a father and son can. You will develop a special bond because you are both on the same team with the same goals in mind. Let your son grow as a player as you grow as a coach. If you take the time to learn the true meaning of being a coach, you and your son will certainly reap the benefits in the future.

Many coaches start coaching simply to be with their child and end up liking it so much that they continue coaching even after their child has moved on. Starting out as an assistant coach with little responsibility is a great opportunity to learn from experience.

You need to keep everything in perspective. You are coaching young men or even young children. Your responsibilities go far beyond winning football games. When you are intimately involved it is hard to objectively view your behavior. Make an effort to evaluate how you handle situations. Better yet when you see another coach say or do something that you don't feel is appropriate, ask yourself, "Have I ever acted that way?" Be truly honest with yourself. Catch your mistakes before they become a routine.

Sometimes it is very hard to admit that you are wrong. Good coaches make many mistakes along the way. Great coaches learn from their mistakes and don't repeat them.

Many coaches who exhibit poor behavior believe they are doing the right thing. The most common example of this is the 'screamer'. If you have spent any time around youth football, you have seen this coach. He is the drill sergeant type. He believes he is building character by degrading and intimidating his players. He believes this is a way to earn the respect of his players. He will even tell you what a tough sport it is and this is why he is so hard on you.

If you spend most of your time screaming and yelling it becomes routine and it will be very hard to make a point when you really need to. If you rarely raise your voice, it will have a significant impact when you do. You should never yell at a player for a fundamental mistake. Yelling at an 11-year-old quarterback because he didn't accurately land a pass will do more harm than good. Do you really believe that boy wasn't trying to throw it right? I'm sure he wanted to do it correctly more than the coach wanted him to. This would be an appropriate time to find a way to teach a way to execute the skill. You need to be a teacher. You will gain nothing by yelling for the sake of yelling. You are actually putting undo pressure on your players, making it harder for them to learn specific skills.

Save the yelling for the right moment. If your team ever acts in an unsportsmanlike manner, this would be an appropriate time to raise your voice. This doesn't mean that this situation requires you to raise your voice. You need to make the point that their behavior was inappropriate and will not be tolerated. Sometimes it doesn't matter what you say, it's how you say it that will determine what type of impact it will have. Don't raise your voice in the wrong situations. Try to catch yourself doing it and correct your behavior. If you think you were ever 'out of line' with your team, bring them together and apologize. Explain to them the point you were trying to make and tell them you went about it the wrong

way. Not only will this gain their respect, but you will also have a chance to reemphasize the point you were trying to make.

An athlete's confidence in his ability will help him to reach his potential much faster. Build your players up rather than constantly tearing them down. If you do tear them down, make sure you build them back up in a relatively short period of time. Teach them the way you want them to do something and find positive things they are doing and make sure you emphasize those positive things. Positive reinforcement is one of the best teachers.

Another poor character quality in a coach is inconsistency. Before the season begins you need to set up parameters. Try to imagine every possible scenario and how you will handle it. Take this a step further and make up a handbook that outlines all your rules and the consequences for breaking these rules. Make sure that not only your players and coaches know what you expect, but also that the parents are aware of your expectations for them and their child. The hard part is standing behind your rules, enforcing them on a consistent basis. Do not give into the pressures of winning or parental pressures. If you treat everyone the same way, you will deal with fewer issues as the season progresses. Do not show favorites. Treat your star athlete the same way you treat the least skilled player on the team. One of the most important things you can do for your entire team is to be consistent.

Many coaches who play favorites may not even know they are doing it. The star players show up late for practice and nothing happens. Another player shows up late and he is disciplined. The fastest kid on the team is last on every lap or sprint and nothing is said to the player. This usually happens on a team where winning is the number one priority. Don't allow any player or parent to act as if they deserve special treatment. If you allow these types of behaviors to exist, you are destroying the entire concept of the word 'team'.

Coaches at all levels exhibit many types of unacceptable behaviors. One of the best things you can do is to evaluate yourself as a coach frequently. Many coaches try to justify their mistakes. They put so much effort trying to put a positive spin on something that they don't take the time to evaluate their performance. Dig deep down and you know in your heart what is right and wrong. All coaches make mistakes, great coaches recognize those mistakes and learn from them. Set your standards high. If you live by high standards then you have the right to expect them from others. "Do as I say, not as I do" will never work on a football field. If you plan to ask your players to strive for greatness, then you must strive for greatness yourself. Be a great coach!

CHAPTER 2

Offense

"A successful coach needs a patient wife, a loyal dog, and a great quarterback—and not necessarily in that order."

-Bud Grant

Offensive Glossary

Abbreviations

C: center

CB: cornerback

DB: defensive back

DE: defensive end

DT: defensive tackle

EMLOS: end man on line of scrimmage

FB: fullback

FS: free safety

G: guard

HB: halfback

ILB: inside linebacker

LB: linebacker

LHB: left halfback

LOS: line of scrimmage

MLB: middle linebacker

NG: noseguard

OLB: outside linebacker

POA: point of attack

QB: quarterback

RHB: right halfback

S: safety

SS: strong safety

TB: Tailback

T: tackle

TE: tight end

WB: wingback

WR: wide receiver

Blocking Terminology

Area: This is a blocking term where the man will take one step to the onside and block that area.

Away: This is a blocking term where the man will block the seam away from POA.

Backer: This is a blocking term where the man will be responsible to block a linebacker.

Boot: This is a pass where the guard opposite the play pulls.

Combo: This is a blocking term where the man will peel off of his part of a double team block for a backer.

Crack: This is a blocking term where the wideout will block the first man inside him.

Down: This is a blocking term where the man will block the first man inside him.

Fire: This man will aggressively block the onside gap and anyone who crosses his path

Hook: This man will block a man by rotating his hips to the outside after he makes contact with the man.

Influence: This is a blocking term where the man will move in a direction to deceive the look of the play.

Lead: This is the down part of a double team block.

Log: This is a blocking term where the man will pull and hook man that is normally trapped.

Pick: This is a blocking term where the man will set up to pass block.

Post: This is the stabilizing part of a double team block.

Pull check: This is a blocking term where the man will cover the area of the blocker next to him who is pulling.

Rule: This refers to blocking assignments of your offensive linemen.

Solid: This is a blocking term that calls off other blocks.

Stalk: This is a blocking term where the man will release off the LOS and block a DB keeping himself under control between the defender and the ballcarrier.

Trap: This is a blocking term where the man will pull down the LOS to block first man outside an area.

Wall-off: This is a blocking term where the man will pull and pt himself in a position to cut-off penetration from middle.

General Terminology

Bag: Tool used to teach blocking or tackling.

Belly: An inside running play that has the ballcarrier crossover (bellies) before hitting LOS.

Buck-up: Running technique that has the man coming from low to high at impact.

Cadence: The words of the signal caller that starts a play.

Chest plate: The portion of the shoulder pads that covers the chest area.

Counter: Backs run opposite the called play. The ballcarrier cuts back after first step.

Cover 2: This refers to 2 deep zone coverage by the defense.

Cover 3: This refers to 3 deep zone coverage by the defense.

Crossover: An initial step to one side that gains only lateral distance.

Dive: An inside running play with no lead blocker.

Drop: This refers to the steps of the QB in the passing game.

Dummy: Tool used to teach blocking or tackling.

Even: This refers to a defensive alignment with no man lined up over center.

Force Area: The area a defender must play to cover the flat vs. pass or the pitchman vs. option.

Freeze: The technique of a runner to follow a blocker without showing his intentions until the block begins.

Gap: The area between the basic alignment of the linemen.

Ghost: Refers to the area a player would line up in a basic set.

Hole: The area at the LOS where the play is directed.

Man: This refers to one-on-one coverage by the defense.

Midline: The imaginary line that splits the axis of the ball and the crotch of both the center and QB.

Motion: The legal movement of a player at the snap of the ball.

North/South: Refers to a direction that is perpendicular to the end zones.

Neutral zone: The area at the LOS that is the width of the ball from nose to nose.

Odd: This refers to a defensive alignment with a man lined up over center.

Offside: Starting at the center this is the area opposite the direction of the play.

Onside: Starting at the center this is the area toward the direction of the play.

Pinnies: Item worn by players to distinguish the positions they are playing.

Playside: Starting at the center this is the area toward the direction of the play.

Reverse Pivot: The first step of the QB when it is opposite the play direction.

Shield: Tool used to teach blocking.

Shift: The formation change of an offense before the start of a play.

Skelly: This term refers to the simulation of a play or series of plays

Split: The distance between linemen in their stance at the LOS.

Start: The first movement of a player at the snap of the ball.

Zone: Refers to an area of responsibility.

Numbering Systems

Most teams use a numbering system to simplify their offense. The numbering system is usually composed of two digits. The first digit dictates the ballcarrier while the second determines the point of attack. In addition, you can add a descriptive term such as Trap, Boot, etc. by which the line and backs may learn their blocking rules. The numbers are usually preceded be some type of formation call (e.g., wishbone 44 counter) In this example, the offense will be in a wishbone formation. The 4 back will get the ball and go to the 4 'hole.'

Figures 2-1 and 2-2 show examples of two types of numbering systems. Figure 2-1 shows the use of an odd-even system to number the hole where the play will go. You can also number the holes 1-9 starting in one direction. In Figure 2-2, the numbers represent a player with numbers 1 and 9 indicating the area outside the end man on the line of scrimmage or outside the area that he would normally line up at if he splits wide. The wing-T is an example of an offense that uses this system.

Figure 2-1. Odd-even numbering system

Figure 2-2

Figure 2-3 is an example of a T-formation backfield. The quarterback is #1, the right halfback is #2, the fullback is #3, and the left halfback is #4.

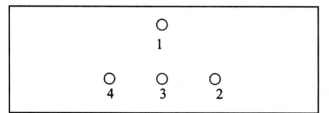

Figure 2-3. T-formation backfield

want penetration right up the middle. Figure 2-4 represents a common line split at the high school level.

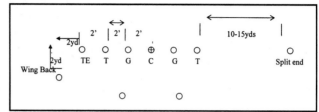

Figure 2-4. Line split

Line Splits

Line splits are the distances between linemen. Advantages and disadvantages exist to the distance you put between your linemen. Wide line splits will spread out the defense. On the other hand, it may make you more vulnerable to a defender who may be stunting into a gap on your line. Small splits make it easier to protect gaps, but it will also bunch the defense making it harder to execute inside running plays.

Some coaches subscribe to the 'accordion theory.' This simply means that you widen your line splits when you run inside and shorten them when you run outside. If you use this theory you also have to take into consideration the defense you are playing against. Sometimes your line splits are determined by the tendencies of your opponent's defense.

You also have to consider the level at which you're coaching. A high school may use two-foot splits as a standard in their offense. It would be tough to pull that off with a team of 9-year-olds. At some levels you will use different splits for different positions. It is not unlikely that the center-guard split will be less than the guard-tackle split at the youth level. This may also be true at older levels depending on the tendencies of your opponent's defense. When you are running a dropback pass you need to create a pocket for your quarterback. The basis of this is for the linemen to force their opponents to their outside; they never

Huddle Procedure

The most important factor in a huddle is paying attention. When the QB reaches the huddle he is the only one who speaks and everyone else pays attention. The huddle should be formed five yards directly behind the ball. It is the center's responsibility to align the huddle properly. He should raise his hand and yell, "huddle" with his back to the ball.

- Everyone hustles to the huddle.
- No one crowds his teammates.
- Everyone is calm and relaxed with hands on their knees.
- No one else talks once the QB steps in.

The QB will enter the huddle on the side closest to your sideline. This allows him to look at the coach

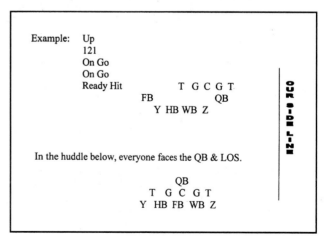

Figure 2-5

or notice a sub entering the game. At the quarter, FB and QB will exchange positions. The QB will step into the huddle and call, "Up." On this command, everyone snaps up to attention and looks at the QB's mouth. The QB will then call the formation and play once along with the snap count. The QB will repeat the snap count and say, "ready pride." The line will mirror the QB by simultaneously calling "pride" and clapping their hands. They will then turn to the inside and sprint to LOS. When breaking the huddle, Z goes in front of all potential receivers and Y goes behind all potential receivers.

Cadence

The following is the cadence used by a high school in New Jersey. It incorporates the ability to time their plays with the options of a deceptive cadence to try to pull teams offside or a quick cadence to keep teams on their heels. Make sure your team's cadence allows for the timing of different types of motion. It should also have a good flow to facilitate a proper takeoff.

The normal cadence to be used:

Huddle: QB says, "On go"

LOS: QB says, "Odd set, (pause), red, (pause), set go"

Notes:

- QB will call odd or even set depending on the defense he sees. Odd means man on C. Even means no man on C.

- If short motion is used, man will leave on "red"

- C snaps the ball on 'G' sound of go

The ball may be snapped on the first sound.

Huddle: QB says, "On sound"

LOS: QB says, "Set"

All shifting or long motion will begin with the QB lifting his heel followed by "Set" when the QB feels the motion man is in proper position.

Huddle: QB says, "On sound"

LOS: QB says, "Set"

"Check cadence" will be used to delay the snap count. The QB will call the normal cadence; however, no snap will take place until the QB says, "Check." The ball will then be snapped on "go" following this call.

Huddle: QB says, "On check cadence"

LOS: QB says, "Odd set, (pause), red, (pause), set go (pause), check, (pause), set go"

"On the line" will be used to:

- Run plays with no huddle

- Package plays–QB calls 21 or 29 on the line in the huddle

- Audible plays–QB calls on the line in the huddle. A live color (blue or white) followed by a play will be used to alert your team what play is to be executed. The snap is always on your normal cadence (go).

Huddle: QB says, "On the line, on go"

LOS: QB says, "Blue 21, (pause), odd set, (pause), red, (pause), set go"

"Now" will be called by the QB twice to audible at the LOS followed by the same procedure as "on the line" at the LOS.

LOS: QB says, "Now, (pause), now, (pause), blue 21, (pause), odd set, (pause), red, (pause), set go"

Offensive Formations

Backfield Formations

Figures 2-6 through 2-14 illustrate basic backfield formations. These examples are only intended to demonstrate the alignment of the backfield. Multiple alignments are possible from each one of these basic formations.

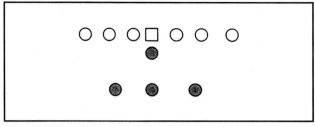

Figure 2-6. Full house or T-formation

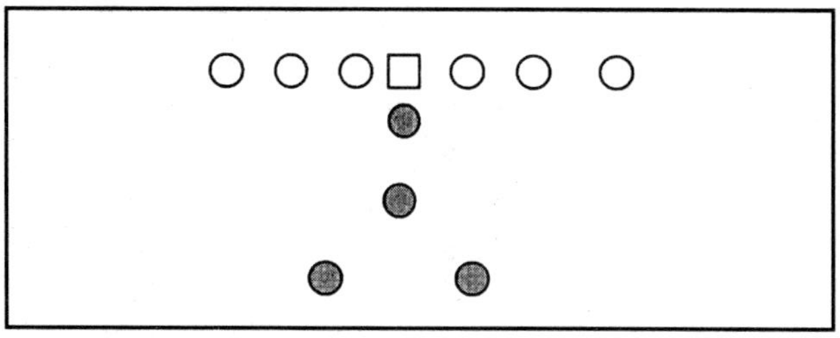

Figure 2-7. Wishbone

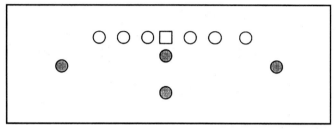

Figure 2-8. One Back or Double Wing or Ace or Double Slot

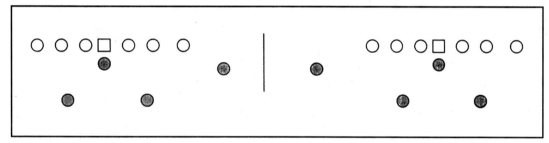

Figure 2-9. Split Backs

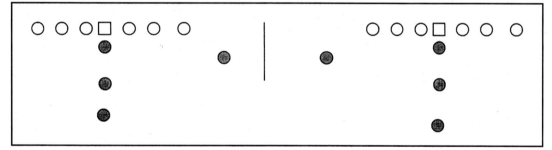

Figure 2-10: I Formation

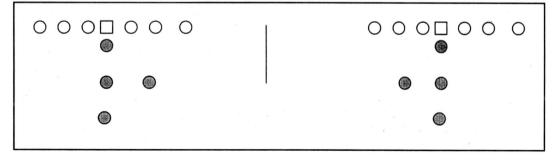

Figure 2-11. Power I

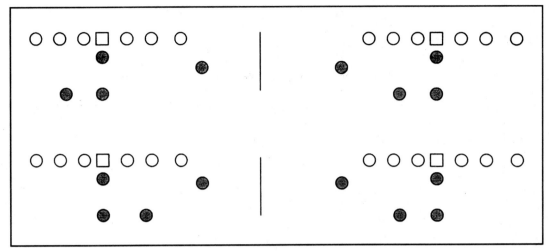

Figure 2-12. Wing-T

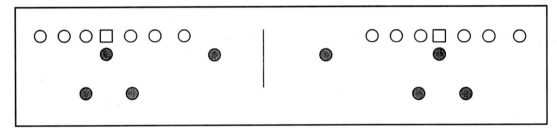

Figure 2-13. Veer

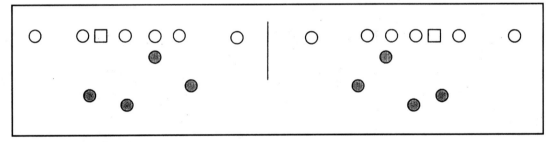

Figure 2-14. Single Wing

Receiver Formations

The following receiver formations show receiver sets. They include wide receivers, tight ends, and backs. They can be used in conjunction with various backfield formations.

Pro

The pro formation has a wingback split wide on the tight end side of the formation. There is a wide receiver split wide on the side opposite the tight end. See Figure 2-15.

Spread

The spread formation utilizes four recievers. There is a tight end and a wing split wide on one side. On the other side you will have a wide receiver split wide with a back lined up in the slot. Figure 2-16 shows one version of a spread. Other variations are possible.

Unbalanced

The unbalanced formation has a wide receiver on the same side as the tight end. Since they are both lined up on the line of scrimmage, the tight end is not an eligible receiver. Therefore, he cannot go downfield on a pass play from this formation. The wing can be lined up on either side but it is best that he is opposite the tight end, which will make it harder for the defense to read the unbalanced formation.

Twins

The twins formation has a wide receiver and a back split wide to one side. The other side may have a tight end or a wide out.

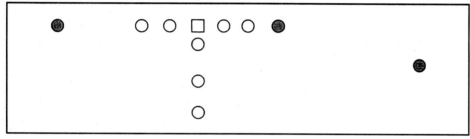

Figure 2-15. Pro

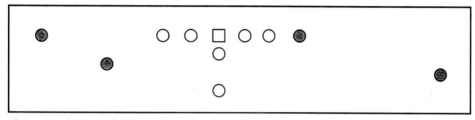

Figure 2-16. Spread

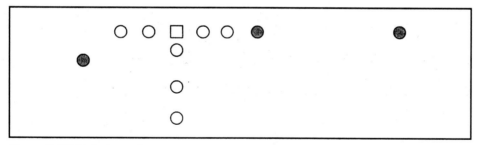

Figure 2-17. Unbalanced

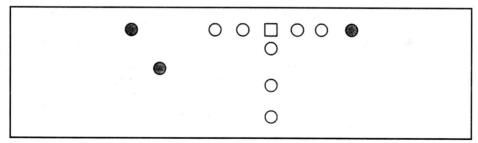

Figure 2-18. Twins

Trips

Trips is a grouping of three receivers to one side. It can have a wide receiver and two backs split to one side or a tight end and two backs to one side.

Quads

The quads formation is a grouping of four receivers to one side. There can be a wide receiver and three backs or a tight end and three backs.

Shifting Formations

A shift in a formation is when your offense lines up in one formation and shifts to another after the quarterback begins his cadence. When a team shifts, every person on the team must be set in his stance for at least one second before the play can start. Teams shift from one formation to another to throw off the defense. Figures 2-21 through 2-23 demonstrate an example of a shift from one formation to another.

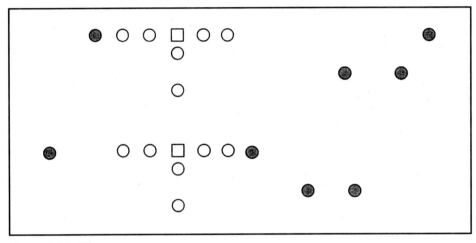

Figure 2-19. Trips

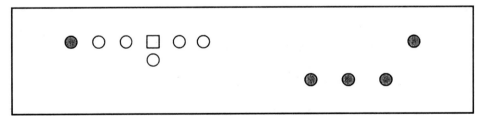

Figure 2-20. Quads

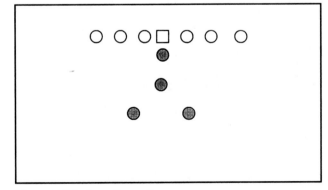

Figure 2-21. Base formation

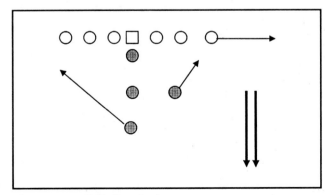

Figure 2-22. Shift directions

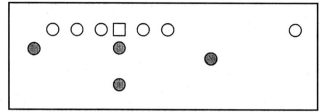
Figure 2-23. New formation

Motion

Motion is the movement of a running back during the snap of the play. Motion is used to change formations and confuse the defense. Terminology varies greatly from offense to offense but the types of motion are similar. The most important thing to remember is that the back cannot be moving forward at the time of the snap. Only one player can be moving at a time. If two players move at once they must reset in their stance along with the rest of the team before the snap. This would be considered a shift, not motion. Motion can begin after a shift as long as the entire team is set for at least one second.

Figure 2-24 shows the wingback going in motion across the formation. On the snap he is located in the wing position on the other side. He has essentially just reversed the formation.

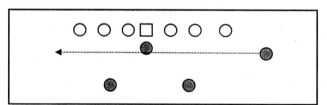
Figure 2-24. Wingback motion across formation

Figure 2-25 shows the wingback crossing over the midline and locating himself behind one of the interior linemen on the snap of the ball. In this case, he has put himself in a position to be a lead blocker on a power type lead play.

Figure 2-26 shows the wingback located short of the midline behind an interior lineman. In this motion he is in a position to attack the line of scrimmage as a lead blocker. He is also in a position to receive the ball on a quick handoff or execute a fake.

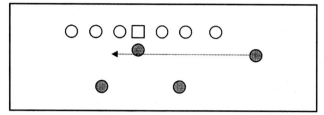
Figure 2-25. Wingback motion crossing over midline

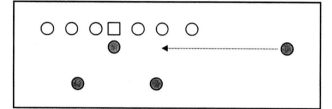
Figure 2-26. Wingback short of midline

Figure 2-27 shows the wingback in motion toward the midline and then reversing field back toward the original spot. This type of motion is used to deceive the defense and perhaps tighten up the outside containment to allow for running a play back to the outside using the wingback as a lead blocker.

Figure 2-28 shows the wingback splitting wide. This essentially shifts the base formation to a pro formation.

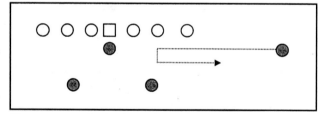
Figure 2-27. Wingback motion toward midline

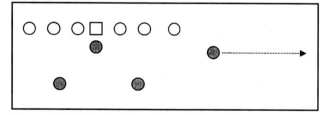
Figure 2-28. Wingback motion splitting wide

Figure 2-29 shows the halfback going in motion toward the strongside of the formation. This is a formation change that can be used to put more players on the side you will be running to or to deceive the defense and run a counter, dive, or reverse type play.

Figure 2-30 shows a formation change. Formation changes are mainly used to deceive the defense.

Figure 2-31 shows the wingback going in motion back toward the halfback position. This is a versatile type of motion. It changes the formation and it also creates deception. The motion man could be setting up to receive the ball, fake receiving the ball, or act as a lead blocker or a pass blocker.

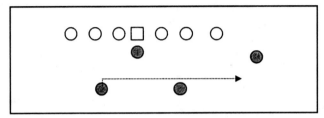

Figure 2-29. Halfback motion toward strongside

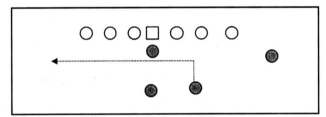

Figure 2-30. Formation change

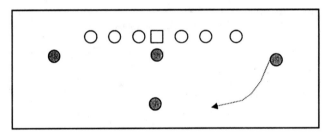

Figure 2-31. Wingback motion toward halfback

CHAPTER 3

Player Fundamentals—Offense

"The strongest human instinct is to impart information, the second is to resist it."

-Kenneth Graham

Quarterbacks

Many variables go into being a quarterback, which makes it a complicated position to teach. This book covers the basic fundamentals, but even these can vary greatly. Some quarterbacks develop their own style of throwing or have a particular grip that works for them.

Intelligence level is something to consider when choosing a quarterback. The QB should have some knowledge of every position on the field. He needs to know everyone's alignment on every play. And as he becomes more advanced, he should develop the ability to "read" and understand various defenses.

Needless to say, a quarterback should be smart, confident, and capable of being a leader. Although he must be a good athlete, he doesn't have to be the most athletic person on the team. The QB just needs to be fundamentally sound and of course, having a great arm is always handy. However, the fact that a kid can throw the ball a mile doesn't mean he will be a great QB. For instance, how many times is a team of 8- or 10-year-olds going to execute the long passing game?

Skills

The skills section is not one to be skimmed over; try to vividly imagine every step. Don't be afraid to bring these notes onto the field with you. Without notes, it is easy to forget a step. nd remember, some players will be more comfortable doing certain things differently than the method outlined. If he can be consistent and achieve the fundamental result you are looking for, this is OK. You're not trying to build robots.

Stance

Following is a description of the different stances you should teach your quarterback:

• Receive the ball from the center with the laces up to quickly allow for a passing grip.

- Plant the feet slightly less than shoulder width apart. Wide stances cause hitch steps.
- Stand flat-footed with your heels slightly off the ground.
- Stand as tall as possible while still staying comfortable (head up, chest out, knees bent). Entire field visibility is important.
- Keep your arms comfortably bent (never straight-armed and tense).
- Press the middle finger of your top hand tightly along the seam of the center's pants with your fingers spread comfortably.
- Thrust your bottom hand down and back at approximately a 135-degree angle. Your thumbs will be over top of each other with the bottom thumb protruding out an inch or so further than the top.

Snap Reception

- Apply constant pressure against the seam of the center's pants giving him a target.
- Do not pull your hands away from the center without full control of the ball.
- Pull the ball into your waist first on every play.
- Adjust the ball for proper fit.

Handoff Exchange

- Receive the ball, pull it into your waist, and protect it until the exchange. Footwork will be discussed later and is usually described in each play.
- Make visual contact with the handoff pocket formed by the ballcarrier.
- Place the ball in the center of the pocket keeping your eyes on the exchange throughout.
- Pull off the ball as the ballcarrier accepts the exchange.
- Keep your eye on the pocket for the first few steps after the exchange.
- When faking, do all the same things listed, especially watching the pocket for a few

steps after the fake exchange. Fakes will be covered later.

Toss Exchange

- In some offenses, the toss is performed from a reverse pivot (see bookmark) as are most plays.
- If tossing right, the first step is a reverse pivot 45-degrees beyond the midline (see footwork) with your left foot.
- Follow up by stepping with your right foot into the direction you will toss the ball.
- Swing your arms like a pendulum with your right leg.
- Softly release the ball with an arc one yard in front of the runner.
- Release the ball just after your right foot hits the ground.
- Never lower the ball below your waist as it causes you to release the ball too high.

Quick Pitch

- Raise the ball to chest level just before pitching it.
- Thrust the ball to your target with both hands.
- Outstretch your arms at the end of the pitch.
- Follow through with your hands beyond the point of release.

Faking

The QB will execute two types of fakes: the one-handed fake and the two-handed fake. The one-handed fake is used mostly in play-action situations allowing the QB to set up quicker. Many coaches feel it minimizes the risk of a fumble. The QB executes this by riding the ball on the soft, inside part of the belly. The free hand enters the handoff pouch and rides it as long as possible. He then gets two hands back on the ball as soon as possible.

The two-handed fake can be more realistic because it entails the identical movements of the real handoff. This fake is frequently used on option plays. This requires the QB to hold the ball firmly. He needs to place the ball softly into the handoff pouch and ride it as long as possible, before pulling the ball back into the stomach. The ball must stay above the belt of the runner so it does not hit his hipbone.

The QB will make other fakes like tosses, pitches, passes etc. The most important thing is for him to execute the same fundamentals on the fake as he does on the real handoff.

Follow-Through

After making a handoff, the QB must place his hand on his outside hip, as if he has the ball, and continue running at full speed. This sets up the keepers, bootleg and play-action passing game. Although this is essentially a faking maneuver, it must be performed consistently and perfectly on every play. This might be the most important thing a QB does. If he does this on every play, he will buy himself a lot of time when he keeps the ball.

Handoff Footwork

When you draw out your plays, the quarterbacks' footwork should be detailed. Every play should have every player's responsibility detailed; the quarterback's steps need to be listed in order to bring perfection to the execution you desire for the play. If you want the quarterback to reverse pivot on a play, then you need to list that. A reverse pivot is when the quarterback's initial turn from the center is opposite the actual playside. This is very important in deceptive offenses like the wing-T. The midline is an excellent point of reference to help a player know exactly where his steps should be.

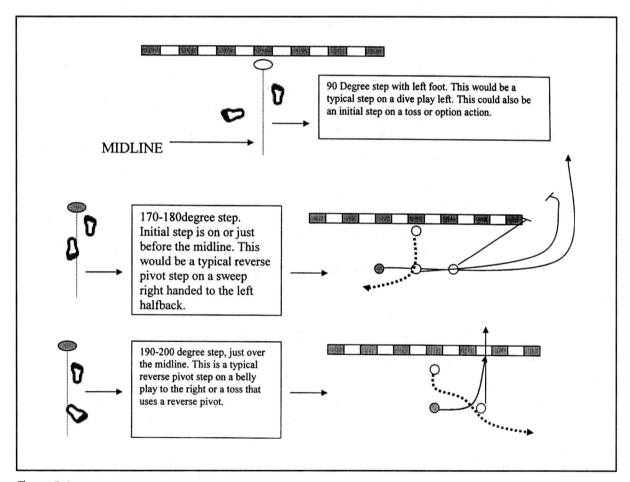

MIDLINE

90 Degree step with left foot. This would be a typical step on a dive play left. This could also be an initial step on a toss or option action.

170-180degree step. Initial step is on or just before the midline. This would be a typical reverse pivot step on a sweep right handed to the left halfback.

190-200 degree step, just over the midline. This is a typical reverse pivot step on a belly play to the right or a toss that uses a reverse pivot.

Figure 3-1

Quarterback Passing

The Grip

How a quarterback grips the football will vary among different players. A smaller-handed QB will hold the ball closer to the end of the ball, while the larger-handed player will grip it more toward the center. Wherever he grips the ball, he still must do the following:

- Spread his fingers wide to help with control and the spiral.
- Extend his index fingers toward the end of the ball.
- Place his last three fingers across the laces.
- Wrap his thumb comfortably around the ball.

Setting Up/Footwork

The three basic dropback steps are 3-,5-, and 7-step drops, although the depth of these steps will vary. Many different play-action, rollout, bootleg and sprint-out passes will vary the number of steps in the set up. The speed at which a quarterback sets up is also important.

While setting up, he should hold the ball outside his chest with two hands, moving the ball from side to side along with his strides. The ball needs to be ready to be cocked quickly for a throw.

No matter how many steps the QB drops back, the last two steps are always the same. They are used to throttle down and plant with the back foot.

Passing Position

- Place your weight on the balls of your feet.
- Always flex your knees rather than bending them.
- Place the ball in front of your chest pointing up and down.
- Keep your elbows down; don't squeeze the ball.
- Maintain wide vision with both eyes on the defense.

- Hips first, shoulders split second later. Push the ball up and out past your ear.
- Follow through with your thumbs down, palm away. Keep your back leg off the ground.

Throwing the Pass

As a quarterback prepares to throw, his weight should transfer from his back foot toward the target. As he propels forward, he releases the ball overhand to his target. His shoulders and hips should have "opened up to the target." He must follow through with his arm, hand, and shoulders after releasing the ball.

A good key to teach your QB is that his index finger should point the ball to the target. His thumb and palm should be facing down as the ball is released. His hand should (turn out) as he follows through. This will help with spiral and accuracy. His index finger should be the last thing to touch the ball and should be pointing toward the target upon release.

Throwing on the Run

Although a quarterback will not likely be able to set his feet properly when throwing on the run, he should still be stepping in the direction he is throwing whenever possible. He must still load (cock back) his shoulders and complete his follow-through on his throwing motion. He must also square his hips toward his target while releasing the pass. This type of pass is usually more of a "touch" pass than a rifle pass.

The Dropback

After a quarterback receives the ball, he drops back from the center and sets up to pass. He usually drops back three, five, or seven steps. Each of these drop steps will be discussed in this section. Quickness should be consistent in every drop. It is very important to set up quickly. The first step, or separation step, is the other thing that is the same in every drop. It is called a separation step because it is important for the QB to get a lot of distance with his first step. In fact, have your quarterback practice his separation step when he is taking warm-up snaps with his center. Be sure that he switches feet each time. His eyes need to always be reading the receiver up the field. He must square his hips and shoulders to his target when he sets up to throw; if not he will improperly throw across his body.

□ The 3-Step Drop

The 3-step drop is used in the short passing game. The receiver is usually running a 10 to 12 yard downfield pass route. A 3-step drop could be used on a five yard out pattern as well. The quarterback should reach a depth of four to five yards depending on his size. The three steps are as follows:

• Step one-The separation step

The right-handed quarterback pivots on his left foot to gain as much distance as possible with the right foot.

• Step two-The crossover step

He crosses over his right foot with his left. He should not gain too much distance and should be plating this foot getting ready to throw.

• Step three-The balance step

The quarterback's momentum will carry him into his third step as he is planting his second step. He should be releasing the ball quickly after coming to balance.

□ The 5-Step Drop

The 5-step drop is used in the medium length passing game. This is perhaps the most widely used drop in many offenses. The quarterback is better protected in the pocket of a 5-step drop. It is easier for linemen to control this area, especially from an outside rush. The blocker can force the outside rusher deeper than the passer and actually open up clearer passing lanes. The quarterback should gain between six to seven yards of depth on this drop.

His focus must be downfield. He must carriage the ball across his chest as he drops back. The five steps are as follows:

• Step one-The separation step

The right-handed quarterback pivots off his left foot to gain as much distance as possible with his right foot.

• Step two-The crossover step

He crosses over his right foot with his left gaining as much distance as possible.

• Step three-The control step

He quickly brings his right leg behind the left trying to get more distance and establish control. This is where he stabilizes and gets ready for the next step.

• Step four-The crossover step

This is the set-up step that will dig in and plant. He must be thinking about the area he is throwing during this step, although he should still have more time to hold the ball than in the 3-step drop.

• Step five-The balance step

This step will happen naturally if he planted his foot properly in the fourth step.

□ The 7-Step Drop

The 7-step drop is merely an extension of the 5-step drop. All the steps are identical, you simply add an extra crossover and control step in the middle to make it a 7-step drop. This drop is used in the long passing game. Keep in mind that there is further exposure to a sack in the 7-step drop. First, it takes longer to set up and the reads are harder for the quarterback. Defensive ends and outside linebackers like to tee-off on quarterbacks this deep. They have a much better trajectory at his set up area. It is also harder for the interior linemen to create a pocket. They are required to protect much more ground, giving the defenders more flexibility in their rush technique.

Quarterback Warm-Up Drills

The quarterbacks and centers should arrive for practice five minutes early every day. Use this time to perform the following warm-up drills. They are all performed with two quarterbacks. The most important thing you can do during these drills is to watch for all the proper fundamental mechanics (i.e., grip, footwork, set up, rotation of hips and shoulders, release, and follow-through).

Follow-through Drill

Description: In this drill, two quarterbacks face each other standing about 10 yards apart and down on one knee. They "load" their shoulders and throw a ball back and forth concentrating on the follow-through.

Coaching Points:

- Make sure the hand pronates (turns inward) after the throw.
- Have players exaggerate their motions.

Figure 3-2. Follow-through Drill

Load Shoulders Drill

Description: In this drill, two quarterbacks face each other 10 yards apart with their feet firmly planted and facing forward. Without moving their feet, they take turns loading their shoulders, cocking their hips and executing a proper throw.

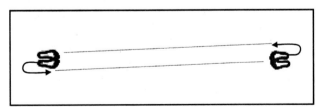

Figure 3-3. Load Shoulders Drill

Shoulders and Hips Drill

Description: In this drill, two quarterbacks face each other 10 yards apart with their feet firmly planted and facing 90 degrees right. Without moving their feet, they take turns loading their shoulders, cocking their hips and executing a proper throw. The drill is then repeated with their feet planted and facing 90 degrees left.

Coaching Points:

- The emphasis in this drill should be the hip rotation. The hips need to come from a 'cocked' position to being parallel with his target.
- The 'loaded' shoulders and hips should be working together in the direction of the pass.

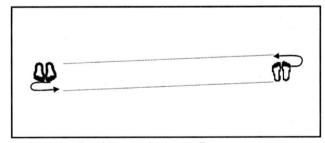

Figure 3-4. Shoulders and Hips Drill

Three-Step Drop Drill

Description: Two quarterbacks stand 10 yards apart facing each other. One player starts as if he were accepting a center snap. He takes a proper 3-step drop and throws the ball to the other QB.

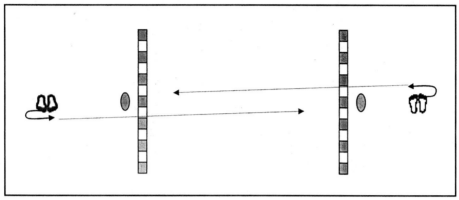

Figure 3-5. Three-Step Drop Drill

Four Corners Drill

Description: In this drill, a 10-yard x 10-yard square is set up on the field. Two quarterbacks line up on opposite sides and on opposite corners. They take turns taking a 5-step drop straight back, turning, and making a proper throw. They should shift corners so that they have to turn in the opposite direction and repeat.

Coaching Points:

- The emphasis needs to be on the proper dropback steps and setting up for a pass opposite their dropback.
- Make sure they readjust their feet in the direction they are throwing.
- Their hips and shoulders should be parallel to their target upon release and they must follow through after the throw.

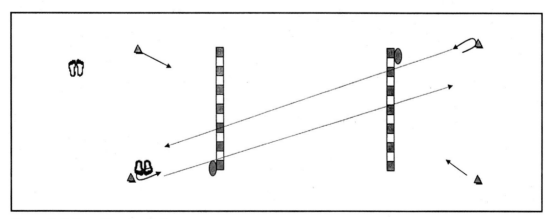

Figure 3-6. Four Corners Drill

Sprint Out Drill

Description: In this drill two quarterbacks stand 10 yards apart each over a yard line. They begin jogging in the same direction down their yard lines. They take turns throwing a ball back and forth as they jog in the same direction. As soon as one player releases the ball, he returns to the line to receive the ball. When they reach the end of the line, they turn around and repeat the drill in the other direction.

Coaching Point:

- Be sure players are loading their shoulders, turning their hips, and stepping in the direction they are throwing.

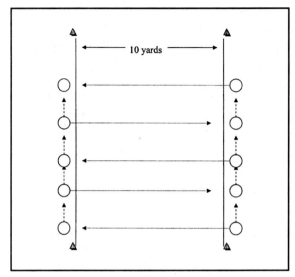

Figure 3-7. Sprint Out Drill

Pass Skelly Drill

Objective: To perfect the timing of your pass offense and teach your quarterback to read coverage.

Description: In this drill, bring together the quarterback, center, running backs, wide receivers, and tight ends to run through your entire passing offense.

Coaching Points:

- Always run this drill using your opponent's defensive scheme. The QB needs to be able to decipher between cover 2, cover 3, and other zone defenses. He should also recognize man coverage.

- Make sure the QB always locates the free safety or potential double coverage. He should also look or mismatches in coverage.

- You can vary this drill by adding defensive backs and linebackers.

- If you prefer not to use the center during this drill, make sure someone is giving the QB a hand snap to simulate an exchange.

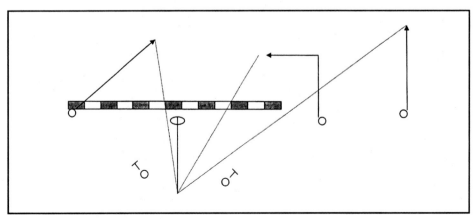

Figure 3-8. Pass Skelly Drill

Long Ball Drill

Description: In this drill, two lines are set up 25 yards apart with your backs and receivers. Each line should have its own quarterback. The first person in each line will take turns running a fly pattern and catching the QB's throw. That player gives the ball to the opposite QB and gets in that line.

Coaching Points:

- Watch the QB for proper throwing mechanics.
- Watch the receivers for proper catching mechanics.
- The ball should be thrown over the inside shoulder of the receiver; therefore it should be caught with palms up and pinkies together.

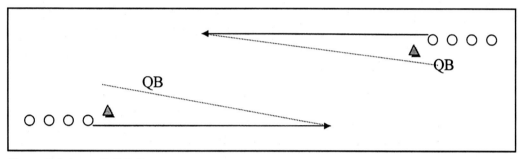

Figure 3-9. Long Ball Drill

Swing Pass Drill

Description: In this drill, a quarterback sets up in between two lines of halfbacks. The first player in each line runs a swing pass out of the backfield. The quarterback executes a 5-step drop and then throws a touch pass over the inside shoulder of the back. Switch lines after every repetition.

Coaching Points:

- Screen action can be used in this drill instead of swing.

- A defender can be added to simulate an outside rush for the QB to throw over.
- Make sure the QB executes a proper 5-step drop.
- The back should take a few lateral steps before arcing his pattern up the field. He will ideally catch the pass around the LOS approximately 8 to 10 yards outside the end man on the LOS. He needs to quickly tuck the ball and sprint five more yards upfield.

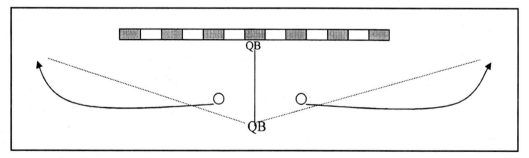

Figure 3-10. Swing Pass Drill

Flat Pass Drill

Objective: To work on the timing of your play action passing game relative to the back coming out of the backfield.

Description: A cone is set up to mark a target for the quarterback to set up and throw. A back comes out of the backfield and gives a forearm to a bag or player at the LOS to simulate traffic delays encountered live. After catching the ball, the running back quickly adjusts his path to get upfield as fast as possible for about five yards. Run this drill in both directions.

Coaching Points:

- Watch the set up and delivery of the quarterback to make sure the play action fake is executed properly.

- A simulated rush can be added so the QB has to redirect and throw on the run.

- The QB also needs to have reps throwing this pass in rush situations. Teach the QB how to make safe throws or get rid of the ball properly if the play breaks down.

- You should always be simulating an actual play action pass that is in your playbook.

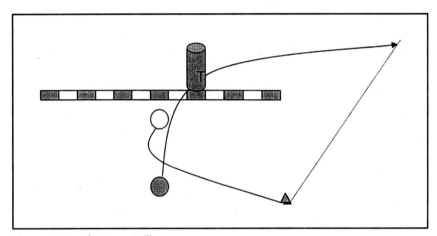

Figure 3-11. Flat Pass Drill

Run Skelly Drill

Objective: To perfect the timing and fundamentals of your running game. To practice all running plays and put in new ones.

Description: In this drill, a line of scrimmage is set up with cones or hose markings for two stations 12 yards behind the other. The first and second string backfields are separated. Simulate a snap to your QB on every play.

Coaching Point:

• This drill can be run by having each set of players run the same play one after the other, or different coaches can work with different groups at their own pace running the drill independently of each other.

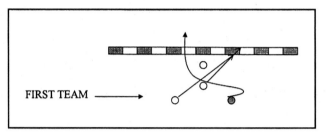

Figure 3-12. Run Skelly Drill

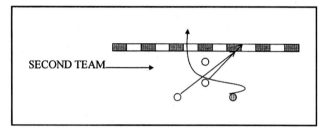

Figure 3-13. Run Skelly Drill

Circle Dril

Objective: To teach the quarterback to throw on the run.

Description: In this drill, two quarterbacks line up facing each other 10 to 15 yards apart. They start running in a clockwise circular motion as they throw the ball back and forth. After a predetermined number of reps, they repeat the drill in a counter-clockwise direction.

Coaching Points:

• Players should stay parallel to each other by maintaining the same speed.

• Players should hold the ball with two hands up by their chest as they run with the ball.

• Make sure they properly rotate their hips and that their shoulders are parallel to their target when they throw. It is important for them to throw the ball with touch and lead the receiver.

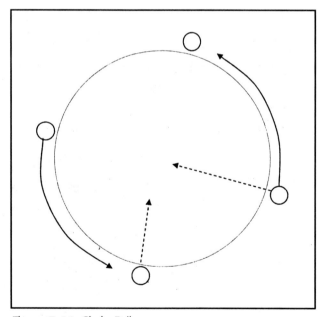

Figure 3-14. Circle Dril

Start Drill

Objective: To teach the quarterback to make a consistent separation step from center.

Description: The quarterback gets in his proper stance with his eyes facing forward. The coach calls out the step for him to execute (e.g., 'left 90' means the QB will take a 90-degree step with his left foot only and so on). His weight should be on his plant foot, which doesn't move. Use a center or simulate a snap to the QB. He should pull the ball into his belly and remain there.

Coaching Points:

- The QB shouldn't stand up; his body position should remain constant from his stance.

- Make sure the QB gets good separation from center.

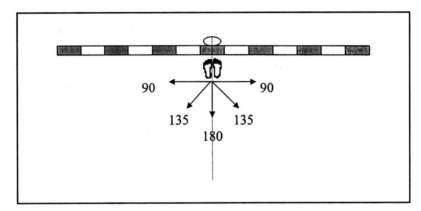

Figure 3-15. Start Drill

Footwork Drill

Description: This drill is the continuation of the Start Drill. In this drill, the quarterback executes his steps in an offensive play. No running backs are used; the emphasis should be on footwork.

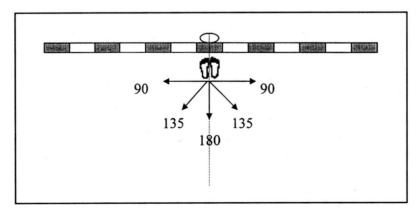

Figure 3-16. Footwork Drill

Running Backs

Depending on the system you use, the backs will start in either a two-point or three-point stance. Each stance has its benefits. For instance, a back in a two-point stance can see the defensive alignment, which can help his run angles. A back coming out of a three-point stance is more explosive and harder to pick-up before the play by the defenders.

Stance

Two-Point Stance

In a two-point stance the running back should:

- Be balanced (i.e., not leaning forward or back or pointing left or right).

- Place extra weight on his push off foot without showing it (e.g., if he were going to take a toss to his right, more weight should be on his left foot).

- Place his palms flat on his thighs with his fingers pointing down.

- Have his head up and his chest out surveying the defense; he should not be hunching over.

- Have all body parts straight ahead with his feet perpendicular to LOS.

Three-Point Stance

In a three-point stance the running back should:

- Distribute his weight evenly between the down hand and both feet; the fingertips of the down hand should be on the ground, not the knuckles.

- Have his back parallel to the ground; it is OK if the butt becomes slightly higher than the shoulders.

- Be consistent with his feet stagger (never more than heel to toe).

- Put the forearm of his free hand across the knee in a manner that can quickly slide up to the stomach and form the handoff pouch.

Takeoff

In a takeoff, acceleration is created with a powerful push off the planted foot and reaching maximum stepping distance with the lead foot. The concentration should be on the power foot or pivot foot. The elbows are kept close to the body upon takeoff. Running backs should take off like an airplane without standing up out of their stance.

Three types of takeoffs of the lead foot should be practiced extensively, first with the right foot then with the left.

- Straight ahead, which would be used in a dive play

- 45 degrees, which would be used on an off-tackle play

- 90 degrees, which would be used on a sweep or toss play

Counter step–When a player takes one step in the opposite direction he is going, looking the same way he steps, then using that jab-step as his new pivot foot to go in other direction.

QB-RB Exchange

The ballcarrier will make a handoff pouch. The arm, which will be on the side of the QB during the exchange, should be held parallel to the ground with that elbow up from about the middle of his chest. The bottom arm is held out on a slight angle just below the waist.

- The ballcarrier's head should be up and reading his "hole" and the defense, while being able to feel the handoff and properly clutch the ball.

- The carrier will fold or close his arms over the ball trying to envelop the ball so that it ends up in the armpit of the lower arm. Every carry must be in an armpit with the hand over the other part of the ball.

Receiving the Pitch or Toss

Concentration is key when a running back receives the pitch or toss from the quarterback. From his very first step he should be intensely staring at the ball in the QB's hands. He should stare at the ball all the way into his hands. His hands should form a basket with his pinky fingers together. Upon receiving the ball, it should be secured in his outside armpit making sure to gain complete control of the ball before attempting any moves. His shoulder should be parallel to the LOS.

The Reverse Hand-off

Some coaches use a basket pouch in the second handoff in a reverse because of the speed of the runners at the time. The basket pouch is similar to the pitch basket pouch. Time it so that you can execute the same consistent exchange throughout your offense.

Ball Security

Proper Carrying

- As previously stated, the hand, fingers, arm, and armpit should envelop the ball.

- The more of the ball that is showing, the greater chance of a fumble.

- The tip of the ball is covered by spread fingers which should be forcing the ball in the armpit like a vise.

- It is important that the elbow be wrapped around the ball. This will allow the arm and hand to give the most coverage of the ball.

- A two handed carry through traffic is essential. A one handed carry with the ball tight in the armpit and the other arm over the ball to protect it. This will bring the ball more in front of the body than the side.

Switching From One Hand to the Other

Typically, when the ballcarrier is in the open field and defenders are coming in their pursuit angles, the ball should be switched to the sideline arm to protect it from contact. The switch takes place by passing through the two-arm carry while the carrying arm forces the ball into the other armpit keeping it secure throughout the switch.

A player should never attempt a switch when a defender is even remotely close to him. And because of the risk of losing the ball, some coaches don't allow arm exchanges at all.

Faking

Faking a handoff is extremely basic. The player doesn't do anything differently than he would if he were to actually receive the ball. He hits the hole like he has the ball, lowers his shoulders, and gets someone to tackle him. Although this sounds simple, it is imperative that you practice this as much as any real handoff. Every detail of a real handoff needs to be executed from the player's hands, shoulders, head, feet, and hips. The player who is executing the fake should:

- Never hunch over (backs with the ball don't hunch)

- Not clasp their hands together quickly out of the pouch (every defender will know it is a fake)

- Run full speed (faking backs have a tendency to slow down quickly)

Running Techniques

You need to develop explosive runners. Teach runners to *explode* out of their stance, explode through the hole, and *explode* through the tackler. Many backs are tentative until they've chosen their path. A hole will close rapidly and runners need to be reminded to keep up the tempo.

Dive Techniques

A dive run means a back is hitting a hole with no lead blocker. This technique is used on dives, counters, draws, etc. The key to a dive run is hitting that hole as quickly and explosively as possible. The back should have a North/South mentality coming off his blockers. He should be at top speed when he hits the hole.

If no hole exists and the runner is at full speed, he will be in a position to blast through for yardage. Give your back a landmark to aim for (e.g., the outside hip of the left tackle). These landmarks will depend on your offensive scheme and blocking schemes for each play. Alignment in the backfield will also change according to your scheme.

Reading the hole that a back will go through starts at the pre-snap. The back should look at the alignment to give him a sense of how his blocks will set up. The back must continue reading the blocker from the snap of the ball until he reaches daylight.

The cutback dive is the quick but small change in directions that are set up by the block. This is where the back's course is altered and he makes a full-speed cut to the inside or outside of his immediate blocker.Again, practice having your players *explode* through the holes.

Freeze Technique

The freeze technique simply means that the ballcarrier runs directly at the defender. This is often done at linebackers. If the runner commits his direction too early, he will surely give up an easy tackle. The key is to make the defender flat-footed, therefore giving the runner the advantage.

The freeze technique is perfect for setting up a blocker. If the player can freeze a LB and make him flat-footed, the blocker doesn't need to make a devastating block for him to get by, which is a major advantage to the blocker. Whenever a player can follow directly behind a blocker until he has made contact, he should be able to get by him. The trick is for the player to not give him any clue as to what direction he is leaning until the blocker makes initial contact. This is an important technique in the I formation.

End Running Technique

The emphasis here should be on north/south running. One of the biggest mistakes made by young running backs is that they tend to angle their running. Most outside runs are designed to create a run lane up the field. The runner must read the blockers and choose the proper lane (i.e., outside the block or inside the block). At that point he needs a north/south mentality.

Some of the best end runs are when a defender is turned out and the runner cuts upfield inside him. This gives fewer defenders a chance to have quality pursuit angles. If your back always tries to get to the sideline in the open field, someone will catch him.

The end runner has to be very disciplined in order to follow his blocks and let his blockers set up the run lane. Many coaches use a one yard by one yard relationship to set up the block. This means the runner is one yard behind the blocker and one yard outside him. It is important to practice this timing. The ballcarrier needs to know who the lead blocker is and the timing it will take to form the correct relationship.

Different offensive schemes will create different angles the runner and blocker will take. Some end runs are done in an arcing pattern while some are east/west with a 90-degree cut when the lane is created. The freeze technique can be executed on end runs as well.

Open Field Running

As with any run, the most important thing for a back to do is explode in a north/south direction while elongating his strides. All cuts should be executed off a north/south running lane. Remember, the more north/south he runs, the fewer defenders will have a shot at him.

When a defender has a good pursuit angle, a last-second cutback against the grain can be very successful. This cutback will only be successful if it comes off a top-speed north/south run.If the running back is perfectly pursued by a defender, or more than one defender, a cutback may minimize the possible yardage he could gain. In this situation, the runner should lower his inside shoulder and drive up and through the shoulder pads of the defender in order to blast himself forward for as much positive yardage as possible. Drills should be performed often so the back can learn when to cut and when to blast forward. Both will only be successful out of a full-speed north/south run.

Dive Surge

The dive surge is used to blast through on critical short yardage situations or on a goal line run. It can be utilized running forward, laterally, or after turning a corner. As in any run, it would most often be used in a north/south direction.

This technique is performed when the runner is trying to squeeze between two defenders and gain necessary yardage. It is executed by dropping the inside shoulder (the arm with ball) to become almost perpendicular to the ground. If the runner squares up in this situation, he will expose too much upper body enabling the defense to stop him. Acceleration, combined with the turned shoulder, will enable the runner to blast through the crack between the two defenders. He must put his surge power right at the gap between the two players; this will give him the advantage.

Spin-out

The spin-out is used when the runner hits a pileup but still sees daylight to one side or the other. To perform this, the runner must be running north/south as he hits the pile with a powerful upward blast. His shoulders should be arching his back and he should use the force of his hit to roll off in the direction he wants. Keeping his feet moving at all times is the key.

Stumble

When a runner loses his balance, he simply uses his free hand to break his fall. Off this move he needs to abruptly thrust his head up, arch his back and pump his knees up high to try and get his feet back under his shoulders.

Dragging a Tackler

This technique is essential to getting that extra couple of yards out of a run. It is performed by running north and south with short choppy steps. A forward body lean and powerfully pumping high knees will make this successful. The ball should be tucked securely when doing this. Blows from other directions will likely be sustained as the runner churns for yardage.

Receiving

Players should always keep their fingers comfortably spread when receiving the ball. They should catch the ball with soft hands like they are catching an egg. Receivers should never use their bodies to help make the catch, rather their hands. The following techniques are used to catch the ball depending on where it is thrown. The receiver's hands should be relatively close together and:

- above the shoulder (thumbs are in and facing down)
- below the shoulder (pinkies are in and thumbs are up)
- over the shoulder (pinkies are together and thumbs are up)

The running back needs to work on his patterns like any other receiver. Their patterns must always be run at full speed. Consistency is the key to success. On play-action patterns they may be called upon to execute a fake handoff reception before completing any pattern.

Blocking

Do yourself a favor and spend a significant amount of practice time on running back blocking. Many young coaches spend all of their time with the running backs working on everything but blocking. Teach the following blocks and work on them as hard as you work on running skills.

Isolation Block

This is usually the blocking of a LB who is left isolated in the blocking scheme. It is best performed using the freeze technique with your runner to put the blocker at an advantage (see Freeze Technique). To execute the isolation block teach the blocker to:

- explode out of his stance
- aim for LB's lower part of the chest plate
- "throttle down" slightly just before contact
- stay in control and widen his stance
- punch up with the palm of his hands just under chest plate from a great power angle (this is referred to as 'stepping on the LB's toes')
- put power in an upward thrust with the lower body
- upon contact, roll his hips under while arching his back
- maintain contact with the LB as he drives him up and back
- if the LB gets by, to execute a 'rip' move on the far side of his chest
- never lunge at the LB, rather to stay in control and focus on executing the proper blow

Kick Out Block

The kick out block is performed on the defensive end. This is a huge block in some offensive systems. This block is used to set up a running lane for the runner to cut back into. Since most defensive ends have 'read and contain' mentalities, the blocker needs to get to him quickly before he reads the play. He should:

- take an inside-out route at full speed toward the defender
- stay low
- keep his elbow in
- rip up through the inside part of the defender's chest
- follow through with his block
- be persistent

If the defensive end closes down hard to the inside, it will be impossible to take him out. If this happens, the blocker needs to blast right over him.

Running Back Drills

Upfield Cut Drill

Description: In this drill, the back takes a handoff running laterally toward the sideline. On the 'cut' command, the back throttles down with short choppy steps and makes a good 90-degree cut upfield for five yards. The quarterback executes a proper handoff with 'boot' follow-through for five yards making sure all his footwork is done properly. He then executes the reverse pivot technique (if this is what your offense normally does). Repeat the drill coming back in the other direction. Do at least two reps in each direction.

Coaching Points:

- Make sure the back drives off his outside foot (pivot foot) when making his cut.
- A cone can be used for the 'cut' reference point rather than a verbal command.

Note: When you execute a drill like this, it is always wise to simulate a play in your offense that would most likely require the use of the skill you are drilling. Use the fire hose or any LOS markers. This will help with proper alignment and help the back time his runs to hit the exact 'hole' or area that the play was designed to hit.

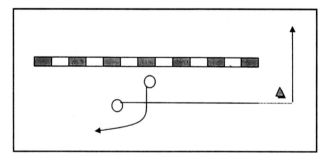

Figure 3-17. Upfield Cut Drill

Cutback Drill

Description: In this drill, the back takes a dive handoff to the right side of the quarterback. He runs north/south at full speed directly at a coach who will be facing him. The coach turns abruptly right or left at the last second. The back must make a quick cut to the coach's backside and continue north/south. Repeat this drill coming back with the handoff to the left side. When the last back is through the line, the QB executes the drill.

Coaching Points:

- Make sure the back doesn't take a wide cut; it should be an abrupt cut and he should continue running north/south with the ball.
- You can use a stand up dummy that a coach or player rocks left or right as the ballcarrier approaches. The ballcarrier must read the dummy and make a sharp cut and get back to his north/south direction quickly.

Note: When you execute a drill like this, it is always wise to simulate a play in your offense that would most likely require the use of the skill you are drilling. Use the fire hose or any LOS markers. This will help with proper alignment and help the back time his runs to hit the exact 'hole' or area that the play was designed to hit.

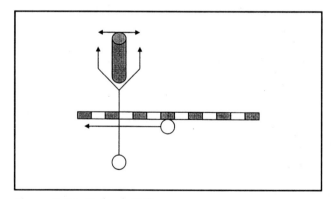

Figure 3-18. Cutback Drill

Exchange Drill

Description: In this drill, the backs form two lines 10 yards apart facing each other. The first back in each line takes off at half-speed toward each other. The back with the ball lays the ball out for a handoff. The other back receives the handoff and then lays it out for the next man in line. The next back in line doesn't takeoff until the other exchange is completed. Continue the drill until the backs receive a sufficient number of reps.

Coaching Points:

• Make sure the back is taking a proper handoff.

• In a proper handoff, their eyes should be straight ahead (never looking at the ball), and they should receive the handoff from the right and left side.

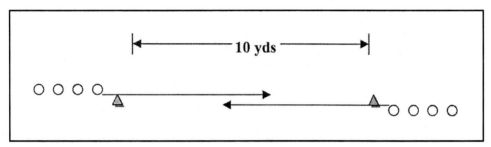

Figure 3-19. Exchange Drill

Cut Drill

Description: In this drill, a series of cones are set up five yards apart and offset by three yards. A runner takes off and cuts around each cone. He carries the ball in his outside arm, switching it with every cut. When he gets to the bag at the end, a coach will dip it right or left and the runner will make a sharp cut and get back upfield.

Coaching Points:

• Make sure the runner plants his outside foot on every cut.

• Make sure the runner is holding the ball and changes arms properly.

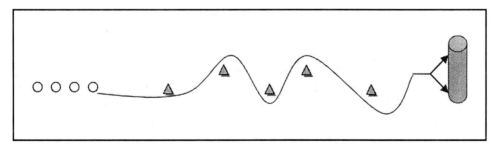

Figure 3-20. Cut Drill

Footwork Drills

Equipment Needed: Five half-rounds; step-over dummies or tackling dummies.

Description: In the footwork drills, the step-over or tackling dummies are placed on the ground parallel to each other with one yard between them. The ballcarrier executes a series of running techniques, over and through the bags.

Note: When you execute drills like this, it is always wise to simulate plays in your offense that would most likely require the use of the skill you are drilling. Use the fire hose or any LOS markers. This will help with proper alignment and help the back time his runs to hit the exact 'hole' or area that the play was designed to hit.

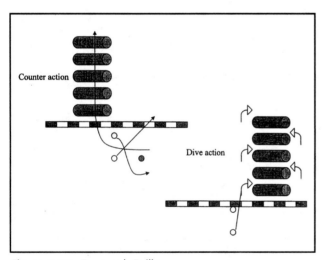

Figure 3-21. Footwork Drills

High-knee Step-overs

Objective: To develop the running back's footwork; improve agility.

Description: In this drill, five bags are set up parallel with each other and one yard apart. A line of players is formed five yards off the bags and facing forward. On the coach's command, the first player in line will step over the bags, alternating feet as they step over each bag. After every player has had a repetition, the drill is repeated having players step with both feet in between each bag.

Coaching Points:

• Make sure players are lifting their knees high between every step.

• Their heads should always be up and facing forward. When they become proficient at this drill, they will be able to perform it without ever looking down.

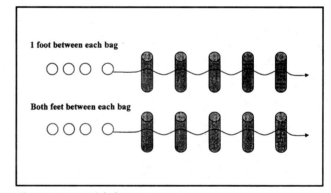

Figure 3-22. High-knee Step-overs

Side Step-overs

Objective: To develop the running back's footwork; improve agility.

Description: In this drill, five bags are set up parallel with each other and two yards apart. A line of players is formed five yards off the end of one of the bags and facing forward. On the coach's command, the player will sidestep over the bag with his first foot, bring his next foot over the same bag, and then bring both feet together in between the bags. He should continue this as quickly as he can until he has completed the drill in that direction. After every player has had an equal number of repetitions, the drill is repeated starting from the other end of the bags, still facing forward.

Coaching Points:

• Make sure players maintain a proper body position throughout the drill.

• Players have a tendency to do this drill standing straight up. It is important that their head is up and facing forward.

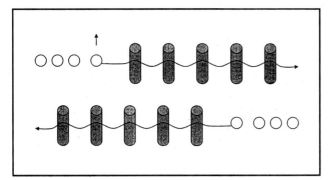

Figure 3-23. Side Step-overs

Shuffle Steps

Objective: To develop the running back's shuffle footwork; improve agility.

Description: In this drill, five bags are set up parallel with each other and two yards apart. A line of players is formed five yards off the end of one of the bags and facing forward. On the coach's command, the first player will shuffle around all the bags. He must remain facing forward throughout the drill.

Coaching Points:

• Make sure the player does not cross his feet at any time.

• Make sure players maintain a proper body position throughout the drill.

• Players have a tendency to do this drill standing straight up. It is important that their head is up and facing forward.

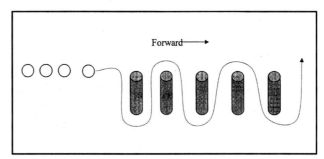

Figure 3-24. Shuffle Steps

Stutter Overs

Objective: To develop the running back's footwork; improve agility.

Description: In this drill, five bags are set up parallel with each other and one yard apart. A line of players is formed five yards off the bags and facing forward. On the coach's command, the first player in line will step over the bags and chop his feet inside the bags simulating four stutter steps. He then steps over the next bag until he has completed the drill. After every player has had a repetition, the drill is repeated by stepping between each bag with both feet.

Coaching Points:

- Make sure the player does not cross his feet at any time.
- Make sure players maintain a proper body position throughout the drill.
- Players have a tendency to do this drill standing straight up. It is important that their head is up and facing forward.

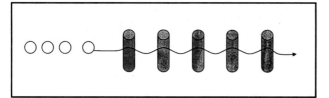

Figure 3-25. Stutter Overs

Bird Dog

Description: In this drill, a line of players takes a three-point stance. On the whistle, they execute coming out of their stances using only the first step. They hold that step for one second and snap back to their stance. The following sequence will be followed for each whistle: right foot forward, left foot forward, right foot 45 degrees, left foot 45 degrees, right foot 90 degrees, left foot 90 degrees. On the seventh whistle blow, the coach will call out a step and the players lead with that step and sprint five yards. Continue this drill until all players have performed the sprint portion of the drill with all six types of lead steps.

Coaching Points:

- When players are sprinting out of the 90-degree step, they should continue in their step direction for three yards before turning upfield to complete the five-yard sprint.
- Players should be stepping with the proper lead foot on every play. The step must be short and quick.
- Players should be frozen momentarily in a low, powerful and balanced position. Don't let them stand up out of their stance.
- Players can tend to get sloppy while doing this drill; if you notice this, make them freeze after their step until you check their body positioning and don't let them back down in their stance until you give them the command.

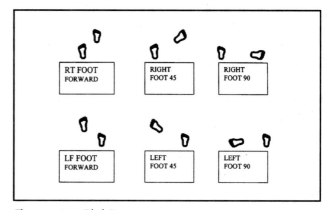

Figure 3-26. Bird Dog

Buck Up Through Drill

Description: In this drill, two bag holders stand side by side with a ballcarrier three yards away. The ballcarrier receives the handoff and explodes up through the bags. The bag holders have three options: they both can hit the ballcarrier; one hits the ballcarrier; neither hit the ballcarrier.

Coaching Points:

- You can replace bags either with a blaster or with players who will use their shoulders but not rap and make tackle.

- You can vary this drill by placing a defender five yards off the bag holders that will approach the runner who will make a cut off him.

- Make sure the runner keeps his head up and his shoulders and butt low for leverage. He should explode up and through the bags with an acceleration step. The ball must be properly protected by the runner at all times; a two-handed carry must be executed at the point of contact.

Note: When you execute a drill like this, it is always wise to simulate a play in your offense that would most likely require the use of the skill you are drilling. Use the fire hose or any LOS markers. This will help with proper alignment and help the back time his runs to hit the exact 'hole' or area that the play was designed to hit.

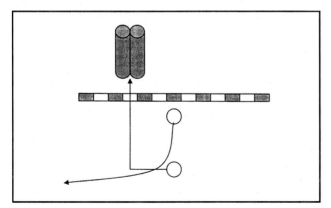

Figure 3-27. Buck Up Through Drill

Lead Blocker Drill (Dive)

Description:

- The blocker will come out of his three-point stance and perform a proper lead block on a bag lined up five yards ahead centered between two cones that are spaced five yards apart.

- A ballcarrier will follow the lead blocker from one to two yards back. He will read the block and make the appropriate cut, then continue upfield in a north/south direction. See Figure 3-28a.

- Run in both directions.

Variation:

- Perform this drill live by replacing the bag with a defender.

Coaching Points:

- The blocker must get low and maintain a properly executed block.

- Make sure the ballcarrier doesn't make too wide of a cut.

- You can alternate running these drills; one day do the dive, on the next day do the sweep.

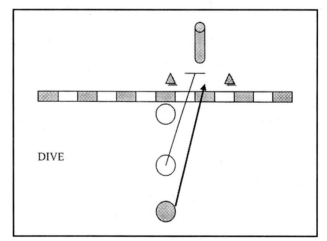

Figure 3-28a. Lead Blocker Drill (Dive)

Lead Blocker Drill (Sweep)

Description:

- The blocker will come out of his stance and perform a lead block on a bag lined up 10 yards to the side and five yards back.
- The ballcarrier will follow the blocker in a 2 x 1 relationship (i.e., two yards back and one yard outside). See Figure 3-28b.
- The ballcarrier will read the block and make the proper north/south cut upfield.
- The blocker and runner should be running an arc motion on the way to the defender. They should not take a course straight out of their stance toward the defender.
- Run in both directions.

Variation:

- Substitute the bag for a live tackler.

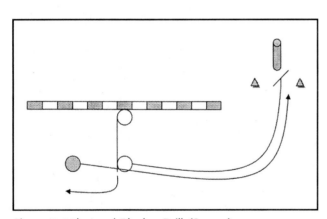

Figure 3-28b. Lead Blocker Drill (Sweep)

Belly Drill

Objective: To perfect the execution of an important offensive play. For halfbacks: to receive live blocking repetitions; for fullbacks: to learn how to read and cut off a lead block; for defenders: to improve the technique of shedding a blocker.

Description:

- Set up a LOS marker (fire hose) and two boundary markers (half rounds) that straddle the area your play will go to. Separate them by three yards.
- A defender (LB) is placed between the boundaries.
- Execute a belly play.
- The lead blocker will block the defender and try to turn him in any direction.
- The ballcarrier must read the block and make the right cut upfield for five yards.
- The defender will try to execute a thud tackle.
- Run in both directions.

Coaching Points:

- For this drill, use any play in your offense that has a lead blocker.
- Make sure that every player is executing his proper footwork on the play.
- Make sure the halfback executes a proper freeze block on the LB; if the LB commits in a direction, he should block him in the direction he is going.
- The FB must keep his head up and attempt to get behind his blocker long enough to read the direction he should cut. If the hips of his blocker turn, he needs to make an immediate cut off his buttocks.

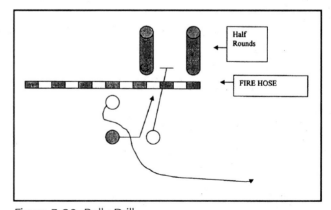

Figure 3-29. Belly Drill

Dive Drill

Objective: To teach a ballcarrier how to read the block of his offensive lineman in a tight area.

Description:

- The ballcarrier will take a dive handoff that simulates a dive action in your offense.

- A blocker that represents a lineman will be in a three-point stance; he will block a defensive lineman or a linebacker lined up over him.

- There will be a one-yard boundary marker on both sides of the blocker. (You can use collapsible cones, pinnies, or half-rounds to create the boundary.)

- The defender will try to make a thud tackle on the runner.

Coaching Points:

- The running back must read the block of his lineman properly. He should be taught to read the buttocks and hips of his blocker and to make his cut off that. The narrow lanes are there to force him to cut and get back up the field in a north/south direction.

- Be sure the handoff is taken properly and the runner has his head up and his eyes focused on the area he must get to.

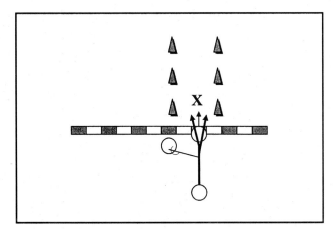

Figure 3-30. Dive Drill

Nutcracker Drill

Objective: To gain as much yardage as possible on the dive technique live, while having to read a block, make the right cut, and prepare for impact with the linebacker.

Description:

- The runner will take a dive handoff and make the appropriate cut behind a blocker on the LOS.

- He will then encounter a linebacker immediately after making his cut.

- This will all be performed within an outlined boundary.

- Perform this drill 100% live.

Coaching Points:

- The most important aspect of this drill is preparing the running back for the immediate impact of the linebacker. He will most likely try and buck up through him. He may also be able to make a good cut on him or be able to make a spin move off him.

- This drill can be a competition to see which back gains the most yardage.

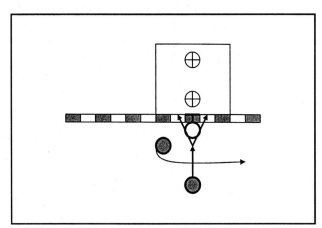

Figure 3-31. Nutcracker Drill

Ultimate Combo Drill

Objective: To improve execution of a play in your offense.

Description:

- The fullback executes a kick-out block on the end man on the LOS. The halfback takes the handoff over the midline and cuts into the LOS inside of the fullback's block.

- The halfback will buck up and through either the blaster, two bags that are held by coaches, or two live players that will lay shoulders into him. He must get his head up and be ready for the next element.

- Through a series of half-rounds, ropes or bags the back will do one of the following: step-overs (one foot over the bags); side cuts (laterally goes around each bag without crossing his feet); stutter steps (four steps between each bag).

- He executes proper cuts around the cones; he always cuts off his outside foot.

- He will either cut off the movement of the bag by the coach or he will drive into the bag and perform a spin move off it.

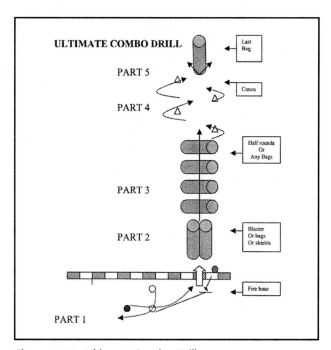

Figure 3-32. Ultimate Combo Drill

Gauntlet Drill

Objective: To teach a ballcarrier how to hold onto the ball in traffic and still gain yardage by keeping his feet and legs moving.

Description:

- Set up two lines of defenders that are parallel to each other.

- Send a runner with a ball to run through the line.

- The first set of defenders (the two in the front of the gauntlet) should lower their shoulders into the runner as he comes through the gauntlet. (You can also use bags to bang the runner instead of live contact.)

- The second set of defenders should slap at the ball trying to jar it loose.

- The third set of defenders use their shoulders again, and the fourth set slap at the ball and so on down the line.

Variation:

- Add a bag or player to the end of the line for the runner to either cut off its movement or drive into and perform a spin move off of it.

Coaching Points:

- Make sure the runner keeps his head up at all times.

- The runner must buck up through the defenders that are lowering their shoulders (or through the bags). He should bring his shoulders up through the defenders from low to high during impact.

- The runner's feet and legs should be pumping powerfully the entire time. He needs to be executing a two-arm carry throughout the gauntlet.

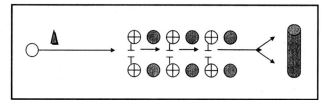

Figure 3-33. Gauntlet Drill

Long Ball

Description:

- Set up two lines 25 yards apart with your backs and receivers. Each line will have its own QB.
- The first person in each line will run a fly pattern and catch the QB's throw.
- After he gets the ball, he gives it to the opposite QB and gets in that line.

Coaching Point:

- Watch the QB and the receivers for proper mechanics. The ball should be thrown over the inside shoulder of the receiver and should be caught with palms up and pinkies together.

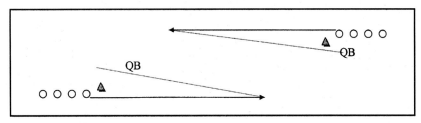

Figure 3-34. Long Ball

Swing Pass Drill (screen)

Description:

- Set up two lines of halfbacks – one on either side of the QB.
- The first player in each line will run a swing pass out of the backfield to the side he is lined up on.
- The QB will execute a five-step drop
- The throw should be a touch pass over the inside shoulder of the back..
- Switch lines after every repetition.

Variations:

- Add a defender simulating an outside rush for the QB to throw over.
- Use screen action instead of swing.

Coaching Points:

- Make sure the QB executes a proper five-step drop.
- The back should take a few lateral steps before arcing his pattern up the field. He will ideally catch the pass around the LOS approximately 8 to 10 yards outside the end man on the LOS. He needs to quickly tuck the ball and sprint five more yards upfield.

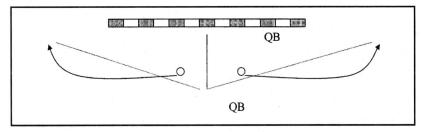

Figure 3-35. Swing Pass Drill (screen)

Flat Pass Drill (Play Action)

Objective: To work on the timing of your play-action passing game relative to the back coming out of the backfield.

Description:

- Set up a cone to mark where you want your quarterback to set up and throw.
- Have the back coming out of the backfield give a forearm to a bag or player at the LOS. (This will better simulate traffic delays encountered live.)
- After catching the ball, the running back must quickly adjust his path to get upfield as fast as possible for about five yards.
- Run in both directions.

Variation:

- Add a simulated rush so the QB has to redirect and throw on the run.

Coaching Points:

- You should always be simulating an actual play-action pass from your playbook.
- Make sure the play-action fake is executed properly.
- Watch the set up and delivery of your QB. Teach the QB how to make safe throws or get rid of the ball properly if the play breaks down.

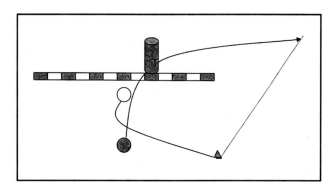

Figure 3-36. Fast Pass Drill (Play Action)

Run Skelly

Objective: To perfect the timing and fundamentals of your running game.

Description:

- Practice all running plays and put in new ones.
- Set up a line of scrimmage with cones or hose markings for two stations 12 yards behind the other. Separate your first and second string backfields.
- Simulate a snap to your QB on every play.

Variations:

- Have each set of players run the same play one right after the other.
- Have different coaches working with different groups at their own pace and running independently of each other.

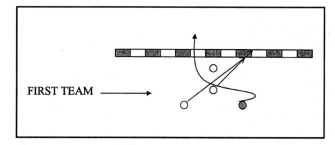

Figure 3-37. Run Skelly

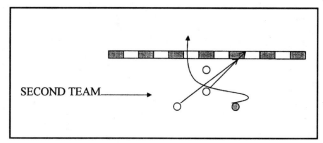

Figure 3-38. Run Skelly

Sideline Run Drill

Objective: To teach the ballcarrier how to run down the sideline and gain maximum yardage.

Description:

• The ball carrier will receive the ball from a sweep or toss action.

• He will turn upfield outside a cone five yards from a sideline.

• Three defenders will use bags to try and hit him off balance.

• The ballcarrier will buck up through the bags and maintain his balance inbounds.

Variations:

• Add a live defender to close in on the ballcarrier from an upfield angle. The ballcarrier must either cut back upfield on him or buck up through and gain the most yards possible.

• This drill demonstrates 'toss' action; run from 'sweep' action as well.

Coaching Points:

• Make sure the ballcarrier uses his inside shoulder to buck up through the bags. He needs to be taught to get from low to high and accelerate through the impact of the bags. Stress the explosiveness of this move.

• When you are using a live defender be sure the runner learns when to cut back upfield versus getting the most yards possible by repeating the explosive buck up and through motion with his inside shoulder. Ill-timed cutbacks will give up potential gains.

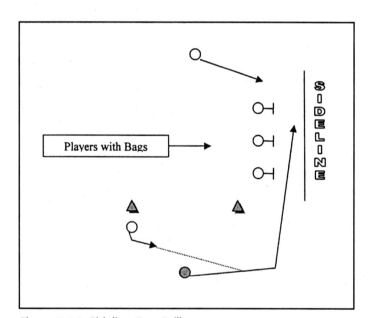

Figure 3-39. Sideline Run Drill

Stumble Drill

Objective: To teach a ball carrier to regain his balance when he stumbles forward.

Description:

- Form two to four lines separated by five yards on any yard line.
- On the coach's command, the backs will take turns running a 25-yard sprint while carrying a football. He will start with the football in his left arm.
- Every five yards he must touch the ground in front of him with his palm, while still running; (this should cause him to stumble).
- He needs to regain his balance by throwing his head up, arching his back, and thrusting his knees up high and toward his chest.
- When he recovers, he needs to switch the ball to his other arm and continue switching until he is finished.

Coaching Point:

- Make sure the players are running fast enough to cause a stumble. Their palm must hit the ground, not just their fingertips.

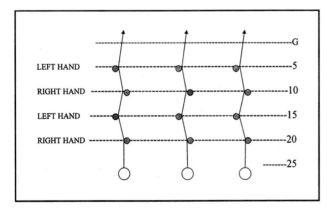

Figure 3-40. Stumble Drill

Mirror Block Drill

Objective: To teach pass blocking to your running backs.

Description:

- Two cones are placed five yards apart.
- A running back and a defender are facing each other two yards apart between the cones.
- Another cone is placed three yards behind the blocker (back) to represent the quarterback, which the back is trying to protect.
- On the coach's command, the defender will shuffle back and forth for five seconds, and then attempt a pass rush at the designated quarterback cone.
- The running back will mirror the defender's every move, and then block him away from the quarterback cone when he rushes.

Coaching Point:

- The running back needs to stay low with his knees flexed. When the defender rushes, he needs to punch up through his chest with both hands and maintain contact with the defender. His shoulders should be lower than the defenders and his base should be slightly wider than his stance.

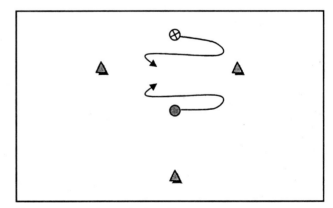

Figure 3-41. Mirror Block Drill

Outside Rush Block

Objective: To teach the running back to pass block in an outside rush situation.

Description:

- Set up a LOS pass situation with a running back and a cone that represents the QB.
- The running back should be lined up approx four yards off the LOS.
- The QB cone should be six to seven yards off the LOS.
- A defender will rush the QB cone from somewhere on the outside of the LOS.
- The running back will execute proper pass block technique on the defender.

Coaching Point:

- The blocker needs to meet the rusher in pursuit; he cannot be back on his heels or he will be bull-rushed. He must mirror his every move. He needs to jam his hands into the chest plate and maintain contact.

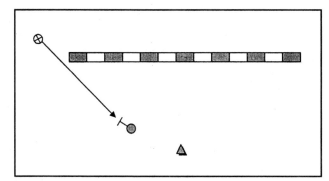

Figure 3-42. Outside Rush Block

Ball Security Drill

Objective: To teach the running back to protect the ball and deliver the blow when impact is inevitable.

Description:

- A running back will secure a football in his left arm.
- A defender will be lined up on an angle to his right.
- On the coach's command the defender will make a thud-type impact with the ballcarrier.
- The ball-carrier will explode into the defender and buck up through with his right shoulder. He must switch to a two-handed carry before impact.
- Perform three to four reps then switch to the left side.

Variation:

- Execute a double shoulder blast with a defender on each side.

Coaching Point:

- The running back must make a two-handed carry on every repetition. He needs to keep his head up at all times and exexute a buck up motion with each shoulder.

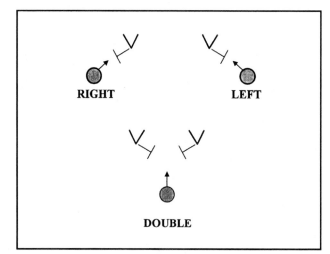

Figure 3-43. Ball Security Drill

Goal Line Score Drill

Objective: To teach the running back how to make the tough yards in goal line or short yardage situations.

Description:

- Set up two boundaries five yards apart with a goal line connecting one end.
- A linebacker will align himself on the goal line and attempt to stop the running back from crossing the goal line.
- A running back who will attempt to score a touchdown will be aligned two yards in front of the linebacker.
- The running back starts the drill whenever he is ready. He will do whatever it takes to score the touchdown.

- The linebacker will start on the back's first movement. He will do whatever it takes to stop the back short of the goal line.

Coaching Points:

- The key to success for both players is to stay low and keep their legs and feet driving. They will both accelerate at the point of impact.
- The back will twist, turn, spin, lunge or do whatever he can after the impact to get the football across the goal line before the whistle.
- The linebacker will try to burst into the football with his facemask if the ballcarrier is running on any type of angle. He will have to explode across the front of his body to accomplish this.

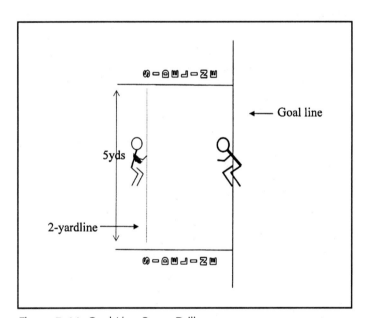

Figure 3-44. Goal Line Score Drill

Wide Receivers

Blocking

In a lot of running situations the receiver is lined up on the offside of the play. This will require him to stalk block. Even when he is aligned on the onside of a running play, he will likely be called on to perform a block somewhere down the field. This simply means he will angle downfield toward the play and try to cut off the safety or DB from getting to the runner if he breaks beyond the LOS. Blocking techniques are performed differently in downfield situations. Most blocks that occur down the field become cutoff blocks, where the defender and the blocker are both moving in the direction of the play.

Downfield blocking should be one of the first things every receiver is taught. These types of blocks are the ones that turn 10-yard gains into touchdowns. These blocks don't need to be devastating hits. The blocker should have a 'screen' mentality, trying to tie up the defender long enough to spring the ballcarrier. He should always aim for the numbers on a defender's jersey as a target for his block. He must first make contact with the defender above the waist. He is then allowed to roll his body below the waist if needed. Teach him to always get his head in front of the man he is blocking. Many touchdowns have been called back for clipping on a receiver blocking downfield. When a receiver has an angle on a defender that is pursuing a play, have him lead with his inside forearm into the chest. This will do two things:

propel his momentum to the proper side of the man in order to cut him off and take away the temptation and/or appearance of holding if the man should turn in a certain direction. Figure 3-45 shows an example of a cutoff block situation.

*Note:*The defender must put him in a position to properly cut this man off. If his angle toward him is incorrect, he will put himself in a position to be called for a clipping and holding call, or he may not be able to make any contact with the defender at all.

Instances will occur when a receiver is in a position to make a devastating block. If he is crossing the field he may have an opportunity to 'pick off' a defender that is totally unaware of his presence. When this situation presents itself, the blocker must seize the opportunity. He should be taught to lower his shoulder and forearm together to make contact just below the chest plate of the defender's shoulder pads. Figure 3-46 is an example of a pickoff block where the receiver will have an excellent opportunity to deliver a devastating blow to the defender in pursuit of the ballcarrier.

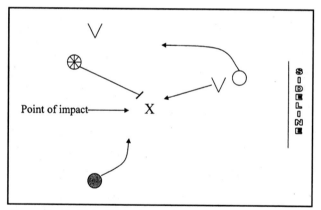

Figure 3-46. Pickoff block

Figure 3-46 shows two receivers downfield in patterns (routes). Both receivers have defenders nearby. This is a typical situation that receivers will find themselves in on a swing pass out of the backfield. Both receivers are running pass patterns down the field in order to draw the defenders away from the swing pass area. As you can see, the receiver coming from the center of the field has an

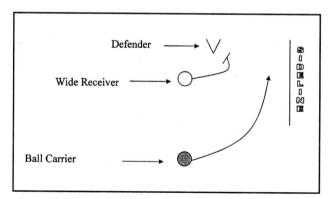

Figure 3-45. Cutoff block situation

excellent opportunity to blindside the pursuing tackler. You should also notice that the receiver closest to the sideline is putting him in a position to cut off the defender penetrating from the middle of the field. Many young receivers would try to chase down the defender that was covering him. However, he is in no position to make a clean block on him so he works himself into a position where he may spring the ballcarrier for a touchdown. He too, may find himself in a position to deliver a devastating block.

Teach your receivers to block smart. They need to always be thinking of the best way to set up the ballcarrier for a big play. Keep in mind that it is the ballcarrier's responsibility to read the block of the receiver. He should take any block he can legally achieve. He shouldn't always assume the ballcarrier needs to get 'outside.' Sometimes a player can screen a defender allowing the ballcarrier to cut to the inside, into a running lane that he just created by simply positioning himself correctly between the two.

Alignment and Takeoff

The most common stance for a receiver is a two-point stance with the outside foot back. His takeoff should be consistent on every play so that the defense will never know if he is running or passing. To be effective, he must be at full speed on every play.

There will be times when a defender will try to jam the receiver at the LOS. One technique to use is the rip technique. Punch your inside fist beyond the defender while taking a long stride with your outside foot. If he is playing off you then you can try a head fake or body shiver to get by him.

Pass Patterns

Pass patterns should be run quickly, consistently, and perfectly every time. Your players can do a variety of things to get open in these routes. Try having them work on head fakes and shoulder fakes when they make their cuts. This can buy an extra step or two from the defender. If you run poor routes you won't get open. Teach receivers to "throttle

down" with short choppy steps before they make a cut on an out route. Figure 3-47 and Figure 3-48 show some pass routes and zone that are common.

Pass Routes/Patterns

Figure 3-48 shows some of the most common pass routes used in many offenses. These should be practiced regularly. On some of these passes timing is extremely important. This is one of the reasons that the receivers need plenty of repetitions with the quarterbacks.

Most patterns can be adjusted depending on the coverage by the defenders. For instance, many slant patterns are adjusted according to the positioning of the defensive backfield. On many slant patterns the runner will be aiming for inside positioning on the defender. On out patterns he cuts toward the sideline and slightly back toward the line of scrimmage. In other words, if he runs a 12-yard out pattern, he should actually catch the ball at a depth of 10 to 11 yards. This will put him in an easier position for the quarterback to make a safe throw by being further away from the defender. When a play is designed to get a first down, be sure that he runs his pattern beyond the first down marker. This way he will have the first down even if he is tackled immediately.

Catching the Ball

When attempting to catch the football, players should always keep their fingers comfortably spread. They should catch the ball with soft hands like they are catching an egg. Their eyes should remain on the ball at all times. They should be able to see the rotation of the ball as it approaches. Teach players to catch the near end of the ball, rather than trying to catch the middle of the ball. As the ball hits their hands it will separate them to some degree. They can compensate for this by making their hands initially contact the ball at the near end just before the first stripe. They should never use their bodies to help make the catch, always the hands. The following techniques are used to catch the ball depending on where it is thrown:

- Above the shoulder-thumbs are in and facing down
- Below the shoulder-pinkies are in, thumbs are up
- Over the shoulder-pinkies are close together with the thumbs up
- Eyes are on the ball
- Hands should be relatively close together
- Catch is made at the end of the ball, the near stripe
- The ball is tucked under the arm immediately after the catch

It is imperative to teach your receivers how to tuck the ball away immediately after the catch and work up the field. In every drill you do, emphasize the importance of protecting the ball quickly. They should get plenty of repetitions catching and tucking the ball all in one motion. It needs to be second nature to them. They should be taught that the securing of the ball after the catch is just an extension of the catch; it is one continuous motion.

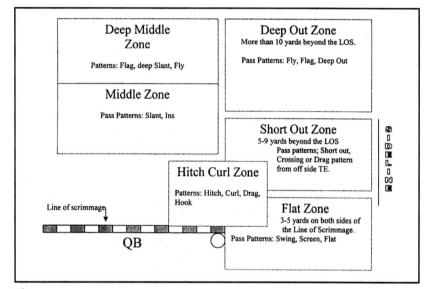

Figure 3-47

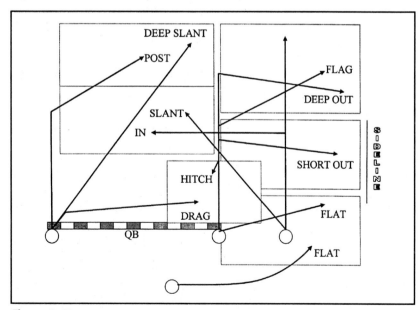

Figure 3-48

Receiver Drills

Around the Clock Drill

Objective: To work on the fundamentals of catching the football when it is thrown to different areas.

Description:

- Two receivers should line up facing each other 10 yards apart.
- They play catch with each other by throwing the ball to different areas of the other receiver's body.
- After every catch they must tuck the ball away immediately as if they were heading upfield after a catch.

Coaching Points:

- The ball should be thrown to areas all the way around the body (nose, chest, waist, knees, etc.).
- The next set of throws should be directly at the receiver's body.
- This drill should be done as a warmup every day.

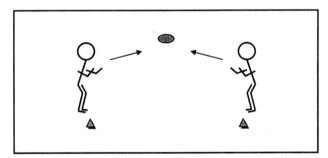

Figure 3-49. Around the Clock Drill

Figure 3-50. Around the Clock Drill

One-Handed Catch Drill

Objective: To teach the receivers to concentrate on the ball and to use 'soft hands' to catch the ball.

Description:

- Form two lines on each side of the line of scrimmage.
- All receivers will start with a proper two-point stance.
- The line on the right will go first followed immediately by the one on the left.
- The coach will say go and the receiver will jog about seven yards forward.
- The coach will thow the ball over the shoulder of the receiver who must catch it with his right hand if he is in the line on the right and the left hand if he is in the line on the left.
- Players should use only the hand to catch the ball, making sure not to trap it against the body.
- The receiver should secure the ball and head upfield.
- Switch lines after each reception.

Variation:

- Change the patterns and the speed of the patterns.

Coaching Points:

- Make sure the receiver is only using his one hand and not trapping the ball. They must focus on the ball at all times. This is a concentration drill; the more intently they concentrate the more successful they will be.

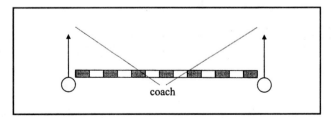

Figure 3-51. One-Handed Catch Drill

Over the Shoulder Drill

Objective: To teach the receiver to catch a pass thrown over the shoulder.

Description:

- Form two lines on on the inside of each hash mark.
- All receivers will start with a proper two-point stance.
- The line on the right will go first followed immediately by the one on the left.
- The coach will say 'go' and the reciever will run a 10- to 15-yard fly pattern at 75 % speed.
- The coach will throw the ball over the shoulder of the reciever who must catch it with his hands only.

- After the catch the receiver should secure the ball and head upfield.
- Switch lines after each reception.

Coaching Points:

- Make sure the receivers are only using their hands and not trapping the ball with their bodies. They must focus on the ball at all times. When catching the ball over the shoulder they must put their hands only inches apart from each other with their palms facing up and their pinkie fingers next to each other.

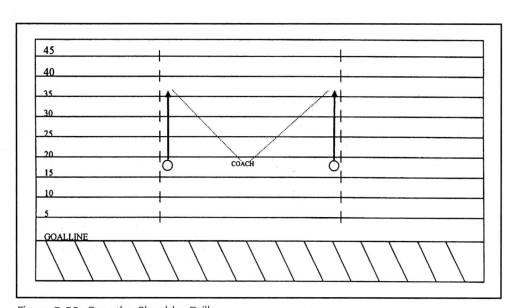

Figure 3-52. Over the Shoulder Drill

Long Ball Drill

Objective: To have the receiver practice 'over the shoulder' catches at full speed.

Description:

- Set up two lines 25 yards apart with your backs and receivers. Each line will have its own QB.

- The first person in each line will run a fly pattern and catch the QB's throw.

- After he gets the ball he gives it to the opposite QB and gets in that line.

- All patterns must be run at full speed.

Coaching Points:

- Watch the QB for proper throwing mechanics. Watch receivers for catching mechanics. The ball should be thrown over the inside shoulder of the receiver; therefore, it should be caught with palms up and pinkies together.

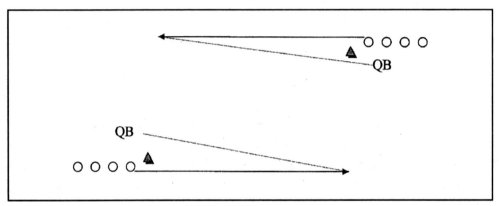

Figure 3-53. Long Ball Drill

Concentration

Objective: To teach the receivers to concentrate on holding onto the ball and at the same time ready themselves for contact.

Description:

- The receiver will run a post pattern at a depth of about 12 yards.

- A coach will be holding a blocking shield or dummy in the area the receiver will catch the ball.

- As soon as the receiver catches the ball the coach will pop him with the bag.

Coaching Points: The most important thing here is catching and holding onto the ball. Concentration is the key to success. The ability to tuck the ball away quickly and protect it must be stressed.

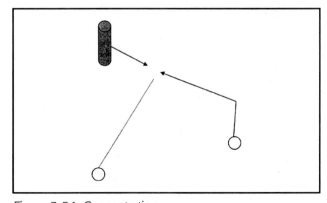

Figure 3-54. Concentration

Out Drill

Objective: To teach the receiver to catch the ball on an out pattern.

Description:

- Form two lines on on the inside of each hash mark.
- All receivers will start with a proper two-point stance.
- The line on the right will go first followed immediately by the one on the left.
- The coach will say 'go' and the receiver will run a 10- to 12-yard out pattern. This means he will catch the ball at a depth of 8 to 10 yards.
- The coach will throw an out pattern to each receiver, varying the positioning of the throws.

- After the catch the receiver should secure the ball and head upfield.
- Switch lines after each reception.

Coaching Points:

- Make sure players run a proper out pattern which requires them to slightly (one to two yards) work their way back toward the line of scrimmage after they have made their cut. The coach should throw passes to different areas. Make sure the receiver always goes to the ball no matter where it is thrown.

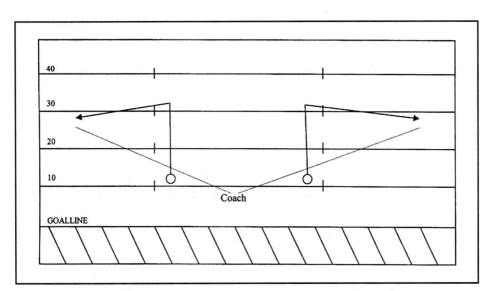

Figure 3-55. Out Drill

69

Find the Ball Drill

Objective: To teach the receivers to look for the ball quickly after making cuts from their patterns; to improve their ability to catch the ball under pressure.

Description:

• Form two receiver lines just inside the hash marks.

• The receiver will run an eight-yard out pattern.

• The quarterback or coach will throw a pass as the receiver is about to make his cut. He will throw the ball to the receiver's outside.

• As soon as the receiver makes his cut he must immediately look for the ball.

• After he catches the ball he will tuck it away and sprint five yards upfield.

• Switch lines after each reception.

Variation:

• Vary the patterns being run by the receiver.

Coaching Points:

• Make sure the receiver makes his proper cut in his pattern. His head should snap back to the passer's direction immediately after his cut.

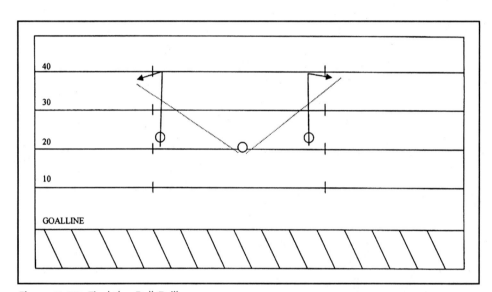

Figure 3-56. Find the Ball Drill

Turn for the Ball Drill

Objective: To teach the receiver to turn and catch a ball that is thrown behind him.

Description:

- Form two receiver lines just inside the hash marks.

- The receiver will run a 12- to 15-yard flag pattern.

- The quarterback or coach will throw a pass to the wrong side of the receiver.

- As soon as the receiver makes his cut he must immediately look for the ball. He will adjust to the throw and make the catch.

- After he catches the ball he will tuck it away and sprint five yards upfield.

- Switch lines after each reception.

Variation:

- Vary the patterns being run by the receiver.

Coaching Points:

- Once the receiver turns to look for the ball he must never turn his back to it. He must adjust his footwork to turn his body and maintain sight of the ball.

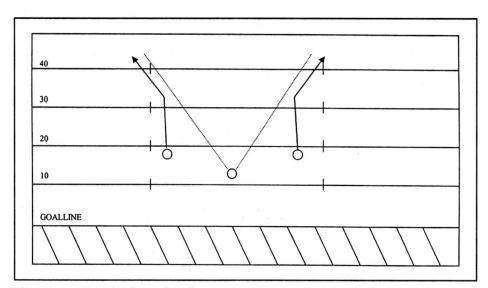

Figure 3-57. Turn for the Ball Drill

Offensive Linemen

This section outlines the skills needed by the five interior linemen and any tight ends in your formations. This is a hand blocking system that requires extensive work on the fundamentals. Contrary to popular belief, these players need to be intelligent. Other than the quarterback, they will have to learn more than any position on the field.

The Delaware wing-T uses "rule" blocking for all linemen. This simply means that on each play, the linemen will execute any one of three different blocks depending on the defensive alignment. For example, a lineman's "rule" on a play may be "post-lead-backer." Simply explained, this means if he has a man aligned over him he has a post block; if a man is aligned over the player inside him, he has a lead block; if there is no player head up on the player inside him or on him, he has backer responsibility. This is all going to seem very overwhelming to you as a coach and to the player. However, it can be learned quickly. As a coach, you should keep a "rules" cheat sheet with you at practice (see Chart 3-1). Take the time to look at the "plays" and their "rules" and you will begin to see that they are common sense. It doesn't matter what offense you run, your linemen's 'rules' should be spelled out on each play. When you practice plays, go through all of the possible defensive scenarios and they will pick it up rather quickly.

If you are using plays that don't have "rules", there are basic principles that you need to adhere to. For example, on an outside running play, the lineman will reach block a player on or outside of him. This means that he will try to hook to the outside of the defender to create an outside running lane. If it is a run inside the lineman, he would try to make a block that would cut off any defender on or outside of him, thus creating an inside run lane. Players are taught the onside and offside of a play, which will alter their assignments. The onside, or playside, is the side of the field the play will be run to using the center as your starting point. The offside is the side the play is not designed to go.

There is also a rule of thumb that will help you tremendously. When your linemen have wide splits (the distance between each lineman) this will spread the defense out more, which may make your inside running game easier. Teams with very small splits bunch the defenders closer together, which can give you an advantage running on the outside. When deciding what splits you use for your team you need to first figure out what type of system you have and what type of personnel you will have before deciding how big your split will be. Some teams will vary their splits depending on the type of play they are running. If you do this you need to be careful. If you are obvious you will create a tendency for other teams to pick up on. Again, consistency is probably your best bet.

The most important thing you can teach young linemen is to take the defender where he wants to go. In other words, stay in control of the defender at all times. If he takes him in the direction he is trying to go then he will help him take himself out of the play. If he executes a block on a defender, which the rule dictates, then he must maintain contact at all times and create a proper run lane. Sometimes, he won't get in the exact position he would like to be in. This is when he will get into a good powerful hitting position and take him where he wants to go. The running back will have to adjust his run lane. Backs are constantly being schooled on adjusting run lanes.

You will hear a lot about "hitting position" and "power angles" in this manual. A proper power angle is the part of the hitting position that will create an advantage for the blocker. The player who uses his power angles properly wins every battle on the field. At the point of contact, every runner, blocker, defender, tackler must explode out of a good hitting position. The power angles utilize the muscles in the legs, hips and buttocks, which are the strongest muscles in the body. Just as you lift a heavy object with your lower body, you block and tackle with the power of your lower body.

A lot of coaches use the phrase "low man wins." This is a completely accurate statement. The problem is that just being lower than someone will not give your players the advantage. A lot of players will drop their heads, which is not only dangerous but will also put them at a fundamental disadvantage. Teach them the proper body positioning that will give them the power advantage. These fundamentals are detailed in the blocking and tackling sections of this manual. If you teach players only one thing, make it proper body positioning.

"Break Your Nose, Not Your Neck"

Simply put, this means 'keep your head up.' A player should never use the crown (top) of his helmet. If you always have your head up, no one will ever be able to make contact with you on the crown of your helmet. If contact with the helmet should occur, it will be the facemask portion of the helmet and not the top. A player should never initiate contact with any part of his helmet, including his facemask. This is not only a safety issue, but it is also a matter of proper fundamentals.

Stance

Be consistent with your stances. You cannot afford to have your players vary their stances from play to play. This is by far the easiest way for a defender to figure out the direction of a play. If you develop different tendencies your opponent will pick them up. When a coach is scouting a team on film, the first thing he looks for are tendencies. This is why your stance must look the same on every type of play.

Young players have a tendency to lean a certain way or put more weight on one foot rather than the other. By doing this he is pointing in the direction he is going. When a young lineman needs to 'pull' on a play, he tends to lean back in his stance, putting very little if any weight on his hand. This often happens when they are pass blocking on a dropback pass play.

The key here is repetition, repetition, and repetition. Everything your players do must start with a proper stance. Always check your players' stances no matter what they are doing. Force them to be

consistently neutral in their stance; never give away their takeoff direction.

All linemen should use a three-point stance. Some coaches feel the linemen to the right of the center should put their right hand down while those to the left would use their left hand. I don't see the advantages of this. I think that a lineman should use the hand he is most comfortable with and the one where they will be most consistent. Balance is extremely important. The following are the key stance fundamentals that should be taught:

- Stand with feet slightly wider than shoulder width.
- Feet should be parallel to the L.O.S. with toes pointing forward.
- Bend at the knees as if going to sit down.
- Reach forward for the ground with the fingertips slightly ahead of the shoulders.
- Knees should be flexed and slightly in front of toes.
- Shoulders should be parallel to the ground and square with the L.O.S.
- Buttocks should be up enough that the back is almost parallel to the ground. They may be slightly lower than shoulders, never higher.
- The hand should be open on inside the knee with that elbow tight to the body.
- Head is up and looking forward with neck bowed.

Run Blocking

Run blocking is performed by using proper positioning of the body. A 'power angle' must be established in order to maintain a proper block. A 'power angle' is created when the blocker executes the proper fundamentals when coming from a position of low to high upon impact with the defender. When a blocker and a defender collide, the player in the best position of 'power' will win.

A proper block is performed when the blocker stays low and balanced while he punches up through the chest of the defender. He should use the power of his hips, buttocks and legs together to drive up and through the defender. The following are the key fundamentals of run blocking.

- Takeoff into block should use short choppy steps.
- Wide base-feet flat and slightly wider than the shoulders.
- Knees and ankles are flexed.
- Elbows are tight to the body.
- Hands open with thumbs up and close to each other.
- Aim hands at chest of defender, with the pressure being applied by the palms as you 'punch up' and through your opponent.
- The thumbs will be just under the chest plate of the defender's shoulder pads.
- Shoulders should be lower than defenders.
- Hips should be rolled up and through in conjunction with the 'punch-up'.
- Keep the head up, chin parallel to the ground and the neck bowed.
- Drive the defender with short choppy steps 6 to 10 inches at a time.

This blocking technique cannot be over practiced. Drill, drill, drill then drill some more. The 'Georgia Southern' drills, which are described in the drill section of this manual, are an excellent teaching tool for these blocks.

Pass Blocking

On a traditional dropback pass the linemen will try and create a 'pocket' for the quarterback to pass from. When they create a pocket, it is best to make the defenders go outside them to rush the passer. A blocker can use his hands as long as they remain within the confines of his body and the defensive player is in front of him. His first step should be back and inside with his inside foot in order to force an outside pass rush. It is extremely important for the blocker to remain between the passer and the rusher. As the rusher moves into him, he should deliver a blow with both hands just under the shoulder pads. As he unloads, he should give a

slight amount of ground and be ready to unload again. The blocker should continue to move his feet throughout the block and be sure not to lunge at the rusher. On the other hand, he cannot be back on his heels at the point of impact. If he is back on his heels, the defender can easily bull rush over him.

Repetition is the key. You should spend time every day working on pass blocking techniques. It all starts with their stance and start. They must quickly set up to perform their block. They should be low and in a position to deliver the blow to the defender.

Pass blocking is usually a zone type block. This means they will set up and defend an area. In a lot of situations, the linemen will know which defender they need to block. If there is no man lined up over them they need to set up and defend their area. If no one threatens their area, they need to look to help out somewhere else along the line. Your plays should be developed so that a pass blocker knows where his second responsibility will be if there is no threat to his area.

The linemen will be called upon to perform play-action pass blocking. When the play is a play-action pass, you will not always set up a traditional pocket for the quarterback to throw out of. The playside linemen's initial step needs to simulate run blocking. When doing so they will never take more than one step into the line of scrimmage. If at that point they don't make contact, they need to set themselves up to block that area from any possible defenders that may attack their area. The offside defenders will usually take an initial step with their playside foot and defend an area from their inside shoulder to anything outside.

Blocking Terminology and Techniques

This section outlines how players should execute blocking techniques. Most have common names that are used in many offenses. Some are called different names but are executed the same way. It is important to have a solid knowledge of the blocking fundamentals, especially the takeoff steps and footwork.

Gap Block: Block the defender on the inside gap. The first step is 45 degrees with the foot closest to the defender. Get his head in front and looking upfield.

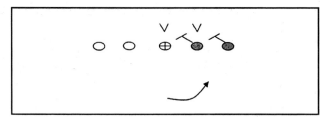

Figure 3-58. Gap Block

Down Block: Block the first man inside him. He may be in his inside gap or head up on the lineman inside him.

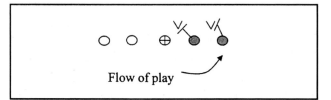

Figure 3-59. Down Block

On Block: Block the defender who is head up or has nose to knee alignment with him away from the point of attack.

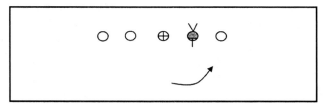

Figure 3-60. On Block

Area Block: Take one step forward, stay low, block anyone that comes in his area and hold for two counts; if no one comes, move forward downfield and block the first defender he encounters.

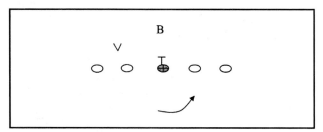

Figure 3-61. Area Block

Post (Post/Lead): This bock is the stabilizing part of a double-team block. The head is on the inside looking upfield; be ready to release if needed to cut off the linebacker after the lead blocker has established control.

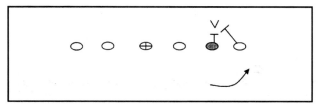

Figure 3-62. Post (Post/Lead)

Lead (Post/Lead): Down part of the double-team. Often this will be the lead blocker on a play. Be very alert; if the man over the post blocker were to commit himself to his offside gap then he would work his way upfield to a backer.

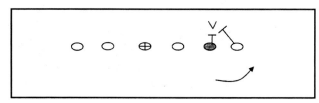

Figure 3-63. Lead (Post/Lead)

Post/Lead: This is the double-team block that combines the post and lead blocks.

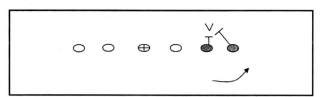

Figure 3-64. Post/Lead

Reach Block: Step laterally down the line of scrimmage and block the onside area; this is a cutoff type block, not a power block. Maintain contact until back is clear. This is a typical offside block as well as an onside block on sweeps and tosses.

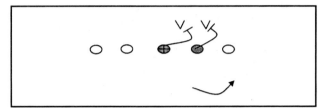

Figure 3-65. Reach Block

Fire Block: Executed like the reach block but is usually performed by offside linemen who will fire to cut off access to the onside.

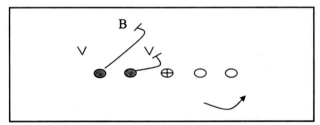

Figure 3-66. Fire Block

Pull Wall Off: Pull and look to block inside after clearing the hole. This block is most likely going to be used to seal off a pursuing backer. When he turns the corner he needs to block the first man that pursues from the inside. If no one shows, he should work his way up the field continuing to look for anyone pursuing from the inside. His takeoff needs to be quick and precise. Stay as low and as close as he can to the buttocks of the linemen in front of him. When he turns the corner he must be as tight to the last man on the LOS as possible. In a lot of circumstances he will turn upfield immediately after a double-team that occurs on the LOS. He is the lead blocker through the hole. Even though his responsibility is to seal inside penetration, he may have a man on him as he turns the corner, who would be your responsibility.

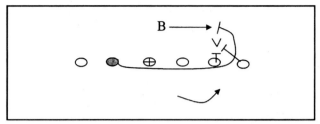

Figure 3-67. Pull Wall Off

Pull Trap/Kick: Pull and kick out the first man he sees penetrate the LOS. If there is no penetration he will turn upfield slightly beyond the point of attack. His initial step is 90 degrees with his playside foot. Stay low and close to his linemen.

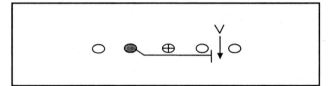

Figure 3-68. Pull Trap/Kick

Pick Block: A pick block is a pass protection type block where the first step is 45 degrees to the inside and the next step is 45 degrees backward with the other foot. He blocks the defenders from the inside out. This means he will block any immediate penetration to the inside; if there is none he will protect the backside. Don't get caught back on his heels. When he reads his block, he should attack it.

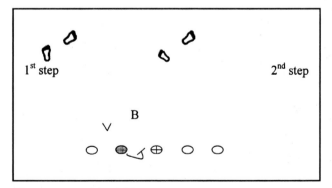

Figure 3-69. Pick Block

Pull Check: Fill quickly for the linemen next to him that is pulling and protect that zone. The takeoff step is 90 degrees. If the pulling lineman has a man over him, he will have to cut him off quickly; it is more important that he cut him off than to try and execute a power block. Get in front of him at all cost. If no defender shows in his area pick the backside.

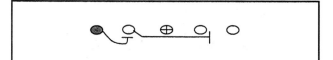

Figure 3-70. Pull Check

Pull Hook Block: This is a pull block that is designed to cut off a defender when the play is designed to get outside him. It is usually the last defender on the LOS.

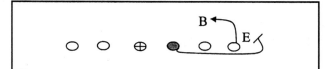

Figure 3-71. Pull Hook Block

Combo Block: This is a combination block that starts with a double-team and has the lead blocker peel off the double-team and perform a seal block on another defender. He must first help the post man establish control before releasing upfield. Have the lead blocker explode into the outside hip of the defender and try to turn him. This is an excellent way to establish quick control for the post blocker.

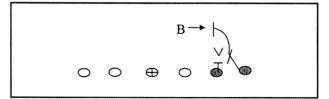

Figure 3-72. Combo Block

Cross Block: This is where adjacent linemen switch responsibilities for blocking the defenders over them on the LOS. They need to make clear who

goes first. The second man must cut quickly off the buttocks of the first man. Essentially, the first man is performing a down or reach type block while the second man is performing a kick type block.

Figure 3-73. Cross Block

Influence: Technically this is not a block. This is more of a fake block to create a false look to the defense. When this is done properly it will set up other blocks and make them easier. It will also force defenders out of position to make a play on the ballcarrier. An 'influence' is usually set up by another play in your offense. For instance, your onside guard may pull on certain plays that are run to the outside. The linebacker may begin to read this movement. You could then run a bootleg that looks similar to that play and have the guard 'influence' the linebacker by pulling to the right as he does on the outside plays, when the play actually has the QB bootlegging to the left. Figure 3-74 is another example of an 'influence' that will also be described.

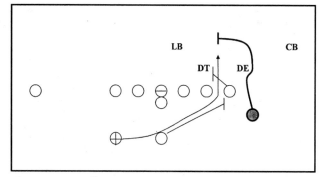

Figure 3-74. Influence

In this play the fullback has to perform a kick out block on the DE. The TE will be blocking down. The ballcarrier will run off tackle between the down block of the TE and the kick out block of the FB. He will crossover the midline by two yards creating the look of an outside run, before making his cutoff tackle. The wingback will perform the influence.' He will do this by approaching the outside shoulder of the DE and then diverting up the field to wall-off the LB. This 'influence' will give the appearance of an outside running play by looking as if his objective is to seal off the DE from the outside. By doing this successfully two things will happen:

- The fullback's kick-out block on the DE will become easier. This will happen because the DE must react to the possible outside running threat created by the appearance of a down block by the wingback. This will momentarily freeze him while he tries to read the play.

- The CB or an OLB, depending on the defensive set, will take himself out of position to make the play. When the CB reads a wingback sealing a defensive end he should read this as a potential outside threat, especially because the back's initial movement is toward the outside. He will then move himself up toward the line of scrimmage to position himself to turn the play in or make the tackle. The ballcarrier will cut up the field, leaving the CB out of position.

Rule Blocking

Rule blocking is where every player knows what blocking technique he needs to perform for every play. Every play is broken down by the players, and every player will have his blocking rules listed. If a player has three rules listed, then they are the order of importance. For instance, if their rule is 'gap-on-area,' the player will first look to see if he has a possible 'gap' block; if there is no one in his gap, he will look to see if he has an 'on' block;, if there is no man on him, he will execute an area block. Figure 3-75 is an example of a rule blocking play. Take the time to go over every players 'rule' and make sure you understand why he is shown blocking his man in this diagram.

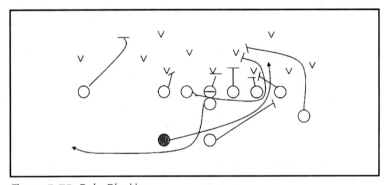

Figure 3-75. Rule Blocking

ONSIDE RULES:	OFFSIDE RULES:
G: gap-area-post	G: pull wall-off
T: gap-area post	T: pull check
C: reach-area-away	TE: stalk
TE: lead-backer-outside	Y: stalk
Y:	
RHB: influence first man on or outside TE wall off backer	
FB: crossover for tail of T, block first man outside T	
LHB: crossover step and receive ball on second step just before midline	
QB: reverse pivot with first step just before the midline, second step on same path, handoff on inside foot of G with shoulders parallel to LOS, bring right shoulder around to hide handoff from DE, fake boot to offside	

Practice Play (Blank)

Draw the offensive and defensive formation shown in Figure 3-76 on a piece of paper. Draw the lines to illustrate every offensive player's responsibility on the play. Do not look at Figure 3-77, which will have the correct lines drawn. This is the same exact play that is outlined in Figure 3-75. In that diagram, the play was being run against a 50 defense; in the practice play shown in Figure 3-76 it is being run against a 40 defense. When you are finished, check your work against Figure 3-77.

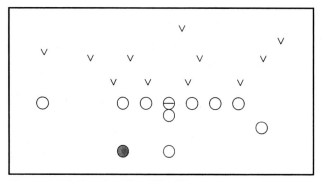

Figure 3-76. Practice Play (Blank)

Practice Play (Completed)

If you know the terminology and you follow your 'rule,' it is very easy to figure out your responsibility.

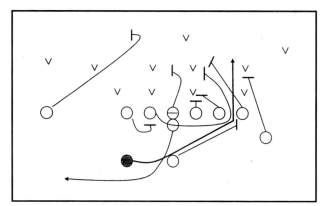

Figure 3-77. Practice Play (Completed)

ONSIDE RULES:	OFFSIDE RULES:
G: gap-area-post T: gap-area post C: reach-area-away TE: lead-backer-outside Y: RHB: influence first man on or outside TE wall off backer FB: crossover for tail of T, block first man outside T LHB: crossover step and receive ball on second step just before midline QB: reverse pivot with first step just before the midline, second step on same path, handoff on inside foot of G with shoulders parallel to LOS, bring right shoulder around to hide handoff from DE, fake boot to offside	G: pull wall-off T: pull check TE: stalk Y: stalk

Blocking Calls

At times, blocking rules for a particular play can be changed to make the play more efficient. The changes are made by having blocking calls. The blocking calls shown in Figure 3-78 will be made by either calling a one-digit number (cross blocks), or a man's name (fold blocks). A one-digit number tells who on the line will be involved in the call based on the numbering system shown in Figure 3-78.

The digit called tells which lineman blocks down (goes first) and the adjacent lineman executes the kick out part of the block. These calls all involve blocks on the LOS (cross blocks).

Figure 3-78 and Figure 3-79 are examples of 'cross block' blocking calls. In the first example, the call was '2', which meant that the TE (2) and the T were going to execute a cross block. Since the TE is the number 2 man, he will go first. The next example has the G and T cross blocking with the right tackle going first since he is the '3' man and so on.

Note: This system works great for teams that use this particular numbering system for its offense. There are certainly other ways to make the same blocking calls.

A man's name describes a fold block which involves a block out on the LOS and then a fold around block on a LB. The first letter in the name tells which lineman does the folding.

The exception is 'down,' which means down block. Any double-team blocks turn into single down blocks.

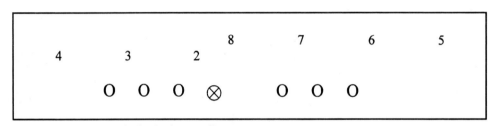

Figure 3-78. Cross Block Blocking Calls

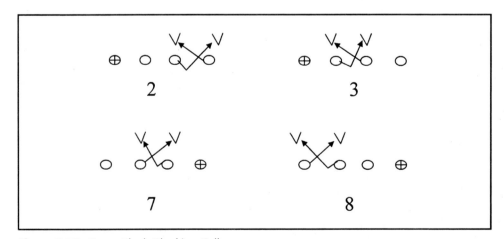

Figure 3-79. Cross Block Blocking Calls

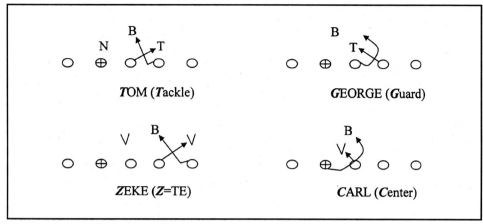

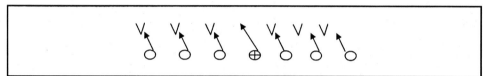

Figure 3-80. Fold Block Blocking Call

Figure 3-81. Down Block Blocking Call

Cheat Sheet

Chart 3-1 is an example of a 'cheat sheet' that players and coaches will keep with them as an aid to remember plays. They can refer to it coming out of the huddle.

Alignment

An excellent instructional aid for alignment uniformity involves the use of a fire hose. During your team's preseason drills, you can place an old fire hose (or mark a chalk line) on the field. The offensive linemen can use this hose as a line marking the offensive edge of the neutral zone. They can then take note of their respective position to their inside teammate as they align as close to the hose as possible. To develop uniformity in a system that utilizes the deeper alignment, you can simply place the ball across the hose. The offensive linemen subsequently can use the hose as a guideline for their foot placement. The hose in Figure 3-82 is marked with the standard spacing along the offensive line and can be used as a

Chart 3-1. Cheat Sheet

teaching tool during the entire season, not only for the offensive line, but also for the running backs when they run their drills without offensive linemen. The fire hose with position markings can be used to teach uniform alignment on the ball. The white space between the position markings represents the line splits you will use.

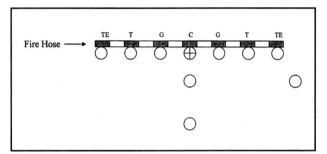

Figure 3-82. Alignments

Identifying Defensive Alignment Techniques

Recognizing the individual alignment techniques of the defensive linemen identifies the alignments of the defensive front. Several different concepts are used to designate the alignment of the defensive linemen throughout the many levels of play. The most recognized system for identifying the defensive front alignments is shown in Figure 3-83. The area in which a defender aligns himself is called a 'technique.'

Defensive Line Techniques

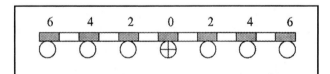

Figure 3-83. Defensive Line Techniques

The even numbers in Figure 3-83 represent defensive linemen in head-up alignment with the offensive linemen. For example, if a man is lined up directly over the guard he is said to be in a '2' technique; head up on the tackle is a '4'; TE '6'; and over center is a '0' technique. If there is a linebacker lined up head-up on a guard he too would be

considered to be lined up in a '2' technique, even if he is line up three yards off the LOS. Some defensive numbering systems will add a zero to the end of the number for the alignment of a backer (e.g., the same linebacker described above would be in a 20 technique).

Note: When there is no tight end in an offensive formation the area that he would normally line up in is very important. The term 'ghost TE' refers to this area. For instance; if there were no Tight End in an offensive formation and the defenders alignment still calls for a '6' technique, the defender would line up over the 'ghost TE'. This simply means that he lines up exactly where he would if the Tight End were there.

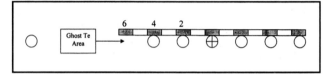

Figure 3-84

The defender aligned in a '6' technique shown in Figure 3-84 is lined up over the 'ghost TE.'

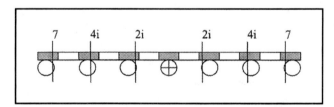

Figure 3-85

The numbers and letters shown in Figure 3-85 describe an inside shade technique by the defensive linemen. This simply means they are lined up on the inside shoulder of the offensive linemen. For example, a man lined up on the inside shoulder of the guard is in a '2I' technique; inside shoulder of the tackle is a '4I' technique; the inside shoulder of the TE is considered the '7' technique.

The numbers shown in Figure 3-86 represent an 'outside shade' technique by the defensive linemen. This means that they are lined up on the outside shoulder of the offensive linemen. No matter which side of the center they are lined up on it is considered a '1' technique. If they are lined up on the outside shoulder of the guard they are in a '3' technique; the outside shoulder of the tackle is a '5' technique; the outside shoulder of the TE is a '9' technique.

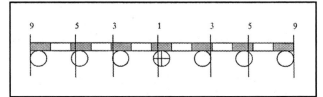

Figure 3-86

Identifying Defensive Gap Assignments

Once you recognize where a defender is aligned, you must recognize the area he is likely assigned. If you knew your defender's assignment it would be a lot easier to block him. Often a defender is assigned to a 'gap' on the LOS. Figure 3-87 shows the 'gaps' on the LOS:

Gap Chart

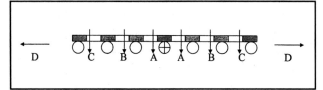

Figure 3-87. Gap Chart

The letters shown in Figure 3-87 represent the 'gaps' on the offensive line. The 'A gap' is the space between the center and the guard. The 'B gap' is the space between the guard and the tackle. The 'C gap' is the space between the tackle and the tight end or ghost TE. The 'D gap' is the entire area outside the tight end or ghost TE.

Note: Every coach should know the technique and gap system outlined in the previous section. The first reason is simplicity. Imagine you are in a game situation and you ask your offensive tackle what the tendencies are of the defender lined up closest to him. Assuming that you thoroughly understand the technique system, which of the following responses sounds easier to work with during game situations?

Defensive Technique and Likely Assignment chart.

TECHNIQUE	GAP ASSIGNMENT	LEVERAGE ARM (FREE ARM)
0	Playside "A" gaps	Playside arm
1	"A" gap	Inside arm
2	"A" gap	Inside arm
3	"B" gap	Outside arm
4	"B" gap	Inside arm
5	"C" gap	Outside arm
7	"C" gap	Inside arm
6	"C" gap	Inside*
9	"D" gap	Outside
8	"D" gap	Outside

*The leverage arm of the 6 technique may vary in response to the blocking scheme.

Figure 3-88

- Technique response–"He is in either a '4' or a '5' and always works to C gap."

OR

- Layman response–"He lines up either head up on me or on my outside shoulder; he seems to always try and control the gap between me and the tight end."

Another important reason to learn this system is for educational purposes. This is the universal language. When you attend any quality coaching clinic, this is the terminology being used. This should be considered basic information. If you don't understand this terminology you will surely be at a loss at these clinics. Many manuals and technical books also use this terminology. The assumption is that most coaches already know it.

Don't underestimate your players; you will be surprised how quickly they will pick this system up. After you start using this terminology, you will never want to go back to the old way you did it.

Line Positions

Guards (2)

In most offenses these players are a little quicker than your tackles. The reasons for this are simple: they will be required to make more open field blocks on LB's because a lot of times they are uncovered; they will pull on tosses and reverses and need to get outside the TE quickly; they are involved in a lot of trap blocks that require quickness. In fact, if you were blessed with a lot of backfield talent, you may want to consider using an extra back on the line if he is also tough. Some kids would rather sacrifice playing the position they prefer in order to get more playing time at another position.

Tackles (2)

These players are usually a little bigger and a little stronger than some of the other positions. Off-tackle plays sometimes take longer to develop, especially counters, and require you to hold your blocks longer.

They still need to be quick out of their stance, as does every lineman. Most of their blocks will be confined to a small area, which makes the quickness of there initial steps more important than their speed. Always work to get those initial steps quicker.

Tight End (1 or 2)

This is a hybrid player. Although his main job is going to be blocking, he'll need some speed and good hands for the passing game. He is a key blocker in your outside game and your off-tackle game, which at the youth level makes up a good percentage of plays. A good TE is a valuable tool. The best TE has the toughness of a lineman combined with the athleticism of a back.

Center (1)

The center might be your smartest lineman. At the higher levels, he will be required to make the line calls, which won't be discussed in this manual. He needs to be coordinated and quick. He will often have a noseguard lined up over him, who is usually a tough player. Look for a player who is tough, confident, and quick. Remember, the center has a lot more to do than just blocking.

Center Stance

Let's start with a proper stance. He must be balanced. His feet should only be slightly more than shoulder width apart. His hips are slightly higher than his back. His neck is bowed and his toes are parallel to the line of scrimmage. His heels can be angled slightly outward. The biggest mistake young centers make is having too wide of a stance. This makes it very hard to get out of the stance to execute the block quickly.

A center can use two types of stances: the three-point stance and the four-point stance. The four-point stance is the preferred stance by many coaches. This stance allows the center to be quicker and more explosive in his blocking. He still only snaps the ball with one hand while the other hand is in an advantageous position to begin the block.

The three-point stance is frequently used for pass blocking. This will have the center put his free hand just inside his knee. If you have a smaller center or prefer quickness, the four-point stance will be the best choice.

Snapping the Ball

The center will grip the ball in the same manner as a quarterback. He will have his thumb on the laces so that he can deliver the ball with the laces up for the quarterback. The first thing you need to instill into your center is to never raise his hips as he snaps the ball. This will significantly affect his ability to properly block after the snap. As he snaps, he should be moving forward into his block. It is the quarterback's responsibility to ride his hands with the center's butt until he is in control of the ball.

The ball should be snapped back in a straight line. The ball should not swing up in a pendulum like motion. The wrist should be flexed as the snap is executed, which will turn the ball enough for the proper delivery. The snap of a right-handed center should skid off his left buttock and vise versa.

It is imperative that the quarterback and the center get plenty of repetitions. They each may need to make small adjustments to compensate for style. Practice is the key. The snap should always be second nature. It must be something that has been practiced so much that it just occurs naturally. The center should spend time with the quarterback in some of his other stations. This is important to the timing of the plays because a snap takes place before any play is executed.

Linemen Drills

□ Linemen Station Warm-up Drills

Circle Up

Objective: To develop coordination, strength, and conditioning.

Description:

- All linemen form a circle lying face down on the ground.
- On the coach's command they will do a set of push-ups. As the season progresses make them place their hands closer and closer together.
- Next, they will perform a step-over drill. One lineman will stand up facing forward and begin stepping over every player until he gets back to his original spot. Never let their legs cross when they step. After a player has been stepped over, he should count to three, stand up and begin stepping over in the same direction.

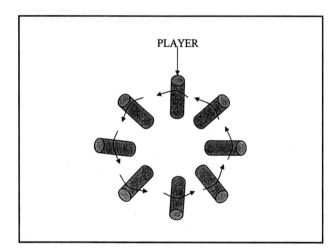

Figure 3-89. Circle Up

Bird Dog

Description:

- A line of players will line up in a three-point stance.

- On the whistle they will execute coming out of their stance using only the first step.

- They will hold that step for one second and snap back to their stance.

- The following sequence will be followed for each whistle blown: right foot forward; left foot forward; right foot 45 degrees; left foot 45 degrees; right foot 90 degrees; left foot 90 degrees. On whistle # 7 the coach will call out a step, when he blows the whistle the player will lead with that step and sprint five yards.

- Continue drill until all players have performed the sprint portion of the drill with all six types of lead steps. When they are sprinting out of the 90-degree step, they should continue in their step direction for three yards before turning upfield to complete the five-yard sprint.

Coaching Points:

This is a critical drill because the player needs to step with the proper lead foot on every play. The step must be short and quick. The player should be frozen momentarily in a low, powerful, and balanced position. Don't let them stand up out of their stance. Players can tend to get sloppy while doing this drill. If you notice this happening, make them freeze after their step until you check their body positioning and don't let them back down in their stance until you give them the command.

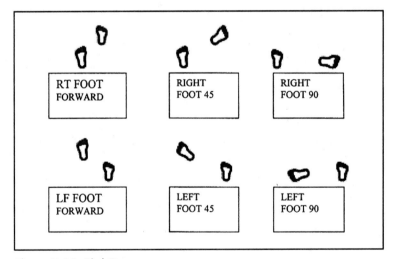

Figure 3-90. Bird Dog

□ Georgia Southerns

These are a series of blocking drills that will teach the hand blocking techniques. During each of these drills the player must do the following: employ proper footwork in their takeoff, take short choppy steps, maintain their power angles when they explode under the chest plate of the defender, keep elbows in and head up, and maintain contact. The offensive player in the drill will drive the defender for 10 yards. The drill is then worked back the other way with the defender becoming the blocker and the blocker becoming the defender. The defender should give 75% resistance allowing the block.

Description: Pairing up the players and put them in a straight line facing their partner. The coach will start at one end of the line. When he blows his whistle the first pair will perform the drill. He will watch the take off and initial impact of the block and stress coaching points if needed. He then works his way down the line starting the next pair of players

and so on. It is best to have another coach start from the other side of the line to expedite the drill. There should also be other coaches watching the drive portion of the blocks. The key to the drive portion is staying low with a wide base, driving with short choppy steps, head up and elbows in. The first two drills are warm-ups. After your team becomes proficient at these drills they can skip the two warm-ups, although it is important to perform the other drills every day. The initial step is listed for every drill. This will describe the takeoff direction of the first step. Every drill must be performed with a right and left foot takeoff.

Coaching Points: Make this drill competitive. The blocker should EXPLODE into the defender trying to knock him on his back with the initial thrust. He must then drive him 10 yards with short choppy steps, widened base, head is up and elbows are in. His shoulders must always be lower than the defenders.

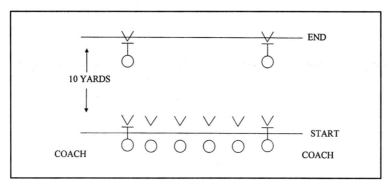

Figure 3-91. Georgia Southerns

Power Drives (Warm-up)

Objective: To teach the lineman the proper power angle.

Description: The offensive lineman gets in a good hitting position with his hands behind his back. The defensive player will put his hands on the chest of the blocker. The blocker will stay low and use a proper power angle to drive the defender 10 yards. The defender will give 75% resistance. To drive the defender the lineman must keep his knees bent, his shoulders out over a widened base, and his head up while his feet are pumping.

Rock and Roll (Warm-up)

Description: The offensive lineman will get in a good hitting position with his hands on the shoulder of the defender. He will drive the man as he did in his power drives. This time the defender will grab the elbows of the blocker and rock him side to side as he is being driven back.

On Block

Initial Step: Right/left foot forward.

Description: The blocker lines up in a three-point stance with the defender one yard off in a three- or four-point stance. On the whistle, the blocker will explode into the defender and execute a proper drive block for 10 yards.

Coaching Points: Make this drill competitive. The blocker should explode into the defender trying to knock him on his back with the initial thrust. He must then drive him 10 yards with short choppy steps, widened base, head is up and elbows are in. His shoulders must always be lower than the defenders.

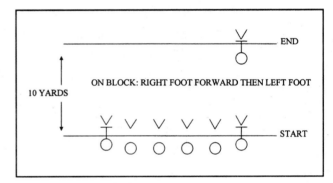

Figure 3-92. On Block

Gap Block

Initial Step: Right/left foot 45 degrees.

Description: The blocker will line up in his three-point stance with a defender one yard off him in the gap to his right. On the whistle, the blocker will take a 45-degree step to his right and explode into the defender and maintain a proper block for 10 yards. Repeat drill with a defender in left gap.

Coaching Points: Make sure that when the blocker takes his 45-degree step to the right he is leading with his right foot and is leading with his left foot when he is blocking his left gap. Make this drill competitive. The blocker should explode into the defender trying to knock him on his back with the initial thrust. He must then drive him 10 yards with short choppy steps, widened base, head is up and elbows are in. His shoulders must always be lower than the defenders.

Backer Block

Initial Step: Right/left foot 90 degrees.

Description: The defender will line up five yards off the blocker lined up as a linebacker. On the whistle the defender will scallop to the blocker's right side. The blocker will use a 90-degree right foot lead, staying low as he takes off upfield, intercept the defender, explode into him and drive him five yards. Repeat drill to left.

Coaching Points: It is very important for the blocker to stay low. He must explode up and through the defender. "Low man wins." Their takeoff should be like an airplane, staying low and rising gradually. Make this drill competitive. The blocker should explode into the defender trying to knock him on his back with the initial thrust. He must then drive him 10 yards with short choppy steps, widened base, head is up and elbows are in. His shoulders must always be lower than the defenders.

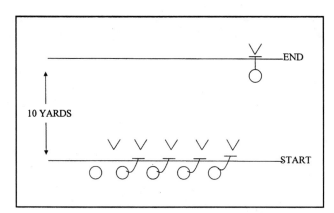

Figure 3-93. Gap Block

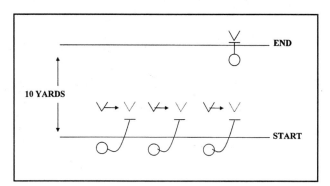

Figure 3-94. Backer Block

Stunt Block Drill

Objective: To teach the lineman how to block when a defender is "shooting the gap."

Description: Have a defender lined up in the right gap of the blocker.

On the whistle, the defender will shoot the gap quickly. To execute this properly, the blocker will take a 90-degree step with his right foot; he must stay low in a proper hitting position. His facemask should aim for the chin of the defender; his right hand will jam under the chest plate of the defender with his left hand under his armpit and he will drive the defender for three seconds.

The defender should be wide enough and close enough to the LOS to get decent penetration before the blocker can make contact. He needs to speed-rush to a spot designated with a cone. Repeat to the left.

Coaching Point: Make it a competition; see which defenders can make it to the cone without being knocked off course.

Run Skelly

Description:

- This is the offense play run through portion of practice.
- A six-man offensive line (center, two guards, two tackles, tight end) is set up at LOS.
- Set up defensive fronts using bags, shields, and coaches.
- Walk through new plays, showing blocking assignments against different fronts.
- Run through old plays at full speed against bags.
- Run each play against different fronts (4-5-6 man fronts with backers).
- Mix in different stunts against plays.

Variation: Run these plays live by substituting players for bags.

Coaching Point: Make sure you teach the players to recognize their assignment against different fronts. Every player must know his assignment for every play against every defense.

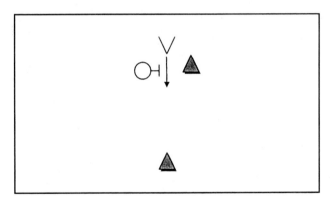

Figure 3-95. Stunt Block Drill

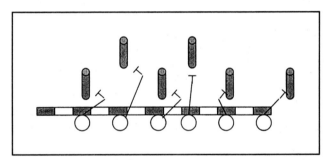

Figure 3-96. Run Skelly

Battle of the Boards

Objective: To teach the proper power angles of a block. To be successful in this drill the blocker will have to exhibit great balance and power, both of which can only come from the execution of proper fundamentals.

Equipment needed: An 8 to 10 foot long board such as a 1 x 8.

Description:

- Two players will line up in a three-point stance facing each other at the center of the board.

- Their feet will straddle the board.

- Their down hands will be on the board.

- On the whistle they will explode out of their stance and try to drive the other player to the end of the board or to the side of the board.

- Once any player's foot touches the board or the ground on the side of the other foot, he loses.

- The winners will be grouped together until all players have participated.

- A second round will be started with only the winners from the first round.

- This process is continued until you can declare a champion.

- You can also separate players into two teams; this can generate extra energy by encouraging players to aggressively root for their teammates. The losing team does push-ups or some other conditioner.

Coaching Points: The key here is explosiveness and balance. Emphasize all the elements in the proper 'power angle' of blocking. Encourage them to use the power of their lower body to drive the man. Quickness is the key. If two blockers are fundamentally equal, the one who gets there first usually wins because he is able to get into the proper positioning.

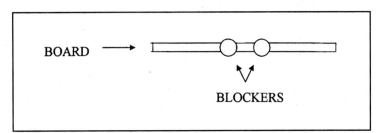

Figure 3-97. Battle of the Boards

□ Blocking Sled Drills

Blocking sled drills are performed on a five- to seven-man sled. If you do not have a sled you can use blocking dummies.

Punch-up Drill

Objective: To teach the explosiveness of the punch-up portion of a block. This is a run blocking technique used by teams that hand block.

Description:

- Form a line of blockers to the left of the sled.
- The first player in line is lined up in front of the first pad of the sled.
- On the first whistle, the player will explode up and through the first pad trying to drive the sled in the air; after one second he will release and set up in front of the second pad. At this time the next man in line quickly sets up in front of the first pad.
- On the next whistle the players will repeat the previous step while moving down the bags in progression.
- Continue this process until every player has performed the punch-up on every bag.
- Keep the pace of this drill rapid. It should only take a couple minutes to complete.

Coaching Points: Make sure that every block is an explosive one. The blocker stays low and at the point of impact drives his hips, buttocks and legs up and through the block. The back should arch. This is all done simultaneously with the punch up and through with the hands.

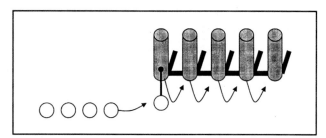

Figure 3-98. Punch-up Drill

Team Explosion Drill

Objective: To emphasize and teach the explosive initial impact of the blocking progression.

Description:

- A player will line up in front of every bag on the sled.
- On the coaches first whistle they will explode up and through the sled, getting the front of the sled off the ground and drive it.
- After two to three seconds the coach will blow the second whistle, which will end that repetition.
- Repeat this drill until every player has had two to three repetitions.

Coaching Points: Make sure that every block is an explosive one. The blocker stays low and at the point of impact drives his hips, buttocks and legs up and through the block. The back should arch. This is all done simultaneously with the punch up and through with the hands.

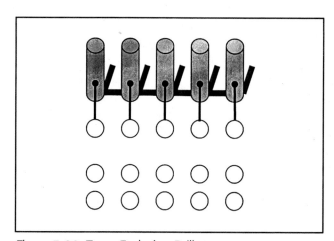

Figure 3-99. Team Explosion Drill

Drive Block Drill

Objective: To work on the drive portion of the blocking progression.

Description:

- A player should be lined up in front of every bag on the sled.
- On the first whistle five players will explode into the sled and drive it until the second whistle.
- The sled should pop up off the ground from the initial impact, and land back down while all linemen maintain contact and continue to drive the sled.
- The sled should be driven five to seven yards before the second whistle is blown.

Coaching Points: Make sure the player uses the proper takeoff into the sled. When the player is driving the sled his head should be up and just above his hands. The knees should be bent while the players stay low and drive the sled with short choppy steps. Their base should be wider than normal as they drive.

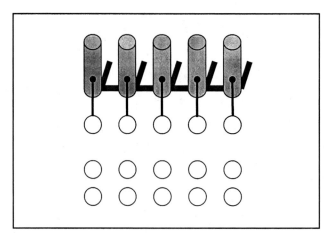

Figure 3-100. Drive Block Drill

Gap Block Drill

Objective: To work on the gap block with a 45-degree initial step.

Description:

- A player should be lined up in gap just to the side of each bag on the sled.
- On the first whistle five players will explode into the sled and drive it until the second whistle.
- Their initial step is 45-degrees in the direction of the bag.
- The sled should pop up off the ground from the initial impact, and land back down while all linemen maintain contact and continue to drive the sled.
- The sled should be driven five to seven yards before the second whistle is blown.
- Repeat in the other direction.

Coaching Points: Make sure the player uses the proper takeoff into the sled. When the player is driving the sled his head should be up and just above his hands. The knees should be bent while the players stay low and drive the sled with short choppy steps. Their base should be wider than normal as they drive.

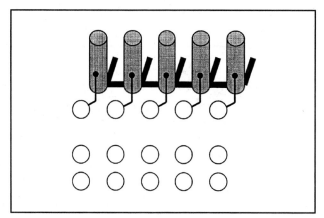

Figure 3-101. Gap Block Drill

Fire Block Drill

Objective: To work on the gap block with a 70-degree initial step, while getting to a defender that is lined up further than normal from him.

Description:

- A player should be lined up in front of the bag to the side of each bag they will be blocking on the sled.
- On the first whistle five players will explode into the sled and drive it until the second whistle.
- Their initial step is 45-degrees in the direction of the bag.
- The sled should pop up off the ground from the initial impact, and land back down while all linemen maintain contact and continue to drive the sled.
- The sled should be driven five to seven yards before the second whistle is blown.
- Repeat in the other direction.

Coaching Points: Make sure the player uses the proper takeoff into the sled. When the player is driving the sled his head should be up and just above his hands. The knees should be bent while the players stay low and drive the sled with short choppy steps. Their base should be wider than normal as they drive.

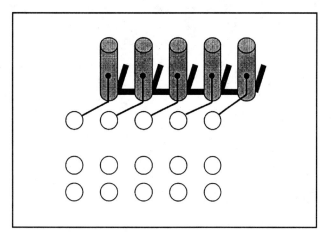

Figure 3-102. Fire Block Drill

Board Drills

Objective: To teach the blocker the fundamentals of drive blocking.

Description:

- Line up four boards 8 to 10 feet long, with a blocking bag sitting on the front of the board.
- A player will line up in front of each station.
- On the whistle the blocker will drive the bag to the end of the board.

Variation: Use a live defender instead of the blocking bag. The defender should give 75% resistance.

Coaching Points: Make sure the player uses the proper takeoff into the bag. When the player is driving the bag his head should be up and just above his hands. The knees should be bent while the players stay low and drive the bag with short choppy steps. His base should be wider than normal as he drives. His feet should never approach the boards. The emphasis here is on widening the base as he drives with short choppy steps.

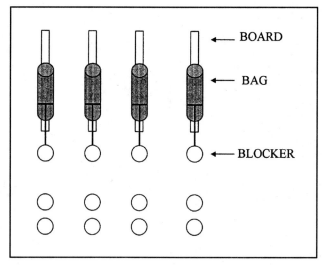

Figure 3-103. Board Drills

□ Pulling Drills

These drills are designed to teach linemen the different types of pulling they will be called on to do in your offense. It is important to get frequent repetitions. Timing is imperative on any play that requires a lineman to pull.

Pull Trap/Counter Drill

Objective: To teach the short pulling action used on inside traps and counter plays.

Description:

• Use a fire hose to represent the line of scrimmage (optional).

• Set up two cones three yards apart that will represent offensive linemen. They should be lined up two feet closer to the line of scrimmage than the feet of the player performing the drill.

• On the whistle the player will execute the trap block on a blocking dummy that will be brought across the line of scrimmage.

• The player will make explosive contact with the bag. The objective is to make contact from low to high and destroy the defender (bag).

• Run this drill to both the right and left side.

Variations:

• Substitute a live defender for the bag. Have him turn into the blocker just beyond the line of scrimmage.

• Have the defender or bag stay on the defensive side of the line of scrimmage forcing the blocker to make a read upfield for his block.

Coaching Points: As with all pulls, the keys are to:

• Get out of the stance quickly.

• Stay low and as close to the backside of your other linemen as possible. Be alert, looking for the first defender that may cross your path, even if it is not the intended defender.

• The block should be performed from low to high, establishing a proper power angle at the point of impact.

• Whenever you are required to turn upfield (when no one shows) stay as tight to the last blocker on the line of scrimmage as possible while making your turn. The turn should be made crisply with the body getting low working up into a block.

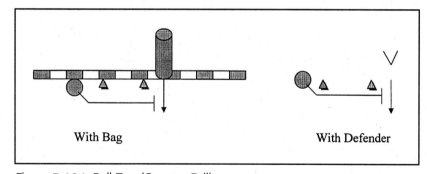

With Bag   With Defender

Figure 3-104. Pull Trap/Counter Drill

Pull Kick/Trap Drill

Objective: To teach the longer pulling action used on long traps, counter plays and some waggle action plays.

Description:

- Use a fire hose to represent the line of scrimmage (optional).

- Set up two cones six to seven yards apart that will represent offensive linemen. They should be lined up two feet closer to the line of scrimmage than the feet of the player performing the drill.

- On the whistle the player will execute the kick block on a blocking dummy that will be brought across the line of scrimmage.

- The player will make explosive contact with the bag. The objective is to make contact from low to high and destroy the defender (bag).

- Run this drill to both the right and left side.

Variations:

- Substitute a live defender for the bag. Have him turn into the blocker just beyond the line of scrimmage.

- Have the defender or bag stay on the defensive side of the line of scrimmage forcing the blocker to make a read upfield for his block.

Coaching Points: As with all pulls, the keys are to:

- Get out of the stance quickly.

- Stay low and as close to the backside of your other linemen as possible. Be alert, looking for the first defender that may cross your path, even if it is not the intended defender.

- The block should be performed from low to high, establishing a proper power angle at the point of impact.

Whenever you are required to turn upfield (when no one shows), stay as tight to the last blocker on the line of scrimmage as possible while making the turn. The turn should be made crisply with the body getting low working up into a block.

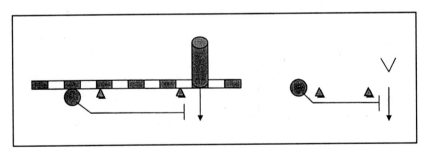

Figure 3-105. Pull Kick/Trap Drill

Pull Wall Off Drill

Objective: To teach the 'wall-off' type-pulling block. This is a pulling block that requires the blocker to turn up the field, looking to seal off linebacker penetration or becoming the lead blocker through a hole.

Description:

- Use a fire hose to represent the line of scrimmage (optional).

- Set up two cones six to seven yards apart that will represent offensive linemen. They should be lined up two feet closer to the line of scrimmage than the feet of the player performing the drill.

- On the whistle the player will execute the kick block on a blocking dummy that will be brought across the line of scrimmage.

- The player will make explosive contact with the bag. The objective is to make contact from low to high and destroy the defender (bag).

- Run this drill to both the right and left side.

Variations:

- Substitute a live defender for the bag. Have him turn into the blocker just beyond the line of scrimmage.

- Have the defender or bag stay on the defensive side of the line of scrimmage forcing the blocker to make a read upfield for his block.

Coaching Points: As with all pulls, the keys are to:

- Get out of the stance quickly.

- Stay low and as close to the backside of your other linemen as possible. Be alert, looking for the first defender that may cross your path, even if it is not the intended defender.

- The block should be performed from low to high, establishing a proper power angle at the point of impact.

Whenever you are required to turn upfield (when no one shows) stay as tight to the last blocker on the line of scrimmage as possible while making the turn. The turn should be made crisply with the body getting low working up into a block.

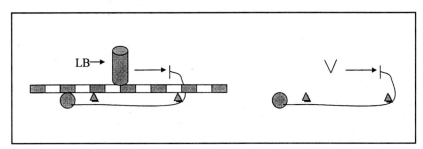

Figure 3-106. Pull Wall Off Drill

Pull Hook Drill

Objective: To teach the 'hook' type pulling block.

Description:

- Use a fire hose to represent the line of scrimmage (optional).

- Set up two cones that will represent the men aligned next to the blocker and the tight end on the playside. They should be lined up two feet closer to the line of scrimmage than the feet of the player performing the drill.

- The blocker will line up as the onside or playside guard.

- On the whistle the player will execute the hook block on a blocking dummy that will be brought across the line of scrimmage.

- The player will make the drive up into the defender and 'wheel' his hips to the outside.

- Run this drill to both the right and left side.

Variations:

- Substitute a live defender for the bag.

- Have the defender or bag stay on the defensive side of the line of scrimmage forcing the blocker to make a read upfield for his block.

Coaching Points: This is a pulling block that requires the blocker to 'hook' the end man on the line of scrimmage. This type of block is used on sweep type plays to prevent the defensive end from containing the play. As with all pulls, the keys are to:

- Get out of the stance quickly.

- Stay low and as close to the backside of the other linemen as possible. Be alert, looking for the first defender that may cross your path, even if it is not the intended defender.

- The block should be performed from low to high, establishing a proper power angle at the point of impact.

Whenever you are required to turn upfield (when no one shows), stay as tight to the last blocker on the line of scrimmage as possible while making the turn. The turn should be made crisply with the body getting low working up into a block.

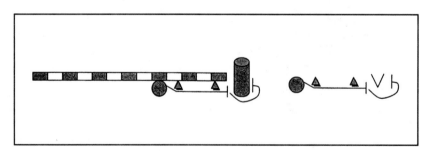

Figure 3-107. Pull Hook Drill

Pull Lead Drill

Objective: To teach the 'lead' type pulling block.

Description:

- Use a fire hose to represent the line of scrimmage (optional).

- Set up two cones that will represent the men aligned next to the blocker and the tight end on the playside. They should be lined up two feet closer to the line of scrimmage than the feet of the player performing the drill.

- The blocker will line up as the offside or playside guard.

- On the whistle the player will execute the lead block on a blocking dummy that will represent an outside linebacker or cornerback.

- The player will make the drive up into the defender trying to maintain contact for as long as possible.

- Run this drill to both the right and left side.

Variation: Substitute a live defender for the bag.

Coaching Points: This is a pulling block that requires the blocker to a 'lead' block outside the end man on the line of scrimmage. This type of block is used on sweeps to the outside. As with all pulls, the keys are to:

- Get out of the stance quickly.

- Stay low and as close to the backside of the other linemen as possible. Be alert, looking for the first defender that may cross your path, even if it is not the intended defender.

- The block should be performed from low to high, establishing a proper power angle at the point of impact.

Whenever you are required to turn upfield (when no one shows), stay as tight to the last blocker on the line of scrimmage as possible while making the turn. The turn should be made crisply with the body getting low working up into a block.

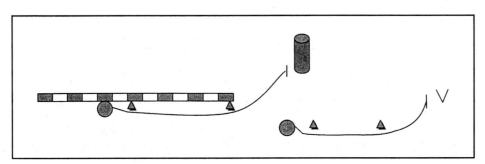

Figure 3-108. Pull Lead Drill

Waggle Drill

Objective: To teach the waggle pulling action by the guards.

Description:

- Use a fire hose to represent the line of scrimmage (optional).

- Align two bags three yards apart that will represent the area where the hook block will be performed. Set up another two bags for the lead block area.

- Two blockers will line up on the line of scrimmage in the guard positions.

- On the whistle the player will execute the hook and lead blocks on live defenders or blocking dummies if you prefer.

- The players will make the drive up into the defenders trying to maintain contact for as long as possible.

- Run this drill to both the right and left side.

Coaching Points: This is a combination drill where the onside guard performs a hook block, while the offside guard is a lead blocker. As with all pulls, the keys are to:

- Get out of the stance quickly.

- Stay low and as close to the backside of the other linemen as possible. Be alert, looking for the first defender that may cross your path, even if it is not the intended defender.

- The block should be performed from low to high, establishing a proper power angle at the point of impact.

- Whenever you are required to turn upfield (when no one shows), stay as tight to the last blocker on the line of scrimmage as possible while making the turn. The turn should be made crisply with the body getting low working up into a block.

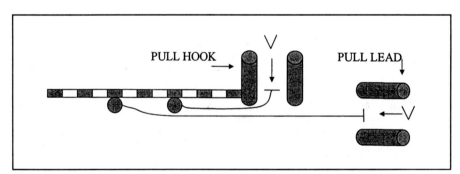

Figure 3-109. Waggle Drill

Combo Blocking Drill (Zone Blocking Drill)

Objective: To teach double-teaming linemen how to read the linebacker's movement so they can determine which player will release to block him.

Description:

- Two linemen will be aligned in there normal splits between two cones set about two yards outside of each lineman. A defensive lineman will be lined up on the inside lineman. A linebacker will be aligned four yards off the line of scrimmage and one yard to the inside of the defensive lineman.

- On the whistle the defensive lineman will charge straight in while the blockers will perform a double-team (post/lead) block.

- The linebacker will hesitate for one second, and then pursue the cone on his left.

- The blockers must read the linebacker's pursuit and perform a combo block. This means that the blocker closest to the pursuing linebacker (the lead blocker) must release from the double team block to engage the linebacker.

- The remaining blocker (the post blocker) must in a position that will allow him to complete the block on the defensive lineman by himself.

- Repeat drill in the other direction.

Coaching Points: This is a typical block in a zone blocking offense. The blockers must execute a proper double-team while maintaining vision beyond that block and reading the movement of the linebacker. The blockers should be hip to hip during the double-team portion. The lead blocker should always keep his outside arm free. He must also extend his inside arm into the defensive lineman as he releases for the linebacker, forcing the defensive lineman into the post blocker.

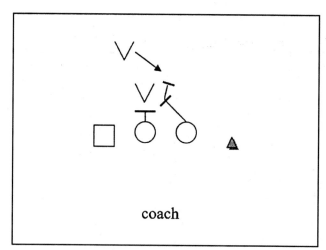

Figure 3-110. Combo Block Drill

Mirror Drill

Objective: To teach proper pass blocking technique on dropback pass plays.

Description:

- An offensive lineman will line up in a three-point stance between two cones separated by five yards.

- A defender will be set up over him.

- On the coach's whistle the defender will try to reach a cone that is set up seven yards behind the line of scrimmage.

- The blocker will take his initial pass blocking step and punch up into the rushing defender. He will maintain this block by continuing to punch up through the defender while trying to drive him as far away from the backfield cone as possible.

- Repeat drill with the defender making initial pursuit in the opposite direction.

Coaching Points: Make sure the blocker demonstrates good balance. His base should be slightly wider than his stance as he is punching up and through the defender. Make sure his shoulders are lower than the defenders.

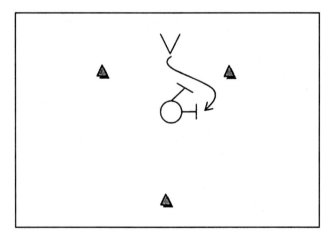

Figure 3-111. Mirror Drill

□ Chute Drills
Stance and Starts

Objective: To improve the blocker's stance and start fundamentals with an emphasis on staying low in the takeoff.

Description:

- Players will get in a three-point stance inside the chute with their heads aligned just inside of the top bar.

- On the whistle they will explode out of their stance and continue for three yards beyond the chute.

- They should not reach a full upright running position by the end of the three yards.

- Keep the pace of the drill as quick as possible. Use every chute station available. The next player in line should be entering the back of the chute on the coach's whistle, getting in his stance and ready to start.

- They will use the following takeoff steps:
  - □ Right foot forward–shoulders are parallel to front bar.
  - □ Right foot 45 degrees–shoulders are parallel to front bar.
  - □ Right foot 90 degrees–shoulders are perpendicular to front bar.
  - □ Repeat all of the above starts with a left foot lead.

Coaching Points: Make sure all players are in a proper three-point stance before each whistle to start the drill. All takeoffs should rise gradually. Remember the airplane takeoff analogy and do not allow them to stand up after exiting the chute area. Their head should be up with their focus upfield.

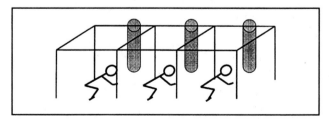

Figure 3-112. Stance and Starts

Explosion

Objective: To teach linemen how to perform the initial contact portion of a block while firing low out of their stance.

Description:

- Set up the chute with a blocking dummy in front of each station.

- The blockers will start in a three-point stance inside the chute.

- On the whistle they will execute the initial contact of the block.

- Their contact must be explosive. They must drive up and through the dummy to bring it off the ground and backwards.

- After two seconds the coach will blow the stop whistle.

Variation: Replace the dummy with a live player giving 75% resistance.

Coaching Points: Use the word 'explode' in every sentence when you describe this drill. Make it a competition. Challenge the blocker to see if he can pancake the defender as he comes out of the chute. Make a big deal out of it if a blocker knocks down the defender or the bag and its holder when he performs this drill. Look for the following fundamentals upon impact with the defender:

- His head should be up and his neck bulled.

- The heels of his open hand should make impact just under the defender's chest plate of his shoulder pads.

- His elbows should be tight to his body as he makes impact and they will drive upward with the arms. It is important that they don't extend their arms straight out when blocking.

- His back will be at a 45-degree angle; upon impact he will arch his back as he drives up and through.

His legs and ankles will be flexed and underneath him in a slightly widened base so that he can use the power of his lower body to propel him up and through the defender.

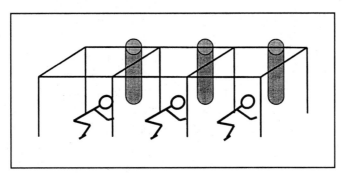

Figure 3-113. Explosion

Drive Blocking

Objective: To teach the blocker to maintain and drive the defender after coming out of his stance in a low and powerful position.

Description:

- Set up the chute with a blocking dummy in front of each station.
- The blockers will start in a three-point stance inside the chute.
- On the whistle they will execute a drive block for five yards.
- Their contact must be explosive. They must drive up and through the dummy, and then drive the dummy with proper fundamentals.

Variations: You can use different starts to work on various footwork techniques. Refer to 'Stance and Start' section of these drills. Replace the dummy with a live player giving 75% resistance.

Coaching Points: The emphasis here is on the drive portion of the block. The key points of drive blocking are as follows:

- Their base should be slightly widened as they are driving the defender.
- Their steps should be short and choppy.
- Their shoulders must be lower than the defenders at all times.
- They should never have their arms 'locked-out.'

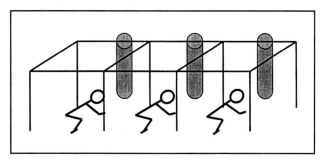

Figure 3-114. Drive Blocking

Backer Cutoff

Objective: To teach the blocker to put himself in a position to cut off the pursuit of a linebacker while taking off properly from his stance.

Description:

- Set up the chute with a blocking dummy on the left side of each station and four yards past the chute.
- The blockers will start in a three-point stance inside the chute.
- The coach holding the dummy (or a live player) will scallop the blocker's right side on the whistle.
- On the whistle the blocker will cut off the defender (dummy or player).
- His initial step should be with the right foot on a 45-degree angle.
- The blocker should make impact with the defender five yards to the right of his starting position.
- Repeat this drill to the left.

Variation: Replace the dummy with a live player giving 75% resistance.

Coaching Points: Make sure the blocker executes the footwork properly. He should not get into an upright position at any time. Upon impact the blocker should wheel his hips to the right. It is more important to be in the right position and maintain the block than it is to make a big hit.

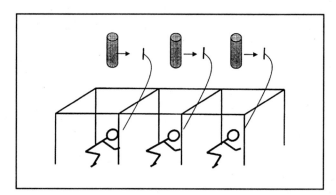

Figure 3-115. Backer Cutoff

Trap Drill

Objective: To teach the blocker to stay low when he executes a block that requires him to pull down the line of scrimmage.

Description:

- Set up the chute with a blocking dummy four yards past the chute.
- The blockers will start in a three-point stance inside the chute. They will be perpendicular to the front of the chute.
- His initial step should be with the right foot on a 90-degree angle.
- He will exit the front of the chute with his shoulders becoming parallel to the front crossbar.
- On the whistle the blocker will cut off the defender (dummy or player).
- He should make explosive impact with the dummy or player.
- Repeat this drill to the left.

Variation: Replace the dummy with a live player giving 75% resistance.

Coaching Points: Make sure the blocker doesn't rise too much before meeting the defender. He should be low enough upon impact to be able to explode up and through the defender without having to dip his shoulders first.

Rapid Fire Drill

Objective: To teach the pass blocker to quickly and accurately react to stunting defenders.

Description:

- Set up three cones in a triangle spaced five yards apart.
- Set up two lines of defenders just inside two cones.
- A blocker will be in a three-point stance in the middle of the linebacker.
- On the whistle the defender on the right will rush the remaining cone behind the blocker.
- The blocker will punch up and through the chest of the defender trying to drive him back; he must release and quickly get back in his three-point stance.
- As soon as the blocker's hand touches the ground the defender in the left line will immediately rush the cone behind the blocker.
- The blocker will repeat the punch up and return to his stance.
- Continue with the drill until the blocker has had to block three defenders to each side.

Coaching Points: Make sure the blocker is getting back to his three-point stance between every block. Every punch up motion should be performed fundamentally; don't allow the blocker to get sloppy.

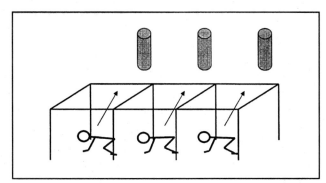

Figure 3-116. Trap Drill

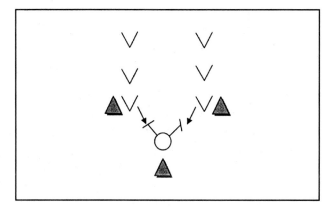

Figure 3-117. Rapid Fire Drill

CHAPTER 4

The Offensive Playbook

RUNNING PLAYS	PASSING PLAYS
• Dive plays	• Play action passing
• Lead plays	• Drop Back Passing
• Counter plays	□ 3-step drop
• Sweeps and Tosses	□ 5-step drop
• Reverses and Bootlegs	□ 7-step drop

Developing an Offensive Scheme

This section of the book will make suggestions for developing the offensive portion of your playbook. In no way does this advocate the use of one system over another. Keep in mind that you can run the same play from various formations. When you are reading through this section you should try to learn the basic concepts that are being demonstrated. The formations are irrelevant. You can adapt the basic concepts of a scheme and adapt them to the formations of your offense.

The first thing you need to do is to develop an offensive philosophy. Are you planning on being a run or pass oriented team? Will you be a finesse team or a power team? Will you be a zone blocking team or will you utilize the rule blocking principle? The answers to some of these questions may change from season to season while others must remain constant every season. For instance, your personnel may change from year to year. You cannot say you are a passing team if you don't have a quarterback who can properly execute your offense. Good coaches will adapt their philosophies to the talent they have available. On the other hand, you will not change your base blocking schemes from year to year.

You need to establish some basic principles whether you're running an offensive system like the wishbone, wing-T, or power I. Otherwise, you will be using multiple sets. The first thing you need is consistency. Your offensive philosophy must be clear and concise. This all starts with the development of your playbook.

When you are developing your playbook you should develop the blocking responsibilities for every player on the team. Don't just draw plays and call it a playbook. You must develop the playbook with the players in mind. Include as many details as possible. The playbook should be more than a culmination of plays. It should outline your philosophy. It should also include other offensive information including some of the following:

- Player expectations
- Inspirational quotes
- Numbering system
- Huddle formation
- Basic line splits
- Cadence
- Blocking calls
- Formations
- Glossary of terms
- Description of block

The remainder of this section of the manual will help you develop your offensive playbook. The plays diagramed are merely examples of the different elements you should include in your playbook. Again, you should concentrate on the concepts that are outlined in each diagram rather than on the play itself.

Basic Dive Plays

The dive play has a running back hit a hole with no lead blocker. This is perhaps the easiest play to teach blocking. Since this is a quick-hitting play the line will be responsible for the man closest to him relative to the play. The rule of thumb for straight forward dive and lead type plays is as follows:

- Onside Rule: Gap on Backer
- Offside Rule: Reach on Backer

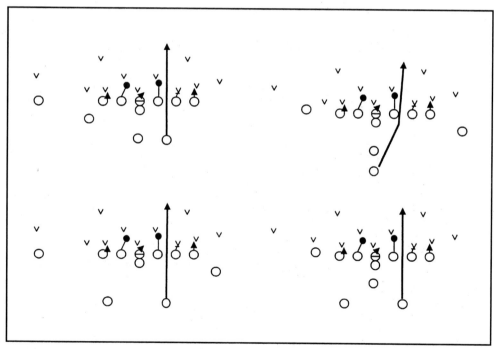

Figure 4-1

In Figure 4-1 the dive play is run from various formations that do not affect the blocking scheme. The look is different yet the execution is the same. Figure 4-2 is a diagram of a dive play from a different formation (4-4). Though the defensive look is different the blocking rules are the same. The blockers just have to remember the simple rules listed before.

Basic Lead Plays

Figure 4-3 shows a lead type play from four different formations. This is a basic way to run a lead. In these leads the lead blocker is a running back that only needs to block the first man he encounters. The linemen are using the same basic rules as in the dive plays shown in Figures 4-1 and 4-2.

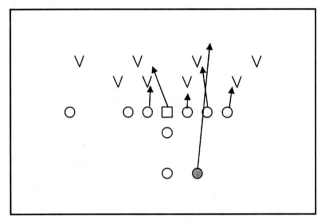

Figure 4-2

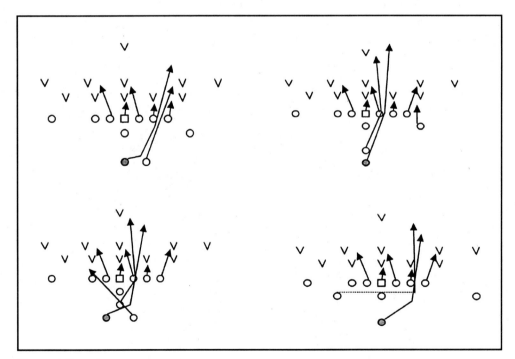

Figure 4-3

Figure 4-4 shows a lead type play against a different defense (4-4). The rules are the same, which makes picking out the man to block very simple. Again, this is the most basic way to run a lead type play.

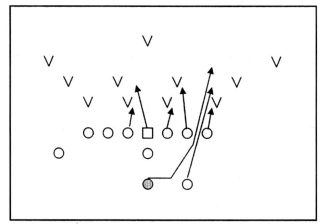

Figure 4-4

Advanced Lead Plays

In the lead play shown in Figure 4-5 there is a double-team at the point of attack. This is a common blocking technique in many offenses. The interior defensive lineman who is the biggest threat to the play is doubled. Many times this block is a combination block where the post or lead blocker will peel for a backer.

It is advisable to use double-teams when you are devising the lead plays for your offense. Two distinct advantages exist to using the double-team. First, you will clear a more distinct 'hole' for your backs by eliminating the most immediate threat on the defensive line. Second, you will set up a freeze block on the linebacker closest to the play. Realize that this linebacker is the most important person in your opponent's run defense. The freeze block is the best way to isolate the linebacker. It is important that the ballcarrier follow the lead blocker without giving any indication of his intended direction. This will 'freeze' the linebacker when the lead blocker initiates contact, making it much easier for the ballcarrier to choose when and where to make a cut up field.

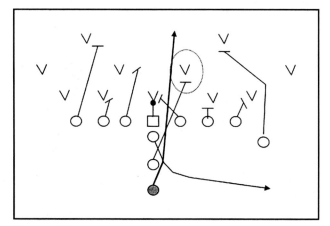

Figure 4-5

You should also make sure your outermost players are working their way upfield, putting themselves in a position to make a block upfield. In Figure 4-5, the offside tight end and the wingback are used to block upfield. The defenders nearest them are not in a position to be an immediate threat to the play. For instance, the offside defensive end likely has outside containment responsibilities. The cornerback and the onside defensive end have to give momentary thought to the possibility that the quarterback may still have the ball on a bootleg type play. The wing back will influence the bootleg possibility by first heading up the field for five yards, as if he were in pass pattern, before breaking on the safety who will also have an eye on him as a potential receiver.

Advanced Lead and Off Tackle Plays

Figure 4-6 illustrates a much more complex lead play. On this play the offside guard becomes the lead blocker through the hole that is still being widened by a double-team at the point of attack. He becomes the person responsible for the onside linebacker. The fullback is still leading the ballcarrier to the line of scrimmage, but on this play he will kick out the end man on the line of scrimmage.

Advantages: The deceptive nature of a play like this is a major advantage. The fullback is attacking

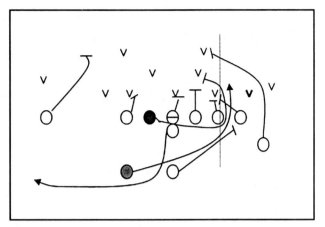

Figure 4-6

the defensive end with the ballcarrier behind him. This has the look of an outside running play. When a lead back blocks a defensive end the play is usually going to the outside. The ballcarrier doesn't cut into the line of scrimmage immediately to help freeze the defensive contain men on the outside. The corner must put himself in a position to contain the outside threat, which will take him out of the play. The significant threat of a bootleg will keep the offside defenders in check.

Although this play may seem complicated, I have seen 11-year-old boys execute this play flawlessly. Look at the elements of this play and understand the concepts behind them. Take these elements and adapt them to your style of offense. These are really just a culmination of several basic blocking schemes that were discussed in the linemen skills section of this book.

Figure 4-8 shows an off tackle lead play from a power I formation. This combines some of the schemes of the previous lead plays. This play shows the double-team and a kick out block from the fullback. You could still pull the offside guard to lead through the hole. If you do that you will need to adjust the paths of the backs in order to properly time the play. Have your backs initially angle more toward the outside and then cut up off tackle. This should give the play just enough time to develop if you choose to run it this way. Do not attempt to use the offside guard if he is not an exceptional athlete.

ONSIDE RULES:	OFFSIDE RULES:
G: gap-area-post	Pull wall-off
T: gap-area post	Pull check
C: reach-area-away	
TE: lead-backer-outside	stalk
Y:	stalk
RHB: wall off backer	
FB: crossover for tail of T, block 1st man outside T	
LHB: crossover step and receive ball on 2nd step just before midline	
QB: reverse pivot w/1st step just before the midline, 2nd step on same path, handoff on inside foot of G with shoulders parallel to LOS, bring right shoulder around to hide handoff from DE, fake boot to offside	

Figure 4-7

He will tend to clog up the play if he doesn't turn the corner upfield quickly. If you do choose to pull him, make sure he cuts up the field very tight to the buttocks of the tight end who has the lead part in the double-team.

You could also run this same play in a more basic way by having the tight end block the defensive end and using the fullback as an

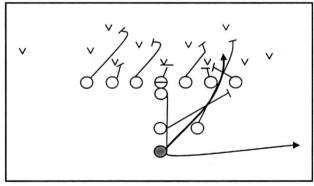

Figure 4-8

additional lead blocker. This can be a very powerful approach. See Figure 4-9.

Another way to utilize both backs as lead blockers would be to use a cross block at the point of attack. In Figure 4-10 the tight end will block down on the defensive tackle while the tackle will cut off his backside to kick out the defensive end. To keep the defensive end in check, it may be wise to have your backs influence the DE by initially taking an outside angle before cutting inside the tackle's kick out block.

Another way to run this play would be as a counter lead. This will combine the counter action with the lead blocking element. In Figure 4-11 the fullback fills for the pulling guard who is performing a kick-out block on the DE. He could also be used to lead through the hole upfield. In that case, the tight end blocks the DE. When you perform this play in this way the lead back will be a much greater distance from the ballcarrier. This will require him to maintain his block longer and eliminates a freeze block situation with the linebacker. The next section will get into greater detail on the counter aspect of the play.

Counter and Trap Plays

Counter and trap plays are essential elements to any offense. Many youth coaches are unduly intimidated by the complexities of a trap play. It is important to learn the blocking concepts involved with these plays. As was previously stated, the formations are not the most relevant information here. You can adapt the concepts to the formations in your offense.

Deception is the most obvious reason to run counters and traps. The best counters and traps accomplish the following three things:

- They effectively eliminate the defensive lineman nearest to the point of attack. This is usually accomplished with a double team block.

- They open big holes by kicking out the next most relevant defensive lineman at the point of attack. This is accomplished by pulling linemen who will usually kick out an unsuspecting defender.

- These plays will usually get the force linebacker off balance. Most linebackers will react to the initial flow of the play. This will make it easier to set up a block on him when he is working back to the ballcarrier.

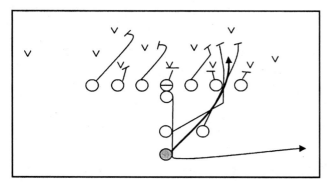

Figure 4-9

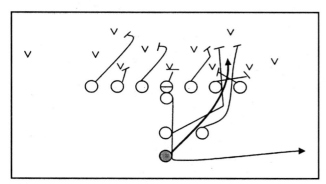

Figure 4-10

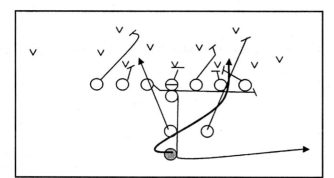

Figure 4-11

Basic Counters

To run a counter play properly, the flow of the backfield has to start opposite the direction of the handoff. Figure 4-12 displays a basic counter play from the I formation. In this example, the wingback is in motion across the formation. The fullback fakes a handoff into the right side of the defense. The halfback takes a jab-step to his right as if he were going in that direction. He pivots on his right foot and cuts back to the left to receive the handoff. He must stay low in his approach to the handoff. The quarterback opens to the offside with a deep step on the midline where he fakes the handoff to the fullback. His next step brings his left foot parallel to his right. His back is to the defense with his shoulder parallel to the line of scrimmage, hiding the ball against his stomach. He hands the ball off to the halfback who comes across tight to his body. He then runs a boot action to the offside.

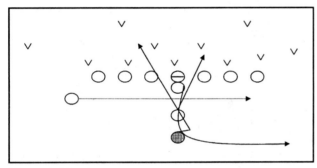

Figure 4-12

Wishbone Counter Lead

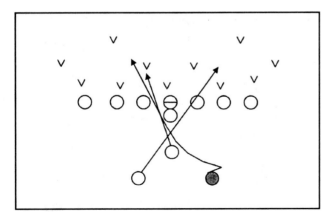

Figure 4-13

Wishbone Counter with Trap

The fullback on this play fills for the offside pulling guard. See Figure 4-14.

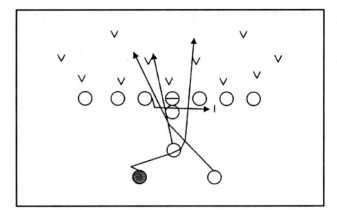

Figure 4-14

Wing T Counter

With the wingback in motion away from the point of attack. See Figure 4-15.

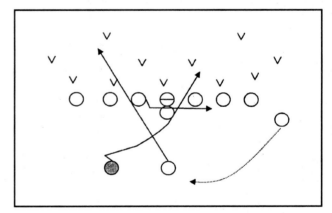

Figure 4-15

Power I Counter (Scissors)

The halfback cuts behind the tailback in this counter. This counter also uses a trap block by the offside guard. You can also run this as a counter lead with the fullback hitting the onside as lead blocker. See Figure 4-16.

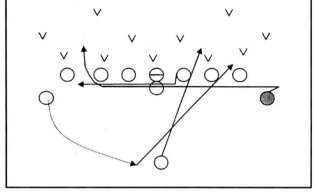

Figure 4-16

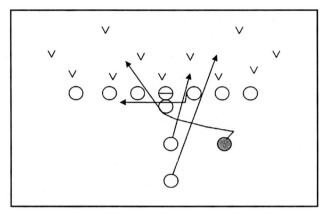

Figure 4-17

Double Wing Counter Criss-Cross

This type of counter is a hybrid between a reverse and a counter. This is still called a counter action because it is designed to cut back into the line of scrimmage. This method also uses trap blocking, which will be detailed next. Figure 4-17 shows the left wing in motion and then performing a fake handoff to the offside. You can also leave the left wing in place and use him to wall off the middle backers. In that case, the fake handoff would be to the tailback to the offside.

Trap Play Progression

Trap plays can be stand-alone plays or performed as part of a counter play. The deception is similar in both types of plays. The difference is that the back who carries the ball does not take a counter step away from the point of attack. He directly hits the hole that the play is designed to hit. The deception comes into play with the other backs in the backfield. The fake to the other back is usually after the handoff to the ballcarrier. You should have another play that uses the identical action where the ball is given to the other back instead. Figure 4-18 is an example of this.

Figure 4-18 shows a trap play to the left side 'A' gap. Immediately after handing the ball to the fullback, the quarterback fakes a handoff to the wing going to the offside. After faking the handoff he runs

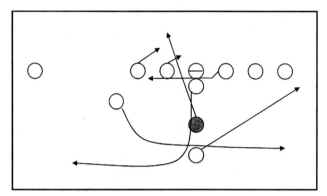

Figure 4-18

a bootleg action to the playside. The play fakes must be executed flawlessly. The defenders should have trouble figuring out if the play was a quick handoff to the fullback, a reverse play to the fullback, or a bootleg by the quarterback.

Figure 4-19 shows the identical formation and action by every one of the backs. This time the quarterback fakes to the fullback and hands the ball off to the wingback on a reverse sweep action. He still fakes the bootleg.

The third part of the play progression is the identical formation and action by the entire backfield. This time the quarterback fakes the handoff to both the fullback and the wingback. He keeps the ball on a bootleg. In this play he has the option of throwing a pass to either the wide receiver or the fullback in the flat. He also has the option of keeping the ball and running up the field.

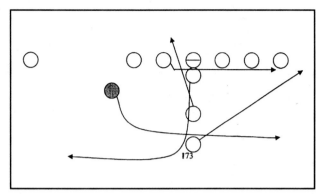

Figure 4-19

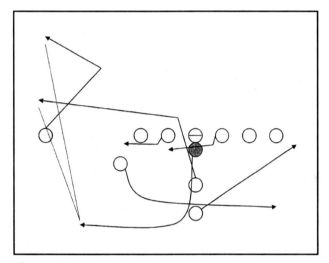

Figure 4-20

You can clearly see that if this series of plays were executed properly, the defense would certainly be conflicted. The inside linebackers have to respect the quick-hitting nature of the trap. The outside defenders on both sides of the defense should be conflicted. In these examples, the one side of the defense has to respect the reverse sweep potential while the other side has to worry about the bootleg potential. The defensive backs need to worry about a potential pass as well as the possibility that the quarterback is keeping the ball.

As stated previously, the formations that are diagramed are irrelevant. This series of plays can be run from many different formations. They can also be run with different elements and points of attack. The important thing here is the concept. When you are making your playbook it is important to 'set up'

your plays. Whether you're setting up the trap play, the sweep, or the bootleg, the only way for these plays to be effective is if you are proficient in the execution of every aspect of the plays. You must also use every one of the plays in the series in order to create the defensive conflicts. Every trap play should be a part of a series of plays.

Developing a Trap Blocking Scheme

Trap plays should be incorporated into every offense. You should have a progression of plays that include a trap as outlined above. You should also have counter plays that include trap blocking. Either way the blocking principles are the same.

In trap blocking, you should be concerned with the defenders at or near the point of attack. In Figures 4-21 and 4-22, the target defenders are outlined in the box. This section will demonstrate the different techniques required to execute the trap with both an odd and an even front.

The middle trap is directed to the left hip of the center. There are always three blocks that must be made in every trap play. They are as follows:

- The clearing block—a down block or post/lead that is used to clear an immediate opening for the ballcarrier to pass through
- The trap/kick block—solidifies the 'hole' for the back who will receive the ball off the backside of this blocker
- The backer block—the block on the playside inside linebacker

The clearing block is performed differently based on the front you are facing. The defender you should be clearing and the blockers involved are circled in Figures 4-23 and 4-24

The clearing block versus the Odd defense will be a post/lead block on the noseguard. The center will post him up and the left Guard will clear him with the lead block shown in Figure 4-25.

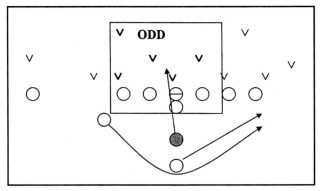

Figure 4-21. Versus 50 defense (odd front)

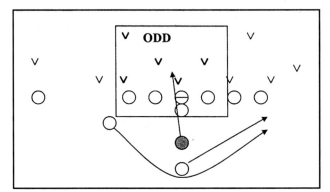

Figure 4-22. Versus 40 defense (even)

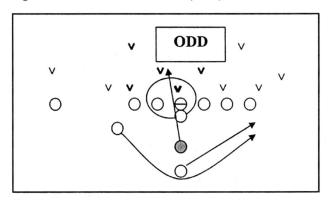

Figure 4-23.

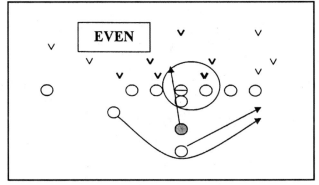

Figure 4-24.

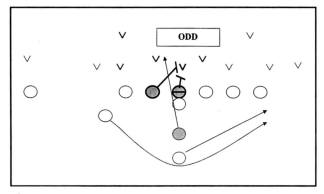

Figure 4-25

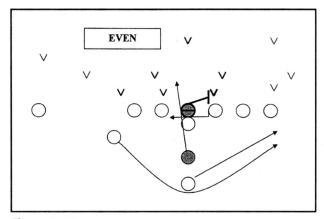

Figure 4-26

The clearing block to use versus an even front is a down block by the center on the defensive tackle to his right. This is an easy way to clear this man since he is located far enough from the point of attack that a double-team block becomes unneeded. The reason you don't want to clear the defensive tackle to the left of the center is because he is the man who will be trapped. The rule of thumb is to always trap block the first man outside the point of attack. Variations of this will be discussed later in this book.

The second part of the trap play is the actual trap block, which should be performed on the first player outside the point of attack. It is important that the lineman who is over the defender you are trapping releases to the inside forcing him to rush from the outside. The trap blocks are shown in Figures 4-27 and 4-28 are highlighted in bold.

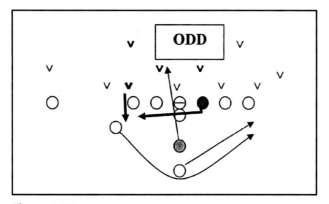

Figure 4-27

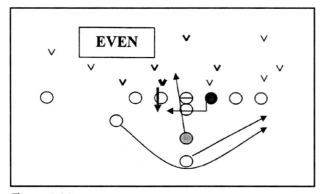

Figure 4-28

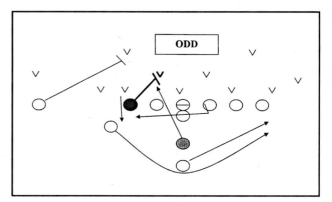

Figure 4-29

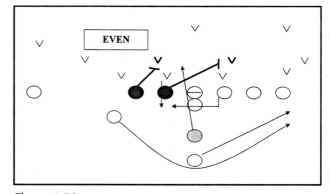

Figure 4-30

The last part of the trap is the backer block. These blocks are performed differently against odd and even defenses. As stated before, the blocker must always release to the inside of the defender lined up on or outside of him. The backer blocking in Figure 4-29 is highlighted in bold.

In the even defense in Figure 4-30 it is important to block both backers. It is unnecessary to block the left defensive end as he will take himself out of the play. This is a tight trap that may require the ballcarrier to adjust his path with the down block of the center.

The Trap Play

Now that you've seen a breakdown of the different elements of the trap play, you can put it all together. The rules are listed in Figures 4-31, 4-32, and 4-33. Read each rule and follow each player through both defenses diagramed. You can see how basic these

plays can be if each player follows his rules. No matter how you mix up the defensive alignments, these rules will always work on trap plays.

Counter Trap Plays

Counter trap plays are labeled just that because the initial flow of the backs is opposite the actual playside. The ballcarrier pivots off his initial step and redirects his path to the playside 'hole.' The blocking scheme uses trap blocking rules. Compare the counter trap plays in Figures 4-34 through 4-36 to the trap plays in Figures 4-31, 4-32, and 4-33, and you will notice the similarities.

Outside Running Plays

This section will focus on two types of outside play: the sweep and the toss. They are similar since they both go in the same direction. They are different in

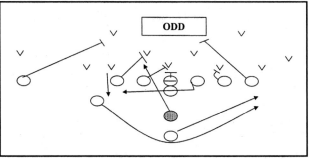

Figure 4-31

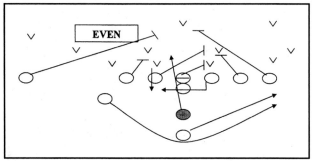

Figure 4-32

ONSIDE RULES:	OFFSIDE RULES:
G: Lead – Backer	G: pull kick 1st man past center
T: 1st Backer from Center	
C: Post - Down	T: Pull check – work up to backer, look for stunting backer
TE: Gap- Backer	
Y: Stalk	
TB: Block 1st Man on or outside TE	TE: Backer or work to safety
FB: Take handoff behind tail of center work behind Backer block	Y:Stalk
LHB: Fake reverse sweep	
QB: Open step at midline, handoff to fullback, turn back to defense fake sweep handoff then bootleg playside	

Figure 4-33

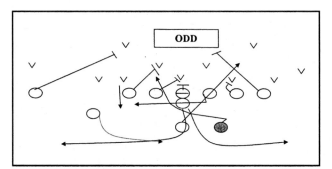

Figure 4-34

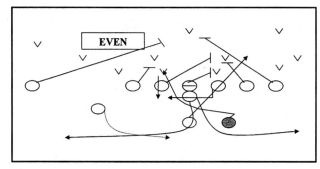

Figure 4-35

ONSIDE RULES:	OFFSIDE RULES:
G: Lead – Backer	G: pull kick 1st man past center
T: 1st Backer from Center	
C: Post - Down	T: Pull check – work up to backer, look for stunting backer
TE: Gap- Backer	
Y: Stalk	
RHB: jab step to offside and cut back to receive handoff	TE: Backer or work to safety
FB: Fake belly type handoff to offside	Y:Stalk
LHB: go in back motion fake toss action to offside	
QB: Reverse pivot Open step at midline, fake to fullback, turn back to defense w/next step, handoff to HB, then bootleg offside	

Figure 4-36

the way they are executed. A sweep play takes longer to develop than a toss play, which creates different blocking strategies. Toss plays are designed to hit the outside quickly.

The biggest misconception with these plays is that the ballcarrier has to get outside of the widest defender. Nothing could be further from the truth. The best strategy for developing outside running plays is to create running lanes. Some of the most efficient outside running plays begin by cutting up the field inside the outermost defender and then angling for the end zone. It is best to reduce the amount of lateral yardage that a runner takes toward a sideline. Figure 4-37 shows an example of an outside running lane that is created by blocking.

In Figure 4-37 the ballcarrier cut up the field between the lead block of the lead back and the receivers block on the pursuing safety. The offside guard performed a hook block on the defensive end and the wing walled off the middle backer. The hook block can be effective on a defensive end because it is unexpected. The guard will cut off the pursuit of the end and wheel his hips to the playside sideline upon impact. The ballcarrier is angling toward the goal line marker as soon as he can. He is doing this to escape the offside support of the defense, which has taken their angle pursuit lanes. Even if they catch him, this method gives him the greatest gain. If he tries to get to the sideline and then work to the end zone, the offside defenders have ample time to catch him.

Sweep Plays

Figure 4-38 shows a sweep play from a wishbone formation. This is a power sweep with two backs and the onside guard lead blocking. You can also use the offside guard instead of the onside guard depending on your philosophy. The onside corner (bold type) will likely pursue this from the outside. Hence, the reason the ballcarrier is shown cutting up the field inside him. If he were to take a more direct route to the ballcarrier the lead block may require the runner to cut outside him.

When you are developing sweep plays for your offense, you need to make sure you have blockers in a position to block the defenders that are going to be in a position to stop the play at or near the point of attack. These defenders are in shown in bold type in Figure 4-38. These defenders can be blocked from multiple formations. You need to devise a way for your players to get to these defenders from your formation. You can use different types of motion to set backs up to be in blocking position. Review the blocks listed in the linemen skills section of this book. See if any of the pulling blocks may be relevant to the sweep plays you are trying to develop.

No matter what scheme you develop, you need to practice the execution as a team. Timing of these plays is very important. Make sure you go over every possible defensive look you may encounter. Make sure there is no confusion in their blocking responsibilities.

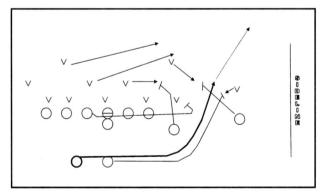

Figure 4-37

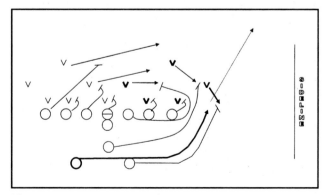

Figure 4-38

Toss Plays

The toss is usually used to get to the outside quickly and take advantage of the speed of a particular back. Because of the quick-hitting nature of the toss it is unlikely you will able to pull any linemen other than the onside tackle, which is shown in Figure 4-39. If you plan on using your tackles to help lead the play, they need to get out there quickly.

The toss play is more likely to turn the outside corner than a sweep play. The ballcarrier must still read the lead block in order to make that decision. He may very well cut up the field in front of that block. Because you may not always get to every defender the way that you can on a sweep, tell your lead blocker to make an attempt to turn the defender in if possible. If you take this play a little wider, there is a better chance for the pursuing defender to get caught up in traffic.

This does not mean the ballcarrier should be heading toward the sideline. He needs to start up the field as quickly as possible. He can accomplish this by influencing the pursuit of the outermost defender, which is usually a cornerback. He can influence this man by running directly at him and cutting around him at the last possible moment. This allows the man blocking him enough time to establish control of his block and, hopefully, wheel his hips to the outside, which should create the outside lane that you are hoping for.

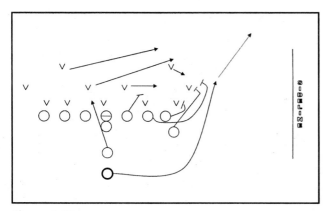

Figure 4-39

Reverse and Bootleg Running Plays

Reverse and bootleg plays are both set up by other plays. The best way to pull off these plays is to devise them from your most successful running plays. The whole idea behind running these plays is to get the defense to flow in one direction while the play goes back in the other direction.

The quarterback plays a pivotal role in both of these plays. This is why he must carry out his bootleg fakes on every handoff he makes. He should act as if he still has the ball on every play. The outside defenders will start to ignore him if he reacts consistently on every running play. This will obviously give him a leg up when he actually keeps the ball on a bootleg. He can also be used as a lead blocker on a double reverse, although some coaches may frown upon their quarterback blocking.

Your linemen will play an important role in the lead blocking of these plays. The defense will watch the initial flow of your backfield, which can give the advantage to a lineman pulling opposite the initial flow of the play.

Figure 4-40 shows a counter play from the I formation. This will be the base play that you will develop a reverse and a bootleg from. In this play, the fullback hits the left 'A' gap and the tailback receives the handoff in the right 'A' gap after his left jab-step.

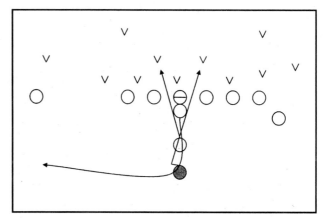

Figure 4-40

Reverse Play

Figure 4-41 shows a reverse play that derives from the counter play shown in Figure 4-40. This time the fullback and the tailback will both fake a handoff. After they get through the line of scrimmage, they are responsible to block the middle linebackers. Hopefully, the linebackers are attempting to tackle them because they properly executed their fakes.

The quarterback opens to the midline with his left foot and after the fake to the fullback he brings his right foot around which causes him to have his back to the defense. At this time, the tailback crosses his path and fakes his handoff. He remains with his back to the defense until the wingback comes across for the reverse handoff. It is the responsibility of the wingback to adjust his path to the location of the quarterback in order to receive the handoff.

The point-of-attack blocking in this play is performed by the receiver and both guards. The receiver takes off on a slant pattern, and then seals off the safety or defensive back in that area. The onside guard hook blocks the defensive end while the offside guard is the lead blocker up the field. The wingback should read this block and adjust his run accordingly.

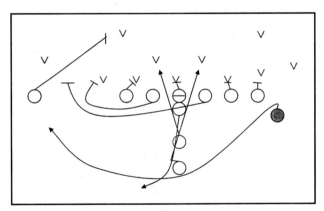

Figure 4-41

This play will work from many different formations. These blocking schemes can be adapted to most offenses.

Double Reverse

The double reverse incorporates two handoffs. Imagine if the tailback in Figure 4-41 was aligned over the left tackle. He takes a handoff going to his right and hands the ball off to the wingback coming back to the left. The blocking scheme may stay exactly the same, or you can now add a lead block by the quarterback around the left end.

Bootleg Play

The bootleg play in Figure 4-42 also derives from the counter shown in Figures 4-34 and 4-35. On this play everything is identical except that the quarterback keeps the ball after his fake to the tailback. He then follows the block of the offside guard who is leading the play.

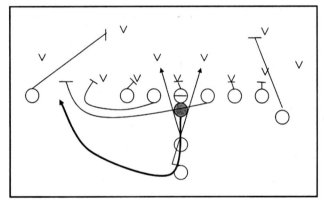

Figure 4-42

Play-Action Passing Plays

The play shown in Figure 4-43 is the play-action version of the bootleg in Figure 4-42. This time the quarterback has the option of throwing a pass in the flat to the fullback or passing to the receiver running a seam-flag pattern. He also has the option of keeping the ball. If he has a clear lane to run the ball, he should opt to run before passing it.

Play-action passes are derived from the running plays in your offense. The more successful you are at the running play, the more successful you will be with your play-action passing game. The best play-action passing plays should look like a running play to the defense. Since you know this is true, you need to use your play-action pass plays in running situations.

Consistency is the most important element when you are developing your play-action pass plays. The quarterback must consistently roll out of every running play the same way that he would roll out if he were throwing the play-action pass off that play. He must always hide his throwing hand during his rollout so that the defenders don't know when he has the ball. The receivers must use the same

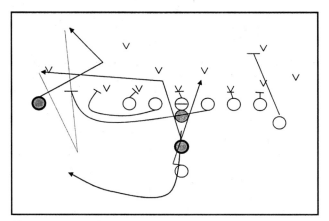

Figure 4-43

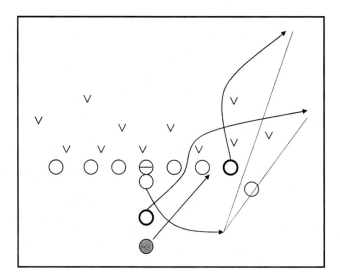

Figure 4-44

takeoff in their stalk block for the running play as they do when they are running a pass pattern. Finally, the running backs must execute their fakes as if they were executing the actual running play.

Figure 4-44 shows a play-action pass that is based on a lead play from the I formation. The fullback on this play slips into the flat. The playside tight end runs a flag pattern and the wingback blocks down on the defensive end.

Figure 4-45 shows another way to run the play action. In this version, the offside tight end is running a drag pattern at an intermediate depth. This creates a flood situation. This can cause coverage conflicts with many zone defenses. The other thing to note is the use of the offside guard to protect backside penetration. Since the tight end is in a pass pattern, the backside becomes vulnerable. You don't have to use this player to do this but you have to protect the quarterback's backside. Any uncovered lineman should check to help in this situation.

Whenever there is more than one eligible receiver, the quarterback should read down. What this means is that his first read should be the deep man; if he is open, he needs to immediately make that throw. The next deepest man would be his next read and so on. The reads on this play are relatively simple since all of the receivers are in the same area,

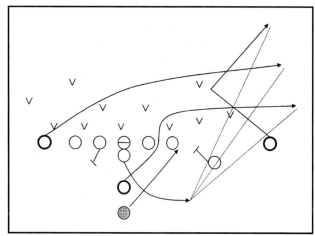

Figure 4-45

just at different depths. These reads should happen very quickly. If he feels that he does not have a safe throw to make, he should attack the flank. At this point, he has a few options. First, he can keep the ball and try to gain as many yards as possible. By attacking the flank, he opens the possibility of a cover man abandoning his coverage to pursue the Quarterback. Or, if he has not crossed the line of scrimmage, he can dump the pass to the open receiver. This will usually be the man on the shortest route. In this case, it would be the fullback in the flat. The man responsible to cover the fullback also has outside run and containment responsibilities.

In the play-action variation in Figure 4-46, the playside safety and corner will be tested if they are in zone coverage. The safety will initially have

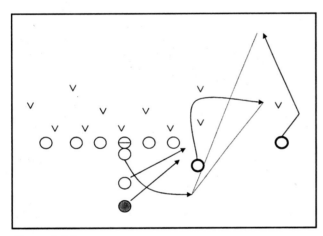

Figure 4-46

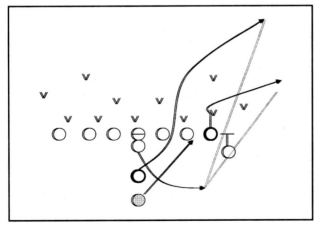

Figure 4-47

coverage of the wingback who will run an 8- to 10-yard out pattern back to a depth of 7 to 8 yards. The cornerback will have initial coverage on the wide receiver who is running a deep pattern. The defenders will have to switch coverage responsibilities or change into man coverage once the play has begun. Either way, this will be tough to pull off leaving one of the two receivers open.

In the variation shown in Figure 4-47 the fullback and the tight end have switched pattern types. The fullback will work up the field for the deep pattern and the tight end will get into the flat on a delay pattern by making quick contact with the defensive end.

Dropback Passing Plays

Dropback passing refers to the quarterback's drop. The three most important drops are the 3-step, the 5-step, and the 7-step drop.

The 3-Step Drop

The 3-step drop is used in the quick passing game. These are mostly timing patterns that don't require much of a post-snap read by your quarterback. Figure 4-48 shows three different patterns that can be used with a 3-step drop. These patterns will require excellent timing in order to be successful. You will need to complete plenty of repetitions in practice to perfect these patterns. The most important thing about these plays is consistency. Since the quarterback is timing his throws, the receiver must be in the same place at the same time every play.

Your line will create a pocket for the quarterback to throw from. Their objective is to not allow inside penetration from the defenders. Since the quarterback is not set very deep, it would be advantageous to force the defenders to take an outside pass rush. To accomplish this, two things are recommended. First, tighten your line splits. Second, make sure that your linemen take a very short initial step to their inside. If penetration comes this way they would block immediately at the line of scrimmage. If there is no immediate inside penetration, they should pivot off that inside step, take a small step back with the outside foot and block any penetration from the defense, forcing it to go as far outside as possible.

- The tight end is running a 6- to 8-yard out pattern.

- The wingback is running to the left flat.

- The wide receiver is running a hitch pattern at a depth of 6 to 8 yards.

The patterns shown in Figure 4-48 are timing patterns. They are relatively safe throws if executed properly. Figure 4-49 shows 3-step drop patterns that require a pre-snap read by the quarterback and the receiver. The quarterback must read the coverage of the defense to determine if the designed play has a chance of success. There should be a safe alternative afforded to him if he feels the play can't work. The receiver must also read the coverage. He may be required to adjust his path depending on the alignment of the defenders.

This needs to be practiced often. The receiver and the quarterback must be on the same page when they feel a pattern adjustment is in order.

The slant pattern shown in Figure 4-49 would be unwise to throw. On the pre-snap read, the quarterback sees the safety and immediately knows that the slant pattern may be in jeopardy. The safe throw here is to the tight end in the flat.

If you had already committed to throwing to the wideout, then you need to draw the coverage of the safety away from the target area. You could accomplish this by running the tight end in a fly or deep flag pattern as shown below in Figure 4-50.

In Figure 4-51, the wingback split wide to the right is the intended target on a fly pattern. In the pre-snap read by the quarterback he notices the defensive back is playing off his receiver with an inside shade. Again, this is not the wisest throw to make. If it is rehearsed in practice, the receiver in this case can make a route adjustment to put himself in a better position to make the catch.

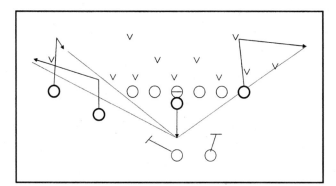

Figure 4-48

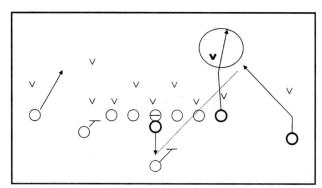

Figure 4-50

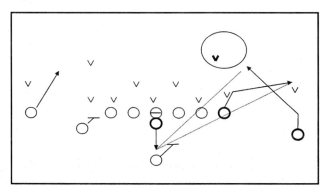

Figure 4-49

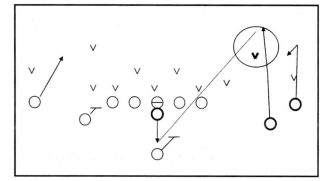

Figure 4-51

In Figure 4-52, the receiver has adjusted his pattern. The important thing he did was to get inside the defender. You would never want this defender between the passer and the receiver. By heading straight up the field for the first five yards, he gives the appearance of a fly pattern. This will have the defender backing up. The receiver then breaks into a short post pattern, putting himself in an advantageous position. The receiver and the quarterback should have some type of signal that indicates the pattern adjustment. They must be 'on the same page' in this situation.

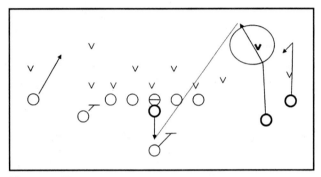

Figure 4-52

The 5-Step Drop

The 5-step drop is the most popular drop in most offenses. It opens up more possibilities than a 3-step drop and it is a lot safer than a 7-step drop. Endless possibilities exist when it comes to pass pattern. Figure 4-53 outlines several possible patterns. Keep in mind that the deeper patterns will take more time to develop.

Pass Routes/Patterns

Countless combinations of patterns are possible that will work with various formations. You should develop a passing scheme that works well with your system. It must also be adapted to the skill level of your quarterback. If you are coaching 11-year-olds, you may not want to put in too many plays that require the quarterback to make reads. This doesn't mean you shouldn't teach them how to read a defense. Young players should start learning the basic pre-snap reads.

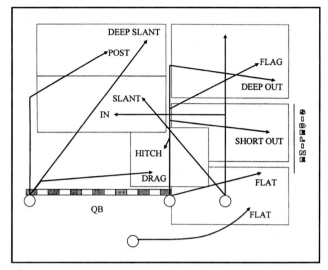

Figure 4-53

Your 5-step passing game should include passes designed for your running backs as well as your other receivers. Since your backs are often your best athletes, it is important to find more ways to get the ball in their hands. Figure 4-54 shows a 'Swing' pass to the right.

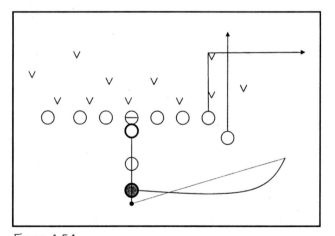

Figure 4-54

Figure 4-55 shows the tailback in a short flat pattern. This pattern can be adjusted to achieve greater depth if you prefer. This pattern can be run immediately out of the backfield with no fakes, or you could have the tailback approach the defensive end as if he were going to block him, then he slips behind him into the flat.

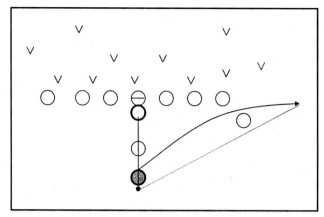

Figure 4-55

Figure 4-56 shows a 'delay' route by the back. In this case, he sets up to block at a distance of approximately three yards from his stance at an angle toward the end. If defensive penetration shows, he should make initial contact and immediately slip into the flat. If no penetration shows after two seconds, he should release into the flat.

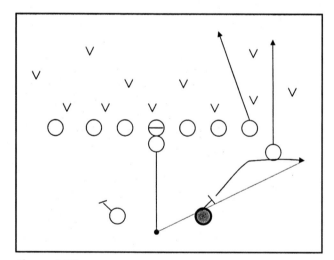

Figure 4-56

Figure 4-57 shows the running back breaking through the line of scrimmage. At this point there are several patterns he can run.

The 7-Step Drop

The 7-step drop is an extension of the 5-step drop. These passes will take slightly longer to develop.

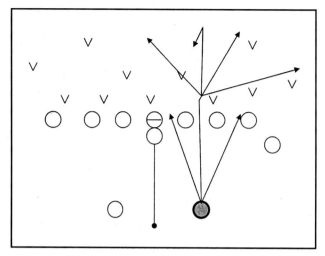

Figure 4-57

The quarterback needs to be making his reads as he is dropping back. It is important that you set up the patterns so that that they have a logical sequence for the quarterback to read. He should never have to make drastic changes in his set-up in order to look for an alternate receiver.

In Figure 4-58, there is a triangle around the three main receivers on this particular play. This 'passing triangle' shows how the quarterback should make his reads. His first read is the post pattern being run by the wide receiver. This is an easy first read because he starts to head toward the middle of the field putting him in a position that the passer can easily follow. If he is not open, he reads from left to right and picks up the wingback on a flag pattern. Finally, he looks for the tight end in the crossing route if no one else is open. This is a logical third pass route to read because of the amount of time it takes for this pattern to develop. It is also a safe throw because he usually slips under coverage since he is crossing two zones, and he is heading toward the sideline allowing the passer to make a safe wide throw. Of course, this will all depend on the amount of time your quarterback has to throw.

When you develop your downfield passing game, draw your own 'passing triangle' and number your receivers. Also, put in a timing pass off the 7-step drop. The best place to throw a timing pass is on the outside. This is a safer place to throw and you're almost guaranteed one-on-one coverage. Your receiver must have a 'ball hawk' mentality on this play. No matter where the ball is thrown, he needs to get to it.

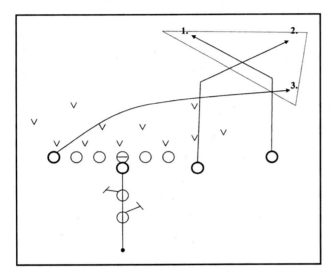

Figure 4-58

If your quarterback has a strong arm, throw the fly pattern to a receiver who is split as wide as possible. The flag play is another excellent timing pattern that works its way to the sideline. You can also time a post pass and a deep slant pass over the deep middle of the field. If you are coaching at a younger level or your quarterback doesn't have the strongest arm, then one of the patterns shown in Figure 4-59 might be your best option. These patterns will not get as deep because they take time developing laterally instead of gaining ground immediately.

Both of these patterns can be thrown at any level. You should adjust the amount of lateral movement needed to suit the throwing ability of the passer.

Figure 4-60 shows two more deep timing patterns that can be incorporated into your offense. The timing of these plays is paramount. They must be practiced repeatedly. Make the necessary adjustments to adapt these patterns to the ability of your passer.

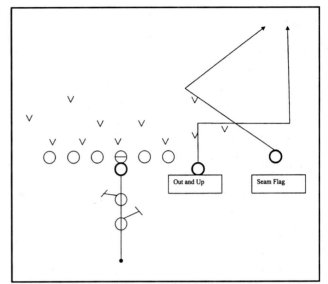

Figure 4-59

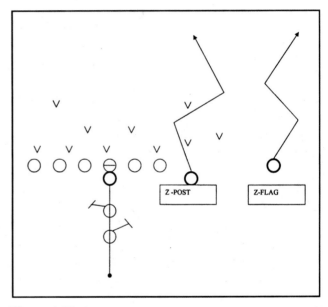

Figure 4-60

Remember the five most important words when you are developing a play to be run by your offense are:

- Repetition
- Repetition
- Repetition
- Repetition
- Repetition

Specialty Plays

The specialty plays described in this book are the type of plays that are rarely run by the offense, but are also essential to the overall scheme of the offense. They are situational type plays. The QB sneak is used on very short yardage plays. The draw play and the screen play are alternatives that can be used in long yardage situations. A quick passing game could be used in time management situations. The 'flea flicker' is another specialty play that every offense should have. They are the plays that are the most fun to develop and the players enjoy running them. These are the plays where you get to use your imagination.

All of these plays need sufficient repetitions in practice. Even if you run these plays once every three games, they will most likely be used in critical situations. The success of a quarterback sneak could be the difference in a touchdown or a field goal, or worse yet, a touchdown or nothing. Imagine it is third down with 15 yards to go for the first down and one minute left in the game and your opponent is in a prevent defense. A screen pass in this situation could make or break the game if the defense isn't prepared for it. The point here is that anything you put into your offense should be perfected in practice before it is used in a game.

The Quarterback Sneak

The biggest reason to run a quarterback sneak is to try to gain a relatively short amount of yardage. For the sake of the play shown in Figure 4-61, let's assume that it is third down and one yard to go for the first. It should be relatively easy to gain that one yard with a sneak if you follow a few principles.

The first thing you need to do is to get a jump on the defense. You can accomplish this in one of two ways. You can go on a silent count where only the quarterback and the center know when to start. They will accomplish this by some type of touch by the quarterback to the center. The other blockers will have to wait for the start of the snap in order to get out of their stance. In some cases, the other blockers never move to try to throw the defense off. In that instance, they are banking purely on the element of surprise. If the defense has not prepared for this scenario, it has a good likelihood of success. Smart defensive teams are looking for things like that in short yardage situations. The best thing may be to go on a quick count. One that is much shorter than your average cadence. You can even go on 'sound.' This means the ball will be snapped on the first sound the quarterback makes. If you decide to do this, the quarterback should make sure everyone is set before he attempts to get under the center.

Perhaps, the most important thing about the sneak play is how you will block at the point of attack. A double-team at the point of attack is advisable. Pick the most immediate threat to your play and destroy it. In Figure 4-61 (sneak 1) the defense is in an even alignment. In this situation, pick the defender to one side of the center and double-team him. The post man in this situation should try to 'cut' the defender by blocking him low while the lead man sends him flying. If the defender

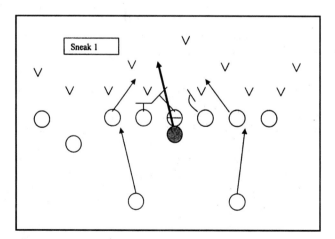

Figure 4-61

goes down on the cut, the post blocker can work up the field for the backer. The offside guard shown in Figure 4-61 should cut-off the pursuit of the man on him. Every other blocker can work his way to the middle of the field. The exterior defenders are irrelevant in this play. There is no reason not to gain a yard here if everyone executes his block.

In Figure 4-62 the defense is in an odd alignment. The right side has one less defender at the area of concern. In this case, double-team the noseguard and have everyone else work to the middle of the field.

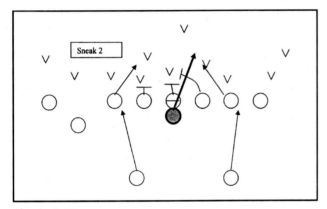

Figure 4-62

The Screen Play

The screen is a very useful tool to an offense. Teams that execute screens well add a significant dimension to their offense. This play requires precision timing. Your linemen must be smart and agile to properly execute this play. It will be very important that your quarterback show a high level of poise on this play. He may have to hold onto the ball until the last minute, which means it may likely require him to take a hit immediately after the release of the ball.

Initially, the quarterback takes a 5-step drop. At this point, he looks at a downfield receiver and hesitates momentarily. He then floats back another three yards, which is where he throws a pass. He does this to change the initial rush angle of the defenders. The halfback will set up to block, brush by the rusher, and set up 3X3 yards, and face the

passer. When he catches the ball, he yells, 'Go' and heads up the field.

The onside linemen and the center hold their blocks for three seconds and then pull to their responsibilities. The tackle pulls and kicks out any outside penetration. The guard pulls out in front of the back and lead blocks up the field while the center pulls wall-off the inside penetration.

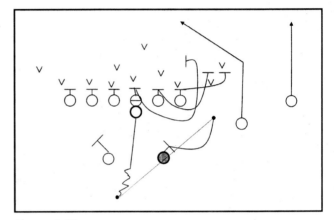

Figure 4-63

Fast-Break Plays

For lack of a better term, plays that happen instantaneously with the snap of the ball have been labeled 'fast-break plays.' The passes require only a 1-step drop (2 at the most). The only handoffs happen immediately upon the snap of the ball.

Teams use these types of plays for various reasons. The most common would be to save time. These plays can be performed with no huddle. The quarterback can read the defense and call these plays at the line of scrimmage. Another reason for running these plays would be the 'element of surprise' or putting your opponent on their heels.

The passing plays shown are all high percentage passes that are fairly safe to throw. The quarterback will know at the line if he is comfortable with one of these plays. If he is not, then he can audible to another one with a higher likelihood of success.

Figure 4-64 is a quick-hitting slant pattern that is run under the fly pattern. To make this play work, the receiver only has to get inside the man covering him. If the defender covering him shades to his inside by a yard or more the QB will audible.

In this play the wingback is being covered by the free safety. You can easily execute this type of play if the defender is playing at least five yards off the receiver.

The play shown in Figure 4-66 is a quick throw to the wideout. The wing runs interference in front of him and he chooses his lane.

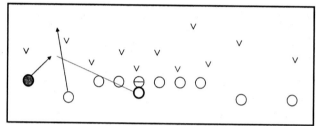

Figure 4-64

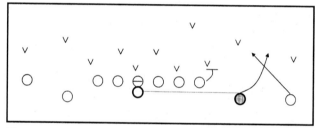

Figure 4-65

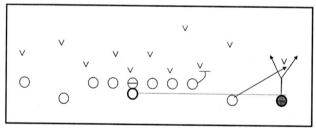

Figure 4-66

The play shown in Figure 4-67 is a quick hitter to the tight end. The safeties in this situation have a habit of 'sitting back' which creates a throwing lane for a quick slant. The inside linebacker is a concern, so the route must be adjusted accordingly. The left wing is in motion to create a diversion and to set up other plays. He could also be setting back up in the

backfield as a blocker and the QB can make a 3- to 5-step drop type play.

The play that is shown in Figure 4-68 is a quick toss play to the wing in motion. He takes off at full speed at the snap, which puts him to receive the toss somewhere behind the tight end area. He will already have momentum as he receives the toss. He must concentrate on receiving the toss before attempting to work up the field.

Figure 4-69 shows a quick handoff to the wingback in motion just behind the line of scrimmage. Since this is an extremely quick handoff, the timing must be flawless. The quarterback opens to his left with a short step. You can also use this action for deception and throw one of the quick passes shown before.

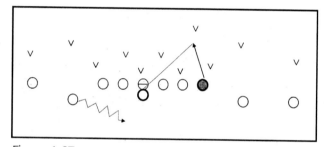

Figure 4-67

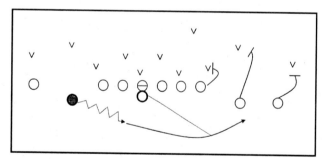

Figure 4-68

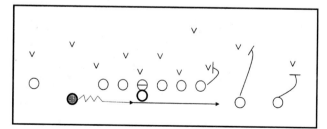

Figure 4-69

CHAPTER 5

Defense

Gaps

It is very important that your defense understands the gap system. Gaps are the designated spaces along the offensive line between the players on the line of scrimmage. Many defensive systems are gap-based systems. These types of defenses assign defenders to gap responsibilities. These responsibilities are called assignments. An offensive blocker has an assignment that gives him a primary blocking responsibility. Defenders should also have assignments that tell them the primary area they are responsible to protect. These areas are called gaps. Figure 5-1 shows where each gap is located.

Gap Chart

The letters represent the gaps on the offensive line.

- The A gap is the space between the center and the guard.
- The B gap is the space between the guard and the tackle.
- The C gap is the space between the tackle and the tight end or ghost TE.
- The D gap is the entire area outside the tight end or ghost TE.

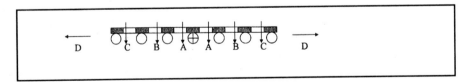

Figure 5-1

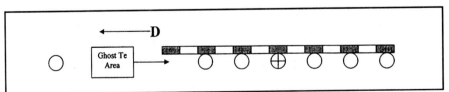

Figure 5-2

Defensive Techniques

This section describes the techniques of a defense. A technique can simply be described as the area in which the defender aligns himself prior to the snap of the ball. This system is a universal defensive language. If you plan on expanding your defensive knowledge base you must learn and understand this system.

If you attend a good coaching clinic, chances are the speaker will be using technique and gap terminology. Many coaching books and videos also use this terminology. The terminology is actually fairly simple. Once you have learned it, use it all the time so that it becomes second nature. Teach it to all your players and encourage them to make it second nature as well.

Figure 5-3 demonstrates the head-up techniques. The even numbers represent defensive linemen in head-up alignment with the offensive linemen. For example, if a man is lined up directly over the guard he is said to be in a 2 technique; head-up on the tackle is a 4 technique; over the TE is a 6 technique; and over the center is a 0 technique. If there is a linebacker lined up head-up on a guard, he too is considered to be lined up in a 2 technique, even if he is lined up three yards off the LOS. Some defensive numbering systems will add a zero to the end of the number for the alignment of a backer. For example, the same linebacker previously described would be in a 20 technique.

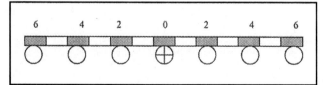

Figure 5-3

Note: When there is no tight end in an offensive formation the area that he would normally line up in is very important. We use the term ghost TE to identify this area.

For instance, if there is no tight end in an offensive formation and the defender's alignment still calls for a 6 technique, the defender lines up over the ghost TE. This simply means that he lines up exactly where he would if the tight end were there.

The defender aligned in a 6 technique, as shown in Figure 5-4, is lined up over the ghost TE.

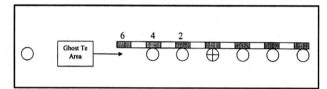

Figure 5-4

The numbers and letters in Figure 5-5 describe an inside shade technique by the defensive linemen. This simply means they are lined up on the inside shoulder of the offensive linemen. For example, a man lined up on the inside shoulder of the guard is in a 2i technique; inside shoulder of the tackle is a 4i technique; and the inside shoulder of the TE is considered a 7 technique.

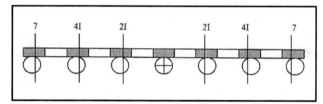

Figure 5-5

The numbers in Figure 5-6 represent an outside shade technique by the defensive linemen. This means that they are lined up on the outside shoulder of the offensive linemen. No matter which side of the center they are lined up on it is considered a 1 technique. If they are lined up on the outside shoulder of the guard, they are in a 3 technique; the outside shoulder of the tackle is a 5 technique; the outside shoulder of the TE is a 9 technique. All of the techniques listed will be broken down in this section.

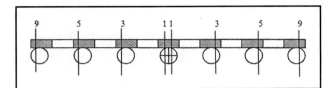

Figure 5-6

The following portion of this section breaks down every technique individually. The base alignment will be demonstrated as well as the likely assignment of the defender.

0 Technique

0 Alignment

- A player who is in a 0 technique is aligned head-up on the center.

- This would be used in an odd defense.

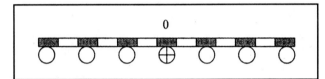

Figure 5-7

0 Assignment

- This technique is widely used in 5-0 defenses. The responsibility of this player can vary. In some base 50 defenses this player would have two gap responsibilities. The two gaps would both be A gaps.

- The key is the center's head; don't allow it to cross the body. Whichever side his head goes to will likely be the playside.

- Other base 50 defenses will require this man to have strongside A gap responsibilities. In this situation, the player doesn't know which gap he is responsible for until the offense is set up and a strongside is determined.

- It would be wise to vary the responsibility of a man aligned in this technique. For instance, if he is responsible for the strongside A gap, then it is

likely that there is a linebacker behind him who is responsible for the weakside A gap responsibility. It may be more beneficial to have your linebacker responsible for the strongside.

1 Technique

1 Alignment

- A player lined up in a 1 technique is lined up in a shade of the center.

- An odd number technique represents an outside shade; both sides of the center could be considered outside.

- The facemask of the defender is aligned with the center of the outside shoulder of the center.

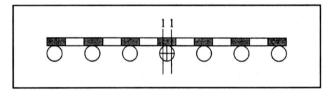

Figure 5-8

1 Assignment

- The base responsibility for a defender in a 1 technique is the A gap to the shade side of the center.

- It is imperative that he never allows the center's head to cross his body.

- If the center blocks down on him, he should work to get himself to the other side of the center's head.

- The guard to the shade side will be the other key. If he tries to block down, the player should work to his outside. This will likely be the playside.

- The defender should not allow himself to be double-teamed. If possible, he would work to the outside of the guard in this situation. He should do whatever it takes to break the double-team.

- If the guard pulls, the defender should read and react quickly in that direction. He will likely lead him to the play.

- On passes he must stay in his rush lane. The rush lane is a direct line between the defender and the outside of the QB's earpiece of his helmet.

2i Technique

2i Alignment

- A player lined up in a 2i technique is lined up in an inside shade of the guard.
- The facemask of the defender is aligned with the center of the inside shoulder of the guard.
- This type of alignment is commonly found in even defenses.

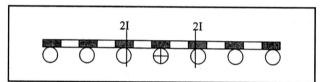

Figure 5-9

2i Assignment

- The base responsibility for a defender in a 2i technique is the A gap.
- It is imperative that he never allows the guard's head to cross his body.
- If the guard blocks down on him he should work to get himself to the other side of his head.
- The center will be the other key. If he tries to block down, the defender should work to his outside. This will likely be the playside.
- The defender should not allow himself to be double-teamed. If possible, he would work to the outside in this situation. He should do whatever it takes to break the double-team.
- If the guard pulls, he should read and react quickly in that direction. Work his way down the line of scrimmage mirroring him until he reads the play. He will likely lead him to the play.
- On passes he must stay in the rush lane. The rush lane is a direct line between the defender and the outside of the QB's earpiece of his helmet.

- If the guard releases beyond the defender for a backer, he should watch for a trap block coming from the opposite side.

2 Technique

2 Alignment

- A player lined up in a 2 technique is lined up head-up on the guard.
- This type of alignment is commonly found in even defenses.

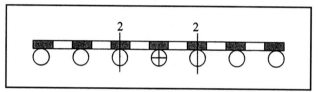

Figure 5-10

2 Assignment

- The base responsibility for this player can vary greatly. The base assignment is either the A or B gap. This will be determined by the base scheme of your defense.
- The 40 defense is an even defense that will vary the assignment according to the defensive call. The backer will always be responsible for the gap opposite the defensive lineman's responsibility.
- It is imperative that he never allows the guard's head to cross his body.
- The center and the tackle will be the other keys. If they try to block down, the defender should work to their outside. This will likely be the playside.
- The defender should not allow himself to be double-teamed. If possible, he would work to the outside in this situation. He should do whatever it takes to break the double-team.
- If the guard pulls, he should read and react quickly in that direction, working his way down the line of scrimmage mirroring him until he reads the play. He will likely lead him to the play.

- On passes he must stay in his rush lane. The rush lane is a direct line between the defender and the outside of the QB's earpiece of his helmet.
- If the guard releases beyond the defender for a backer, he should watch for a trap block coming from the opposite side.

3 Technique

3 Alignment

- A player lined up in a 3 technique is lined up in an outside shade of the guard.
- The facemask of the defender is aligned with the center of the outside shoulder of the guard.

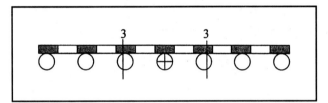

Figure 5-11

3 Assignment

- The base responsibility for a defender in a 3 technique is the B gap.
- It is imperative that he never allows the guard's head to cross his body.
- If the guard tries to reach block him, he should work to get himself to the outside.
- The tackle will be the other key. If he tries to block down, the defender should work to his outside. This will likely be the playside.
- The defender should not allow himself to be double-teamed. If possible, he would work to the outside in this situation. He should do whatever it takes to break the double-team.
- If the guard pulls, he should read and react quickly in that direction, working his way down the line of scrimmage mirroring him until he reads the play. He will likely lead him to the play.

4i Technique

4i Alignment

- A player lined up in a 4i technique is lined up in an inside shade of the tackle.
- The facemask of the defender is aligned with the center of the inside shoulder of the tackle.

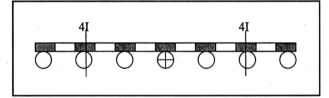

Figure 5-12

4i Assignment

- The base responsibility for a defender in a 4i technique is the B gap.
- It is imperative that he never allows the tackle's head to cross his body.
- If the tackle blocks down on him, he should work to get himself to the other side of his head.
- The guard will be the other key. If he tries to block down, the defender should work to his opposite side. This will likely be the playside.
- The defender should not allow himself to be double-teamed. If possible, he would work to the outside in this situation. He should do whatever it takes to break the double-team.
- If the guard or tackle pulls, he should read and react quickly in that direction, working his way down the line of scrimmage mirroring him until he reads the play. He will likely lead him to the play.

- On passes he must stay in his rush lane. The rush lane is a direct line between the defender and the outside of the QB's earpiece of his helmet. He should never spin to his inside unless he is blocked beyond the passer.
- If the guard releases beyond the defender for a backer, he should watch for a trap block coming from the opposite side.

4 Technique

4 Alignment

- A player lined up in a 4 technique is lined up head up on the tackle.
- This technique is commonly used in both 50 and 60 defenses.

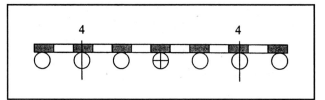

Figure 5-13

4 Assignment

- The base responsibility for this player can vary greatly. The base assignment is either the A or B gap. This will be determined by the base scheme of your defense.
- This player would have C gap responsibility in many 50 base defenses. This defense may vary the responsibility depending on alignment and assignment of the linebackers.
- It is imperative that he never allows the tackle's head to cross his body.
- The guard and the tight end will be the other keys. If they try to block down, he should work to their outside. This will likely be the playside.
- He should not allow himself to be double-teamed. If possible, he would work to the outside

in this situation. He should do whatever it takes to break the double-team.
- If the guard or tackle pulls, he should read and react quickly in that direction, working his way down the line of scrimmage mirroring him until he reads the play. He will likely lead him to the play.
- On passes he must stay in his rush lane. The rush lane is a direct line between the defender and the outside of the QB's earpiece of his helmet.
- If the guard releases beyond the defender for a backer, he should watch for a trap block coming from the opposite side.

5 Technique

5 Alignment

- A player lined up in a 5 technique is lined up in an outside shade of the tackle.
- The facemask of the defender is aligned with the center of the outside shoulder of the tackle.

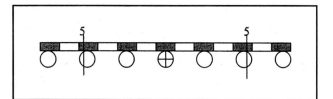

Figure 5-14

5 Assignment

- The base responsibility for a defender in a 5 technique is the C gap.
- It is imperative that he never allows the tackle's head to cross his body.
- If the tackle tries to reach block him, he should work to get himself to the outside.
- The tight end will be the other key. If he tries to block down, the defender should work to his outside. This will likely be the playside.

- He should not allow himself to be double-teamed. If possible, he would work to the outside of the down block in this situation. He should do whatever it takes to break the double-team..

- On passes he must stay in his rush lane. The rush lane is a direct line between the defender and the outside of the QB's earpiece of his helmet.

- If the tackle releases beyond the defender for a backer, he should watch for a trap block coming from the opposite side.

7 Technique

7 Alignment

- A player lined up in a 7 technique is lined up in an inside shade of the tight end or ghost tight end. Some defensive schemes may call for him to slide into a 5 technique if there is no tight end.

- The facemask of the defender is aligned with the center of the inside shoulder of the tight end or ghost area.

- He should align on the tight end up to a three-yard split from the tackle. If he is any further, consider it a ghost situation.

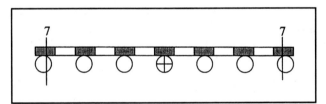

Figure 5-15

7 Assignment

- The base responsibility for a defender in a 7 technique is the C gap.

- If the tight end blocks down on him he should work to get himself to the other side of his head.

- The tackle will be the other key. If he tries to block out, the defender should work to his opposite side. This will likely be the playside.

- He should not allow himself to be double-teamed. If possible, he would work to the outside of the down block in this situation. He should do whatever it takes to break the double-team.

- On passes he must stay in his rush lane. The rush lane is a direct line between the defender and the outside of the QB's earpiece of his helmet. He should never spin to the inside unless he is blocked beyond the passer.

- If the tight end releases beyond the defender for a backer, he should watch for a trap block coming from the opposite side. This may also indicate a play-action passing situation.

6 Technique

6 Alignment

- A player lined up in a 6 technique is lined up head-up on the tight end or ghost tight end area. Some defensive schemes may call for him to slide into a 5 technique if there is no tight end.

- This technique is commonly used in even defenses.

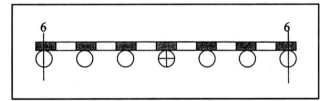

Figure 5-16

6 Assignment

- The base responsibility for this player can vary greatly. The base assignment is either the C or D gap. This will be determined by the base scheme of your defense.

- It is imperative that he never allows the tight end's head to cross his body.

- He should never allow the tight end to release from the LOS cleanly. He should jam him at the line and mirror his initial movements

- If the tight end blocks down the line, he should jam down on his outside shoulder and work down with him. He should look for a kick out block from a back or pulling lineman. If he encounters this, drive the kick blocker back into the ballcarrier that is likely following him.

- On passes he must stay in his rush lane. The rush lane is a direct line between this player and the outside of the QB's earpiece of his helmet.

- He should align on tight end up to a three-yard split from the tackle. If he is any further, consider it a ghost situation.

9 Technique

9 Alignment

- A player lined up in a 9 technique is lined up in an outside shade of the tight end. This player will likely be in a two-point stance.

- The facemask of the defender will be aligned with the outside shoulder of the tight end.

- If there is no tight end, but there is a slot back in his area, he should align himself with the slot back as he would have the tight end.

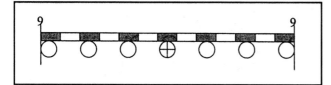

Figure 5-17

9 Assignment

- The base responsibility for a defender in a 9 technique is the D gap. This means he has outside containment responsibilities. On outside running plays, he is responsible to either turn the play inside or string it out-of-bounds.

- It is imperative that he never allows the tight end's head to cross his body. If the tackle tries to reach block him he should work to get himself to the outside.

- The near back will be the other key. If he releases toward the outside of the tight end, he will release the tight end and work to the outside shoulder of the back.

- If the tight end blocks down the line, he should jam down on his outside shoulder and work down with him. He should look for a kick out block from a back or pulling lineman. If he encounters this, drive the kick blocker back into the ballcarrier that is likely following him.

- On passes he must stay in his rush lane. The rush lane is a direct line between this player and the outside of the QB's earpiece of his helmet. He should never allow himself to get deeper than the ball.

Defensive Formations

The following section outlines some basic defensive alignments. The common way that they are described is with numbers. An example would be a '52' defense. The first number (5) represents the number of defensive linemen in the formation. The second number (2) represents number of linebackers. The rest of the players are defensive backs. Their alignment will vary greatly depending on the offensive formation and the coverage package called.

Base 52

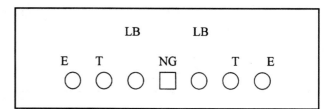

Figure 5-18

- Ends—Aligned in a 9 technique.

- Tackles—Aligned in a 5 technique.

- Noseguard—Aligned in a 0 technique.

- LB—Aligned in a 2 technique three to four yards off the LOS.

Base 53

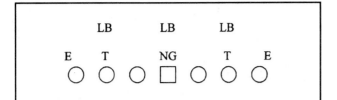

Figure 5-19

- Ends–Aligned in a 9 technique.
- Tackles–Aligned in a 4 technique.
- Noseguard–Aligned in a 0 technique.
- LB–Aligned in a 2 or 4 technique three to four yards off the LOS, stacked behind lineman.

Base 44

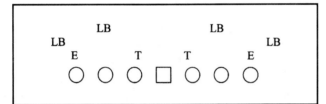

Figure 5-20

- Ends–Aligned in a 6 technique.
- Tackles–Aligned in a 2i technique.
- Outside linebackers–Aligned in a 9 technique with a 2 x 2 yard relationship with the tight end.
- Inside linebackers–Aligned in a 4 technique approximately four yards off the ball.

Base 44 Stack

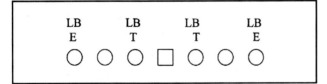

Figure 5-21

- Ends–Aligned in a 6 technique.
- Tackles–Aligned in a 2 technique.

- Outside linebackers–Aligned in a 6 technique stacked approximately two yards behind the end.
- Inside linebackers–Aligned in a 4 technique approximately four yards behind tackles.

Base 43

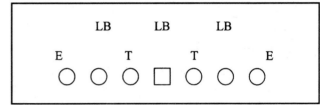

Figure 5-22

- Ends–Aligned in a 9 technique.
- Tackles–Aligned in a 2 technique.
- Linebackers–Aligned in 0 and 2 techniques approximately four yards off the ball.

Base 34

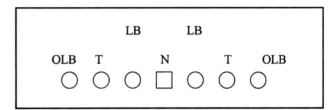

Figure 5-23

- Noseguard–Aligned in a 0 technique.
- Tackles–Aligned in a 4 technique.
- Inside linebacker–Aligned in a 2 technique four yards off the ball.
- Outside linebacker–Aligned in a 9 technique.

Base 62

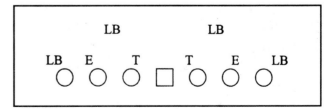

Figure 5-24

- Ends–Aligned in a 5 technique.
- Tackles–Aligned in a 2i technique.
- Outside linebackers–Aligned in a 9 technique.
- Inside linebackers–Aligned in a 4i technique four yards off the LOS.

Base 61

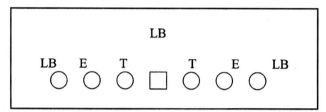

Figure 5-25

- Ends–Aligned in a 5 technique.
- Tackles–Aligned in a 2 technique.
- Outside linebackers–Aligned in a 9 technique.
- Inside linebacker–Aligned in a 0 technique four yards off the LOS.

Base Coverage Packages

This section diagrams the basic coverage packages found in most defenses. They will only be shown from one defensive formation. The same coverage concepts can be adapted to most defensive alignments. The defensive keys and techniques involved in these coverage packages will be detailed in Chapter 7.

Cover 2

The cover 2 is a two-deep zone defense. This simply means that there are two defenders responsible for the deepest zone. They each are responsible for half of the field in that zone. Figure 5-26 is an example of a cover 2 zone defense.

- In this alignment there are two safeties; they are responsible for the deep zone.
- The linebackers are responsible for the middle intermediate and short zones.

- The cornerbacks are responsible for the outside intermediate zone.
- The defensive ends will pick up the flat in the backfield.

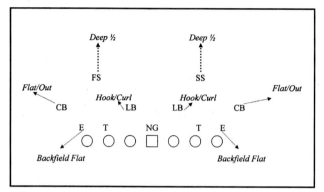

Figure 5-26

Cover 3

The cover 3 is a three-deep zone defense. This simply means that there are three defenders responsible for the deepest zone. They each are responsible for one-third of the field in that zone. Figure 5-27 is an example of a cover3 zone defense.

- In this alignment there is one safety and two cornerbacks; they are responsible for the deep zone.
- The linebackers are responsible for the middle, intermediate, and short zones.
- The outside linebackers are responsible for the out and flat zones.

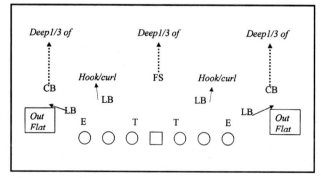

Figure 5-27

Cover 1

A cover 1 defense is also called man defense. This means that every potential receiver will have a defender that will cover him man-to-man. In this situation, all defensive linemen are using a pass rush mentality. The linebackers and the defensive backs are responsible for coverage. There will always be one or two cover guys (linebackers or defensive backs) that may not have a cover responsibility. In these cases, they will either rush the passer, cover a hot zone, or double cover a chosen receiver.

To determine which man the defender will cover, they must communicate. The best way to do this is to label every potential receiver. A very common way to do this would be to number the eligible receivers as shown in Figure 5-28. First you must split the offense in half by using the midline as the dividing point. Then, you will number every eligible receiver starting from each sideline and ending at the midline.

Most defenders will know which receiver they are responsible for when their coverage package is called in the huddle. If there is any confusion, they can communicate with each other by pointing and by calling out a receiver's number.

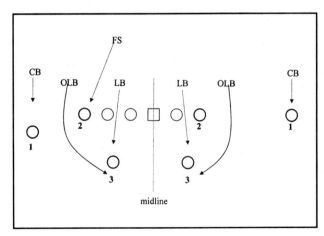

Figure 5-28

Tackling

Tackling is the most important skill for every defensive player. You should designate a large portion of time at every practice to work on tackling technique. Every player should get as many tackling repetitions as possible at every practice. In every other sport, the best players get a significant number of repetitions in order to master the skills needed for their sport. Baseball players will take hundreds of swings a day in batting practice. A golf player will spend a lot of time on the driving range. Basketball players take hundreds of shots at the net at every practice. Why wouldn't a defensive football player get all the possible tackling repetitions possible at every practice?

The first thing you need to do is teach the proper tackling technique. You can make your players do all the repetitions you want, but if they don't do them properly, they won't make any progress. Following are 10 important aspects of tackling that your players should learn. If they can become proficient with these 10 aspects of tackling, your defense will be incredible no matter what scheme you employ.

• Be aggressive.

This may be the most important aspect, even though it is the most abstract. Tackling can be considered 20% technique and 80% attitude and desire. Anyone can learn the proper mechanics of tackling. Truly great tacklers are the ones that are so focused on making the tackle that the see nothing else on the field. Everything else that happens during their pursuit of the ballcarrier is just another obstacle to overcome to meet the ultimate goal. A fire burns inside of them; they are relentless. When that moment of impact comes, they are not going to tackle that man—they are going to destroy him. They explode through the ballcarrier not into him. Then they get up and get themselves ready to destroy the ballcarrier on the next play.

You can help develop this attitude among your players. When you are running drills, keep the tempo up; make it a competition. When someone makes that explosive tackle you're looking for, recognize it in a big way. Get in his face and get excited, letting him know that was exactly what you were looking for. Not only will this fire that player up, everyone in the drill should now feel the excitement involved in an explosive tackle. They want to get that same type of recognition. I truly believe that when a player feels the adrenaline rush involved in a situation like this, they will never forget it. They will hunger for the next time they have an opportunity to make a tackle.

Whenever you talk about tackling to your players, use the words explode and destroy. Develop a mentality to go along with tackling. Reward the big tackles. After every game you should reward the crushing tackles as if they were the biggest moments in the game. If you're watching films with the team and you review a big tackle, pause the tape and make a big deal over it. This type of mentality will take you a long way.

• Keep your eyes on the jersey number of the ballcarrier.

As the tackler approaches the ballcarrier, he should focus on his jersey numbers since this is where he should make impact with him. Some players watch for a player's head, which can deceive him and also cause him to hit the man too high. His chest is the point of impact so the tackler needs to know exactly where it will be when he explodes into it. Be wary about telling players to watch the hips of the ballcarrier. Many believe that the body must go in the direction the hips are going. However, this can create a fundamental problem. Players that focus on their opponent's hips tend to put their own heads down. You definitely want the tackler's head up at the point of impact.

• Break down under control with short choppy steps; your back should be at a 45-degree angle before contact.

The tackler should approach the ballcarrier balanced and under control. Do not interpret this to mean slowing down. In fact, it will be just the opposite: he will always accelerate through a tackle. This simple means that his base will widen slightly and steps will shorten up. If his base is too close together upon impact, there is a good chance the runner will win the battle and knock him back. If his steps are too elongated, he will also compromise his balance, which could give the advantage to the runner.

The other part of this aspect is the positioning of his back. It should be close to a 45-degree angle because this is the proper hitting position in football. If he creates the right power angle upon impact, his back position will direct the force of the impact in the proper direction—up and through the ballcarrier. Too many tacklers think that all they need to do is run through the ballcarrier. They must be taught to drive up and through him. The ultimate tackle will have the ballcarrier's feet coming off the ground upon impact and before the tackler plants him on his back.

• Get as close to him as possible before beginning the tackle–("Step on his toes").

Tackles should never be attempted too soon. The best tackles are made with the tackler's legs driving through the tackle as it is being made. He should never leave his feet to make a tackle unless it is his last resort. This is one of the biggest reasons for missed tackles. "Step on his toes" simply means that they should get as close to the runner as possible before exploding up and through him.

• Explode into the runner by accelerating your footwork as you drive up and through him.

Whenever you teach tackling, use the word explode when you talk about the initial contact of the tackle. You need to emphasize the fact that they should explode up and through the runner and not just through him. The way that they will create this explosion is to accelerate at the point of impact. Most young tacklers have a tendency to slow down or stop just before impact with the runner.

Using tackling dummies in practice is an excellent way to get in tackling repetitions without the wear and tear of live tackling. It is also a less intimidating way to teach the explosiveness that we are looking for in our tackles. Several tackling dummy drills are outlined later in this section.

• Your facemask should drive right through the football.

At the point of impact with the ballcarrier, the tackler's facemask should slide across the body and into the football. This takes into consideration that the runner is carrying the ball in his outside arm. As the facemask is making contact with the ball, the tackler's chest plate will be making contact just under the chest plate of the runner. Not only is this a fundamentally sound way to make a tackle, but it could also cause a fumble by impacting the ball with the facemask. This does not mean that the tackler should use the facemask as a battering ram. The tackler's impact is with his shoulder and chest. He should never make initial contact with his facemask on the runner's body.

• Recoil—Your hips should drive forward as your back is straightening, and you come up and through the ballcarrier.

At the point of impact with the runner, the tackler's back is at a 45-degree angle. His hips are driving forward as his back is straightening and he is accelerating through the runner. This is the action that will cause the tackler to come up and through the ballcarrier to make the tackle.

• Wrap him up by shooting your arms around him and try to clasp them.

When making a tackle, the defender should never wind up with his arms. His elbows should always remain in front of his body. He will shoot his arms around the ballcarrier. He should wrap the ballcarrier as tightly as possible. He should try to clasp his hands or arm if possible.

• Never stop chopping your feet and driving until he is on his back.

As we have already pointed out, the tackler must accelerate at the point of contact. This acceleration should continue until the tackle is complete. In fact, the ultimate tackle would have the defender's feet still touching the ground as the ballcarrier's back is hitting the ground. If he can accomplish this, then he was truly driving his feet through the tackle until it was complete. These are the types of tackles that highlight films are made of.

• If you are not in the proper tackling position upon contact, do whatever it takes to bring him down (except pulling him down by his facemask).

At times, the perfect tackle is just not possibleand a defender will count on shear will and determination to get the job done. He must grab onto anything he can (other than the facemask). He could pull him down, slow him up or cause him to stumble. He should be relentless and do whatever it takes.

Tackling Drills

Tackling Progression Drill

Objective: To teach the proper mechanics of tackling.

Description:

- Line up as many players as you like in pairs, facing each other, two yards apart.
- One line is designated the tacklers and the other line will stand there and allow the tackler to execute each move on him.
- The coach will call out a number that will correlate to a step involved in the tackle and the tackler will execute that step. The four steps are outlined in Figure 5-29.
- The coaches will inspect each step for proper form before calling out the next step.
- Repeat drill with partners switching rolls.

Step 1—Fit up. The tackler will set up in front of the other man in pre-tackle form and freeze in that position.

- □ His facemask should be inches away from man's jersey numbers.
- □ His back should be at a 45-degree angle.
- □ His arms should be bent and in front of his body.

Figure 5-29

Step 2—Engage man in tackling form.

- □ His arms should shoot around the man and clasp other wrist just beyond his buttocks.
- □ His facemask will slide to one side of the man.
- □ The top of the tackler's chest plate will be in contact with the bottom of the other man's chest plate.
- □ His back is still at a 45-degree angle.
- □ His feet are under his shoulders with a base slightly wider than shoulders.

Step 3—Lift the man in the air. The tackler should be using his legs to lift the man not his back. This will happen naturally if he is the correct body position. They must also remain chest to chest.

Step 4—Carry the man. He should carry the man for three to five yards. They must remain chest to chest throughout the carry.

Variation: You could add a fifth step by having them bring the man to the ground after three yards of carrying. When they do this, they must remain chest to chest and the tackler's feet should remain on the ground until the other mans' back is hitting the ground. You may want to use some sort of pad for landing.

Lift Drill

Objective: To teach the proper fundamental techniques of tackling, with an emphasis on the wrap and lift part of the tackle.

Description:

- Line up two players seven yards apart; one man is designated the tackler.
- The tackler will begin in a linebacker-like stance.
- On the coach's whistle they will jog toward each other.
- Just before impact, the other player will jump slightly in the air and the tackler will execute basic tackling fundamentals.
- They must time this so that the initial contact of the tackle occurs while the others players' feet are coming off the ground.
- The tackler will carry the other player for 2 yards.
- Players should switch lines after each repetition.

Coaching Points: This drill should be performed at a rapid pace. You must watch all of the tackling fundamentals. Check the following things:

- Upon impact the tackler's facemask should be on the other man's side, where the football would be carried by a ballcarrier.
- Upon impact the tackler's base should be slightly widened with his steps shortening.
- Upon impact the tackler's back is at a 45-degree angle that straightens as his hips drive forward in the lift portion.
- Upon impact the tackler should be high chest to lower chest with the man.
- Tackler's arms will shoot around the other man's body and wrap, never winding up.

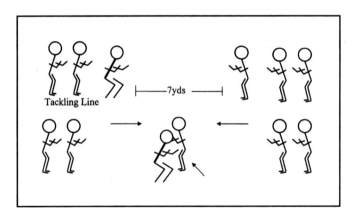

Figure 5-30

Tackling Triangle

Objective: To teach the fundamentals of tackling on an angle.

Description:

- Set up three cones in an equilateral triangle with all cones 10 yards apart.

- Set up a tackling line in the center of two cones.

- Set up a ball carrying line behind the cone that is across from the tackling line.

- On the coach's whistle the ballcarrier will run directly at one of the other cones. When he is contacted by the tackler, he will slow up and give a little ground to the tackler. He must carry the ball in his outside arm.

- The tackler will execute proper tackling techniques approximately two yards in front of the cone the ballcarrier is heading to. He will drive the ballcarrier back for three yards and release him. He does not take him to the ground.

- Players will switch lines between every repetition.

Coaching Points: This drill is run at full speed by both players; the ballcarrier will slow down only after impact from the tackler. Make sure the tackler employs all of the proper tackling fundamentals. Stress the importance of the tackler getting his head in front of the runner. His head should slide across the ballcarrier's chest, still using the football as an aiming point. This drill is run at full speed, although the tackler will not complete the tackle. He will not take the ball carrier to the ground.

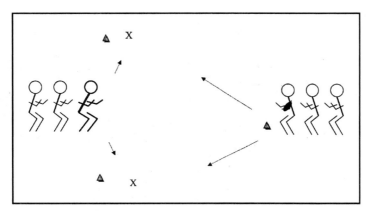

Figure 5-31

Bag Tackling Drills

This section includes a series of drills designed to teach the fundamentals of tackling. They are designed to give your player tackling repetitions without the constant pounding of an actual tackle. This will allow you to do more repetitions in a shorter period of time.

The keys to these drills are tempo and intensity. There should be near rapid-fire repetitions performed at the highest intensity levels. Make the players grunt and groan upon impact with the bag. Make it a competition. See who can perform the drill with the most intensity. Have any player who is not performing the drill 'hooting and hollering' while he is waiting his turn. The coaches should be at a peak intensity level during these drills and encouraging the players to not only show intensity, but also to execute the drills with the proper fundamentals.

Description:

- These are team-tackling drills.
- Set up four to five tackling bags approximately five yards apart on any yard line.
- Try to use heavy bags that are appropriate for the level you are coaching. If you do not have heavy bags, any bag will do.
- Form a line five yards in front of each bag.
- Players should be in a three-point stance or a linebacker stance in the ready position.
- The bags can be held by coaches or the last player to tackle the bag.
- The bags must be retuned to the original yard line quickly between reps.

Coaching Point:

- Feel free to improvise these drills and add your own twists. Keep them moving and keep them fun.

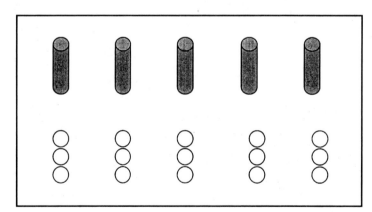

Figure 5-32

Bag Lift Drill

Objective: To teach the tackler the proper fundamentals of the impact and lift portion of a tackle in a low-impact environment.

Description:

- Set up four to five tackling bags approximately five yards apart on any yard line.
- Form a line five yards in front of each bag.
- Players should be in a three-point stance or a linebacker stance in the ready position.
- The bags can be held by coaches or the last player to tackle the bag.
- On the coach's whistle the tackler will aggressively attack the bag and simulate an explosive tackle without bringing the bag to the ground.
- The tackler explodes up and through the bag causing it to come off the ground as it is driven back.
- The tackler's head should slide to the right side of the bag. After sufficient reps, switch the drill so they are sliding their head to the left of the bag.
- He will carry the bag approximately three yards and return it to its original spot.

Variation: You can add a coach with an arm shield to 'chuck' the tackler during his pursuit of the bag.

Coaching Points: Make sure the tackler gets the bag up off the ground upon impact. The emphasis should be on the proper body mechanics of tackling.

- Upon impact the back should be at a 45-degree angle and will straighten out as the hips come under the shoulders.
- The base will be slightly wider than shoulder width just before impact and footwork will accelerate upon impact.
- His chest must maintain contact with the bag throughout the drill.
- His feet should remain on the ground through the completion of drill.
- His hands and arms will shoot around bags and clasp; he should never wind up with his arms.

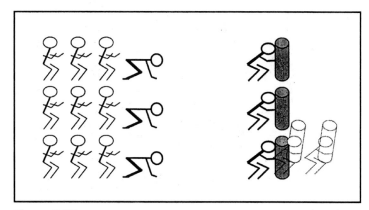

Figure 5-33

Bag Tackle Drill (Forward)

Objective: To teach the tackler proper fundamentals of a tackle in a low-impact environment.

Description:

- Set up four to five tackling bags approximately five yards apart on any yard line.
- Form a line five yards in front of each bag.
- Players should be in a three-point stance or a linebacker stance in the ready position.
- The bags can be held by coaches or the last player to tackle the bag.
- On the coach's whistle the tackler will aggressively attack the bag and simulate an explosive tackle.
- The tackler explodes up and through the bag causing it to come off the ground as it is driven back and to the ground.
- The tackler's head should slide to the right side of the bag. After sufficient reps, switch the drill so they are sliding their head to the left of the bag.
- After completing the tackle he will return the bag to its original spot.

Variation: You can add a coach with an arm shield to 'chuck' the tackler during his pursuit of the bag.

Coaching Points: Make sure the tackler gets the bag up off the ground upon impact and his feet should remain on the ground as he is planting the bag on the ground. The emphasis should be on the proper body mechanics of tackling.

- Upon impact the back should be at a 45-degree angle and will straighten out as the hips come under the shoulders.
- The base will be slightly wider than shoulder width just before impact and footwork will accelerate upon impact.
- His chest must maintain contact with the bag throughout the drill.
- His feet should remain on the ground through the completion of drill.
- His hands and arms will shoot around bags and clasp; he should never wind up with his arms.

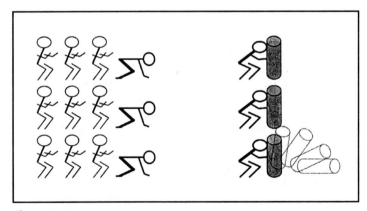

Figure 5-34

Roll and Tackle Bag Drill

Objective: To teach the tackler to recover quickly if knocked down and still make the tackle.

Description:

- Set up four to five tackling bags approximately five yards apart on any yard line.

- Form a line five yards in front of each bag.

- Players should be in a three-point stance or a linebacker stance in the ready position.

- The bags can be held by coaches or the last player to tackle the bag.

- On the coach's whistle the tackler will execute a forward roll in route to the bag and get up as quickly as possible to tackle the bag.

- The tackler explodes up and through the bag causing it to come off the ground as it is driven back and to the ground.

- The tackler's head should slide to the right side of the bag. After sufficient reps, switch the drill so they are sliding their head to the left of the bag.

- After completing the tackle he will return the bag to its original spot.

Variation: You can add a coach with an arm shield to 'chuck' the tackler during his pursuit of the bag.

Coaching Points: Teach the player to tuck his chin against his chest just before he begins his roll. The emphasis should be on the proper body mechanics during the tackling portion of this drill.

- Upon impact the back should be at a 45-degree angle and will straighten out as the hips come under the shoulders.

- The base will be slightly wider than shoulder width just before impact and footwork will accelerate upon impact.

- His chest must maintain contact with the bag throughout the drill.

- His feet should remain on the ground through the completion of drill.

- His hands and arms will shoot around bags and clasp; he should never wind up with his arms.

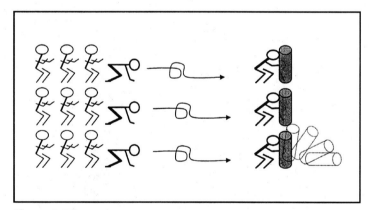

Figure 5-35

Bag Tackle Drill (With Blocker)

Objective: To teach the tackler how to release off a block and make a tackle.

Description:

- Set up four to five tackling bags approximately five yards apart on any yard line.
- Form a line five yards in front of each bag.
- Players should be in a three-point stance or a linebacker stance in the ready position.
- The bags can be held by coaches or the last player to tackle the bag.
- On the coach's whistle the tackler will shed the blocker and then aggressively attack the bag and simulate an explosive tackle.
- The tackler explodes up and through the bag causing it to come off the ground as it is driven back and to the ground.
- Tacklers should release to the right side of the blocker. After sufficient reps they should be instructed to release to the left of the blocker.
- Blocker will hold the block for two to three seconds then release the man.
- After completing the tackle he will return the bag to its original spot.

Variation: You can have the tackler use a specific release technique in order to shed the blocker before pursuing the ball.

Coaching Points: The emphasis should be getting off the block as quickly as possible. They should take a direct route to the bag after release.

- Upon impact the back should be at a 45-degree angle and will straighten out as the hips come under the shoulders.
- The base will be slightly wider than shoulder width just before impact and footwork will accelerate upon impact.
- His chest must maintain contact with the bag throughout the drill.
- His feet should remain on the ground through the completion of drill.
- His hands and arms will shoot around bags and clasp; he should never wind up with his arms.

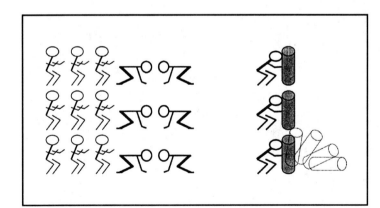

Figure 5-36

Hurdle and Tackle Drill

Objective: To teach the tackler how to set up quickly in order to make a tackle.

Description:

- Set up four to five tackling bags approximately five yards apart on any yard line.

- Form a line five yards in front of each bag.

- Players should be in a three-point stance or a linebacker stance in the ready position.

- The bags can be held by coaches or the last player to tackle the bag.

- A player will set up in a six-point stance between the tackler and the bag.

- On the coach's whistle the tackler will hurdle over the man who is in a six-point stance, get

  himself under control, and then properly tackle the bag.

- The last player to hold the bag will set up in a six-point stance between bags.

- The tackler explodes up and through the bag causing it to come off the ground as it is driven back and to the ground.

- The tackler's head should slide to the right side of the bag. After sufficient reps, switch the drill so they are sliding their head to the left of the bag.

- After completing the tackle he will return the bag to its original spot.

Variation: You can use a dummy to hurdle over instead of a player.

Coaching Points: Make sure the tackler gets himself set up in the proper body positioning prior to tackling the bag. The emphasis should be on the proper body mechanics of tackling when he tackles the bag.

- Upon impact the back should be at a 45-degree angle and will straighten out as the hips come under the shoulders.

- The base will be slightly wider than shoulder width just before impact and footwork will accelerate upon impact.

- His chest must maintain contact with the bag throughout the drill.

- His feet should remain on the ground through the completion of drill.

- His hands and arms will shoot around bags and clasp; he should never wind up with his arms.

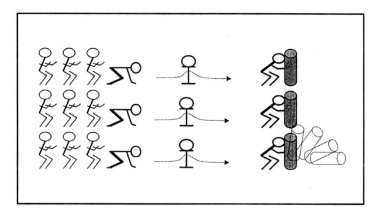

Figure 5-37

Angle Tackle Drill

Objective: To teach the tackler proper fundamentals of a tackle in a low-impact environment.

Description:

- Set up four to five tackling bags approximately five yards apart on any yard line.
- Form a line five yards back from and five yards to the left of the bag they will tackle.
- Players should be in a three-point stance or a linebacker stance in the ready position.
- The bags can be held by coaches or the last player to tackle the bag.
- On the coach's whistle the tackler will tackle the bag offset to his left.
- The tackler will employ proper tackling fundamentals.
- The tackler's head should slide across the front of the bag upon impact.
- After completing the tackle he will return the bag to its original spot.
- Repeat the drill with the bags offset to the players right side.

Variations:

- You can add a coach with an arm shield to 'chuck' the tackler during his pursuit of the bag.
- You can add a forward roll before the tackle.

Coaching Points: Make sure the tackler goes across the front of the bag before the shoulder and chest make impact. The emphasis should be on the proper body mechanics of tackling during the tackling portion.

- Upon impact the back should be at a 45-degree angle and will straighten out as the hips come under the shoulders.
- The base will be slightly wider than shoulder width just before impact and footwork will accelerate upon impact.
- His chest must maintain contact with the bag throughout the drill.
- His feet should remain on the ground through the completion of drill.
- His hands and arms will shoot around bags and clasp; he should never wind up with his arms.

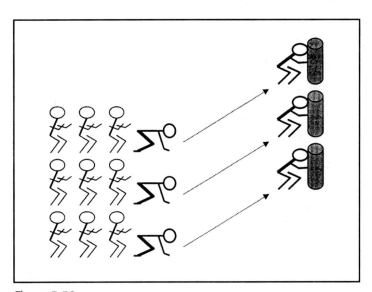

Figure 5-38

Popsicle Drills

This section outlines tackling drills that are performed on a one-man sled, also known as a popsicle. A popsicle is an excellent tool for teaching tackling and for low-impact tackling repetitions. I highly recommend the use of these sleds. If you plan on getting one, make sure it is the appropriate size and weight for your age level.

Pop and Lift Drill

Objective: To teach the tackler the proper fundamentals used during the initial impact of a tackle with an emphasis on driving up and through the ballcarrier.

Description:

- Set up a line of tacklers five yards in front of the popsicles.
- The first player in line will be in a two- or three-point stance.
- On the coach's whistle the player will explode up and through the popsicle forcing it to rise up onto the back portion of the sled rails.
- He will release the sled after one second.
- His head should slide to the right of the sled upon impact.
- Repeat the drill with the head sliding to the left of the sled.

Coaching Points: Make sure that the initial impact of the sled is low and the player drives up and through the sled. This will cause the sled to come off the ground and be driven backwards at the same time. The proper fundamentals of tackling should be employed on every repetition.

- Upon impact the back should be at a 45-degree angle and will straighten out as the hips come under the shoulders.
- The base will be slightly wider than shoulder width just before impact and footwork will accelerate upon impact.
- His chest must maintain contact with the bag throughout the drill.
- His feet should remain on the ground through the completion of drill.
- His hands and arms will shoot around bags and clasp; he should never wind up with his arms.

Figure 5-39

Drive Tackling Drill

Objective: To teach the tackler to keep his feet driving and accelerating through a tackle.

Description:

• Set up a line of tacklers five yards in front of the popsicles.

• The first player in line will be in a two- or three-point stance.

• On the coach's whistle the player will explode up and through the popsicle forcing it to rise up onto the back portion of the sled rails.

• He will then drive the sled back five yards.

• His head should slide to the right of the sled upon impact.

• Repeat the drill with the head sliding to the left of the sled.

Coaching Points: Emphasize the fact that the tackler must accelerate his footwork while driving the sled back. Make sure that the initial impact of the sled is low and the player drives up and through the sled. This will cause the sled to come off the ground and be driven backwards at the same time. The proper fundamentals of tackling should be employed on every repetition.

• Upon impact the back should be at a 45-degree angle and will straighten out as the hips come under the shoulders.

• The base will be slightly wider than shoulder width just before impact and footwork will accelerate upon impact.

• His chest must maintain contact with the bag throughout the drill.

• Feet should remain on the ground through the completion of drill.

• His hands and arms will shoot around bags and clasp; he should never wind up with his arms.

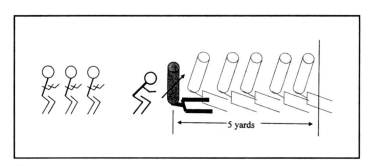

Figure 5-40

Drive and Finish Drill

Objective: To teach the tackler to keep his feet driving and accelerating through a tackle and getting the leverage to finish the tackle.

Description:

- Set up a line of tacklers five yards in front of the popsicles.
- The first player in line will be in a two- or three-point stance.
- On the coach's whistle the player will explode up and through the popsicle forcing it to rise up onto the back portion of the sled rails.
- His head should slide to the right of the sled upon impact.
- He will then drive the sled back five yards.
- He will then drive the sled to the ground; it should land on its left side.
- Repeat the drill with the head sliding to the left of the sled; the sled will then go down on its right side.

Coaching Points: Emphasize the fact that the tackler must drive the sled down to the opposite side of his head. His feet should remain on the ground until the sled has been completely turned on its side. The proper fundamentals of tackling should be employed on every repetition.

- Upon impact the back should be at a 45-degree angle and will straighten out as the hips come under the shoulders.
- The base will be slightly wider than shoulder width just before impact and footwork will accelerate upon impact.
- His chest must maintain contact with the bag throughout the drill.
- His feet should remain on the ground through the completion of drill.
- His hands and arms will shoot around bags and clasp; he should never wind up with his arms.

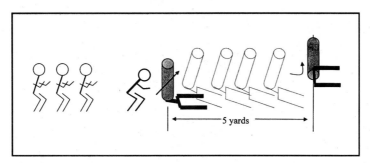

Figure 5-41

Head-to-Head Drill

Objective: To teach tackling and to get live tackling repetitions in a controlled area.

Description:

- Use collapsible cones or any markers to create two parallel boundaries two yards apart and five yards long.
- Form two lines at either end of the boundaries: a tackler line and a ballcarrier line.
- The first player in each line will lie in the center of the boundaries head-to-head on their backs. Their heads should be about one yard apart.
- On the coach's whistle they will both get to their feet as quickly as possible.
- The ballcarrier will try to score by getting past the tackler.
- The tackler will execute proper tackling fundamentals in his attempt to stop the ballcarrier from scoring.
- The participants will switch lines after completing their repetition.

Coaching Points: This drill should be performed at a rapid pace. You must watch all of the tackling fundamentals. Check the following things:

- Upon impact the tackler's facemask should slide to the football.
- Upon impact the tackler's base should be slightly widened with his steps shortening yet accelerating through the runner.
- Upon impact the tackler's back is at a 45-degree angle that straightens as his hips drive forward in the lift potion.
- Upon impact the tackler should be high chest to lower chest with the man.
- The tackler's arms will shoot around the other man's body and wrap; he should never be winding up.

Figure 5-42

Team Gauntlet Drill

Objective: To practice tackling repetitions in a high-intensity environment.

Description:

- Set up 12 collapsible cones or pinnies as markers five yards apart, three wide and four deep. This will set up two alleyways for you to run this drill.
- Set up a tackler between every set of cones except the first.
- Set up a line of ballcarriers in front of both alleyways.
- The ballcarrier will run on an angle to one of the first series' of markers.
- The first tackler will make a tackle before the runner gets to the first cone.
- The runner will get up from the ground and run on an angle to the next marker where he will be met by the next tackler, and so on.

- After the runner has carried the ball through the end of the gauntlet, he will take the place of the last tackler who will move up one spot in the tackling line. The first man in the tackling line will go to the end of the ballcarrier's line.
- If the tackler does not bring down the ballcarrier immediately after impact, he will release him and allow him to continue through the gauntlet.

Coaching Points: Make sure that every tackle in this drill is executed properly. The ballcarrier should try to break every tackle by bucking up and through each tackler. Make a competition out of the drill. Keep it up-tempo with a lot of intensity. You can make the drill longer by adding more markers

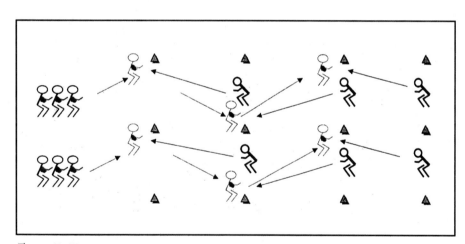

Figure 5-43

Team Circle Drill

Objective: To work on angle pursuit tackling at a high intensity level.

Description:

- Line up the entire team in a circle.
- The coach will call out the name of a ballcarrier.
- The ballcarrier will run clockwise around the inside of the circle.
- The coach will then call out the name of a tackler.
- When the runner passes the tackler, he will cross the circle at the proper angle and make the tackle.
- If the tackle is not fundamentally sound, the coach will instruct the runner to start running again. The tackler will take the angle again and make a proper tackle.
- The tackler will become the ballcarrier after he completes the tackle the correct way.
- The coach will call out another name for the tackler and the drill will continue until everyone has had at least one repetition as a tackler.

Coaching Points: Do not allow the tackler's repetition to end until he has executed all of the proper tackling techniques. The biggest emphasis should be on getting the tackler across the front of the runner's body to make the tackle.

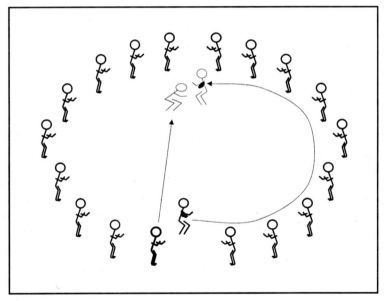

Figure 5-44

CHAPTER 6

Player Fundamentals—Defense

Defensive Line

This is a position with variable alignments that depend on the fronts and stunts of a particular defense. However, at some levels of football it may be the least coached position. Do you have a defensive line coach? How much time do you set aside for a defensive line station? Most defensive coaches tell their defensive players the alignment at the time they put the defense in as a team. You need to develop the fundamental skills of the position.

"Get in the backfield and make something happen." Although it sounds great, it is one of the biggest mistakes young coaches make. They tell their interior defensive lineman to "do whatever it takes, just get into the backfield." If you take this approach, against weak teams you will look like a defensive genius. Even against quality teams you will have a couple of big plays in the backfield. However, more often than not, this mentality in big games will burn you. By doing this, players abandon their run lanes to take the easy way into the backfield, setting up big holes for the offense, essentially taking them out of the play.

Even if you stunt your linemen a lot, they need to take a disciplined route. You have to teach gap assignments. Someone has to be responsible for every gap. Refer to the gaps and technique chart shown in Figure 3-87 in Chapter 3. If your defensive tackle lines up in a 2 technique and shoots the B gap, then there better be a linebacker who is responsible for the near A gap. Every gap needs to be accounted for on every play.

This brings up another problem. When you stunt a lineman, he must stay in the stunt lane. Young linemen will loop wider than desired because it is the easy way in. Teach them the technique and the quickness to stunt a gap and control that gap at the same time.

Personnel

Before choosing your defensive linemen, you must first have a defensive scheme and philosophy. This will help you determine the type of player you would prefer at each position. For instance, if you run a gap control 50 defense, the noseguard and tackles will likely be strong run stoppers. These players will be called on to control the line of scrimmage. They must be strong enough to handle staying with and shedding blockers at the appropriate times. Many teams rely on their linebackers to make the tackles. The interior linemen are used to clog up holes and tie up the blockers. The linebackers are responsible to read the play and make the tackles.

Figure 6-1 is an example of a 50 defense that is pursuing a basic power running play. The interior lineman in this situation had to control his gap responsibility by jamming the blocker in that gap. As he reads the flow of the play, he will work off his blocks and work his way down the line of scrimmage to the play. The linebackers are reading and reacting to the flow of the play. For defenses that frequently run this type of scheme, the big strong interior linemen are best suited for this system.

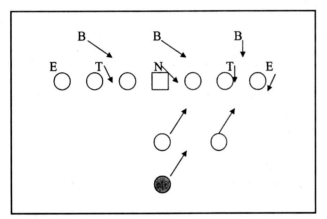

Figure 6-1

The ends are the other defensive linemen that are used in the defense shown in Figure 6-1. These players have D gap responsibility. They will be aligned in a two-point stance. This player must be quick and agile, as well as strong. This could be considered a hybrid position. This player is 25% lineman and 75% linebacker.

Defensive ends that have D gap responsibility are required to cover a lot of ground. They are also given an enormous amount of responsibility. The first thing this player must do is control the tight end. He will have to take him on without allowing himself to be flanked. If other players pursue his flank, he will have to release the blocker and take on the new threat to the outside, always working to contain the run.

Figure 6-2 is an example of containment. The end must always keep his outside shoulder free in order to release the blocker and continue to contain the outside.

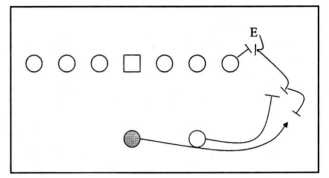

Figure 6-2

Figure 6-3 is an example of a gap control 40 defense. The tackles in this alignment have A gap responsibility. Again, these players will be the strong lumbering type of player. They will mainly be called upon to clog up the interior of the line. They are also very vulnerable to double-team blocks. Many traps, counters and straight ahead power plays will double-team the defender that is closest to the point of attack on the line of scrimmage.

The defensive ends have C gap responsibility in most base 40 defenses. The defensive ends in the 50 defense were described as a lineman/linebacker hybrid. The ends in the 40 defense should also possess some linebacker like skills. The defensive end in the base 40 defense has to be at least 75% lineman and about 25% linebacker.

The defensive ends will also have a lot of responsibility. Their core assignment will be to

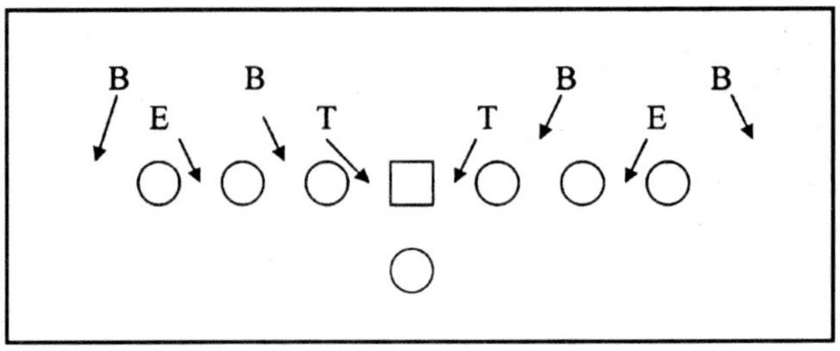

Figure 6-3

control the C gaps, which is where the offenses off-tackle plays will go. Most running teams run off-tackle more than anywhere else. These types of plays are often preceded with a lead blocker. The defensive end must try to make the play at the line of scrimmage. It is preferable that he not let the play bounce outside him.

At times he will be called upon to control the D gap. Stunt calls will force him to switch responsibility with the outside linebacker on his side. And there will also be many situations where there is no tight end aligned on his side of the line of scrimmage. Although he would still have C gap responsibility, this gap will constitute the outside on his side of the line of scrimmage. In those situations he needs to make sure that he is never hook blocked by anyone on the line of scrimmage. As he is pursuing the play, he should not allow anyone to flank him on the outside.

Finally, he will be the primary pass rusher in passing situations. He will be responsible to not only diligently rush the quarterback, but he must also contain him if he tries to escape the pocket. You can see how he must still be a versatile player.

Stance and Starts

Down lineman will be in a quality three- or four-point stance with their weight on the balls of their feet. Their free arm needs to be poised to deliver a quick blow. Starts are similar to offensive starts. The player should know which direction he is going first and he should lead off with that foot in the proper direction.

How many times have you heard a coach tell a defensive lineman to "watch the ball" being snapped so he doesn't go offside? If the defensive end is in a three-point stance, lined up in a 6 technique and he is watching the ball being snapped, he has definitely given the advantage to the man assigned to block him. The blocker knows the snap count. Therefore, the defensive lineman's head should not be turned away from his assignment at the beginning of the play. He will always have a key offensive lineman to watch in every play.

The DL should be focused on the OL's hand and his head. When the offensive lineman picks up his hand, the DL should be exploding into his target that he is already looking at. If he waits for the first move, he will never be offside. If the noseguard is lined up over the ball, he should definitely be watching the ball. If he is not, he should be watching the keys. Keep in mind that his peripheral vision will allow him to see at least one other blocker and potentially two.

The blocker's head is another key place to watch as soon as he starts. His head will oftentimes go to the side that the ball is going. This is especially true with teams that use shoulder-blocking techniques. It is the nature of a shoulder block to get the head to the ballcarrier side of the man you are blocking. If his head is going to a distinct side, the player should work to get positioning on the blocker to control that side. He should not allow a blocker to get his head across his body. It will take many practice repetitions to become proficient at working off the blocker.

Alignment and Assignment

Some defenses will require the linemen to have a two-gap responsibility if they are lined up head up on a man. In many defensive schemes they will be responsible for only one gap. This doesn't mean they can't shutdown the other gap, it simply tells them what their first read is. Make sure every player knows the techniques and gaps. Refer to the gaps and techniques chart shown in Figure 3-87 in Chapter 3. These techniques are the universal defensive language. You should know it, teach it, and use it.

The lineman's alignment in most cases will be six to eight inches off the ball. Some defensive alignments call for them to align as much as 18 inches off the line. They feel this gives them an advantage over the blocker as long as their approach is low. Offensive linemen have a tendency to stand up if they have a distance to travel to make a block. This is not etched in stone; if you have a defensive lineman who is slower to react than you like, moving him back off the ball will give him more time to read and react.

Figure 6-4 shows defensive linemen that are aligned in an inside shade technique. They will usually be assigned to control the gap to which they are shaded. They will execute their assignment by exploding out of their stance, delivering the blow to the inside chest of the blocker aligned on them. They will try to stand their man up while maintaining a balanced base. They should be able to read and react to the play swiftly.

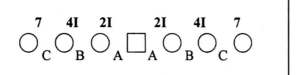

Figure 6-4

Figure 6-5 shows the defensive lineman in head-up techniques. Their base assignment will vary based on the philosophy of the defense. In a gap control defense their assignment will be directly affected by the alignment and assignment of the linebackers.

Figure 6-5

Figure 6-6 shows a 4-4 defense with the four linemen in head-up, even techniques. In this situation their assignment would be the gap inside them; this is due to the fact that the linebackers are all aligned outside of them. The linebackers will always be responsible for the opposite gap of the lineman closest to them.

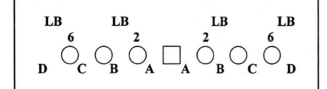

Figure 6-6

In the defensive formations shown in Figure 6-7 and Figure 6-8, the linebackers are aligned directly behind the defensive linemen. In these alignments the gap responsibilities are not clearly defined. Many times they are defined by the strength of the offensive formation. Some teams will shift toward the strength of the offense, which would then establish a more clear assignment to the defender. Most teams will shift a shade to the strength of the defense, which is shown in Figure 6-9.

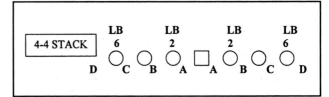

Figure 6-7

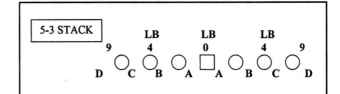

Figure 6-8

The alignment shown in Figure 6-9 is shifting to the strength of the offensive formation. When this is done, the base gap assignments are clearly defined.

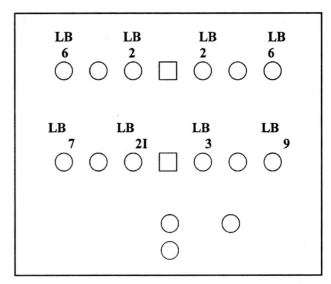

Figure 6-9

Figure 6-10 is an example of a stacked defense that does not shift to the strength of the offensive formation, although it reacts to its strength. In this example, the defensive linemen have maximized the opportunity for one of the linebackers to make the play if they are unable to do so. At the same time, they did not tip-off the offensive blockers to their assignments.

All of the previous assignment examples were out of base defenses. This means they were the most basic ways that a defense will align. Many defenses will incorporate stunt and blitz packages that are designed to confuse an offense. The other benefit of stunting is that it clearly defines the assignments of the defenders. Figure 6-11 shows an extreme blitz package. A defense may incorporate all or part of this package. Some defenders could have the base assignment that is called in the huddle, while other player's assignments are defined by the stunt package called. A countless number of stunt packages can be incorporated into every defensive

alignment. Be sure that if you incorporate stunt packages, everyone on the defense clearly understands their assignment.

Gap Control Techniques

To control the gaps a defensive lineman should explode out of his stance and into the blocker. He should take control of the blocker quickly. He should be lower than him, driving his hands or forearm right up through him and standing him up to make the read.

- His shoulders and feet should stay parallel to the LOS.
- His hands and arms should be kept between himself and the blocker.
- His back should maintain a 45-degree angle.
- His head is up looking for the ball.
- The blocker's head should not get past his shoulders.

If the blocker's head is going hard to the outside, the DL needs to work to the outside, never allowing the blocker's head past his shoulders.

Pursuit

Coaches, tell your players to do the following:

- Stay in your lane.
- Work through a blocker.
- Never spin out or run around the blocker.
- Throw the blocker off–don't stay blocked.
- Move laterally as the ball comes to your area.
- Be disciplined in your pursuit of the ball.
- Take away the run angles–force him to cut back–keep the ball in front of you or your pursuit angle.
- Run to the ball on every play–make the tackle– strip the ball–be there!

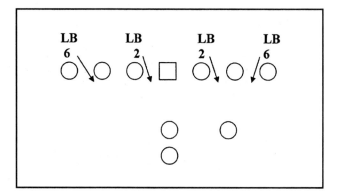

Figure 6-10

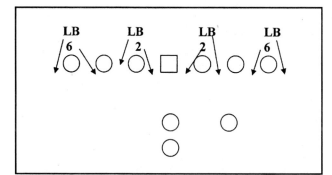

Figure 6-11

Tackling Tips

Coaches, tell your players to do the following:

• "Step on his toes"–most missed tackles are caused from starting too far away.

• Square up, eyes on the numbers–make him run through you.

• Keep your back at a 45-degree angle.

• Break down under control, use short choppy steps.

• Explode into the runner by accelerating your footwork as you drive up and through him. Hit through him not just the front of him.

• Your facemask should drive right through the football.

• Recoil–your hips should drive forward as your back is straightening and you come up and through him.

• Wrap him up–never wind up with your arms.

• Never stop chopping and driving until he is on his back.

Stunt Rushes

Players may be required to stunt a gap. This may be done alone as in a slant or crash. It may also be done in conjunction with a backer who is also stunting the opposite gap. Coaches, tell your players to do the following:

• Know the gap you are stunting.

• Get out of your stance quickly.

• Drive through the outside/inside shoulder of the man you are stunting. Never loop or be blocked wide to that side. Use the rip or swim technique.

• Your goal should be to get one yard into the backfield and read the play.

• Stay in control.

• Do not fire deep into the backfield.

• Never get deeper than the ballcarrier.

• Protect your gap.

• Pursue the ballcarrier.

The most common mistake that young defensive linemen make when they stunt a gap is to penetrate too deeply and too quickly. A good rule of thumb is for them to be one yard behind the line of scrimmage. This means that the lineman that is stunting the B gap in Figure 6-12 should aim for the spot one yard behind the man he is stunting past.

Figure 6-13 is an example of a basic stunt package. This could be called slant strong in the huddle. This call means that every lineman would slant to the strongside of the formation. A slant is a stunt that is performed in the gap on the strongside.

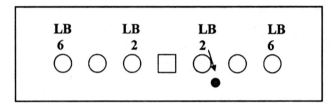

Figure 6-12

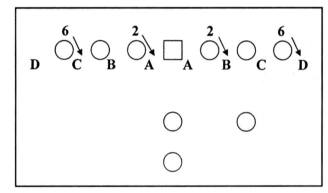

Figure 6-13

Shedding the Blocker

This section covers the techniques used to shed a blocker: the bull rush, the rip move, and the swim move. Although this is a short list of techniques, these moves are the ones you should master first.

The Bull Rush

The most common style of rush used is the bull rush. With this style the DL simply tries to run over or through the blocker. The trick is to catch a blocker back on his heels and he will be easily beat. This rush is used in passing situations. A lot of pass blockers start out by taking a step back to set up for the block.

The Rip Move

The rip move is the most widely used escape technique. It is especially useful on stunt rushes. Following is an example of a defender using a rip move in an attempt to get to the right side of the defender. Obviously, you would reverse it when going left.

- The left arm is held at a 90-degree angle with hand fisted.
- The left foot should explode just to the left side of the blockers' while staying low.
- The left arm will punch up and through the left side of the blocker's body at the same time.
- At the moment of the punch and step he should be perpendicular to the LOS. This is only for a split second.
- The right foot needs to follow quickly. If performed with explosion and proper fundamentals he will be right where he wants to be. If he tries to loop or go wide this technique will fail. He must go straight at him, and then at the last second perform this technique.

Swim Move

The swim move is used when the blocker is controlling the DL with his arms when the DL is trying to control a gap at the LOS. This is also a good pass rush technique. Again, it will be described to the right.

- The DL should land with a strong left-foot stride tightly to the side of the blocker.
- At the same time, the fisted left arm will explode over the arms of the defender.
- The upper body momentum must be forward.
- At the top of his swing, his hand should be up in the air and his upper arm parallel to the ground.

- Leading with the elbow, he should pull that arm down as hard as he can which will break his arm from his body.
- He should regain control with a quick step with the right foot.

Defending the Trap

The trap play is a staple inside running play for many teams. Many inexperienced defenses are unable to properly read and defend the trap. Defending the trap play will require a lot of practice repetitions. Defensive linemen need to be able to read a trap play instinctively.

Explain to your linemen that they don't need to make the tackle to stop a trap play. The most important thing they will do is to jam up the running lane for the ballcarrier. These plays are designed to cut inside the trap blocker's block. Do not allow your linemen to be kicked out by the trap man.

The technique used to stop this is rather simple. Figure 6-14 shows the basic elements of a trap play. The defender in bold is the man being trapped. The guard lined up over him will release inside him to block a linebacker. The defensive tackle in this situation needs to jam down on the outside shoulder of the guard while looking for the trapping guard pulling down the line. As soon as he locates him, he must attack him in the backfield. He will jam him with his outside shoulder and forearm, keeping his inside shoulder free. This will put him in a position to make the tackle if the running back were to continue on his planned path. If the running back is forced

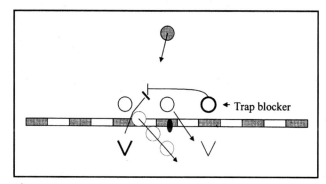

Figure 6-14

outside the trap blocker, the play will break down quickly meaning the defender did his job properly.

Spend a fair amount of practice time teaching this technique. Work on live drills that will incorporate these skills. If you can stop the trap, you may take away an offenses' strength.

Pass Rushing

When you know it's a pass, you need your defenders to get to the passer. Employ one of the moves mentioned previously to get to the quarterback quickly. The defenders should rush him under control and not make it easy for him to sidestep. If he begins his throwing motion, the defensive linemen should get their arms up in his way trying to knock his pass down.

Make sure they stay in their pass lanes when rushing the passer. A pass lane is defined by the angle which you pursue the passer. All defensive linemen should pursue the passer in a similar fashion. When they read a pass, they should pursue the passer by any means necessary. They should aim for the outside ear of the passer. By doing this, they are also in a position to stop the passer if he tries to escape the pocket.

They should never rush deeper than the ball or allow themselves to be blocked beyond the quarterback. If they do get deeper than the quarterback, they can spin to release off the block.

If the quarterback releases the ball during the rush, the DL must pull up. He must make every attempt to avoid contact with the passer once he releases the ball. If his momentum takes him into the quarterback after he releases the ball, he will likely avoid the penalty as long as he made every effort to avoid him. The other thing he must avoid is diving at the knees of the passer. He should execute a thundering tackle whenever possible making sure to employ proper tackling fundamentals.

Defensive Line Drills

Stance and Start Drill

Objective: To teach the proper stance and start fundamentals for defensive linemen.

Description:

- Form two lines of players facing each other in pairs. One line will be defensive linemen while the other line will be blockers.
- Both lines will get in their stances facing each other across an imaginary line of scrimmage.
- The coach will stand behind the defensive linemen. He will show the offensive linemen the snap count by holding up that many fingers.
- On the designated snap count, the blockers will come out of their stance to simulate a block on the defender. They will block at three-fourths speed.
- The defensive linemen will react to the movement of the blocker's hand. As soon as the blocker's hand moves, he will explode into him driving him back and up while getting his arms extended to create seperation.

- They will freeze once they have extended their arms from the blocker.
- The coaches will check their form.
- Repeat the drill with defenders and blockers switching roles.

Coaching Points: Make sure the defensive linemen are using proper fundamentals throughout the drill.

- Emphasize the explosion into the blocker.
- The defensive linemen must win the leverage battle.

He will accomplish this by aiming for the chest plate of the blocker with his open hands. As he drives into the blocker, his hips should be driving underneath him.

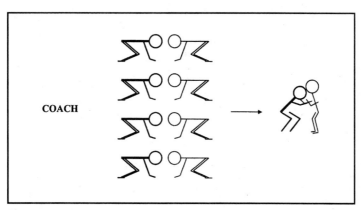

Figure 6-15

Sled Punch Drill

Objective: To perfect the explosive punch-up motion used by defensive linemen.

Equipment Needed: A football that is attached to a rope. It doesn't matter if it is inflated or not. You will use this to simulate a snap.

Description:

- Form a line in front of every blocking pad on your sled.
- The first line will line up in front of the sled in their proper stance.
- A coach who is standing behind the sled will simulate the snap of the ball by yanking on the rope attached to a football.
- The players will punch up and through the sled, driving it up into the air.
- They will freeze with the sled in the air.
- The coaches will check for form.

Coaching Points: When you are checking the form of the defenders make sure:

- they have their arms extended
- their head is up
- their body is not leaning forward
- their base is slightly widened

Don't ever allow defensive linemen to move on any sound. They must always have a visual key to start.

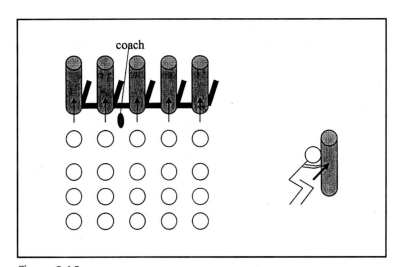

Figure 6-16

Read and React Drill

Objective: To teach defensive linemen how to read and react to the flow of the play.

Description:

- Form two lines of players facing each other in pairs. One line will be defensive linemen while the other line will be blockers.

- Line up a coach or a player four yards behind the blockers that will simulate a ballcarrier.

- Both lines will get in their stances facing each other across an imaginary line of scrimmage.

- The coach will stand behind the defensive linemen. He will show the offensive linemen the snap count by holding up that many fingers. He will then point in a direction which represents the direction the ballcarrier will go.

- On the designated snap count, the blockers will block the defensive linemen attempting to seal them off from the playside.

- The simulated ballcarrier will run in the direction of the play.

- The defensive linemen will react to the play and work themselves to the playside of the blocker getting themselves in a position to make a tackle. There will be no contact with the simulated ballcarrier.

- Repeat the drill with defenders and blockers switching roles.

Coaching Points: The defender must read the head of the blocker. He must work toward the blocker's head, never allowing the blocker to square off on him and screen him from the playside.

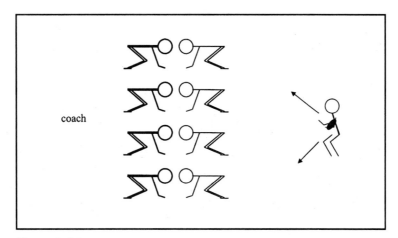

Figure 6-17

Two-Gap Drill

Objective: To teach defensive linemen how to neutralize a blocker while reading the gaps on either side of him.

Description:

• Form two lines of players facing each other in pairs. One line will be defensive linemen while the other line will be blockers.

• Line a ballcarrier four yards behind the blocker.

• The first person in each line will get in their stances facing each other across an imaginary line of scrimmage between two cones, four to five yards apart.

• The coach will stand behind the defensive linemen. He will show the offensive linemen the snap count by holding up that many fingers. He will then point in a direction which represents the direction the ballcarrier will go.

• On the designated snap count, the blocker will block the defensive lineman attempting to seal him off from the playside.

• The ballcarrier will run in the direction of the play. He must hit the hole on the playside without making any cuts.

• The defensive linemen will react to the play and work themselves to the playside of the blocker getting themselves in a position to make a tackle.

• They will make initial contact with the ballcarrier without tackling him to the ground.

• Repeat the drill with defenders and blockers switching roles.

Coaching Points: The defender must read the head of the blocker. He must work toward the blocker's head never allowing the blocker to square off on him and screen him from the playside.

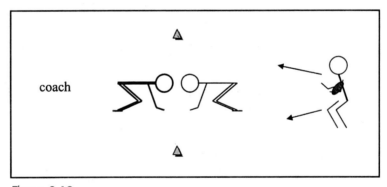

Figure 6-18

Shoot the Gap Drill

Objective: To teach defensive linemen how to effectively stunt (shoot) gaps on the offensive line.

Description:

• Form two lines of players facing each other in pairs. One line will be defensive linemen while the other line will be blockers.

• Both lines will get in their stances facing each other across an imaginary line of scrimmage.

• A coach will stand behind the defensive linemen. He will show the offensive linemen the snap count by holding up that many fingers.

• A coach will stand behind the offensive linemen pointing to the side they will stunt to.

• On the designated snap count, the blockers will attempt to drive block the defender.

• On the first movement by the blockers, the defensive linemen will stunt to the gap on the side designated by the coach.

• He will try to reach a point that is one yard beyond the outside shoulder of the blocker on the stunt-side gap.

• Repeat the drill with defenders and blockers switching roles.

• Make sure every defender gets repetitions shooting the gaps in both directions.

Coaching Points: The emphasis must be on getting to the target spot on a tight line from their stance. They must never try to loop around the blocker. They need to use the proper leverage to be in the proper positioning.

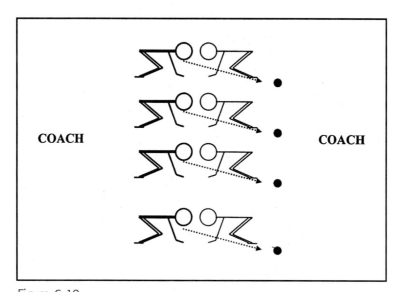

Figure 6-19

Bull Rush Drill

Objective: To properly teach defensive linemen how to bull rush past a blocker on the line in pass rush situations.

Description:

- Form two lines of players facing each other in pairs. One line will be defensive linemen while the other line will be blockers.

- Both lines will get in their stances facing each other across an imaginary line of scrimmage.

- The coach will stand behind the defensive linemen. He will show the offensive linemen the snap count by holding up that many fingers.

- A cone will be set up five yards beyond the LOS, representing the QB.

- On the designated snap count, the blockers take an initial step back and set up to pass block the defender.

- The defensive linemen will react to the movement of the blocker's hand. As soon as the blocker's hand moves, he will explode into him trying to knock him back in his stance and get past him as quickly as possible trying to get to the cone in the backfield.

- Repeat the drill with defenders and blockers switching roles.

Coaching Points: The emphasis needs to be on getting out of their stances quickly and trying to contact the blocker as he steps back and before he can properly set up to block. The defender should never be allowed to loop too wide around the blocker. This drill can be run at full speed or at three-fourths speed when first teaching this technique.

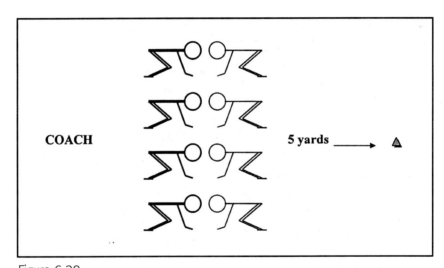

Figure 6-20

Rip Drill

Objective: To teach proper defensive linemen how to perform the rip move to get beyond a blocker.

Description:

- Form two lines of players facing each other in pairs. One line will be defensive linemen while the other line will be blockers.

- Both lines will get in their stances facing each other across an imaginary line of scrimmage.

- The coach will stand behind the defensive linemen. He will show the offensive linemen the snap count by holding up that many fingers.

- A cone will be set up five yards beyond the LOS, representing the QB.

- On the designated snap count, the blockers take an initial step back and set up to pass block the defender.

- The coach will call left or right to determine which foot the blocker will step back with on his initial step.

- The defensive linemen will react to the movement of the blocker's hand. As soon as the blocker's hand moves, he will explode out of his stance and perform a rip move to the side called, trying to take the tightest path possible to the QB cone.

- Repeat the drill with defenders and blockers switching roles.

Coaching Points: The emphasis needs to be on getting out of their stances quickly.

- When going to the left, the defender must rip with his right arm as he steps through with his right leg.

- When going to the right, the defender must rip with his left arm as he steps through with his left leg.

- Have the blocker working at three-fourths speed when first teaching this technique.

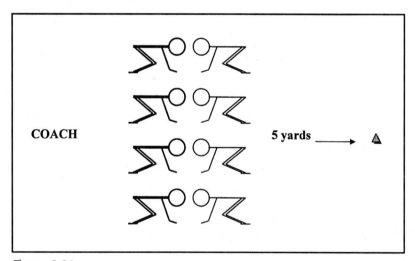

Figure 6-21

Swim Drill

Objective: To teach proper defensive linemen how to perform the swim move to get beyond a blocker.

Description:

- Form two lines of players facing each other in pairs. One line will be defensive linemen while the other line will be blockers.
- Both lines will get in their stances facing each other across an imaginary line of scrimmage.
- The coach will stand behind the defensive linemen. He will show the offensive linemen the snap count by holding up that many fingers.
- A cone will be set up five yards beyond the LOS, representing the QB.
- On the designated snap count, the blockers take an initial step back and set up to pass block the defender.

- The coach will call left or right to determine which foot the blocker will step back with on his initial step.
- The defensive linemen will react to the movement of the blocker's hand. As soon as the blocker's hand moves, he will explode out of his stance and perform a swim move to the side called, trying to take the tightest path possible to the QB cone.
- Repeat the drill with defenders and blockers switching roles.

Coaching Points: The emphasis needs to be on getting out of their stances quickly. Make sure that the swim move fundamentals are executed properly. Have the blocker working at three-fourths speed when first teaching this technique.

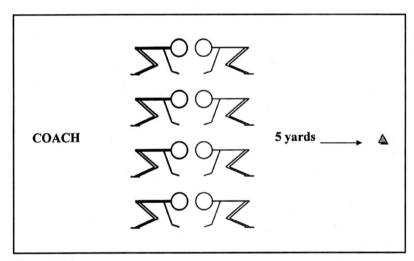

Figure 6-22

174

Popsicle Punch Drill

Objective: To teach the defensive linemen the proper fundamentals used during the initial impact of a start with an emphasis on driving up and through the blocker until the arms are extended.

Equipment Needed: A football that is attached to a rope. It doesn't matter if it is inflated or not.

Description:

- Set up a line in front of the popsicles.
- The first player in line will be in a three- or four-point stance directly in front of the sled.
- The coach will start the drill by pulling the football on a rope.
- The player will punch up on the sled until his arms are extended.
- The sled should be up in the air resting only on the back rails.

Coaching Points: Make sure that the initial impact of the sled is low and the player drives up and through the sled. He should explode into the sled causing it to go backwards as well as up in the air. Don't ever allow defensive linemen to move on any sound. They must always have a visual key to start.

Popsicle Punch and Rip Drill

Objective: To teach the defensive linemen the proper fundamentals of the rip move after they have stood up the blocker.

Equipment Needed: A football that is attached to a rope. It doesn't matter if it is inflated or not.

Description:

- Set up a line in front of the popsicles.
- The first player in line will be in a three- or four-point stance directly in front of the sled.
- The coach will start the drill by pulling the football on a rope.
- The player will punch up on the sled until his arms are extended.
- The coach will blow the whistle and the player will execute a rip move to the right of the sled.
- Repeat drill using a rip move to the left of the sled.

Coaching Point:

- Don't ever allow defensive linemen to move on any sound. They must always have a visual key to start.

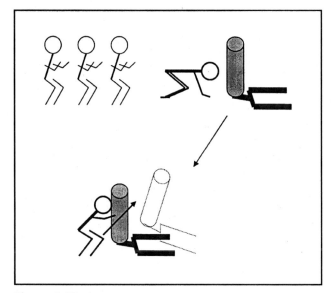

Figure 6-23

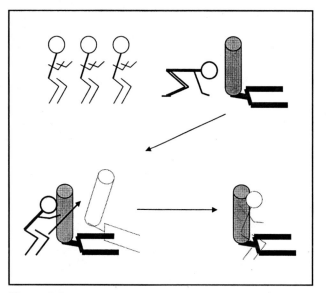

Figure 6-24

Popsicle Punch and Swim Drill

Objective: To teach the defensive linemen the proper fundamentals of the swim move after they have stood up the blocker.

Equipment Needed: A football that is attached to a rope. It doesn't matter if it is inflated or not.

Description:

- Set up a line in front of the popsicles.
- The first player in line will be in a three- or four-point stance directly in front of the sled.
- The coach will start the drill by pulling the football on a rope.
- The player will punch up on the sled until his arms are extended.
- The coach will blow the whistle and the player will execute a swim move to the right of the sled.
- Repeat drill using a rip move to the left of the sled.

Coaching Points: Make sure that the player executes the swim move with the proper fundamentals. Since there is no live contact, the player should exaggerate the swim movements. He should try to move his arms and feet as quickly as possible. Don't ever allow defensive linemen to move on any sound. They must always have a visual key to start.

Forearm Lift Drill

Objective: To teach the defensive linemen the technique used to fend off blockers that are coming at them from angles.

Description:

- Form a triangle with three players that are three yards apart in a two-point stance.
- One player is designated as the defensive lineman while the other two players are blockers.
- On the coach's whistle one of the blockers will start toward the defender.
- The defender will attack the blocker and will drive him away with his inside shoulder and forearm.
- The defender will recoil back to his original spot and then the other blocker will start toward him and he will repeat the separation move with his inside shoulder and forearm.
- He will continue this until he has worked both sides three times.

Coaching Points: Make sure that the defensive lineman is attacking the blocker. He should be the aggressor at the point of impact. He must have a low base and explode up and through the blocker not just into him

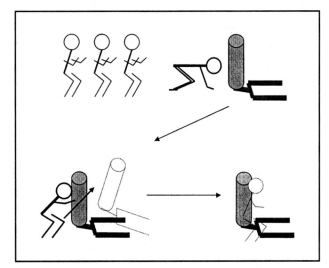

Figure 6-25

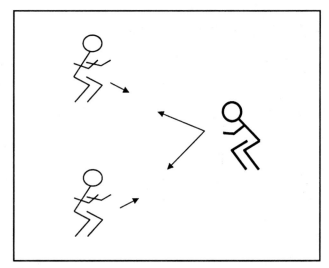

Figure 6-26

Stop the Trap Drill

Objective: To teach the defensive linemen how to look for and defend the trap play.

Description:

- Line up four players (two guards, one center, and one defensive tackle) on the line of scrimmage over one of the guards.

- On the snap count, the covered guard will release down to the inside of the defender while the other guard will pull down the LOS to execute a trap block.

- The defensive tackle will jam down on the outside shoulder of the guard that is blocking down. When he reads the trapping guard he will release and jam the inside shoulder of the pulling guard while he is still in the backfield.

- Reverse the drill with the defensive tackle lined up on the other guard.

Coaching Points:

- The defensive tackle can never let the pulling guard get to his inside shoulder, which must remain free to stop the trap play.

- Teach him that if he can't make the tackle, he should force the play to the outside.

- Make sure he initiates the contact with the guard as far into the backfield as possible, with the hopes of jamming the play.

- You can replace the center with a cone or a football if you prefer.

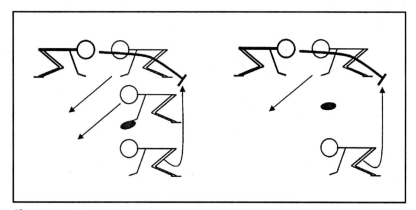

Figure 6-27

Power Scrimmage

Objective: To work on the skills needed by the interior defensive linemen and inside linebackers to stop the inside running game of their opponent.

Description:

- This is a live full-contact scrimmage in a controlled area.

- Set up an offensive line that includes one center, two guards and one tackle.

- Set up a backfield with two running backs and a quarterback.

- Set boundary markers one yard on each side of the last man on the end of the line of scrimmage.

- Set up two defensive linemen and two linebackers in your teams' defensive alignment.

- The offense should run interior running plays including dives, leads, counters, traps, and sneaks.

- The defense should stay in a base alignment, reading and reacting to the plays.

Coaching Points: Have enough coaches available to monitor every player. Make it a competition. Get both sides of the ball playing at an intense level. You can use a coach as the quarterback if you prefer.

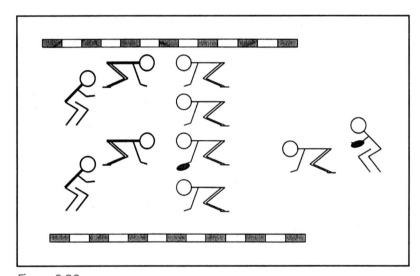

Figure 6-28

Bag Contain Drill

Objective: To teach defensive ends and outside linebackers how to contain the outside running game.

Description:

- Set up three blocking dummies, three yards apart and three yards deep.
- A defensive end will line up on the first dummy.
- On the start of the drill he will jam into the bag from the outside half of it driving it back one yard.
- He will release the first dummy and work his way down the line repeating this technique until he gets to the cone.
- Work this drill in both directions.

Coaching Points: Emphasize to the defensive contain men that they should never get flanked by anyone. They must work to the outside of every blocker. You can use coaches or players with blocking shields rather than dummies if you prefer.

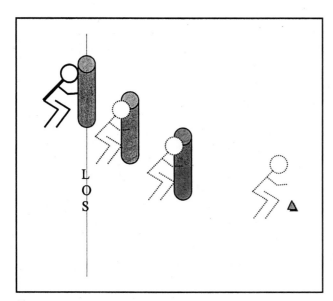

Figure 6-29

End Reach Drill

Objective: To teach the defensive end how to stop the tight end's reach block.

Description:

- Line up a tight end and a defensive end on the end of the line of scrimmage.
- Have a ballcarrier in the backfield. It can be a live ballcarrier or a coach simulating the carry.
- On the start of the drill the tight end will attempt to reach block the defensive end.
- The ballcarrier will try to run outside the end.
- The defensive end will jam the outside shoulder of the tight end with his inside shoulder and forearm.
- The defensive end will make the tackle on the ballcarrier. He can also just make a thud hit on the ballcarrier or just touch him if it is a coach simulating the carry.
- Repeat the drill to the other side.

Coaching Points: The defensive end must keep his head up and his base should be slightly widened upon impact with the blocker. He should never give ground to the blocker.

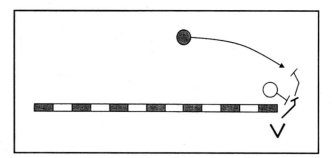

Figure 6-30

Two-Man Contain Drill

Objective: To teach the defensive end or the outside linebacker how to contain the outside running play by working off one block and into the next.

Description:

- Line up a tight end and a defensive end on the end of a line of scrimmage.
- Have a ballcarrier and a lead blocker in the backfield. It can be a live ballcarrier or a coach simulating the carry.
- On the start of the drill the tight end will attempt to reach block the defensive end.
- The ballcarrier will follow his lead block to try to run outside the end.
- The defensive end will jam the outside shoulder of the tight end with his inside shoulder and forearm.
- When he sees the lead blocker coming out of the backfield, he will release from the tight end and jam the outside shoulder of the lead blocker.
- He will try to force the running back all the way to the sideline.
- The running back must try to get outside the end. He is not permitted to cut back in this drill.
- The defensive end will make the tackle on the ballcarrier. He can also just make a thud hit on the ballcarrier or just touch him if it is a coach simulating the carry. Repeat the drill to the other side.

Coaching Points: It is imperative that the ballcarrier is stopped from turning the outside corner. You cannot stress the importance of this enough.

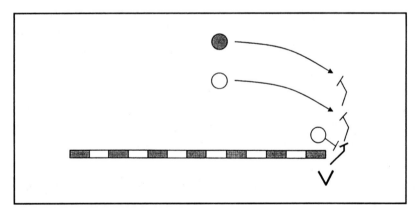

Figure 6-31

Goal Line Surge Drill

Objective: To teach the defensive linemen how to surge into the backfield in goal line situations.

Description:

- Line up two blockers with only a two- to three-inch spread.

- A defensive lineman will be lined up in a four-point stance in the gap of the two blockers and as close to the line of scrimmage as possible.

- On a designated count the blockers will double-team the defensive lineman.

- The defender will surge into the backfield as low as possible.

Coaching Points:

- The defender's main objective is to break through the double-team block and get into the backfield.

- He should be aiming for the area between the lower thighs of the blockers.

- His head should stay up.

- He needs to stay as low to the ground as possible.

- He is setting up the linebackers to make the tackle in these situations.

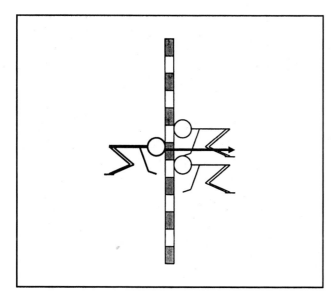

Figure 6-32

Linebackers

The linebacker may be the most important position on the field. Spend plenty of time teaching the fundamentals and the reads of this position. Not only will these be some of your best athletes, but they will also possess many intangibles. The biggest intangible is good instincts. Your defensive captain will most likely be one of your LB's. Make sure you run plenty of drills during LB's stations at practice.

The following six tips are useful for linebackers:

- Maintain good body position.

- Protect yourself—avoid or play off of other blockers.

- Make quick, lateral, and forward movements.

- Improve your ability to change directions.

- Make tackles.

- Know where the runner is and where he is going.

Stance

The linebacker's stance must be very balanced. He needs to be able to move in any direction. His feet should not be planted into the ground. The basic stance fundamentals for a linebacker are listed below:

- His feet are spread at shoulder width.

- His knees are flexed slightly with the hips.

- His weight is on the balls of the feet.

- His back is at about a 45-degree angle.

- His arms and hands are in front of the knees and ready.

- His shoulders are parallel to the LOS.

- His eyes are focused.

Keys

Outside LB's first key is the TE if there is one on his side. His first moves will indicate the play direction. He should read through the TE to the near back and the triangular running lane in his zone as shown in

Figure 6-33. A tight end blocking down may indicate an outside play. If he releases downfield it may mean a pass.

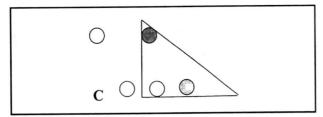

Figure 6-33

Middle linebackers need to see through the linemen they are lined up over to the near back. Their keys are found in the read triangle shown in Figure 6-34. They need to read potential blockers coming at them as well as locate where the ball is going. He should focus on a pulling guard; he will take him to the play. A down block by a lineman surely means the play is going outside him. The head of the guard may likely take him to the play. They cannot rely on this key alone. Great linebackers are able to see other things going on at the same time.

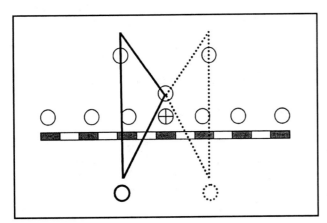

Figure 6-34

Alignment

Alignment is dependent largely on what defense you are running. In most defenses the middle LB's are the same distance from the LOS as the halfbacks in the offense.

Some stack defenses call for the linebacker to stack only one yard behind their defensive linemen as shown in Figure 6-36.

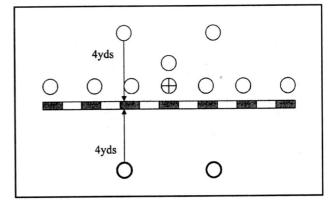

Figure 6-35

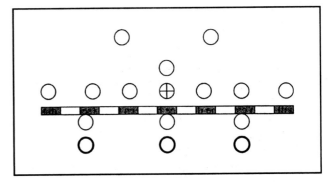

Figure 6-36

Assignment

In most defensive systems the linebackers are assigned to a gap. The gap they are assigned to can change depending on the strength of the offensive formation. Figure 6-37 is an example of gap assignments based on the strength of the offensive formation. If the strength of the formation is to the other side, the assignments of the noseguard and both inside linebackers would be reversed.

Linebacker assignment can vary greatly from system to system. Some defenses never move to the strength of the offensive formation. Some defensive systems don't assign gaps to their linebackers. These teams use many variables on the line and allow their linebackers to read and react at their own discretion.

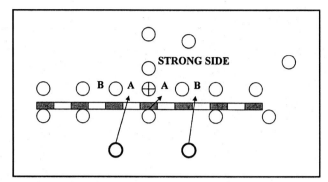

Figure 6-37

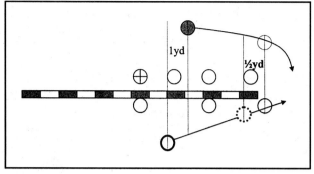

Figure 6-38

Run Responsibility

Lateral movement is the key. They must always keep their shoulders parallel to the line of scrimmage. Knowing when to break for the ballcarrier is a key element for a linebacker. Many young linebackers get themselves caught in bad situations by breaking for the runner too soon. When an inside linebacker pursues a ballcarrier that is moving laterally, he must mirror his movement by remaining one yard or so behind him depending on the distance between he and the ballcarrier. As they are moving laterally, the linebacker will try to close the distance between them as shown in Figure 6-38.

Outside linebackers pursue the ballcarrier differently. Assuming they have D gap responsibility, they cannot allow a ballcarrier to get outside. Their mentality is to turn the play inside where they have the support of other defenders. Their angle of pursuit can vary by situation. In Figure 6-39, the outside linebacker must get outside positioning on the lead blocker. He cannot allow the blocker to get positioned outside him or the back will have a clear break around him.

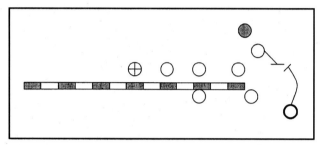

Figure 6-39

In Figure 6-40, the outside linebacker is pursuing a ballcarrier with no lead blocker. In this situation he is trying to force him all the way to the sideline without giving him an opportunity to cut back into the field. He does this by pursuing him on an angle that puts him just far enough inside that he can't cut back, and yet not far enough inside to allow him to get outside. This will likely force him out-of-bounds or the linebacker will make the tackle sometime before reaching the sideline. By stringing this play out to the sideline it will allow other defenders to recover and pursue the ballcarrier. If the linebacker happens to miss the tackle, there will likely be other defenders in a position to make the tackle.

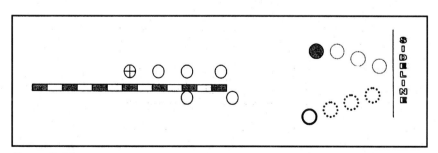

Figure 6-40

Shedding Blockers

The first thing he should try is avoiding blockers altogether; if he can't, then he should square up to his blocker. If he comes at him high, he should get under him. He should jam him while he is shuffling toward the play, shake him, and make the tackle. If he comes at him low, he keeps his feet moving and will jam down on his shoulders, pushing him into the ground as he continues to pursue the ballcarrier.

The linebacker must never turn his back to the player or spin to get off a block. He should work to the outside of the block even if he has to give up some ground to the runner. He should never take the easy way to the ballcarrier. The easy way usually means it is too late to catch up to him. Figure 6-41 is an illustration of this concept.

Pass Responsibility

Pass responsibility can vary greatly. The base coverage will vary in different defensive schemes. The coverage package called by a defense will also change the responsibilities of your linebackers.

Defenses that feature two inside linebackers will many times use the base zone package shown in Figure 6-42, which is a base 40 defense. This example features both inside and outside linebackers. Inside LB's have hitch/curl responsibilities in the zone defense, while the outside linebackers are responsible for the out/flat routes.

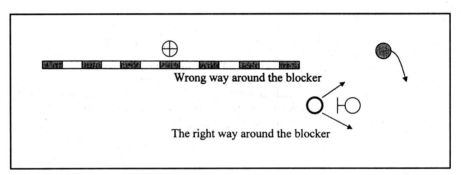

Figure 6-41

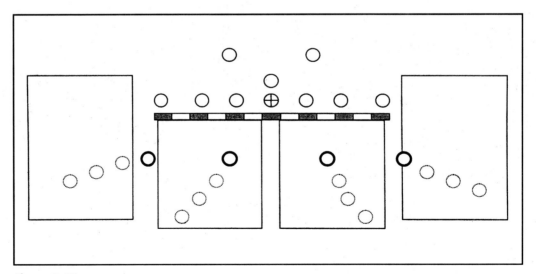

Figure 6-42

Stunt/Blitz

Stunts, or blitzes as they are also called, will vary greatly depending on the defensive scheme. Some defenses are based on a great number of stunts while other defenses rely on very few. Some coaches rarely ever stunt. These coaches believe in playing basic fundamental football. Stunts can also be used based on a given situation. When a defensive coordinator picks up on an offensive tendency, he may call an automatic stunt to a particular area that will be used only when the defense recognizes that particular tendency.

A few basic principles should be followed when you execute stunts. You don't want to tip-off your stunt moves. You will usually be stunting in conjunction with a defensive lineman. He may be going right with your player is going left. The first step should be forward allowing the lineman to make the first move. He then takes the stunt route as fast and hard as he can while maintaining a good hitting position.

Linebacker Footwork Drills

Linebackers have to be able to move and change directions quickly. Agility is a great asset for a linebacker to possess. They need to learn how to move in different ways. When they are pursuing a play and working their way down the line of scrimmage they will shuffle their feet, never taking a crossover step. When they pursue a ballcarrier beyond this area, they will need to use the crossover step to gain greater speed. The following drills will help with stance and footwork.

High Knee Step-overs

Objective: To develop the linebacker's footwork; to improve agility.

Description:

- Set up five bags parallel with each other and one yard apart.

- Form a line of players five yards off the bags and facing forward.

- On the coach's command the first player in line will step over the bags alternating his feet as he steps over each bag.

- After every player has had a repetition, repeat the drill by having the players step with both feet between each bag.

Coaching Points: They should lift their knees high between every step. Their heads should always be up and facing forward. When they are proficient at this drill they will be able to perform it without ever looking down.

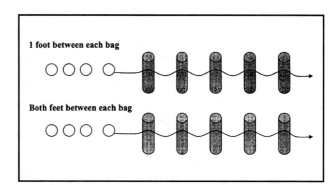

Figure 6-43

Side Step-overs

Objective: To develop the linebacker's footwork; to improve agility.

Description:

- Set up five bags parallel with each other and two yards apart.
- Form a line of players five yards off the end of one of the bags and facing forward.
- On the coach's command the player will side-step over the bag with his first foot; he will then bring his next foot over the same bag, and then bring both feet together in between the bags.
- He will continue this as quickly as he can until he has completed the drill in that direction.
- After every player has had an equal number of repetitions, repeat the drill starting from the other end of the bags still facing forward.

Coaching Points: Make sure that they maintain a proper body position throughout the drill. Players will have a tendency to do these standing straight up. It is important that their heads are up and facing forward.

Shuffle Steps

Objective: To develop the shuffle footwork employed by a linebacker; to improve agility.

Description:

- Set up five bags parallel with each other and two yards apart.
- Form a line of players five yards off the end of one of the bags and facing forward.
- On the coach's command the first player will shuffle around all the bags.
- He must remain facing forward throughout the drill.

Coaching Points: The player is not allowed to cross his feet at any time throughout the drill. Make sure that they maintain a proper body position. Players will have a tendency to do these standing straight up. It is important that their heads are up and facing forward.

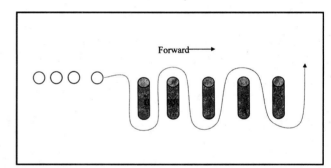

Figure 6-45

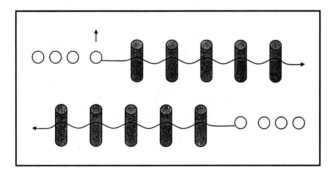

Figure 6-44

Around the Bag Drill

Objective: To develop the linebacker's footwork; to improve agility.

Description:

- Set up five bags parallel with each other and two yards apart.

- Form a line of players five yards off the end of one of the bags and facing forward.

- On the coach's command the player will shuffle-step over to the first bag.

- He will then run backwards to the end of the first bag. He will shuffle over two yards still facing forward, and then sprint to the end of the bag. He will repeat these steps until he has completed the drill.

- The next player in line will begin the drill when the first player is halfway through the drill.

Coaching Points: Make sure that they maintain a proper body position throughout the drill. Players will have a tendency to perform these standing straight up. It is important that their heads are up and facing forward. When they are running backwards they must flex at the waist and knees; their shoulders should be over their feet. If their shoulders are too far back they will lose their balance.

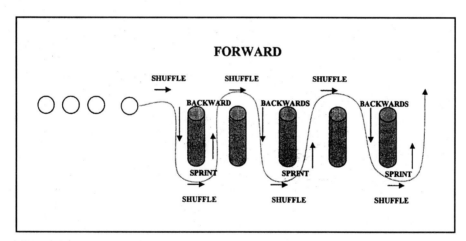

Figure 6-46

Pursuit Drill

Objective: To develop the shuffle and crossover footwork employed by a linebacker; to improve agility.

Description:

- Set up five bags parallel with each other and two yards apart.
- Form a line of players five yards off the end of one of the bags and facing forward.
- On the coach's command the first player will shuffle around all the bags.
- When he gets to the cone at the end of the bags he will employ crossover steps to the next cone.
- He will turn and face the next set of bags and shuffle around them.

- When he gets to the next cone, he will finish the drill by crossover-stepping to the next cone.
- He must remain facing forward throughout the drill.

Coaching Points: Make sure that they maintain a proper body position throughout the drill. Players will have a tendency to perform these standing straight up. It is important that their heads are up and facing forward. They should always face the bag when shuffling.

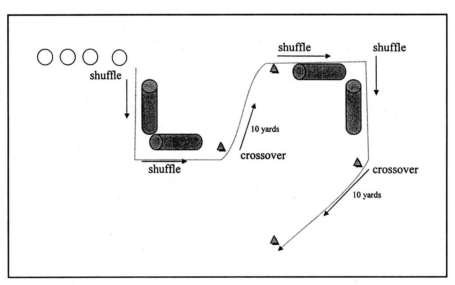

Figure 6-47

Quarter Turn Drill

Objective: To teach linebackers how to change directions quickly; to improve footwork and agility.

Description:

- Form four lines of linebackers facing a coach.
- From a good stance, the player will make a quick quarter turn and maintain an excellent hitting position.
- The coach's command will be left or right.
- The player will make the appropriate turn without jumping or stepping.
- On the 'go' command or whistle, the player will sprint five yards maintaining good hitting position.

Coaching Points: Make sure the player doesn't hop or jump his turns. He rotates his hips quickly when his feet are barely off the ground. He should maintain a good linebacker position throughout the drill.

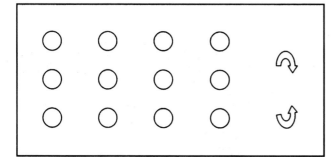

Figure 6-48

Shuffle Drill

Objective: To teach the linebacker how to shuffle laterally; to improve agility.

Description:

- Form four lines of linebackers facing a coach.
- From a good stance, the players in the front row start chopping their feet on the coach's command.
- The coaches will use a football to show the direction the linebacker must move in. If he moves the ball to the player's left, they will shuffle left; if he moves the ball to their right, they will shuffle right.
- They must keep their feet chopping throughout the drill.
- The player will make the appropriate movement without crossing his feet.
- On the 'go' command or whistle, the player will sprint five yards maintaining good hitting position.
- The next group in line will begin the drill.

Coaching Points: Make sure the player never crosses his feet. Quickness is the key to this drill. Challenge them to move as quickly as possible throughout the entire drill. They should maintain a good linebacker position throughout the drill. They should never pick their feet up too far off the ground.

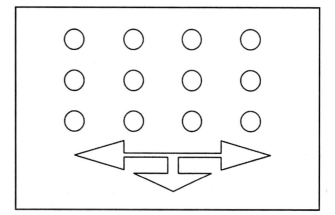

Figure 6-49

Crossover Drill

Objective: To teach the linebacker how to quickly pursue a play that will cover a greater distance; to improve footwork and agility.

Description:

- Form four lines of linebackers facing a coach.

- From a good stance the players in the front row start chopping their feet on the coach's command.

- The coaches will use a football to show the direction the linebacker must move in. If he moves the ball to the player's left, they will crossover to the left; if he moves the ball to their right, they will shuffle right. When he moves the ball back to the center of his body they must keep their feet chopping in place until the next command.

- On the 'go' command or whistle, the player will sprint five yards maintaining good hitting position.

- The next group in line will begin the drill.

Coaching Points: Quickness is the key to this drill. Challenge them to move as quickly as possible throughout the entire drill. They should maintain a good linebacker position throughout the drill.

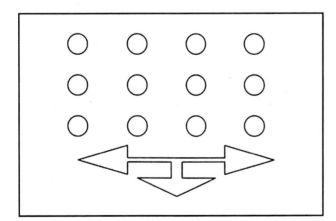

Figure 6-50

Body Position Drills

Objective: To develop the ability of the linebacker to maintain their stance position while running.

Description:

- Form four lines.

- From a good stance they will sprint forward on the coach's whistle. On the next whistle they will freeze.

- They should still be in a good hitting position when they freeze.

- The coach will inspect their hitting position, correct any mistakes, and blow the whistle to continue.

- The next player in line will begin on the next whistle.

Coaching Points: Make sure the players start and finish in the same stance. The players must never stand erect when they are running forward toward the ballcarrier. Check for the following:

- Heads are up and facing forward.

- Knees and waist are slightly bent.

- Arms are hanging loosely with their hands just outside the knees.

- Backs are straight—never arched.

- Shoulders are square.

- Weight is on the balls of their feet.

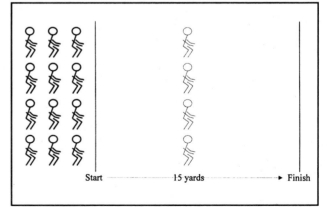

Figure 6-51

Combination Drill

Objective: To teach the linebacker how to change directions quickly; to improve footwork and agility.

Description:

- Form four lines of linebackers facing a coach.

- From a good stance, the players in the front row start chopping their feet on the coach's command.

- The coaches will use a football to show the direction the linebacker must move in. If he moves the ball to the player's left, they will shuffle left; if he moves the ball to their right, they will shuffle right. If he drops it down, they will hit the ground and immediately bounce back to their feet and start chopping again. If he pulls it up high, they will throw their hands up and jump in the air as if they were blocking a pass.

- They must keep their feet chopping throughout the drill.

- The player will make the appropriate movement without crossing his feet.

- On the 'go' command or whistle, the player will sprint five yards maintaining good hitting position.

- The next group in line will begin the drill.

Coaching Points: Make sure the player never crosses his feet. Quickness is the key to this drill. Challenge them to move as quickly as possible throughout the entire drill. They should maintain a good linebacker position throughout the drill.

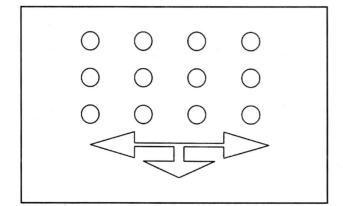

Figure 6-52

Mirror Challenge Drill

Objective: To develop the linebackers' footwork in a competitive environment; to improve agility.

Description:

- Choose two captains to lead the drill and divide the rest of the players into two lines.

- If you have seven players or fewer participating in the drill, choose only one captain and the remainder of the players will form one line in front of him.

- From a good stance, the captain who is out in the front will start chopping his feet. The players in the front row will do the same.

- The captain will shuffle left or right, hit the ground and rebound or shoulder roll left or right. The players in the first row will mirror his movements.

- The captain will make certain everyone is back on their feet and chopping before he makes another move.

- The captain moves in any direction he wishes and performs any of the moves listed above at any time.

- To end the drill the captain will turn his back to his group and sprint five yards.

- The next group in line will begin the drill.

Coaching Points: Make sure you choose the most energetic players as captains. If someone is truly hustling, give him an opportunity to be the captain the next day. Challenge players to keep up with the captain throughout the entire drill. They should maintain a good linebacker position throughout the drill.

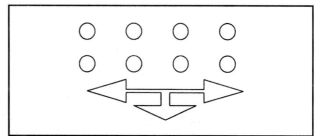

Figure 6-53

Mirror Shuffle Drill

Objective: To develop the linebackers' ability to move laterally without crossing their feet.

Description:

- Two bags are set up five yards apart.
- On one side, a back will run left or right and continue reversing his direction at different times until the whistle blows.
- The linebacker will mirror him maintaining a good hitting position without crossing his feet.
- The coach will blow a second whistle to stop the drill.

Coaching Points: The linebacker must maintain a good linebacker stance throughout the drill. He should never stand up. Check for the following:

- His head is up and facing forward.
- His knees and waist are slightly bent.
- His arms are hanging loosely with his hands just outside the knees.
- His back is straight—never arched.
- His shoulders are square.

Mirror Score Drill

Objective: To develop the linebackers' ability to move laterally without crossing their feet, and then move forward to make a tackle.

Description:

- Four bags will be lined up, creating three running lanes.
- A back will run back and forth on one side until the coach says, "Score," and then he will cut up one of the lanes.
- The linebacker will be shuffling laterally and mirroring the back.
- When he tries to score, he steps up into the run lane and makes proper contact and drives the runner backward, not finishing the tackle.
- The hit will need to be explosive to drive him back.

Coaching Points: The linebacker must maintain a good linebacker stance throughout the drill. He should never stand up. When he steps up to make the tackle he must execute a tackle using all the proper fundamentals.

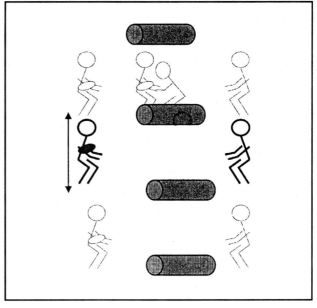

Figure 6-55

Figure 6-54

Shed the Bags Drill

Objective: To teach the linebacker how to shed a blocker while pursuing a ballcarrier.

Description: Line up four bags five yards apart. Three bags should be on one line to simulate blockers and one bag should be offset five yards to simulate the ballcarrier. Form a line in front of bag #1. On the coach's whistle the first player will attack bag #1, shed the bag upon impact, shuffle back two steps and pursue bag #2; he will shed bag #2 and retreat two steps to pursue bag #3, shed bag # 3 and retreat two steps to pursue bag # 1 again; he sheds bag #1 and pursues bag #4, which he will tackle.

Variation: Replace the first three bags with players that will jam the linebacker as he approaches.

Coaching Points: The key to shedding a blocker is keeping the outside shoulder and arm free whenever possible. When they are shedding bags #1 and #2, they should make impact with their right shoulder and arm, using their left arm to push off with. Bags #3 and #4 will be impacted with the left shoulder and forearm. Make sure they apply all the proper fundamentals on the tackle portion of the drill.

Forearm Lift Drill

Objective: To teach the linebackers the technique used to fend off blockers that are coming at them from angles.

Description:

- Form a triangle with three players three yards apart in a two-point stance.
- One player is designated as the defensive lineman while the other two players are blockers.
- On the coach's whistle one of the blockers will start toward the defender.
- The defender will attack the blocker and will drive him away with his inside shoulder and forearm.
- The defender will recoil back to his original spot and then the other blocker will start toward him; he will repeat the separation move with his inside shoulder and forearm.
- He will continue this until he has worked both sides three times.

Coaching Points: Make sure that the defensive lineman is attacking the blocker. He should be the aggressor at the point of impact. He must have a low base and explode up and through the blocker not just into him.

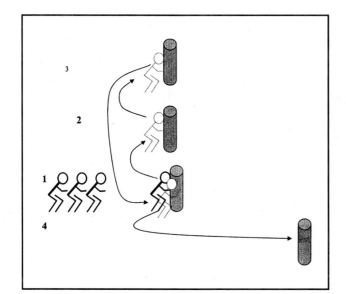

Figure 6-56

Figure 6-57

Side Cut Drill

Objective: To develop the ability of a linebacker to react quickly in a direction, and then step up and make a tackle.

Description:

- Set up two cones five yards apart.

- Lay down two bags next to each other centered between the cones with the ends of the bags on the line between the cones.

- Form two lines on each end of the bags. A ballcarrier line and a linebacker line on the cone end of the bags.

- The ballcarrier will start by setting up a half-yard in front of his end of the bags.

- He will start the drill by picking a side and running toward the line between the cones.

- He must stay inside the cones.

- The linebacker, who is lined up a half-yard behind the other end of the bags, will read the ballcarrier's move, shuffle quickly in that direction, step up and make a driving tackle without bringing the ballcarrier to the ground.

- The ballcarrier is at full speed until impact, when he will then give 75% resistance.

- The players will switch lines after each repetition.

Variation: Make this a competition by going 100% live. The ballcarrier will try to score by crossing the line between the cones, while the linebacker must stop him.

Coaching Points: The linebacker must maintain a proper stance throughout the drill. He must accelerate through the tackle. Emphasize the importance of winning that battle when he makes impact with the runner. He wins that battle by using all the proper tackling fundamentals combined with the instinct to explode through the runner, not into the runner.

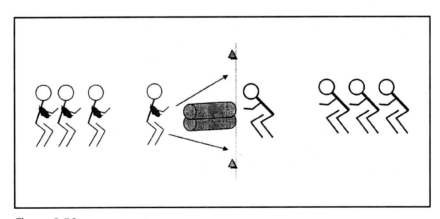

Figure 6-58

Bag Contain Drill

Objective: To teach defensive ends and outside linebackers how to contain the outside running game.

Description:

- Set up three blocking dummies three yards apart and three yards deep.

- A defensive end will line up on the first dummy.

- On the start of the drill he will jam into the bag from the outside half of it driving it back one yard.

- He will release the first dummy and work his way down the line repeating this technique until he gets to the cone.

- Work this drill in both directions.

Coaching Points: You can use coaches or players with blocking shields rather than dummies if you prefer. Emphasize to the defensive contain men that they should never get flanked by anyone. They must work to the outside of every blocker.

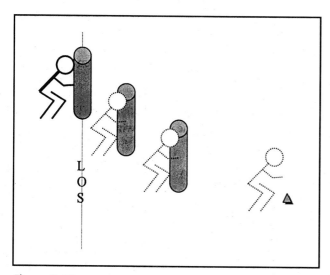

Figure 6-59

End Reach Drill

Objective: To teach the linebacker how to stop the tight end's reach block.

Description:

- Line up a tight end and a linebacker on the end of a line of scrimmage.

- Have a ballcarrier in the backfield. It can be a live ballcarrier or a coach simulating the carry.

- On the start of the drill, the tight end will attempt to reach block the defensive end.

- The ballcarrier will try to run outside the end.

- The defensive end will jam the outside shoulder of the tight end with his inside shoulder and forearm.

- The defensive end will make the tackle on the ballcarrier. He can also just make a thud hit on the ballcarrier or just touch him if it is a coach simulating the carry.

- Repeat the drill to the other side.

Coaching Points: The defensive end must keep his head up and his base should be slightly widened upon impact with the blocker. He should never give ground to the blocker.

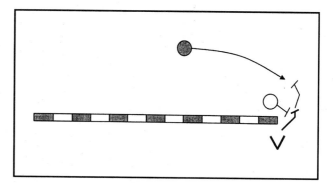

Figure 6-60

Two-Man Contain Drill

Objective: To teach the defensive end or the outside linebacker how to contain the outside running play by working off one block and into the next.

Description:

- Line up a tight end and a defensive end on the end of a line of scrimmage.
- Have a ballcarrier and a lead blocker in the backfield. It can be a live ballcarrier or a coach simulating the carry.
- On the start of the drill the tight end will attempt to reach block the defensive end.
- The ballcarrier will follow his lead block to try to run outside the end.
- The defensive end will jam the outside shoulder of the tight end with his inside shoulder and forearm.

- When he sees the lead blocker coming out of the backfield, he will release from the tight end and jam the outside shoulder of the lead blocker.
- He will try to force the running back all the way to the sideline.
- The running back must try to get outside the end. He is not permitted to cut back in this drill.
- The defensive end will make the tackle on the ballcarrier. He can also just make a thud hit on the ballcarrier or just touch him if it is a coach simulating the carry.
- Repeat the drill to the other side.

Coaching Points: It is imperative that the ballcarrier is stopped from turning the outside corner. You cannot stress the importance of this enough.

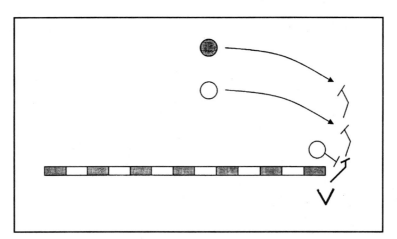

Figure 6-61

Fill the Hole Drill

Objective: To develop the ability of the linebacker to step up into the line of scrimmage and make a driving tackle.

Description:

- Four bags and a cone will be lined up, creating three running lanes and an outside marker.

- A back will run down the line of bags at 75% speed and step up into each running lane and make low impact contact with the LB. He backpedals out of the lane and continues down around the cone.

- The linebacker will be shuffling laterally and mirroring the back.

- When the back enters the lane, he steps up into the run lane and makes proper contact and drives the runner backward. Without finishing the tackle, he continues until he makes the angled tackle at the cone at the end.

- The hit will need to be explosive to drive him back.

Variation: The last tackle beyond the cone can be a full-speed completed tackle.

Coaching Points: Make sure the linebacker employs all the proper stance and footwork fundamentals during the pursuit portions of the drill. Watch all tackling fundamentals during the tackle portions. Stress the initial contact portion of the tackle. The linebacker will shoot his arms around the ballcarrier, never allowing them to wind up. The initial impact with the ballcarrier needs to be explosive enough to drive the ballcarrier back a yard; then he releases him and continues with the drill.

Figure 6-62

Angle Shuffle Drill

Objective: To develop the ability of the linebacker to pursue a ballcarrier through traffic; to improve footwork.

Description:

- Set up four bags on the ground one yard apart and on a 45-degree angle. Place a cone five yards beyond the last bag.

- A linebacker will face forward and shuffle down the line of bags. When he gets past the last bag he will run to the cone using crossover steps and make a thud tackle. He drives through the runner and doesn't complete the tackle.

- A ballcarrier is lined up five yards in front of the last bag. When the tackler gets past the last bag he will take off to the cone. At impact he will give 75% resistance allowing the tackler to drive him back.

- Repeat the drill by switching the cone and start sides, and by facing the other direction.

Variation: You can replace the thud tackle at the end with a live tackle to completion.

Coaching Points: The linebacker must maintain good body position throughout the drill. His head should be up and his eyes focused forward. Make sure that he executes the proper angle tackling techniques at the end of the drill. His head must get across the front of the ballcarrier's body.

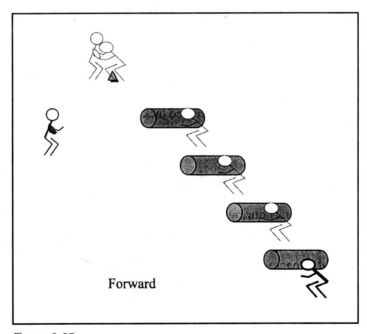

Figure 6-63

Bull in the Ring

Objective: To develop the ability of the linebacker to fend off blockers from all angles in their pursuit of the ballcarrier.

Description:

- Form a circle of players 8 to10 yards in diameter. The players around the perimeter of the circle are designated as blockers.

- A player will enter the center of the circle and he will be the designated linebacker.

- The coach will randomly call out the name of a player who is aligned in the outside circle. That player will charge the linebacker in an attempt to block him.

- The linebacker will use his near shoulder and forearm to fend off the blocker.

- The coach will continue to call out names until he feels the linebacker has had sufficient repetitions.

- After he is finished, he will join the circle as a blocker.

- A new linebacker will be placed in the middle and the drill will be repeated. The drill will continue until every player has had an opportunity to be the linebacker in the middle.

Coaching Points: The linebacker must always keep his outside shoulder free. Make sure that he plants on his front foot just before making contact with the blocker. It should be the same foot as the shoulder. In other words, if he is using his right shoulder and forearm, then he will plant with his right foot, leaving his left shoulder free.

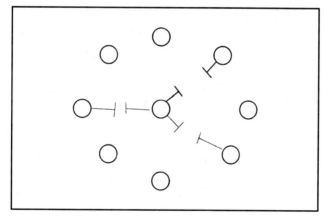

Figure 6-64

Separation Drill

Objective: To develop the ability of the linebacker to get separation from a blocker while in pursuit of a play.

Description:

- Line up three players in a line three yards apart from each other. These players will be designated as blockers.
- Line up a linebacker five yards across from the center blocker.
- A coach will align behind the linebacker.
- To start the drill the coach will point to one of the three blockers who will step up to block the linebacker. After initial contact with the linebacker they will backpedal back to their original position.
- The linebacker will attack, and then separate himself from the blocker as he would in a game situation. He will then backpedal back to his original spot.
- The coach will point to another blocker and the linebacker will repeat the above step.
- The drill will continue until the coach feels the linebacker has had enough repetitions.
- Repeat this drill until every linebacker has had a turn.

Coaching Points: To separate from the blocker in a game-like situation, the linebacker will react as if the play is going outside the blockers on each end and he must stand the center man straight up, assuming the ballcarrier is behind him and has not committed to a side. The following rules would apply to the blockers:

- He would impact the blocker on his left with his right shoulder and forearm.
- He would impact the blocker on his right with his left shoulder and forearm.
- He will jam his palm up into the middle of the center player's chest plate with his arms fully extended.

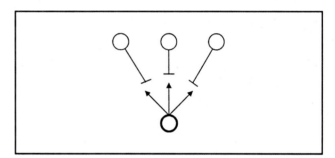

Figure 6-65

Bust the Line Drill

Objective: To develop the linebackers' ability to bust through a double-team while in pursuit of a play.

Description:

- Line up two blockers two feet apart.
- Line up a linebacker three to four yards from the center of the blockers.
- On the coach's command the linebacker will try to bust through the two blockers who will try to stop him from getting through.
- Continue the drill until every player has had an equal number of repetitions.

Coaching Points:

- The linebacker will need to bust through with his shoulder leading the way.
- Since there is no designated side to get through, the linebacker can use whichever shoulder he is most comfortable with.
- Make sure his shoulders are not square to the line of scrimmage upon impact.
- He will have to 'make himself skinny' by turning to one shoulder just before impact.
- He must come from low to high as they make contact.
- He must accelerate upon contact and explode through the blockers.

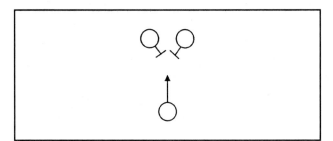

Figure 6-66

Tackling Triangle

Objective: To teach the fundamentals of tackling on an angle.

Description:

- Set up three cones in an equilateral triangle with all cones 10 yards apart.
- Set up a tackling line in the center of two cones.
- Set up a ball carrying line behind the cone that is across from the tackling line.
- On the coach's whistle the ballcarrier will run directly at one of the other cones. When he is contacted by the tackler, he will slow up and give a little ground to the tackler. He must carry the ball in his outside arm.
- The tackler will execute proper tackling techniques approximately two yards in front of the cone the ballcarrier is heading to. He will drive the ballcarrier back for three yards and release him. He does not take him to the ground.
- The player will switch lines between every repetition.

Coaching Points: This drill is run at full speed by both players, although the tackler will not take the ballcarrier to the ground. The ballcarrier will slow down only after impact from the tackler. Make sure the tackler employs all of the proper tackling fundamentals. Stress the importance of the tackler getting his head in front of the runner. His head should slide across the chest of the ballcarrier, still using the football as an aiming point. This drill is run at full speed.

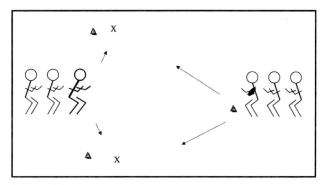

Figure 6-67

Popsicle Drills

Popsicle drills are tackling drills that are performed on a one-man sled, also known as a popsicle. A Popsicle is an excellent tool for teaching tackling and for low impact tackling repetitions. If you plan on getting one of these sleds, make sure it is the appropriate size and weight for your age level.

Pop and Lift Drill

Objective: To teach the tackler the proper fundamentals used during the initial impact of a tackle with an emphasis on driving up and through the ball carrier.

Description:

- Set up a line of tacklers five yards in front of the popsicles.
- The first player in line will be in a two-point stance.
- On the coach's whistle the player will explode up and through the popsicle forcing it to rise up onto the back portion of the sled rails.
- He will release the sled after one second.
- His head should slide to the right of the sled upon impact. Repeat the drill with the head sliding to the left of the sled.

Coaching Points: Make sure that the initial impact of the sled is low and the player drives up and through the sled. This will cause the sled to come off the ground and be driven backwards at the same time. The proper fundamentals of tackling should be employed on every repetition.

- Upon impact, the back should be at a 45-degree angle and will straighten out as the hips come under the shoulders.
- The base will be slightly wider than shoulder width just before impact and footwork will accelerate upon impact.
- His chest must maintain contact with the bag throughout the drill.
- His feet should remain on the ground through the completion of the drill. His hands and arms will shoot around bags and clasp. He should never wind up with his arms.

Figure 6-68

Drive Tackling Drill

Objective: To teach the tackler to keep his feet driving and accelerating through a tackle.

Description:

- Set up a line of tacklers five yards in front of the popsicles.
- The first player in line will be in a two-point stance.
- On the coach's whistle the player will explode up and through the popsicle forcing it to rise up onto the back portion of the sled rails.
- He will then drive the sled back five yards.
- His head should slide to the right of the sled upon impact. Repeat the drill with the head sliding to the left of the sled.

Coaching Points: Emphasize the fact that the tackler must accelerate his footwork while driving the sled back. Make sure that the initial impact of the sled is low and the player drives up and through the sled. This will cause the sled to come off the ground and be driven backwards at the same time. The proper fundamentals of tackling should be employed on every repetition.

- Upon impact the back should be at a 45-degree angle and will straighten out as the hips come under the shoulders.
- The base will be slightly wider than shoulder width just before impact and footwork will accelerate upon impact.
- His chest must maintain contact with the bag throughout the drill.
- His feet should remain on the ground through the completion of the drill.
- His hands and arms will shoot around bags and clasp. He should never wind up with his arms.

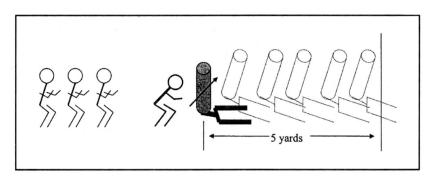

Figure 6-69

Drive and Finish Drill

Objective: To teach the tackler to keep his feet driving and accelerating through a tackle and get the leverage to finish the tackle.

Description:

- Set up a line of tacklers five yards in front of the popsicles.

- The first player in line will be in a two-point stance.

- On the coach's whistle the player will explode up and through the popsicle forcing it to rise up onto the back portion of the sled rails.

- His head should slide to the right of the sled upon impact.

- He will then drive the sled back five yards.

- He will then drive the sled to the ground; it should land on its left side.

- Repeat the drill with the head sliding to the left of the sled; the sled will then go down on its right side.

Coaching Points: Emphasize the fact that the tackler must drive the sled down to the opposite side of his head. His feet should remain on the ground until the sled has been completely turned on its side. The proper fundamentals of tackling should be employed on every repetition.

- Upon impact the back should be at a 45-degree angle and will straighten out as the hips come under the shoulders.

- The base will be slightly wider than shoulder width just before impact and footwork will accelerate upon impact.

- His chest must maintain contact with the bag throughout the drill.

- Feet should remain on the ground through the completion of drill.

- His hands and arms will shoot around bags and clasp. He should never wind up with his arms.

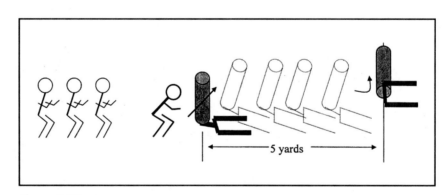

Figure 6-70

Shuffle and Fill Drill

Objective: To teach the tackler to keep his feet driving and accelerating through a tackle.

Description:

- Set up a line of tacklers five yards in front of and five yards to left of the popsicles.
- The first player in line will be in a two-point stance. On the coach's whistle the player will shuffle five yards to the front of the bag, and then attack and explode up and through the popsicle forcing it to rise up onto the back portion of the sled rails.
- He will then drive the sled back five yards.
- Repeat the drill starting five yards back and to the left of the sled.

Coaching Points: The linebacker must employ proper body positioning throughout the drill. Emphasize the fact that the tackler must accelerate his footwork while driving the sled back. Make sure that the initial impact of the sled is low and the player drives up and through the sled. The proper fundamentals of tackling should be employed on every repetition.

- Upon impact the back should be at a 45-degree angle and will straighten out as the hips come under the shoulders.
- The base will be slightly wider than shoulder width just before impact and footwork will accelerate upon impact.
- His chest must maintain contact with the bag throughout the drill.
- His feet should remain on the ground through the completion of the drill. His hands and arms will shoot around bags and clasp. He should never wind up with his arms.

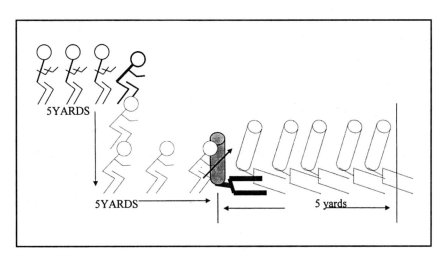

Figure 6-71

Head-to-Head Drill

See Figure 5-42 in Chapter 5.

Pick a Lane Drill

Objective: To develop the ability of the linebacker to read and fill for a ballcarrier who is working his way down the line of scrimmage.

Description:

- Set up four bags two yards apart and parallel to each other.

- Place a cone one yard outside each bag.

- Divide your players up into two lines, linebackers and ballcarriers.

- The ballcarrier will start on the side of the bags with the cones. They will run down the line and cut into any lane just beyond a cone. Once they make any cut they must square up to the line and continue straight forward. They are running full speed until they make contact with the linebacker, at which time they will give 75% resistance as they are driven back.

- The linebackers will mirror the ballcarrier until he makes a move toward the line, at which time they will step up and make a drive tackle on him.

Variation: You can use a live tackle to completion instead of the thud-type tackle. If you do this, you should replace the bags with other soft boundary material to prevent injury.

Coaching Points: The proper body position must be maintained throughout the drill. You must watch all of the tackling fundamentals.

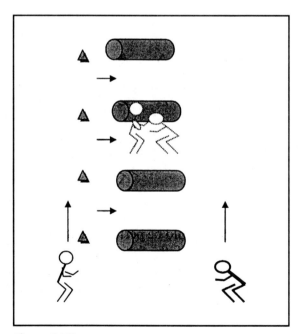

Figure 6-72

Attack the Blocker Drill

Objective: To develop the ability of the linebacker to ward off a blocker while in pursuit of a play.

Description:

- Line up two lines of blockers five yards apart from each other.
- Line up one player five yards across from the center of the blockers.
- To start the drill the player in the right line will roll and get up to try and block the linebacker.
- The linebacker will attack him as he begins his roll; he will jam him back before he has his total balance. He will then look for the man in the other line who will begin as soon as the linebacker makes contact with the other player.
- As soon as he sees him, he will attack him in the same fashion.

- The drill will continue until the coach feels the linebacker has had enough repetitions.
- Repeat this drill until every linebacker has had a turn.

Coaching Points: To separate from the blocker in a game-like situation, the linebacker will react as if the play is going inside the blockers since his next move will be to the man inside him. The following rules would apply to the blockers:

- He would impact the blocker on his left with his left shoulder and forearm.
- He would impact the blocker on his right with his right shoulder and forearm.

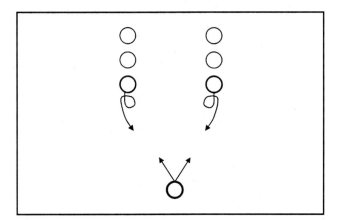

Figure 6-73

Sideline Tackle Drill

Objective: To teach the player how to make tackles at the sideline.

Description:

- Set up a cone five yards from the sideline.

- Set up two lines, a ballcarrier line and a tackler line three to five yards away from the cone and outside the cone.

- On the coach's command the ballcarrier will run between the cone and the sideline. He will try to get beyond the pursuing tackler.

- The tackler will make a sideline tackle without allowing the ballcarrier to cut back into the field of play.

- If the ballcarrier is forced out-of-bounds, the whistle is blown to end that repetition.

- Players will switch lines after every repetition.

- Run this drill from both sidelines.

Coaching Points: The linebacker must take an inside-out pursuit angle toward the ballcarrier. When he is pursuing the runner, he should never let himself get beyond the ball carrier's inside shoulder. At the start of the drill when they are further apart from each other, he should be as much as one yard inside the man as he pursues him. He closes that gap as they get closer to the sideline. The emphasis is to not allow the ballcarrier to cut back into the field of play before going out-of-bounds.

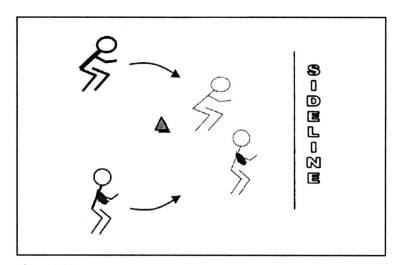

Figure 6-74

Goal Line Tackling Drill

Objective: To teach the linebacker how to make a tackle in goal line or short yardage situations.

Description:

- Set up two boundaries five yards apart with a goal line connecting one end.
- A linebacker will align himself on the goal line. His objective will be to stop the running back from crossing the goal line.
- A running back will be aligned two yards in front of the linebacker. His objective will be to score a touchdown.
- The running back will start the drill whenever he is ready. He will do whatever it takes to score the touchdown.
- The linebacker will start on the back's first movement. He will do whatever it takes to stop the back short of the goal line.

Coaching Points: The key to success for both players is to stay low and keep their legs and feet driving. They will both accelerate at the point of impact. The back will twist, turn, spin, lunge or do whatever he can after the impact to get the football across the goal line before the whistle. The linebacker will try to burst into the football with his facemask if the ballcarrier is running on any type of angle. He will have to explode across the front of his body to accomplish this.

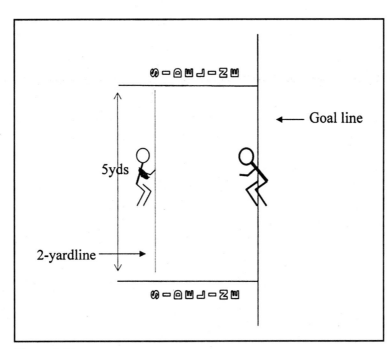

Figure 6-75

Lead Blocker Drill (Dive)

Objective: To teach the linebacker to take on a lead blocker, shed him, and make the tackle.

Description:

- Set up a running lane on the line of scrimmage five yards apart with two cones.
- A linebacker will set up two yards off the line of scrimmage and between the cones.
- A backfield will be set up with a lead blocker and a running back.
- A coach or a quarterback will start the drill on a quick cadence.
- The blocker will come out of his three-point stance and perform a proper lead block on a linebacker.
- A ballcarrier will follow the lead blocker from one to two yards back. He will read the block and make the appropriate cut, and then continue upfield in a north/south direction. Once he makes the cut off his blocker, he may not make any more cuts. He must continue straight up the field.
- The linebacker will shed the blocker and make the tackle.

Coaching Points: The blocker must get low and maintain a properly executed block. Make sure the ballcarrier doesn't make too wide of a cut. The linebacker should try to drive the blocker into the ballcarrier until he has chosen his side. At this time, the linebacker will put himself in a position to make the tackle.

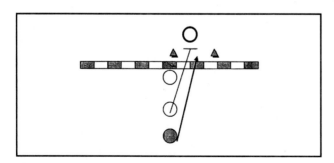

Figure 6-76

Lead Blocker Drill (Sweep)

Objective: To teach the outside linebacker to take on a lead blocker, shed him, and make the tackle.

Description:

- Set up a running lane on the outside of the line of scrimmage five yards apart with two cones.
- A linebacker will set up two yards off the line of scrimmage and between the cones.
- A backfield will be set up with a lead blocker and a running back.
- A coach or a quarterback will start the drill on a quick cadence.
- The blocker will perform a proper lead block on a linebacker.
- A ballcarrier will follow the lead blocker from one to two yards back. He will read the block and make the appropriate cut, and then continue upfield in a north/south direction. Once he makes the cut off his blocker, he may not make any more cuts. He must continue straight up the field.
- The linebacker will shed the blocker and make the tackle.
- Run in both directions.

Coaching Points: The linebacker should try to drive the blocker into the ballcarrier from his outside shoulder until he has chosen his side. At this time, the linebacker will put himself in a position to make the tackle. It is very important that he never gets beat to the outside.

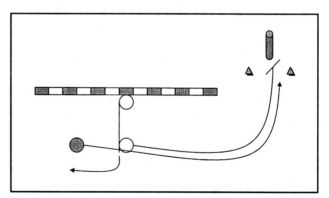

Figure 6-77

Dive Drill

Objective: To teach a linebacker how to read the block of the offensive lineman in a tight area.

Description:

- The ballcarrier will take a dive handoff that simulates a dive action in your offense.

- A blocker that represents a lineman will be in a three-point stance; he will block a linebacker lined up over him.

- There will be a two-yard boundary marker on both sides of the blocker. You can use collapsible cones, pinnies, or half-rounds to create your boundary.

- The defender will try to make a thud tackle on the runner.

Coaching Points: The running back must read the block of his lineman properly. The narrow lanes are there to force him to cut and get back up the field in a north/south direction. The linebacker should attack the lineman as he comes out of his stance. The linebacker must be the aggressor in order to control the blocker.

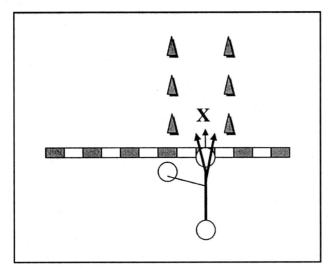

Figure 6-78

Nutcracker Drill

Objective: To teach the linebacker how to read and stop the dive play in a realistic environment.

Description:

- Set up a controlled scrimmage with a defensive lineman lined up over an offensive lineman. There will be a running back lined up three yards behind the lineman.

- The runner will take a dive handoff and make the appropriate cut behind a blocker on the LOS.

- He will then encounter a linebacker immediately after making his cut.

- This will all be performed within a drawn boundary.

Coaching Points: The most important aspect of this drill is preparing the linebacker to make the tackle as close to the line of scrimmage as possible. He will most likely try and buck up through him. The running back's objective should be to gain as much yardage as possible under the situation. The linebacker wants to hold him to as few yards as possible.

- Perform this drill 100% live.

- Make it a competition to see which back gains the most yardage.

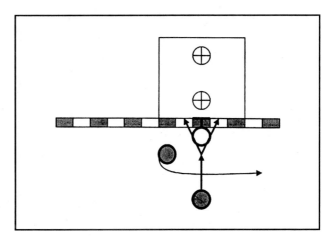

Figure 6-79

Power Scrimmage

Objective: To work on the skills needed by the interior defensive linemen and inside linebackers to stop the inside running game of their opponent.

Description:

- This is a live, full-contact scrimmage in a controlled area.
- Set up an offensive line that includes one center, two guards, and one tackle.
- Set up a backfield with two running backs and a quarterback.
- Set boundary markers one yard on each side of the last man on the end of the line of scrimmage.
- Set up two defensive linemen and two linebackers in your teams' defensive alignment.
- The offense should run interior running plays including dives, leads, counters, traps, and sneaks.
- The defense should stay in a base alignment, reading and reacting to the plays.

Coaching Points: Have enough coaches available to monitor every player. You can use a coach as the quarterback if you prefer. Make the drill a competition. Get both sides of the ball playing at an intense level.

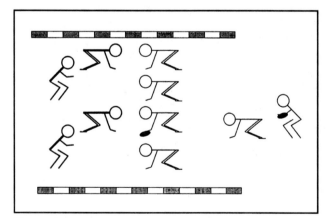

Figure 6-80

Break for the Ball Drill

Objective: To teach the player the proper way to break for the football when it is thrown.

Description:

- Form four lines five yards apart.
- The first player in every line will turn and face the coach.
- On the whistle they will sprint backwards keeping their head up and their eyes focused on the coach.
- The coach will throw a football to a player in a random direction after the players have backpedaled six to eight yards.
- The player will break for the ball.
- If one of the players catches it, he will tuck the ball away and sprint 10 yards down the field as if he had intercepted a pass.

Coaching Points: Make sure the player is using the proper fundamentals when he is backpedaling. They must all sprint to the ball. Once the ball is in the air, they should focus only on the ball.

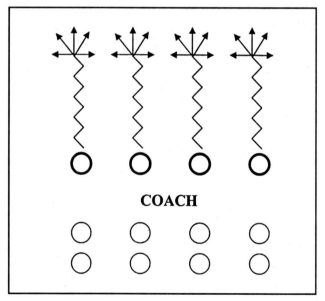

Figure 6-81

Interception Drill

Objective: To teach the player the proper way to make an interception.

Description:

- Form a line next to the coach.
- The first player in line will line up five yards from the coach, and then turn and face him.
- On the whistle he will sprint backwards keeping his head up and his eyes focused on the coach.
- The player will backpedal and break in a predetermined direction.
- The coach will throw a football after the player makes his break.
- The player should catch the ball, tuck it away, yell and sprint 10 yards down the field as if he had intercepted a pass. You can choose any word you would like him to yell.

Coaching Points: Make sure the player is using the proper fundamentals when he is backpedaling. Once the ball is in the air, he should focus only on the ball. It is important that the player tucks the ball away very quickly. He must yell as loud as he can to alert his teammates that he has intercepted the ball. Whatever word you have him yell, the team should recognize that this word means the ball was intercepted. Be consistent.

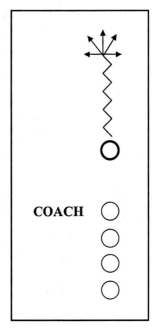

Figure 6-82

Defensive Backs

Defensive backs are also known as cornerbacks, safeties, strong safeties, and free safeties. These players have a 'pass first' mentality. Their first steps are usually two steps backward while they are reading and reacting to the play. They must be great openfield tacklers. Most defensive drills and skills taught in the defensive back stations at practice should be geared to open-field tacklers and pursuit angles. Pass coverage skills are a must.

The skills required are the same for linebackers. Alignment and assignment will be the big differences. They need to be able to shed blockers and make tackles.

A defensive back should never allow a runner to cut back on him in the open field. He must maintain a pursuit angle that will keep him on a collision course with the runner, but at the same time take away his cutback lane. He shouldn't get back on his heels; he should continue to attack and pursue.

Stance

The defensive back's stance must be very balanced. He needs to be able to move in any direction. He has to be 'light on his feet.' His feet should not be planted into the ground. The basic stance fundamentals are:

- Feet are spread at shoulder width.
- Knees are flexed slightly with the hips.
- Weight is on the balls of feet.
- Back is at about a 45-degree angle.
- Arms and hands are in front of knees and ready.
- Shoulders are parallel to the LOS.
- Eyes are focused.

Keys

The keys for defensive backs can vary greatly depending on the formation of the offense. The one constant for a defensive back is the tight end, if one exists. If he blocks to his outside, the assumption would be that there will either be a running play inside or he is pass blocking. Once this type of play is read, the defensive back must then read down the line of scrimmage until he finds the ball. If the tight end tries to hook or reach block, then the play is likely going outside.

Alignment

The alignment is dependent largely on what type of defense your team is running. The base defense is shown in Figure 6-83. This is a 5-2 defense, which means there are five linemen, two linebackers, and four defensive backs. The defensive backs consist of two cornerbacks, a strong safety, and a free safety.

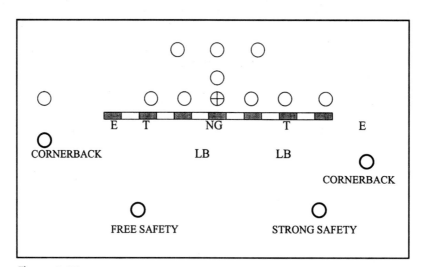

Figure 6-83

Assignment

A defensive back must have a 'pass first' mentality. This means that a defensive back should always assume the play is going to be a pass. As soon as he reads a running play he will put himself in a position to make a tackle. The defensive back's initial steps should be backwards. Assignments will be covered in the following run/pass responsibility sections.

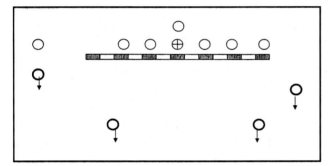

Figure 6-84

Run Responsibility

Movement is the key for a defensive back. They must be ready to move in or change directions at any time. Knowing when to break for the ballcarrier is also a key element for a defensive back. As a basic rule, defensive backs will usually be called on to close down a running lane. In Figure 6-85, there is a defensive end in place to turn the play in, which would create a running lane inside him.

In this case, there is a cornerback aligned outside this area. He will pursue the ballcarrier from the outside inward. He needs to be aware of the possibility of the runner to get outside the running lane. He will always close in the ballcarrier as if he has outside responsibility. If the man were to get outside him, he would have the entire sideline to cut up into.

The safety in Figure 6-85 is sealing the lane from the middle of the field. He will pursue the ballcarrier from the inside outward. He must never over pursue the ballcarrier which would open up the entire middle of the field. He will close in on the

ballcarrier in the same fashion an inside linebacker would. He would keep a one- to two-yard inside relationship that would reduce as he closes in on the runner.

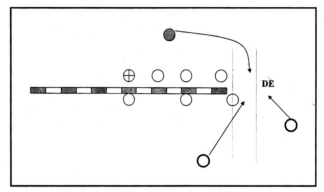

Figure 6-85

In Figure 6-86, the defensive back is pursuing a ballcarrier that has outflanked him to the sideline. In this situation, he is trying to force him all the way to the sideline without giving him an opportunity to cut back into the field. He does this by pursuing him on an angle that puts him just far enough inside him that he can't cut back, and yet not far enough inside to allow him to get outside him. This will likely force him out-of-bounds or the linebacker will make the tackle sometime before reaching the sideline. By stringing this play out to the sideline, it will allow other defenders to recover and pursue the ballcarrier. If the defensive back happens to miss the tackle, there will likely be other defenders in a position to make the tackle.

Shedding Blockers

The first thing a defensive back should do is try to avoid blockers; if he can't, then he should square up to his blocker. If the blocker comes at him high, he should get under him. He should jam him while he is shuffling toward the play, shake him, and make the tackle. If he comes at him low, he keeps his feet moving and jams down on his shoulders, pushing him into the ground as he continues to pursue the ballcarrier.

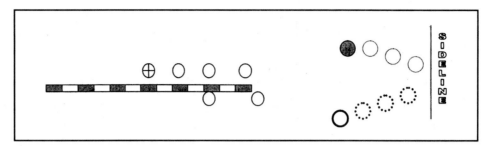

Figure 6-86

The defensive back must never turn his back to the play. He should never spin to get off a block. Instead, he should work to the outside of the block even if he has to give up some ground to the runner. He should never take the easy way to the ballcarrier. The easy way usually means it is too late to catch up to him. Figure 6-87 is an illustration of this concept.

Pass Responsibility

Pass responsibility can vary greatly. The base coverage will vary in different defensive schemes. The coverage package called by a defense will also change the responsibilities of your defensive backs.

Defenses that feature two inside linebackers will often use the base zone package shown in Figure 6-88, which is a base 40 defense. This example features both inside and outside linebackers. Inside LB's have hitch/curl responsibilities in the zone defense, while the outside linebackers are responsible for the out/flat routes.

The defensive backs in this defense are the two cornerbacks and the one safety. This particular base defense is a cover 3 zone package. This is a 3 deep zone. The cornerbacks are responsible for the deep outside third of the field and the safety is responsible for the middle third of the field.

Figure 6-89 is an example of a base 5-2 defense in a cover 2 zone coverage package. This means that it is a 2 deep zone. The safeties, in this case, are each responsible for one deep half of the field. The cornerbacks have out responsibility on each side.

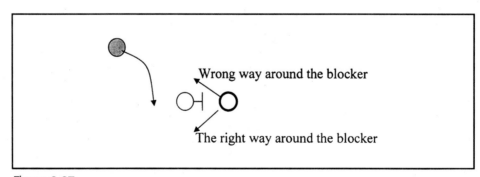

Figure 6-87

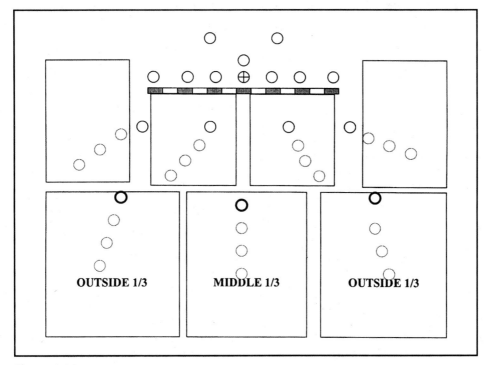

Figure 6-88

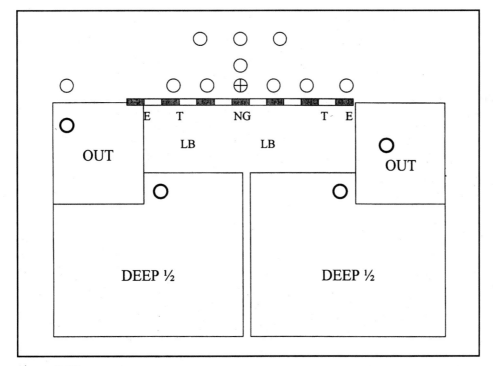

Figure 6-89

Defensive Back Drills

Backpedal Drill

Objective: To teach the defensive backs the proper way to run backwards.

Description:

- Form four lines facing a marker 10 yards away.
- The first player in every line will turn and face the coach.
- On the whistle they will sprint 10 yards backwards keeping their heads up and their eyes focused on the coach.

Coaching Points: Running backwards requires the same body movements as running forward; they are just performed in the opposite direction. The following skills must be emphasized to the defensive backs:

- Bend at the knees and waist.
- Place your weight on the balls of your feet.
- Bend your arms at a 90-degree angle and swing them in a pendulum motion as you do when you run forward.
- Pull your body over your feet as you step backwards.

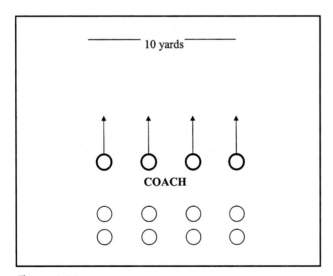

Figure 6-90

Backpedal and Break 45 Drill

Objective: To teach the defensive backs the proper way to break out of backpedaling to cover a man or break on the ball at a 45-degree angle.

Description:

- Form four lines.
- The first player in every line will turn and face the coach.
- On the whistle they will sprint backwards keeping their heads up and their eyes focused on the coach.
- The coach will be holding a football in front of his chest. When he pulls it up as if to throw, the player will break on a 45-degree angle to the coach's right.
- Repeat the drill with the player breaking 45 degrees to the coach's left.

Variation: Have the coach throw the ball after the player breaks out of his backpedal.

Coaching Points: Make sure the player is using the proper fundamentals when he is backpedaling. The moment he breaks on his 45-degree angle he must sprint full speed in that direction.

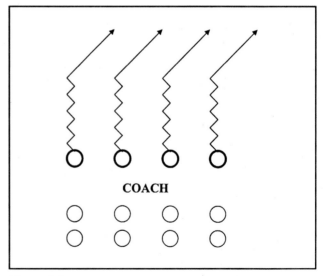

Figure 6-91

Backpedal and Break 90 Drill

Objective: To teach the defensive backs the proper way to break out of backpedaling to cover a man or break on the ball at a 90-degree angle.

Description:

- Form four lines.
- The first player in every line will turn and face the coach.
- On the whistle they will sprint backwards keeping their heads up and their eyes focused on the coach.
- The coach will be holding a football in front of his chest. When he pulls it up as if to throw, the player will break on a 90-degree angle to the coach's right.
- Repeat the drill with the player breaking 90 degrees to the coach's left.

Variation: Have the coach throw the ball after the player breaks out of his backpedal.

Coaching Points: Make sure the player is using the proper fundamentals when he is backpedaling. The moment he breaks on his 90-degree angle he must sprint full speed in that direction.

Backpedal and Fly Drill

Objective: To teach the defensive backs the proper way to break out of backpedaling to cover a man who is trying to get beyond him with a fly pattern.

Description:

- Form four lines.
- The first player in every line will turn and face the coach.
- On the whistle they will sprint backwards keeping their heads up and their eyes focused on the coach.
- The coach will be holding a football in front of his chest. When he pulls it up as if to throw, the player will break into a sprint as if a receiver were trying to run a fly pattern past him on his right side.
- Repeat the drill with the player breaking his left.

Variation: Have the coach throw the ball after the player breaks out of his backpedal.

Coaching Points: Make sure the player is using the proper fundamentals when he is backpedaling. The moment he breaks, he must turn in the direction of the receiver and sprint full speed. He would keep his eyes on the receiver at all times after he breaks with him.

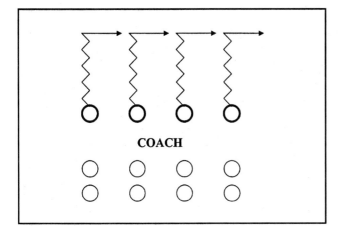

Figure 6-92

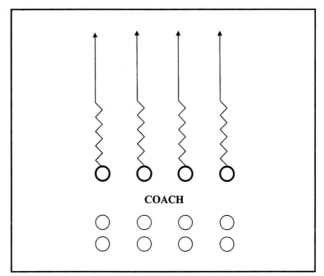

Figure 6-93

Change Direction Drill

Objective: To teach the defensive backs the proper way to change directions when they are running, without turning their back to the play.

Description:

- Form four lines facing a marker 40 yards away.
- The first player in every line will turn and face the coach.
- On the whistle they will sprint 40 yards keeping their heads up and their eyes focused on the coach.
- They will be looking back at the coach from their right side at the start. This means they will be looking at the coach over their right shoulder as
- they are running.
- The coach will pull a football from one side of his body to the other, which is when the runner will turn and look from his left side. He will never turn his back to the coach.
- The coach will have them turn at least four times during their 40-yard run.

Coaching Points: If you were to break down the footwork in this drill, the steps for the defensive back are as follows: one, if he is looking over his right shoulder and wants to turn, he will step forward and pivot on his left foot; two, he will open his hips and shoulders to the coach by stepping around with the right foot, and then crossover step with the left. He should be looking at the coach over his left shoulder.

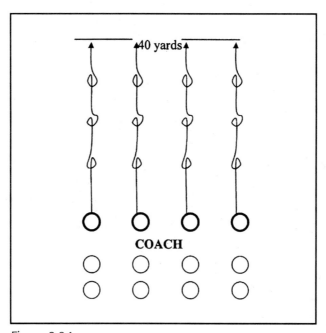

Figure 6-94

Turn For the Ball Drill

Objective: To teach the player to turn and catch a ball that is thrown behind him.

Description:

- Form two lines just inside the hash marks.
- The player will run a 12- to 15-yard flag pattern. If he is a DB, he is simulating the coverage of a man running a flag pattern.
- The quarterback or coach will throw the pass to the wrong side of the player.
- As soon as the player makes his cut, he must immediately look for the ball. He will adjust to the throw and make the catch.
- After he catches the ball he will tuck it away and sprint five yards upfield.
- Switch lines after each reception.

Variation: You can vary the patterns being run by the player.

Coaching Points: Once the player turns to look for the ball, he must never turn his back to it. He must adjust his footwork to turn his body and maintain sight of the ball, much like an outfielder does when he is tracking a fly ball.

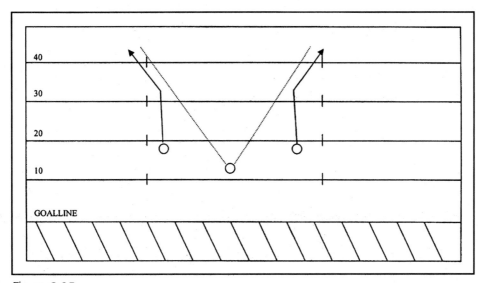

Figure 6-95

Break For the Ball Drill

See Figure 6-82.

Interception Drill

See Figure 6-83.

Coverage Skelly

Objective: To work on pass coverage skills.

Description:

- Form two receiver lines just inside the hash marks.
- The first player in line will move out five yards and turn and face the next man in line. He will be the defensive back.
- The receiver will run a pattern given to him by the coach or QB.
- The quarterback or coach will throw the pass to the receiver.
- The defensive back will break for the ball to intercept it. If he is not in a position to get the ball, he will thud tackle the receiver as soon as he touches the ball.

- If he intercepts the ball, he will tuck it away and sprint five yards upfield.
- After each repetition, the receiver will become the defensive back for the same line he came out of and the defensive back will go to the back of the other line.

Coaching Points: This drill should be run simulating actual pass patterns. If you have a scouting report of your opponent, use their patterns. The defensive back should never let any receiver get past him. If he has an opportunity to get to the ball, he must take it.

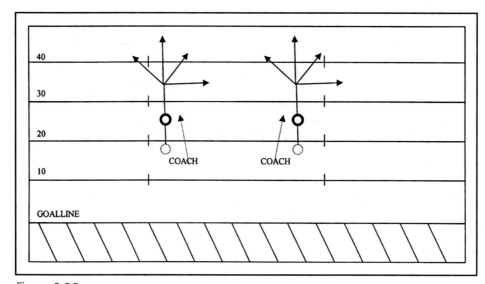

Figure 6-96

Strip the Ball Drill

Objective: To teach the defensive player to strip the ball from the receiver as he makes the catch; to develop the ability to complete the tackle if the ball is not stripped.

Description:

- Form two receiver lines just inside the hash marks.

- The first player in line will move out five yards and turn and face the next man in line. He will be the defensive back that will cover the receiver.

- The receiver will run a 12- to 15-yard flag pattern.

- The quarterback or coach will throw the pass to the receiver.

- As soon as the receiver touches the ball, the defender will attempt to strip the ball with his outside arm.

- If he is unsuccessful, he will complete the tackle.

- Switch lines after each reception.

Variation: You can vary the patterns being run by the receiver.

Coaching Points: The emphasis of this drill should be on stripping the ball. The player should reach around the receiver with his outside arm and try to make contact with the ball. His inside hand should be in contact with the receiver as soon as he touches the ball. This hand will be the stabilizer to allow him to smack at the ball, and yet still be in a good position to make the tackle if he is unsuccessful.

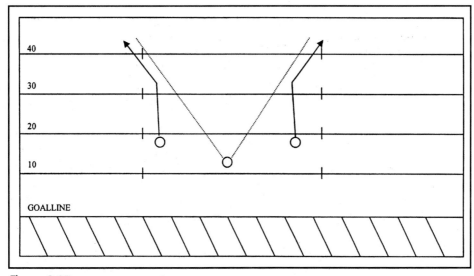

Figure 6-97

Footwork Drills

These footwork drills emphasize all the elements that will be used by defensive backs in their pursuit of the play.

The following drills are the same ones used by the linebackers. They were outlined earlier in this chapter:

- High Knee Step-overs (Figure 6-43)
- Side Step-overs (Figure 6-44)
- Shuffle Steps (Figure 6-45)
- Around the Bag Drill (Figure 6-46)

Tackling Triangle

Objective: To teach the fundamentals of tackling on an angle.

Description:

- Set up three cones in an equilateral triangle with all cones 10 yards apart.
- Set up a tackling line in the center of two cones.
- Set up a ball carrying line behind the cone that is across from the tackling line.

- On the coach's whistle the ballcarrier will run directly at one of the other cones. When he is contacted by the tackler, he will slow up and give a little ground to the tackler. He must carry the ball in his outside arm.
- The tackler will execute proper tackling techniques approximately two yards in front of the cone the ballcarrier is heading to. He will drive the ballcarrier back for three yards and release him. He does not take him to the ground.
- Players will switch lines between every repetition.

Coaching Points: This drill is run at full speed by both players; the ballcarrier will slow down only after impact from the tackler. Make sure the tackler employs all of the proper tackling fundamentals. Stress the importance of the tackler getting his head in front of the runner. His head should slide across the chest of the ballcarrier, still using the football as an aiming point.

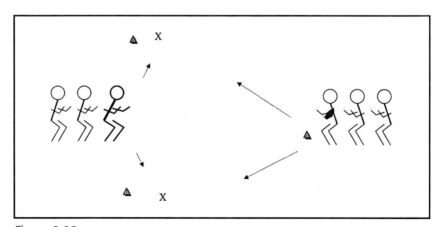

Figure 6-98

Popsicle Drills

Popsicle drills are tackling drills that are performed on a one-man sled, also known as a popsicle. The following popsicle drills were outlined earlier in this chapter:

• Pop and Lift Drill (Figure 6-68)
• Drive Tackling Drill (Figure 6-69)
• Drive and Finish Drill (Figure 6-70)
• Lead Blocker Drill (Sweep) (Figure 6-78)
• Sideline Tackle Drill (Figure 6-75)
• Goal Line Tackling Drill (Figure 6-76)
• Separation Drill (Figure 6-65)
• Attack the Blocker Drill (Figure 6-74)

Openfield Tackle Drill

Objective: To develop the defensive players' ability to make tackles in the openfield.

Description:

• To set up this drill, lay a bag parallel to a line on the field. Set up sideline markers starting five yards from each end of the bag that widen as they gain depth. If you use cones as markers, make sure they are the soft, collapsible type.

• Set up a defender four yards from the bag on the cone side.

• A line of ballcarriers will be four yards from the bag on the other side.

• The first ballcarrier will start the drill by taking off in either direction and try to get past the defender.

• The defender will react to the ballcarrier's move and tackle him for as little gain as possible.

• After the repetition, the ballcarrier will become the defender while the defender will go to the end of the ballcarrier line.

Coaching Points: The defender must pursue the ballcarrier from the inside out. He will begin the drill one yard inside the ballcarrier and close that gap as he gets closer to him. This will take away his cutback lane. He should force the player to the sideline and either make the tackle there or force him out-of-bounds.

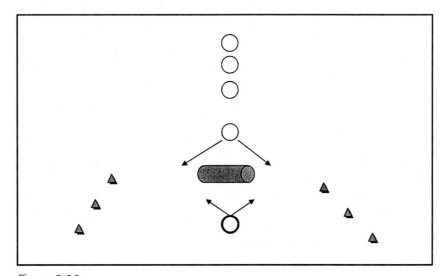

Figure 6-99

Angle Pursuit Drill

Objective: To teach the defender how to recognize the proper angle of pursuit.

Description:

- In the center of the field, line up a ballcarrier three yards behind the ball. Line up a defender three yards off the line of scrimmage and three yards outside the midline.

- You can use other markers if you don't have a lined field.

- The ballcarrier will run beyond the hash mark and angle toward the sideline and up the field. He will never cut back.

- The defender will count one second after the ballcarrier's initial movement, and then he will take the proper angle of pursuit and tackle him. If you prefer, the defender can start the drill immediately without any count.

- Repeat the drill to the other side of the field.

Coaching Points: When you first start doing this drill, you will need to do extra repetitions until the defender can judge the proper angle to pursue the ballcarrier. It is not important how many yards are yielded to the runner. It is more important to take an angle that will give you an opportunity to make the tackle.

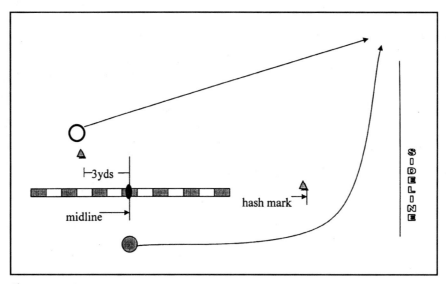

Figure 6-100

Secondary Angle Pursuit Drill

Objective: To teach the defensive secondary how to recognize the proper angle of pursuit.

Description:

- In the center of the field line up your defensive secondary.

- You can use other markers if you don't have a lined field.

- The ballcarrier will be lined up three yards behind the line and three yards outside your widest defender.

- The ballcarrier will run beyond the hash mark and angle toward the sideline and up the field. He will never cut back.

- The defender will count one second after the ballcarrier's initial movement, and then he will take the proper angle of pursuit and tackle him. If you prefer, the defender can start the drill immediately without any count.

- Repeat the drill to the other side of the field.

Coaching Points: When you first start doing this drill, you will need to do extra repetitions until the defenders can judge the proper angle to pursue the ballcarrier. It is not important how many yards are yielded to the runner. It is more important to take an angle that will give you an opportunity to make the tackle.

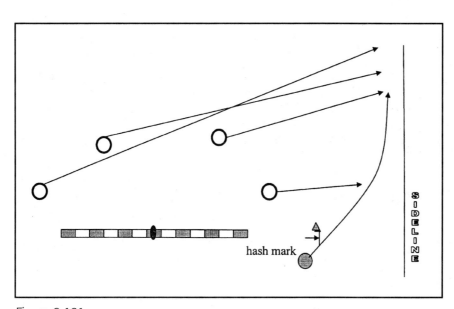

Figure 6-101

CHAPTER 7

The Defensive Playbook

This chapter describes different ways to structure your defense. The emphasis will be on the base alignment and assignment of the players. Every defense will have different stunts and blitzes that will be diagramed and explained. The base coverage for the secondary will be outlined as well.

4-4 Defense

The 4-4 defense is a cover 3 (3 deep zone coverage) defense that employs four linebackers. This is a gap control defense that is very strong against the run. The coverage is very basic and works well against many types of passing attacks. It shows some weaknesses against pass-oriented teams that have a tendency to spread the field and flood a zone.

Many different versions of the 4-4 defense exist. This is a defense that can have many different looks. This section covers a base alignment and shows the different alignment calls that you can use in this defense. The coverage packages will be described last.

Even Defense

Figure 7-1 is an example of the base alignment for the even 4-4 defense.

The names of the positions can be anything you choose. Some coaches will come up with a name for every linebacker and defensive back. For instance, many coaches call their inside linebackers Mike and Will. Mike is the strongside linebacker while Will is the weakside linebacker. Mike and Will may swap alignments depending on the strength of the offensive formation. Many coaches will always leave Mike on the left and Will on the right. There are advantages and disadvantages to both. In this defense, the linebackers will remain on their respective sides. The abbreviations used are as follows:

E = End

T = Tackle

B = Linebacker (inside)

S = Sam (strongside outside linebacker)

R = Rover (weakside outside linebacker)

C = Corner

FS = Free Safety

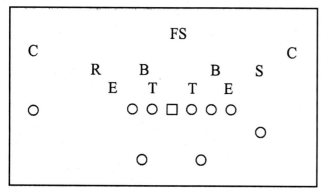

Figure 7-1

Even Alignments (Cover 3)

(Refer to the technique charts outlined in Chapter 3, Figure 3-88).

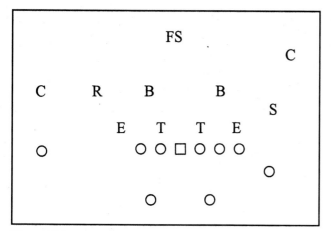

Figure 7-2

Defensive Ends:

versus tight end: 6 technique

versus wide receiver: ghost 6 technique

Defensive Tackles: 2 technique

Inside Linebackers: 40 technique—Heels should be 4.5 yards off the ball.

Outside Linebackers:

versus tight end: 2 x 2 yards off tight end

versus wide receiver or split end: Five yards off the line of scrimmage, split the difference

between the end man on the line of scrimmage and the wide player

versus wingback: outside shade of wing, two yards off the line of scrimmage.

Corners:

versus tight end: seven yards off and three yards wide

versus wide out: five yards off and 1yd wide

Free Safety: Twelve yards from the ball.

Even Base Responsibilities Versus Run and Pass (Cover 3)

(Refer to the gap and coverage charts outlined in Chapter 3, Figure 3-87).

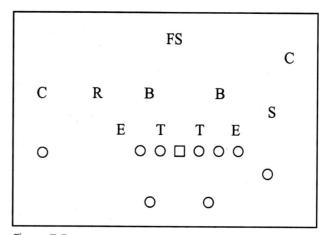

Figure 7-3

Defensive Ends:

versus run: C gap

versus pass: Pass rush, aim for outside ear of QB

Defensive Tackles:

versus run: A gap

versus pass: Pass rush, aim for outside ear of QB

Inside Linebackers:

versus run: B gap

versus pass: On TE and flanker side, hook to curl responsibility. On single receiver side, curl responsibility

Outside Linebackers:

versus run: D gap, contain responsibility, turn everything inside.

versus pass: curl to flat responsibility

Corners:

versus run: Outside support

versus pass: Deep one-third of the field

Free Safety:

versus run: Alley support

versus pass: Deep middle of the field; never allow anyone to get deeper than you.

Even Stunts and Blitzes

Figure 7-4 and Figure 7-5 are stunts and blitzes that can be called from the even package of the 4-4 defense. Although a name is attached to each one, you can call them anything you wish. All diagrams will show the alignment technique for the linemen and the linebackers that are involved in the stunt/blitz called. Remember 'S' is for the Sam (left) outside linebacker and 'R' is for the Rover (right) linebacker.

Coaches, teach your players the following: Stunting linemen should never loop around a blocker. The proper technique is to drive through the stuntside shoulder of the blocker you are aligned on. You should aim for a point that is one yard deep in the backfield, find the ball, and pursue. Never get deeper than the ball. Blitzing linebackers should not give any indication for the hole they are blitzing until the ball is snapped. The exception to this rule is when you see the word 'now' after the call which means the linebacker will align himself on the line of scrimmage right over top of the gap they will shoot.

Strength Call: Many stunts will be called to the strongside or the weakside of a formation. This is why the strongside of the offensive alignment must be identified on every play. The word 'rip' will be used when the strength is to the right side of the defense. And the word 'liz' will be used when the strength is to the left side of the defense.

Note: All examples are shown from a 'liz' (left) call. Reverse responsibilities for a 'rip' (right) call.

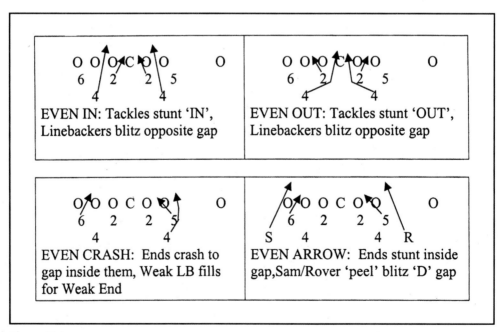

Figure 7-4

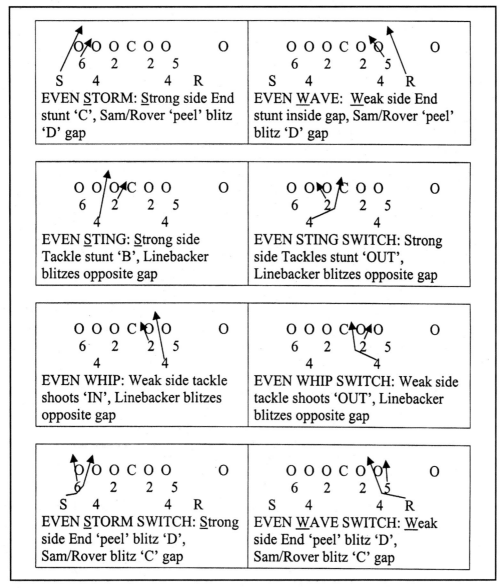

EVEN STORM: Strong side End stunt 'C', Sam/Rover 'peel' blitz 'D' gap	EVEN WAVE: Weak side End stunt inside gap, Sam/Rover 'peel' blitz 'D' gap
EVEN STING: Strong side Tackle stunt 'B', Linebacker blitzes opposite gap	EVEN STING SWITCH: Strong side Tackles stunt 'OUT', Linebacker blitzes opposite gap
EVEN WHIP: Weak side tackle shoots 'IN', Linebacker blitzes opposite gap	EVEN WHIP SWITCH: Weak side tackle shoots 'OUT', Linebacker blitzes opposite gap
EVEN STORM SWITCH: Strong side End 'peel' blitz 'D', Sam/Rover blitz 'C' gap	EVEN WAVE SWITCH: Weak side End 'peel' blitz 'D', Sam/Rover blitz 'C' gap

Figure 7-5

Note about the peel blitz: When blitzing from the outside, the LB must pursue toward the outside shoulder of the nearest back in the backfield, never allowing anyone to outflank him at any time. He should make contact with anyone trying to leave the backfield on his side.

Even Option Responsibilities

The option responsibilities for the even package are listed by position:

• Tackles

Tackles always have dive responsibility.

• Ends

The defensive ends have dive to QB responsibilities. His responsibility will be determined by the block of the tight end or the offensive tackle if he is aligned on the split end side of the offensive alignment. If he is on the tight end side, he reads the tight end's block. If the tight end blocks down, he will take the dive. If the tight end were to on block or release off the line of scrimmage, he would have QB responsibility.

• Outside Linebackers

The outside linebacker's first responsibility is to force the QB to pitch the ball. He will work closely with the defensive end. If the defensive end is in a position to get to the QB, he will close in on the QB from the outside in, stopping his ability to pitch yet getting in a position to assist the defensive end. If the defensive end vacates his area for the dive, the outside linebacker must work the QB in a way that will require him to pitch the ball, yet still keep himself in a position to pursue the pitch man by forcing him as far outside as possible.

• Inside Linebackers

The inside linebackers have to check everything from dive to QB to pitch. Their first read is dive. If a teammate closes the dive, then they work down to the QB. If the QB pitches, they must be in a position to pursue him from the inside out, ready for a cutback.

• Corners

The corner will have outside support on the pitch man. He will always have contain responsibility, never allowing the play to get outside him.

• Free Safety

The free safety is the alley player. He has QB to pitch responsibility.

Stack Package

The stack package has the four linebackers stacked two yards behind the correlating defensive linemen. The exception would be on a split end or wing side of the offense, where the outside linebacker will make the same alignment adjustment as in the even package. In fact, this way is identical to the even package except the alignment of the linebackers. This package will give another look to the offense and cause confusion in the blocking schemes of the offense.

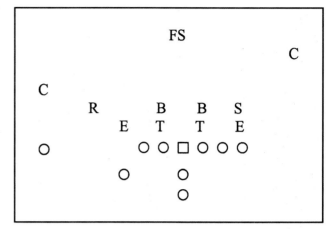

Figure 7-6

Defensive Ends:

    versus tight end: 6 technique

    versus wide receiver: ghost 6 technique

Defensive Tackles: 2 technique

Inside Linebackers: 20 technique–stacked two yards behind tackle.

Outside Linebackers:

    versus tight end: Stacked two yards behind end.

    versus wide receiver or split end: Five yards off the line of scrimmage; split the difference between the end man on the line of scrimmage and the wide player

    versus wingback: Outside shade of wing, two yards off the line of scrimmage.

Corners:

    versus tight end: seven yards off and three yards wide

    versus wide out: Five yards off and one yard wide

Free Safety: Twelve yards from the ball.

Stack Stunts and Blitzes

This is the type of defensive package that encourages a lot of stunting and blitzing. The key to this defense is to mix up the calls and keep the offense off balance. All stunts and blitzes in the even package can be employed in the stack version.

Figure 7-7 shows a list of stunts and blitzes that are very effective from the stack defense.

In the stunts shown in Figure 7-7, every lineman was involved. You can take this a step further by labeling each lineman. For instance, if you number them 1-4 and the left end is #1, you can stunt just that player by calling his number and a command; '1 gap in' would have the left end stunt the inside gap. You can mix this call up by calling out more than one person at a time. If you decide to do this, you can label the corresponding linebackers 1-4 so that there will be no confusion when stunts or blitzes are called.

The blitzes shown in Figure 7-8 were accomplished by simply calling the linebacker's name and the direction of the gap he is stunting. The linebacker must tap the hip of the linemen in front of him, which indicates the gap direction the linebacker will blitz. This also notifies the lineman that he must stunt the opposite gap. Following is a list of other stunt combinations using the same principles listed in Figure 7-8.

- Sam Out: Sam blitzes the outside or D gap and the end stunts the C gap.

- Rover Out: Rover blitzes the outside or D gap and the end stunts the C gap.

- Sam In: Sam blitzes the C gap and the end stunts the D gap.

- Rover In: Rover blitzes the C gap and the end stunts the D gap.

Note: If you call a Sam/Rover In and they end up on a split end side, the stunt should be called off automatically. Sam/Rover will yell, "Off, off."

Combination Blitzes: Call out any combination of linebackers and they will execute their stunts using all the same principles listed previously. Following is a list of possible calls:

- Sam and Will Out
- Mike in-Will out
- All out
- Mike and Will in
- All in

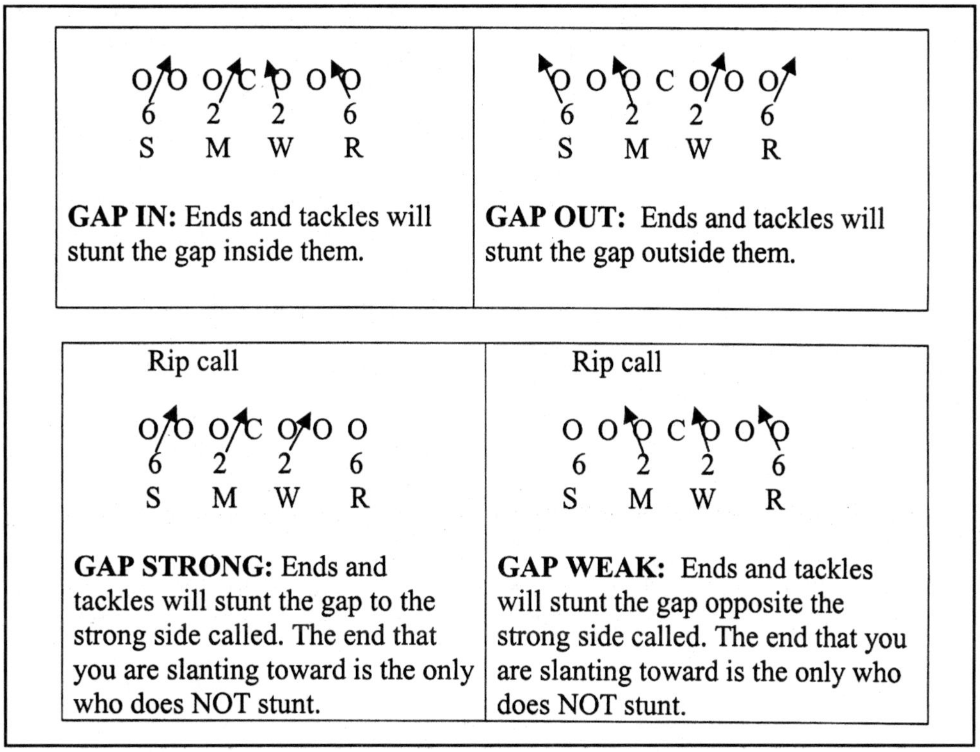

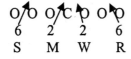

GAP IN: Ends and tackles will stunt the gap inside them.

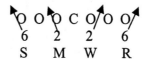

GAP OUT: Ends and tackles will stunt the gap outside them.

Rip call

6 2 2 6
S M W R

GAP STRONG: Ends and tackles will stunt the gap to the strong side called. The end that you are slanting toward is the only who does NOT stunt.

Rip call

6 2 2 6
S M W R

GAP WEAK: Ends and tackles will stunt the gap opposite the strong side called. The end that you are slanting toward is the only who does NOT stunt.

Figure 7-7

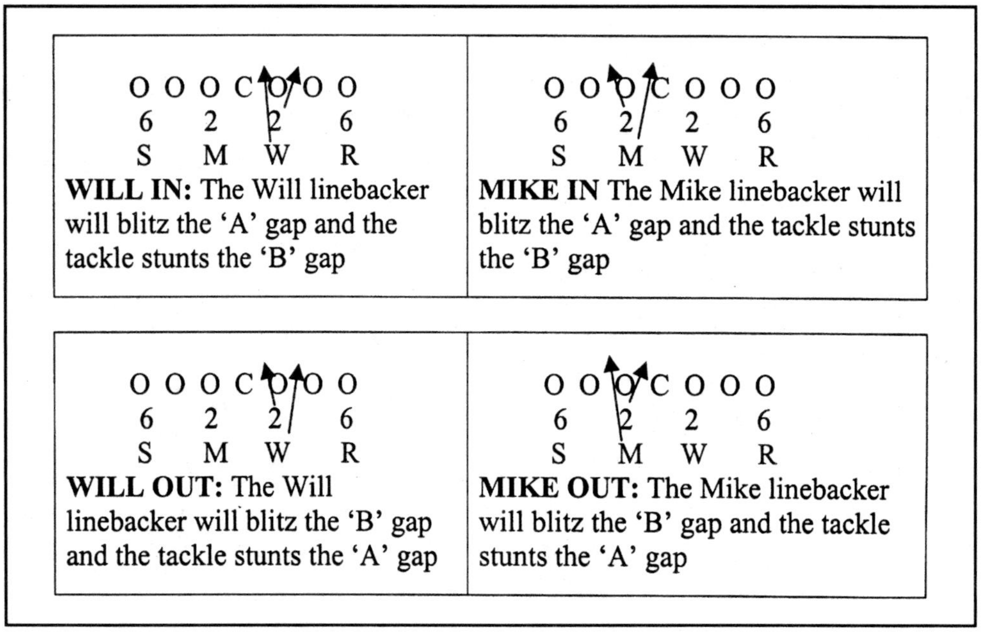

```
    O O O C O O O            O O O C O O O
    6   2   2   6            6   2   2   6
    S   M   W   R            S   M   W   R
```

WILL IN: The Will linebacker will blitz the 'A' gap and the tackle stunts the 'B' gap

MIKE IN The Mike linebacker will blitz the 'A' gap and the tackle stunts the 'B' gap

```
    O O O C O O O            O O O C O O O
    6   2   2   6            6   2   2   6
    S   M   W   R            S   M   W   R
```

WILL OUT: The Will linebacker will blitz the 'B' gap and the tackle stunts the 'A' gap

MIKE OUT: The Mike linebacker will blitz the 'B' gap and the tackle stunts the 'A' gap

Figure 7-8

As you can see, you can mix up the blitzes any way you like to confuse the offensive blocking schemes and keep your opponent guessing.

Stack Option Responsibilities

The option responsibilities for the stack package are listed by position:

• Tackles

Tackles always have dive responsibility.

• Ends

The defensive ends have dive to QB responsibilities. His responsibility will be determined by the block of the tight end or the offensive tackle if he is aligned on the split end side of the offensive alignment. If he is on the tight end side, he reads the tight end's block. If the tight end blocks down, he will take the dive. If the tight end were to on block or release off the line of scrimmage, he would have QB responsibility.

• Outside Linebackers

The outside linebacker's first responsibility is to force the QB to pitch the ball. He will work closely with the defensive end. If the defensive end is in a position to get to the QB, he will close in on the QB from the outside in, stopping his ability to pitch yet getting in a position to assist the defensive end. If the defensive end vacates his area for the dive, the outside linebacker must work the QB in a way that will require him to pitch the ball, yet still keep himself in a position to pursue the pitch man by forcing him as far outside as possible.

• Inside Linebackers

The inside linebackers have to check everything from dive to QB to pitch. Their first read is dive. If a teammate closes the dive, then they work down to the QB. If the QB pitches they must be in a position to pursue him from the inside out, ready for a cutback.

- Corners

The corner will have outside support on the pitch man. He will always have contain responsibility, never allowing the play to get outside him.

- Free Safety

The free safety is the alley player. He has QB to pitch responsibility.

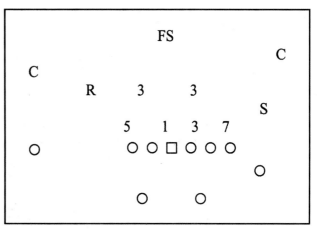

Figure 7-9

Call Side	Away Side	Alignment/Assignment
Defensive End	7 tech/C gap	5 tech/C gap
Defensive Tackle	3 tech/B gap	1 tech/A gap
Inside Linebacker	30 tech/A gap	30 tech/B gap
Sam and Rover	Same as even *vs 2 TE's	9 tech
Corner	Base cover 3, or called coverage	
Free Safety	Base cover 3, or called coverage	

Odd Package

The odd package is another adjustment to the 4-4 Defense. It is called an odd defense because there will be a man on the weakside shade of the center. This package will make you stronger against the run. This defensive alignment makes it harder for the offense to block the linebackers, especially when using the stunt package associated with the odd defense. The blitzes are harder for the offense to recognize in this package.

The callside in this example is liz, which indicates the offensive formation strength is to the left side of the defense. The away side (weakside) is to the right side of this defense. If the offense aligns in a two tight end formation, the weakside outside linebacker would align in a 9 technique at the line of scrimmage, which would put the defense in a 50 front.

Odd Stunts and Blitzes

If the offense aligns in a two tight end formation, the weakside outside linebacker would align in a 9 technique at the line of scrimmage, which would put the defense in a 50 front. The secondary would slide to a cover 2 alignment opposite the way the front shifted. This coverage is called cover 2 weak since it was rolled to the weakside of the call. Figure 7-12 is an example of these situations. Coverage packages for this defense are outlined in this section.

Odd Option Responsibilities

The option responsibilities for the odd package are listed by position:

- Tackles

Tackles always have dive responsibility.

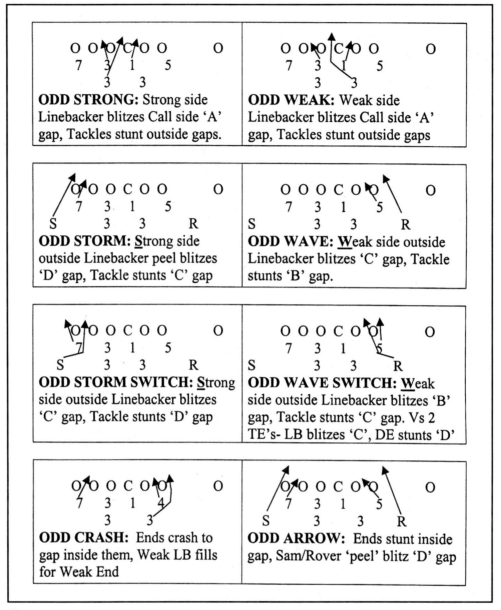

ODD STRONG: Strong side Linebacker blitzes Call side 'A' gap, Tackles stunt outside gaps.

ODD WEAK: Weak side Linebacker blitzes Call side 'A' gap, Tackles stunt outside gaps

ODD STORM: Strong side outside Linebacker peel blitzes 'D' gap, Tackle stunts 'C' gap

ODD WAVE: Weak side outside Linebacker blitzes 'C' gap, Tackle stunts 'B' gap.

ODD STORM SWITCH: Strong side outside Linebacker blitzes 'C' gap, Tackle stunts 'D' gap

ODD WAVE SWITCH: Weak side outside Linebacker blitzes 'B' gap, Tackle stunts 'C' gap. Vs 2 TE's- LB blitzes 'C', DE stunts 'D'

ODD CRASH: Ends crash to gap inside them, Weak LB fills for Weak End

ODD ARROW: Ends stunt inside gap, Sam/Rover 'peel' blitz 'D' gap

Figure 7-10

• Ends

The defensive ends have dive to QB responsibilities. His responsibility will be determined by the block of the tight end or the offensive tackle if he is aligned on the split end side of the offensive alignment. If he is on the tight end side, he reads the tight end's block. If the tight end blocks down, he will take the dive. If the tight end on blocks or releases off the line of scrimmage, he would have QB responsibility.

• Outside Linebackers

The outside linebacker's first responsibility is to force the QB to pitch the ball. He will work closely with the defensive end. If the defensive end is in a position to get to the QB, he will close in on the QB from the outside in, stopping his ability to pitch yet getting in a position to assist the defensive end. If the defensive end vacates his area for the dive, the outside linebacker must work the QB in a way that

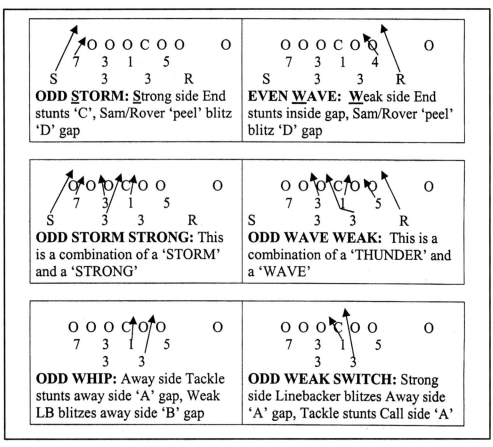

ODD STORM: Strong side End stunts 'C', Sam/Rover 'peel' blitz 'D' gap

EVEN WAVE: Weak side End stunts inside gap, Sam/Rover 'peel' blitz 'D' gap

ODD STORM STRONG: This is a combination of a 'STORM' and a 'STRONG'

ODD WAVE WEAK: This is a combination of a 'THUNDER' and a 'WAVE'

ODD WHIP: Away side Tackle stunts away side 'A' gap, Weak LB blitzes away side 'B' gap

ODD WEAK SWITCH: Strong side Linebacker blitzes Away side 'A' gap, Tackle stunts Call side 'A'

Figure 7-11

will require him to pitch the ball, yet still keep himself in a position to pursue the pitch man by forcing him as far outside as possible. If he is aligned in a 9 technique versus two tight ends, he will read the tight end's block, which will determine if he has dive or QB.

• Inside Linebackers

The inside linebackers have to check everything from dive to QB to pitch. Their first read is dive. If a teammate closes the dive, then they work down to the QB. If the QB pitches, they must be in a position to pursue him from the inside out, ready for a cutback.

• Corners

The corner will have outside support on the pitch man. He will always have contain responsibility, never allowing the play to get outside him.

• Free Safety

The free safety is the alley player. He has QB to pitch responsibility.

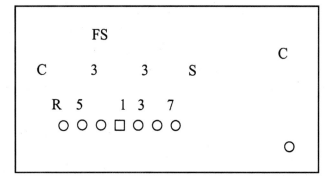

Figure 7-12

237

Tight Package

The tight package is another adjustment to the 4-4 defense. This is basically an adjustment to the even package. The linemen are squeezed down the line of scrimmage while the outside linebackers are moved up on the line of scrimmage in a 9 technique. This defense is very effective against the run. This is also the package that would be used in goal line situations.

The callside in this example is liz, which indicates the offensive formation strength is to the left side of the defense. The away side (weakside) is to the right side of this defense.

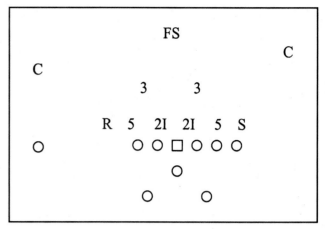

Figure 7-13

Call Side	Away Side	Alignment/Assignment
Defensive End	5 tech/C gap	5 tech/C gap
Defensive Tackle	2i tech/B gap	2i tech/A gap
Inside Linebacker	30 tech/A gap	30 tech/B gap
Sam and Rover	9 tech/D gap	9 tech/D gap
Corner	Base cover 3, or called coverage	
Free Safety	Base cover 3, or called coverage	

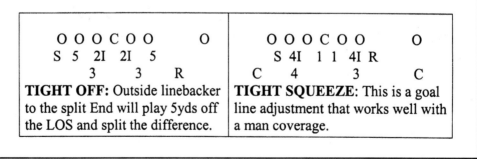

Figure 7-14. Tight alignment adjustments

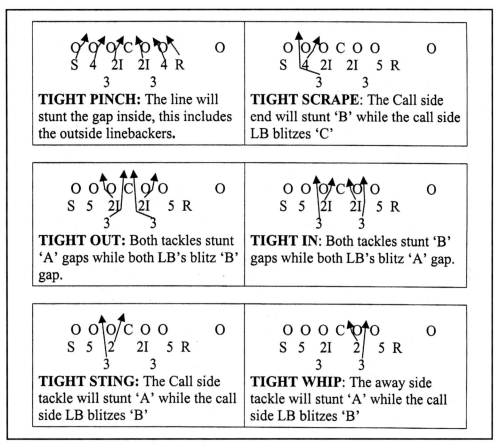

TIGHT PINCH: The line will stunt the gap inside, this includes the outside linebackers.

TIGHT SCRAPE: The Call side end will stunt 'B' while the call side LB blitzes 'C'

TIGHT OUT: Both tackles stunt 'A' gaps while both LB's blitz 'B' gap.

TIGHT IN: Both tackles stunt 'B' gaps while both LB's blitz 'A' gap.

TIGHT STING: The Call side tackle will stunt 'A' while the call side LB blitzes 'B'

TIGHT WHIP: The away side tackle will stunt 'A' while the call side LB blitzes 'B'

Figure 7-15. Tight stunts and blitzes

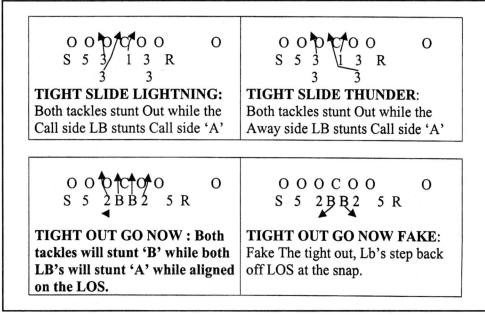

TIGHT SLIDE LIGHTNING: Both tackles stunt Out while the Call side LB stunts Call side 'A'

TIGHT SLIDE THUNDER: Both tackles stunt Out while the Away side LB stunts Call side 'A'

TIGHT OUT GO NOW : Both tackles will stunt 'B' while both LB's will stunt 'A' while aligned on the LOS.

TIGHT OUT GO NOW FAKE: Fake The tight out, Lb's step back off LOS at the snap.

Figure 7-16. Tight stunts and blitzes

Disco

Disco is a term that is used for linebackers who are 'dancing' at the line of scrimmage. The linebackers will threaten different gaps by approaching the line then retreating. They will sometimes pause momentarily, or they may continually jab-step at the line. They will do this to fake different stunts and confuse blocking schemes at the line of scrimmage. You can also use disco when you are blitzing a gap in order to further confuse the blockers. If the linebacker is using disco as a fake, he must make sure that he prepares himself at the snap of the ball to be in a position to read and pursue the play.

Switch

Switch can be added to any stunt that includes action by a lineman and a linebacker. They will simply switch roles when this is called. An example of the switch in the tight defense would be a sting switch. The sting has the callside tackle stunt the A gap while the linebacker blitzes the B gap. On the sting switch, the callside tackle will stunt the B gap while the linebacker blitzes the A gap.

Tight Option Responsibilities

The option responsibilities for the even package are listed by position:

- Tackles

Tackles always have dive responsibility.

- Ends

The defensive ends have dive to QB responsibilities. His responsibility will be determined by the block of the offensive tackle. If the offensive tackle were to block down, then he must take dive. If the tackle blocks on, then he has QB responsibility.

- Outside Linebackers

The outside linebacker will read the block of the tight end if there is one on his side. If the tight end blocks down, then he has dive first responsibility. If the tight end blocks on or tries to release down the field, then he has QB responsibility.

- Inside Linebackers

The inside linebackers have to check everything from dive to QB to pitch. Their first read is dive. If a teammate closes the dive, then they work down to the QB. If the QB pitches, they must be in a position to pursue him from the inside out, ready for a cutback.

- Corners

The corner will have outside support on the pitch man. He will always have contain responsibility, never allowing the play to get outside him.

- Free Safety

The free safety is the alley player. He has QB to pitch responsibility.

Coverage Packages

This section outlines a coverage package that can be used with the 4-4 defense. The secondary of the 4-4 consists of two corners and a safety. All four linebackers will be used in coverage as well. The outside linebackers will be called upon to play different roles depending on the coverage that is called. That is why these players must be very athletic. At times, they will be called on to plug like a linebacker. And on the next play, they will be given contain/pass responsibilities similar to a cornerback.

The following coverages will be outlined:

- Cover 1—Man coverage
- Cover 2—Two deep zone coverage
- Cover 3—Three deep zone coverage
- Cover 5—Five deep zone coverage—pass prevent coverage

Certain things will remain constant throughout any of the coverage packages. Every player will break on the ball on every pass. Defenders should sprint to the spot where the ball is thrown as soon as the ball is released by the quarterback. Also, certain calls have to be made when certain things are spotted. The following are examples of the calls that should be made:

- Yell "run" or "pass"
- Yell description of run type: "sweep," "reverse," "option," and "bootleg"
- Yell "ball" when the pass is released
- Yell "fire" when a pass is intercepted and everyone becomes blockers.

All coverages should be disguised whenever possible. Our team uses a technique we call "prowl." This is when you roll your secondary into the called coverage from a different alignment. By doing this, you may confuse the quarterback's pre-snap read. When you are in a cover 3 defense, your corners will likely play five to seven yards off the split end. Have your corner align at the line of scrimmage over top of the receiver and then 'prowl' back to his called alignment. To accomplish this, you must have a feel for the quarterback's cadence. All players must be in their proper alignment at the snap of the ball.

Cover 3

The base coverage package for any 4-4 defense is cover 3. This is a three deep zone. The outside linebackers are responsible for the area from curl to flat and the corners and free safety are each responsible for a deep one-third of the field. The interior middle zone is covered by the inside

linebackers who have hook to curl responsibility. This is the coverage package that you would check to when there is any confusion or change when other coverage packages have been called.

☐ Cover 3 Responsibilities
- Corners

Align one yard wide and five yards deep off any wide receiver. He has pass first responsibility. His first two steps should be backwards; if he reads run, he has outside support responsibilities. If he reads pass, he will run back to his deep one-third pass responsibilities. If the wide receiver is trying to crack block inside him on an outside running play, he would yell "crack" to alert the other defenders of the potential crack back block coming their way. Versus a tight end, the corner would align three yards outside and seven yards deep. The run and pass responsibilities remain the same for both corners.

- Outside Linebackers (Sam and Rover)

Versus a tight end, the outside linebacker will align two yards deep and two yards outside. Versus a wide receiver, they will align five yards deep and split the difference between the wide receiver and the end man on the line of scrimmage. If there is a tight end and a wingback, they would align themselves in an outside shade of the wing. They

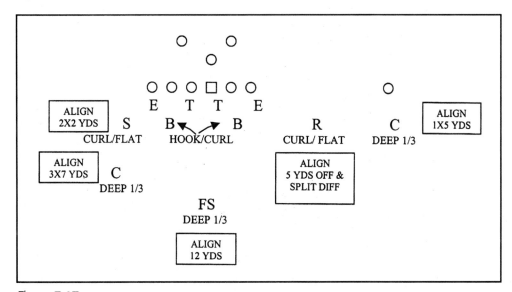

Figure 7-17

have force /contain responsibilities on running plays. They should never allow themselves to be outflanked by anyone aligned inside them at the snap of ball. They should attack the first threat that approaches them taking on blockers from the outside in so that they will turn the runner inside if they are unable to make the tackle. Outside linebackers must have a run first mentality. Versus the pass, they have the curl to flat zone. They should always key the near back in the backfield watching for him to run routes out of the backfield (i.e., swing, flair, and screen routes).

• Free Safety

Align 10 to 12 yards off the ball. Versus the run, this will be the alley player who will pursue the play from the inside out. Versus a pass, they have the deep middle one-third zone.

• Linebackers

Both inside linebackers will assume their regular alignment that was called. They have run first responsibility. When they read pass, they have hook to curl responsibility. If the offense has a split receiver and a tight end on his side, he will go immediately to hook. If there is only a split receiver threatening his side, he must go to curl responsibility. If there is no split receiver, he will go immediately to hook.

Cover 2

Cover 2 is the two deep coverage package for the 4-4 defense. By making this adjustment, the defense will essentially be in a 4-3 defensive alignment. This alignment will have a free safety and a cornerback responsible for the deep zones. Each one will be responsible for a deep half of the field. The cornerback that is responsible for the deep coverage will be determined by the call that is made by the defense. The secondary could make their own directional call to determine which corner plays up and which corner plays the deep half with the free safety. The other way to determine the alignment is to use the strength call that has already been called on the field. In this case, we use two directions to roll the corners; the calls are weak and strong or cover 2 weak and cover 2 strong. The corner that is rolled up in coverage will be in bump and run coverage. This means they will jam the split receiver hard at the line of scrimmage, trying to disrupt their route. They will jam them from the outside in so that they are in a good position for their containment responsibilities in the case of an outside run. In Figure 7-18, the secondary is rolled away from the callside. In Figure 7-19, the secondary is rolled to the callside.

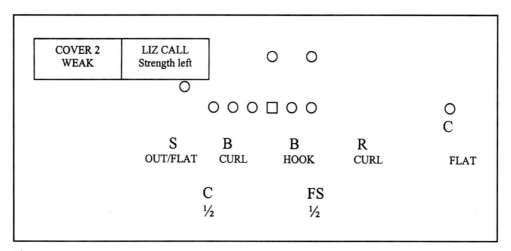

Figure 7-18

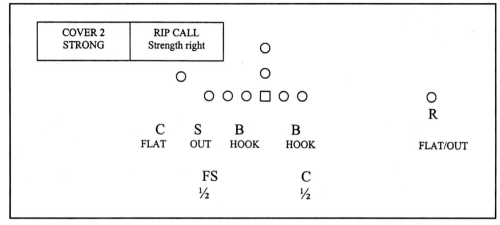

Figure 7-19

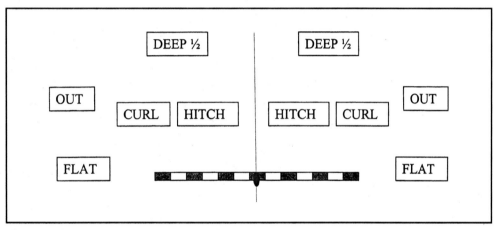

Figure 7-20

◻ Cover 2 Responsibilities

• Corners

Callside–A corner should align head-up on the split receiver (#1 receiver). He should jam him at the line of scrimmage with a good chuckmaking sure not to extend their arms. The receiver can easily release from a defender if he is jammed with extended arms, the defender needs to get his body involved. As he jams the #1 receiver, he will work toward the flat while reading the #2 receiver. If the #2 receiver runs into the flat, the corner will pick him up. If there is no threat to the flat, the corner will work back to cover the out area responsibilities. If the corner reads run, he has outside containment responsibilities. Versus the option he is responsible for the pitch man.

Away side–A corner should align 10 to 12 yards off the ball splitting the difference between the #1 and #2 receiver if the ball were in the middle of the field. If the ball is placed on a hash mark, he will never align past that hash mark. When he drops into coverage, he should remain within four yards of the hash mark on either side of it until the quarterback releases the pass. He should be dropping to his deep half responsibility as he reads pass. His key to the play would be his nearside tackle. He will key him to determine run or pass. If he reads run, he pursues as an alley tackler. This means he must attack from inside to outside. Versus the option, he is responsible for quarterback to pitch.

• Outside Linebackers (Sam & Rover)

Callside–He should align five yards off the #2 receiver and two yards outside him. Read #2 for pattern recognition. Keep an eye for #1 receiver for the threat of a curl, which is his responsibility. There can also be a backside crossing threat or a backfield threat to his area that must be checked. Versus an option, he has quarterback to pitch responsibilities.

Away side–He should align head-up on the split receiver (#1 receiver). He should jam him at the line of scrimmage with a good chuck. As he jams the #1 receiver, he will work toward the flat while reading the #2 receiver. If the #2 receiver runs into the flat, the outside linebacker will pick him up. If there is no threat to the flat, the outside linebacker will work back to cover the out area responsibilities. If he reads run, he has outside containment responsibilities. Versus the option, he is responsible for the pitch man.

• Free Safety

He should align 10 to 12 yards off the ball splitting the difference between the #1 and #2 receiver if the ball were in the middle of the field. If the ball is placed on a hash mark, he will never align past that hash mark. When he drops into coverage, he should remain within four yards of the hash mark on either side of it until the quarterback releases the pass. He should be dropping to his deep half responsibility as he reads pass. His key to the play would be his nearside tackle. He will key him to determine run or

pass. If he reads run, he pursues as an alley tackler. This means he must attack from inside to outside. Versus the option, he is responsible for quarterback to pitch.

• Linebackers

Both inside linebackers will assume their regular alignment that was called. They have run first responsibility. When they read pass, they have hook to curl responsibility. If the offense has a split receiver and a tight end on his side, he will go immediately to hook. If there is only a split receiver threatening his side, he must go to curl responsibility because the outside linebacker will jam that receiver and then stay home for the flat/out responsibility. If there is no split receiver, he will go immediately to hook.

□ Cover 2 Adjustments

• Cover 2 versus Twins

The cover adjustment to twins is similar to the adjustment to any two-receiver side. The corner will play up in bump and run coverage and maintain the flat to out coverage. The most immediate pass threat to him is the quick screen to the slotback or the wide receiver or a hitch pattern.. He should jam the wide receiver from the outside in at the line of scrimmage while he reads pass or run. On a running play, he has outside contain responsibilities. When he reads pass, he will focus on his immediate threats, while at the same time reading his

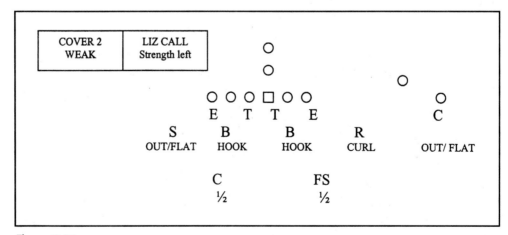

Figure 7-21

secondary threat, which is a back out of the backfield. The back may run a screen, swing, or flair pattern out of the backfield, which would become the corner's responsibility.

The outside linebacker to the twins' side will drop to the curl area if he reads pass. The most immediate threats to his area are a curl or slant from either split receiver. If the quick screen were thrown to the slotted back, the outside linebacker would be responsible to fill and make the tackle. The corner would likely have to force the play inside. The nearback would be the key run read for the outside linebacker. If he reads toss to his side, he must pursue quickly, without being outflanked by a lead back or pulling lineman. The other likely threat on a toss play would be the crack back block from one of the twins' receivers. The corner should read this and yell, "crack" to the outside linebacker. The outside linebacker should work to the outside shoulder of the crack back blocker, which should put him in a position to make the play or turn the play in for a safety or linebacker who will fill from the alley.

• Cover 2 versus Trips

The adjustment to the trips formation is very similar to the twins adjustment. In this case, the outside linebacker will play man-to-man coverage on the 1 receiver side of the formation. This may be a tight end or a wide out. This is called a lock, when you are playing man coverage with only one of your defenders. If this man were to run a crossing pattern

into the strongside zone, he would release him about midway and assume the deep middle one-third pass zone responsibility.

If you notice, the corner that is rolled back to the safety area and the free safety have the deep one-third of the field instead of the deep half of the field. They will be shifted to the trips side of the formation. The backside corner will play 10 to 12 yards off the center, while the free safety will play 10 to 12 yards off the #3 receiver. He will never align himself inside the hash mark at the start of a play.

The rest of the defenders will play this the same as any cover 2 situation. This can be a very good time to stunt and blitz one of the middle linebackers. Since there is only one immediate running threat that is aligned in the backfield, it will be a fairly safe and effective time to blitz one of your backers. Since you are in a lock on the one receiver side of the formation, this may be a good time to blitz the linebacker on that side of the formation. Your blitz strategy should be determined by your scouting report. You should determine which gap he is most likely to attack on a running play and then blitz that gap. Because this is the tight end side and because of the way the defense has aligned, this may be the safest area for them to run. The locked outside linebacker must make sure to maintain his outside contain responsibilities. If he gets outflanked, there is big play potential outside of him.

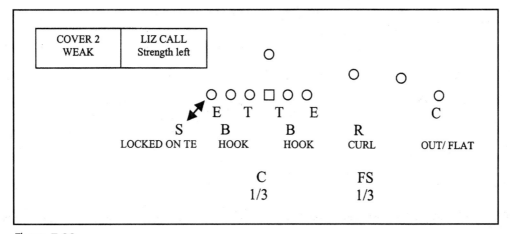

Figure 7-22

- Cover 2 versus Two Tight Ends

In Figure 7-23, the defense is running cover 2 versus two tight ends. In this particular case, their backfield is balanced, which means there is no strength call based on formation. The defense will make its strength call based on the wide side of the field or an offensive tendency in the scouting report. The defense shown in Figure 7-23 called the strength left (liz). The front is shifted to the left and the secondary is shifted to the right. This formation will make the defense as balanced as the offense. It may be wise to have the secondary roll to the wide side of the field since the outside linebacker will be in a 9 technique and will also have a corner outflanking him, which aligns two players in a position to contain an outside running threat, which will likely go to the wide side of the field.

The outside linebacker that is playing the 9 technique will key the nearback as he always should. If he reads pressure coming his way from this back, he must make immediate steps to get to his outside shoulder, never allowing himself to be outflanked by anyone.

Cover 1

Cover 1 is a man-to-man cover package with a free safety. In this coverage, every defender will call out the number of the player he is covering. You always start from the outside when you are numbering receivers. The cornerback is responsible for #1; the outside linebacker is responsible for #2; and the middle linebacker on that side is responsible for the #3 man. The running back aligned behind the quarterback can be covered by either side linebacker, which is why it is very important to call out the numbers so that there is no confusion who has the responsibility for each player. If there are two backs aligned behind the quarterback, as in an I formation, the tailback is counted first, and then the fullback in front of him is counted. The free safety will take the responsibility of a blitzing linebacker, if a blitz were called. Figure 7-24 is an example of cover 1.

- Alignment

- Split End—Five yards off, one yard inside

- Tight End or wing—Five yards off, one yard outside

- Inside the five yard line—Split the difference between the receiver and the goal line.

- Versus Trips—Check coverage to a zone coverage (cover 2 or cover 3) depending on the game plan and the tendencies of your opponent.

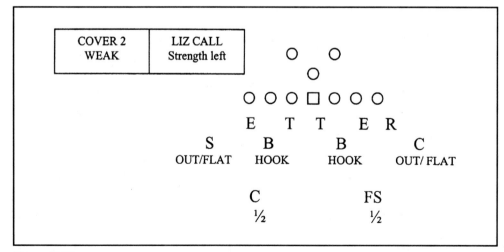

Figure 7-23

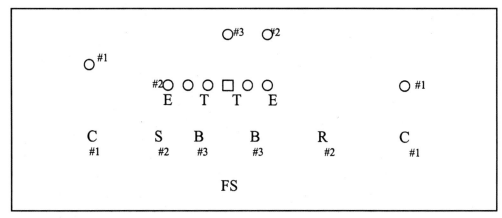

Figure 7-24

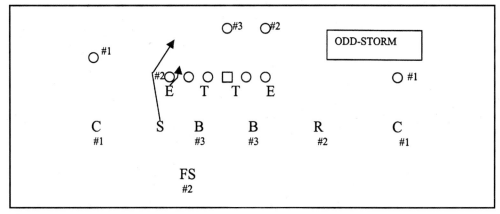

Figure 7-25

The free safety would pick up a man that would be left uncovered by a blitz. Figure 7-25 is an example of a storm blitz where the free safety will cover #2 since the outside linebacker (Sam) is blitzing.

□ Motion

In Figure 7-26, the spread win is going in motion across the line. Before he goes in motion, he is the # 1 man on the left side of the defense. His motion action causes him to become the #2 man on the left side. This means that the Rover outside linebacker now has the responsibility to cover this man. Figure 7-26 depicts what the coverage would be after the motion takes place.

Note: When motion causes confusion in the coverage, the defense should always check to a zone coverage (cover 2 or cover 3) depending on the game plan that week.

Cover 5 or Pass Prevent

This is the pass prevent package in the 4-4 defense. It is a five deep zone coverage package that is designed to stop the deep pass forcing the quarterback to throw underneath the coverage. This package would be used at the end of a half or the end of a game when the offense only has time for one more play before time expires.

• Corners

They should align 12 yards off the line on the numbers between each hash mark. They are responsible for one-fifth of the field.

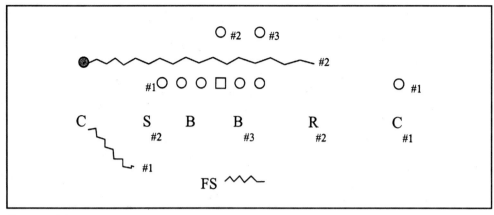

Figure 7-26

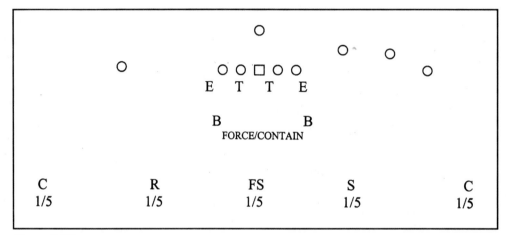

Figure 7-27

- Outside Linebackers

They should align 12 yards off the line and one yard inside the hash marks. They are responsible for their deep one-fifth of the field.

- Free Safety

They should align 12 to 15 yards off the line and in the middle of the field. They are responsible for their deep one-fifth of the field.

- Middle Linebackers

They should align seven yards off the line in a 50 technique. They should mirror the quarterback. They have force/contain responsibilities versus the run.

4-5 Run Stopper Defense

This is a run stopping adjustment to the 44 defense. This would be used in run stopping situations, usually against teams that employ two tight ends. If you were being overpowered by a teams' running game, you may want to try this defensive set. This is also very similar to a 4-3 defensive set. The difference between the two would be personnel. The 45 employs outside linebackers who are strong run stoppers, while the 4-3 has two corners in their place and two safeties for deep coverage. The free safety is the key to this set. He aligns four to five yards off the nose of the ball. His primary responsibility is run defense. He will likely be unblocked, allowing him free pursuit to the play. Mix this package in with other defensive sets for diversity.

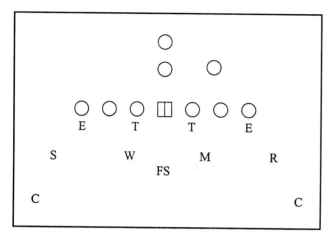

Figure 7-28

Base Alignment and Assignment

Ends: 6 technique alignment with C gap responsibility

Tackles: 2 technique alignment with two-gap responsibility

Outside Backers: Sam and Rover (left and right) aligned 3.5 yards off and one yard outside the tight end or wingback. They have outside contain versus run and out/flat versus pass.

Inside Backer: Mike and Will (strong and weak) aligned two to three yards off the line in a 30 technique with B gap responsibility.

Corners: Align 8 x 2 versus wing or tight end. Cover 2 responsibilities versus the pass.

Free Safety: Align four to five yards off the line. Free roam and attack the run.

Stunts and Blitzes

(Same as the 4-4 stack from 4-5 alignment)

The key to running this defense is to keep the offense off balance with stunts and blitzes. With the free safety playing the run, you are in a position to take more chances. The stunts and blitzes called should be changed from play to play in order to keep the offense off balance. All of the stunts and blitzes are based on gap assignment. No matter

what you call, every gap will be accounted for. Plus, you will have the extra run stopper with the free safety. This is similar to a stack defense. The defensive lineman directly correlates to a backer behind him. This means that they are always responsible for opposite gaps. Middle backers and tackles always have A or B gap, while outside backers and ends always have C or D gap. This means that if a tackle is called upon to stunt the A gap, then the corresponding middle backer is responsible for the B gap.

In the stunts shown in Figure 7-29 and Figure 7-30 every lineman was involved. You can take this a step further by labeling each lineman. For instance, if you number them 1-4 and the left end is #1, you can stunt just that player by calling his number and a command; '1 gap in' would have the left end stunt the inside gap. You can mix this call up by calling out more than one person at a time. If you decide to do this, you can label the corresponding linebackers 1-4 so that there will be no confusion when stunt or blitzes are called.

The blitzes shown in Figure 7-31 and Figure 7-32 were accomplished by simply calling the linebackers name and the direction of the gap he is stunting. The linebacker must tap the hip of the linemen in front of him, which indicates the gap direction the linebacker will blitz. This also notifies the lineman that he must stunt the opposite gap. Following is a list of other stunt combinations using the same principles listed previously.

- Sam Out: Sam blitzes the outside or D gap and the end stunts C gap.

- Rover Out: Rover blitzes the outside or D gap and the end stunts the C gap.

- Sam In: Sam blitzes the C gap and the end stunts the D gap.

- Rover In: Rover blitzes the C gap and the end stunts the D gap.

Note: If you call a Sam/Rover In and they end up on a split end side, the stunt should be called off automatically. Sam/Rover will yell, "Off, off."

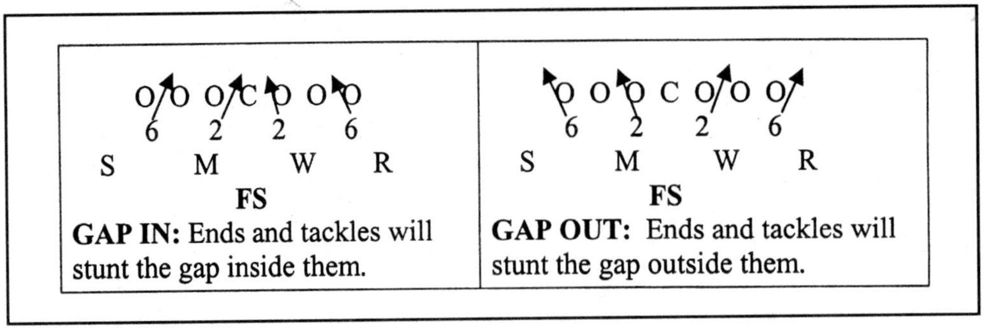

O/O O/C O O O/
6   2   2   6

S   M   W   R
FS

GAP IN: Ends and tackles will stunt the gap inside them.

O O O C O/O O/
6   2   2   6

S   M   W   R
FS

GAP OUT: Ends and tackles will stunt the gap outside them.

Figure 7-29

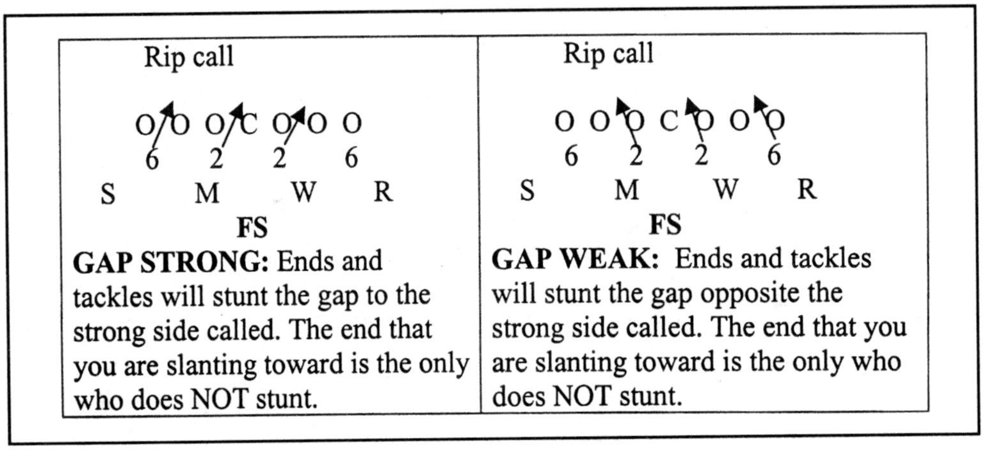

Rip call

O/O O/C O/O O
6   2   2   6

S   M   W   R
FS

GAP STRONG: Ends and tackles will stunt the gap to the strong side called. The end that you are slanting toward is the only who does NOT stunt.

Rip call

O O O C O O O
6   2   2   6

S   M   W   R
FS

GAP WEAK: Ends and tackles will stunt the gap opposite the strong side called. The end that you are slanting toward is the only who does NOT stunt.

Figure 7-30

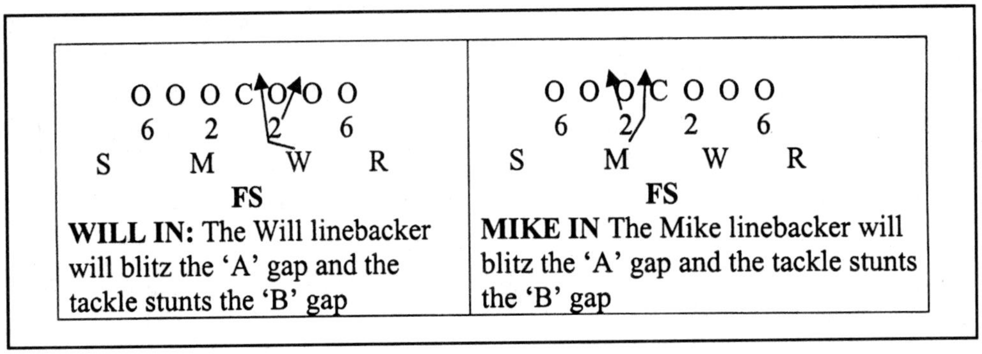

O O O C O O O
6   2   2   6

S   M   W   R
FS

WILL IN: The Will linebacker will blitz the 'A' gap and the tackle stunts the 'B' gap

O O O C O O O
6   2   2   6

S   M   W   R
FS

MIKE IN The Mike linebacker will blitz the 'A' gap and the tackle stunts the 'B' gap

Figure 7-31

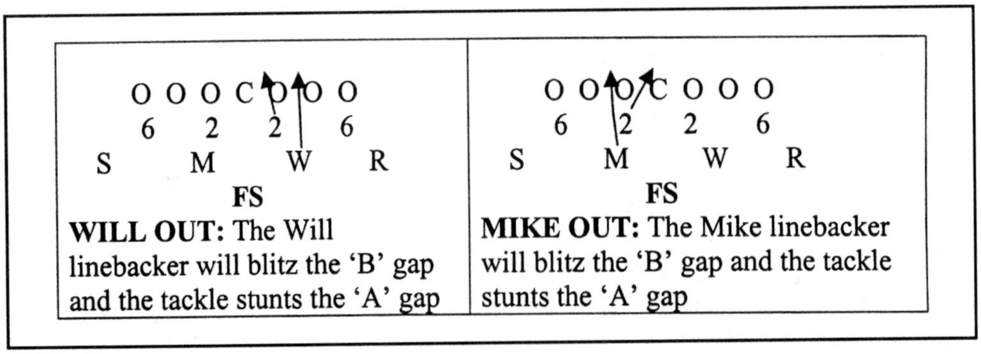

O O O C O O O
6   2   2   6

S   M   W   R
FS

WILL OUT: The Will linebacker will blitz the 'B' gap and the tackle stunts the 'A' gap

O O O C O O O
6   2   2   6

S   M   W   R
FS

MIKE OUT: The Mike linebacker will blitz the 'B' gap and the tackle stunts the 'A' gap

Figure 7-32

Combination Blitzes: Call out any combination of linebackers and they will execute their stunts using all the same principles listed previously. Following is a list of possible calls:

- Sam and Will out
- Mike in-Will out
- All out
- Mike and Will in
- All in

As you can see, you can mix up the blitzes any way you like to confuse the offensive blocking schemes and keep your opponent guessing.

Coverage Package

This is a cover 2 base defense. You should always prowl to this alignment from a 4-4 cover 3 look. This is not the best coverage package versus teams that like to put out multiple receivers and flood zones. It is likely that you will be using this package against run oriented teams. This means that their passes will likely be play-action passes that may use fewer receivers or take longer to develop. Since you will stunt and/or blitz on every play when you use this package, the coverage should be adequate if you can rush the quarterback.

- Sam and Rover—Out to flat pass responsibility
- Mike and Will—Hitch to curl pass responsibility
- Corners—Deep half of the field pass responsibility.
- Free safety—Fill in for a stunting inside backer during pass play.

50 Defense

Two packages in the 50 defense will be discussed in this section: the 5-2 and the 5-3 packages. Both packages will have a noseguard, two defensive tackles, and two stand-up defensive ends on the line of scrimmage. The first package is the base 5-2 responsibilities and adjustments. The next package is the 5-3 with all the possible adjustments that can be made from the base formation.

5-2 Package

The base 5-2 defense employs two inside linebackers and four defensive backs. This base coverage of the 5-2 defense is cover 2. Two corners and two safeties are used in the secondary. The base alignment for the 5-2 package is shown in Figure 7-34. The inside linebackers can always remain on one side of the defense or they can swap responsibility based on the strength of the offensive formation or the tendencies of the opposing offense. If you will be swapping them, they should be labeled. In the examples for this package, the strongside inside linebacker is Mike (M), and the weakside linebacker is Will (W). When you are choosing personnel, it should be noted that the defensive ends in any 50 defense are hybrid linebackers. They are called upon to perform many of the tasks of the linebacker combined with the size and power of a lineman. The ends may also

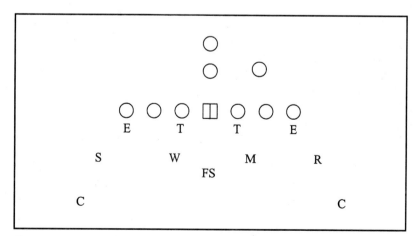

Figure 7-33

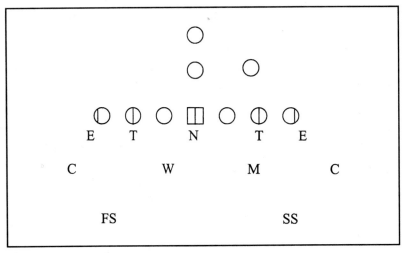

Figure 7-34

swap alignment based on the strengths of the offense. The more athletic of the two is often aligned to the strength of the offense or to the wide side of the field, depending on the defensive philosophy or the tendencies of the opponent.

The base alignment and assignments for each position are listed as follows:

• Noseguard (N)

The noseguard is aligned in a 0 technique, head-up over the center. He has two-gap responsibility that includes both A gaps. He will accomplish this by reading the center's head. He should jam up under and into the center while working in whatever direction the center's head is going. The moment he reads pass, he will pursue the passer in a direct line to the middle of his body.

• Tackles (T)

The base alignment for the tackles, with a tight aligned on their side, is a 4 technique, head-up over the offensive tackle. If they are aligned on the split end side with no tight end, they will align in a 3 technique. His base assignment from the 4 technique is the C gap, although he will read the head of the tackle he is aligned over. If the tackle blocks down, he will squeeze down with him and read the play. He must never be outflanked by the

tackle. If the man attempts to reach block him, he will immediately work the blocker's outside shoulder looking to make a play which will likely be to the outside of his alignment. When he is aligned in a 3 technique, he is responsible for the B gap. If he reads pass, he will pursue the passer from his alignment to the outside ear of the passer.

• Ends (E)

The base alignment for the ends is a 9 technique versus tight end, and a 5 technique on the split end side with no tight end. These players are always aligned in a two-point linebacker stance. They have force/contain responsibility on the outside. This means that their main objective is turn outside plays to the inside. Their initial steps should be to jam down on the outside shoulder of the tight end, putting them in a position to release to the outside if needed. They should never get outflanked by a tight end or a back that comes out of the backfield. They will read the nearback in the backfield. If he comes toward him, he must try to make contact with that back without getting outflanked by him. If the nearback works away from him, he works toward the play looking for a counter, reverse, or bootleg.

Ends have flat/rush responsibility versus the pass. They are responsible for the immediate flat on their side. They will jam or cover any back out of the backfield for a potential screen, swing, or flair pass. They will rush the passer from the outside inward if no back is releasing into their flat. They must never allow the quarterback to rollout to their side.

• Inside Linebackers

The inside linebackers in the base 5-2 will align in a 30 technique, 3.5 yards from the line of scrimmage. Linebackers always have run first responsibility. Their first move should always be toward the initial flow of the backfield key. If the flow is toward the linebacker's side, he is attacking the flow. If the flow is away from the linebacker's side, then he will pop his feet in that direction, slightly hesitating only long enough to read for a potential counter or reverse, then he will continue on his pursuit of the play. No matter which direction the play is going, your linebackers should always pursue downhill. This means that their pursuit should always be moving forward from their original alignment. They should never be backing up on any running play. When the inside linebacker reads pass, he will drop back to his zone which is hook/curl.

• Corners

The corners alignment will vary against different alignments. They are always aligned with the widest offensive player on their side. Versus a tight end or a wing, they will align 4.5 yards off and three yards

outside. Versus a split receiver, they will align 4.5 yards off and one yard outside. There is an up call where they will align on the outside shoulder of the receiver at the line of scrimmage, jamming him to the inside at the snap of the ball. The up call can be made at any time, or may be used automatically against a certain team or player based on the scouting report and the defensive game plan for that week. Some coaches will always play their corners up. No matter where they align, they always have contain responsibilities on the outside. No running play should ever get outside them.

• Safeties

The safeties are aligned 9 to 12 yards off the line of scrimmage. They have a pass first mentality, yet they are crucial in defending the run. They are the alley player that should make the tackle on the runner that has been turned in by the corners. They pursue from the inside outward. They will have the opportunity to make the big hits in the open field. This is why these players must possess the speed and instincts to cover the pass, yet have the guts to make the big hits on the ballcarrier cutting across the field. The base coverage of the 5-2 is cover 2, which means the safeties will each be responsible for a deep half of the field. They must never let a receiver get past them on a pattern.

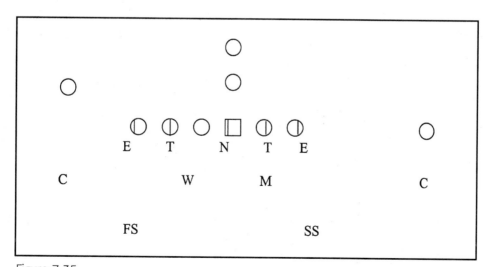

Figure 7-35

Slide Adjustment

The slide adjustment in the 5-2 package is designed to make the defense stronger against the run when there is only one tight end in the formation. The line will slide to the strength of the formation, which is the tight end of the formation. It also allows the defense to cover every gap with its line and inside linebackers. Figure 7-35 is an example of a slide adjustment.

The chart shown in Figure 7-36 lists the alignment and gap assignment for the defensive line and inside linebackers in the slide adjustment.

5-2 Package Stunts and Blitzes

5-2 Option Responsibilities

The option responsibilities for the 52 package are listed by position:

- Noseguard

Noseguards always have dive responsibility.

- Tackles

Tackles always have dive responsibility.

- Ends

The defensive ends' first responsibility is to slow the play down to get support. If the defensive end is in a position to get to the QB, he will close in on the QB from the outside in, stopping his ability to pitch yet getting in a position to make the tackle at the line of scrimmage.

- Inside Linebackers

The inside linebackers have to check everything from dive to QB to pitch. Their first read is dive. If a teammate closes the dive, then they work down to the QB. If the QB pitches, they must be in a position to pursue him from the inside out, ready for a cutback

- Corners

The corner will have outside support on the pitch man. He will always have contain responsibility, never allowing the play to get outside him.

- Safeties

The free safety is the alley player. He has QB to pitch responsibility.

| | ALIGNMENT | | ASSIGNMENT | |
	Strong side	Weak Side	Strong side	Weak Side
Defensive End	'9' tech	'5' tech	'D' gap	'C-D' gap
Defensive Tackle	'4' tech	'3' tech	'C' gap	'B' gap
Nose Guard	'1' tech		'A' gap	
Inside Linebacker	'30' tech	'20' tech	'B' gap	'A' gap

Figure 7-36

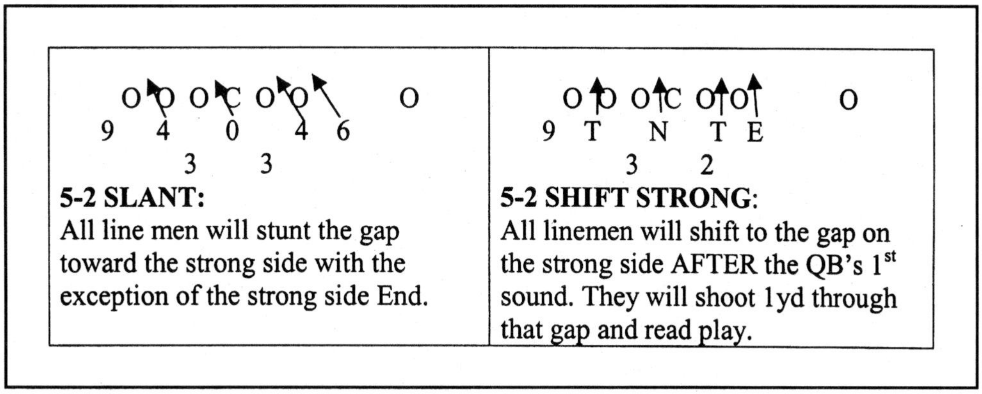

O O O C O O   O
9   4   0   4   6
     3   3

5-2 SLANT:
All linemen will stunt the gap toward the strong side with the exception of the strong side End.

O O O C O O   O
9   T   N   T   E
     3   2

5-2 SHIFT STRONG:
All linemen will shift to the gap on the strong side AFTER the QB's 1st sound. They will shoot 1yd through that gap and read play.

Figure 7-37

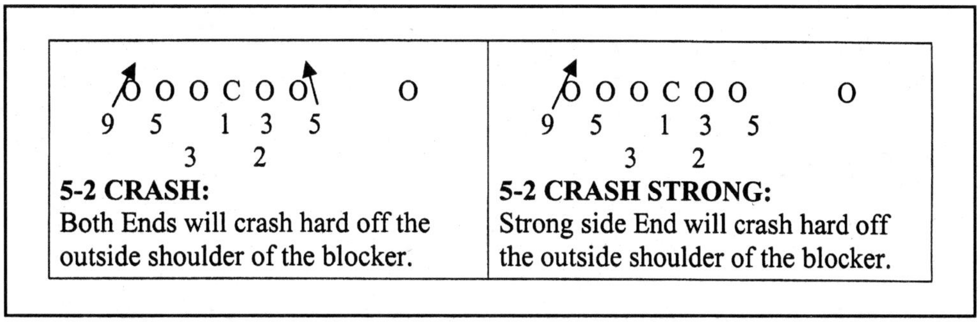

O O O C O O   O
9   5   1   3   5
     3   2

5-2 CRASH:
Both Ends will crash hard off the outside shoulder of the blocker.

O O O C O O   O
9   5   1   3   5
     3   2

5-2 CRASH STRONG:
Strong side End will crash hard off the outside shoulder of the blocker.

Figure 7-38

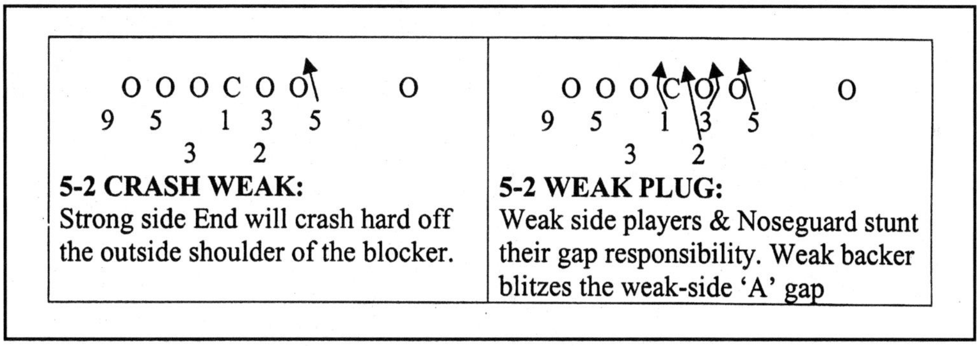

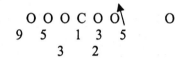

O O O C O O   O
9   5   1   3   5
     3   2

5-2 CRASH WEAK:
Strong side End will crash hard off the outside shoulder of the blocker.

O O O C O O   O
9   5   1   3   5
     3   2

5-2 WEAK PLUG:
Weak side players & Noseguard stunt their gap responsibility. Weak backer blitzes the weak-side 'A' gap

Figure 7-39

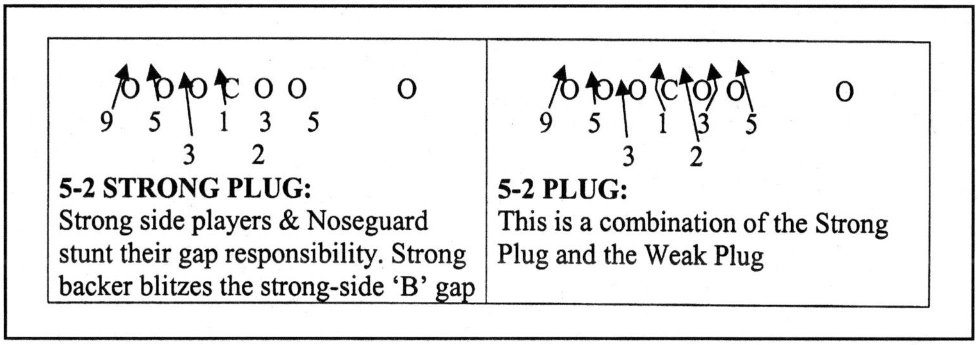

O O O C O O   O
9   5   1   3   5
     3   2

5-2 STRONG PLUG:
Strong side players & Noseguard stunt their gap responsibility. Strong backer blitzes the strong-side 'B' gap

O O O C O O   O
9   5   1   3   5
     3   2

5-2 PLUG:
This is a combination of the Strong Plug and the Weak Plug

Figure 7-40

5-3 Package

The base 5-3 defense employs three inside linebackers and three defensive backs. This base coverage of the 5-3 defense is cover 3. Two corners and one safety are used in the secondary. The base alignment for the 5-3 package is shown in Figure 7-41. The outside linebackers can always remain on one side of the defense or they can swap responsibilities based on the strength of the offensive formation or the tendencies of the opposing offense. If you will be swapping them, they should be labeled. In the examples for this package, the strongside outside linebacker is Strong (S), and the weakside linebacker is Weak (W). When you are choosing personnel, it should be noted that the defensive ends in any 50 defense are hybrid linebackers as they are in the 5-2 package. All of the defensive linemen have the same base alignment and assignment as they do in the 5-2 package.

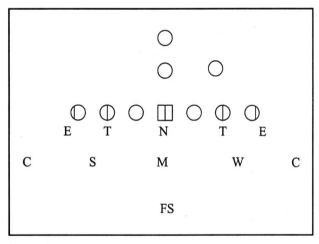

Figure 7-41

The base alignment and assignments for each position are as follows:

- Noseguard (N)

Same as 5-2

- Tackles (T)

Same as 5-2

- Ends (E)

Same as 5-2

- Inside Linebacker

The inside linebackers, (Mike) in the base 5-3, will align in a stack 0 technique behind the noseguard, 3.5 yards from the line of scrimmage. Linebackers always have run first responsibility. Their first move should always be toward the initial flow of the backfield key. This should be your best pure linebacker. He should have a good 'nose' for the ball. He has A gap responsibility, which is determined by the assignment of the noseguard. If the noseguard has one A gap, then Mike has the other. Sometimes the coach will have both the nose and the Mike backer with two-gap responsibilities, requiring them to read the play and flow to the proper A gap.

- Outside Linebackers

The outside linebackers in the base 5-3 will align in a 50 technique, 3.5 yards from the line of scrimmage. Linebackers always have run first responsibility. Their first move should always be toward the initial flow of the backfield key. If the flow is toward the linebacker's side, he is attacking the flow. If the flow is away from the linebacker's side, then he will pop his feet in that direction, slightly hesitating only long enough to read for a potential counter or reverse, then he will continue on his pursuit of the play. No matter which direction the play is going, your linebackers should always pursue downhill. This means that their pursuit should always be moving forward from their original alignment. They should never be backing up on any running play. When the inside linebacker reads pass, he will drop back to his zone which is hook to out.

- Corners

The corners alignment will vary against different alignments. They are always aligned with the widest offensive player on their side. Versus a tight end or a wing, they will align 4.5 yards off and three yards outside. Versus a split receiver, they will align five to seven yards off. They should have a pass first mentality. They should backpedal two to three steps, then read and react to the play. Versus the run, they have outside containment responsibilities. Versus the pass, they have the deep one-third zone on their side of the field.

- Safety

The safety is aligned 9 to 12 yards off the line of scrimmage. They have a pass first mentality, yet they are crucial in defending the run. They are the alley player that should make the tackle on the runner that has been turned in by the corners. They pursue from the inside outward. They will have the opportunity to make the big hits in the open field. This is why these players must possess the speed and instincts to cover the pass, yet have the guts to make the big hits on the ballcarrier cutting across the field. They will be responsible for the deep middle one-third of the field when they are in pass coverage.

5-3 Stunts and Blitzes

5-3 Option Responsibilities

The option responsibilities for the 5-3 package are listed by position:

- Noseguard

Noseguards always have dive responsibility.

- Tackles

Tackles always have dive responsibility.

- Ends

The defensive end has QB to pitch responsibilities. His responsibility will be determined by the block of the tight end or the offensive tackle if he is aligned on the split end side of the offensive alignment. If he is on the tight end side, he reads the tight end's

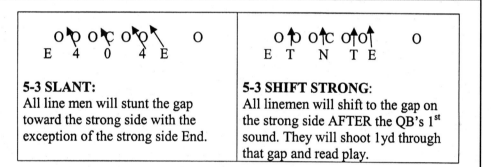

5-3 SLANT:
All line men will stunt the gap toward the strong side with the exception of the strong side End.

5-3 SHIFT STRONG:
All linemen will shift to the gap on the strong side AFTER the QB's 1st sound. They will shoot 1yd through that gap and read play.

Figure 7-42

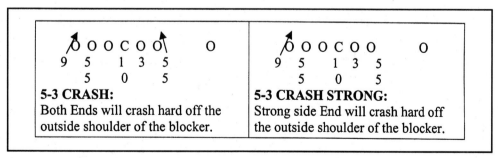

5-3 CRASH:
Both Ends will crash hard off the outside shoulder of the blocker.

5-3 CRASH STRONG:
Strong side End will crash hard off the outside shoulder of the blocker.

Figure 7-43

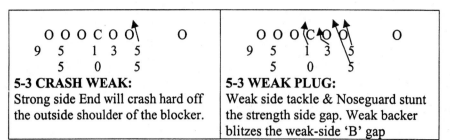

5-3 CRASH WEAK:
Strong side End will crash hard off the outside shoulder of the blocker.

5-3 WEAK PLUG:
Weak side tackle & Noseguard stunt the strength side gap. Weak backer blitzes the weak-side 'B' gap

Figure 7-44

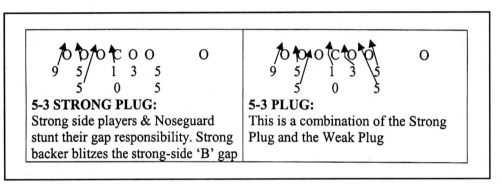

5-3 STRONG PLUG:
Strong side players & Noseguard stunt their gap responsibility. Strong backer blitzes the strong-side 'B' gap

5-3 PLUG:
This is a combination of the Strong Plug and the Weak Plug

Figure 7-45

block. If the tight end blocks down, he will take the dive. If the tight end on blocks or releases off the line of scrimmage, he would have QB responsibility.

• Outside Linebackers

The outside linebacker's first responsibility is to force the QB to pitch the ball. He will work closely with the defensive end. If the defensive end is in a position to get to the QB, he will close in on the QB from the outside in, stopping his ability to pitch yet getting in a position to assist the defensive end. If the defensive end vacates his area for the dive, the outside linebacker must work the QB in a way that will require him to pitch the ball, yet still keep himself in a position to pursue the pitch man by forcing him as far outside as possible.

• Inside Linebackers

The inside linebackers have to check everything from dive to QB to pitch. Their first read is dive. If a teammate closes the dive, then they work down to the QB. If the QB pitches, they must be in a position to pursue him from the inside out, ready for a cutback.

• Corners

The corner will have outside support on the pitch man. He will always have contain responsibility, never allowing the play to get outside him.

• Free Safety

The free safety is the alley player. He has QB to pitch responsibility.

Coverage Packages

There are two basic coverage packages in the 50 defense: 52 cover 2, and 53 cover 3. Certain adjustments must be made for different formations that the offense will use. These adjustments will be detailed in this section along with a man-to-man coverage package and a pass prevent package.

52 Cover 2

This is the base coverage package of the 5-2 package.

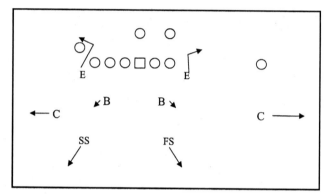

Figure 7-46

Ends—Responsible for the flat behind the line of scrimmage (i.e., screens, swings etc.). He should rush the passer while keying the nearback. If the nearback were to release into the flat, the end is responsible for the coverage.

Backers—Hook to curl responsibility

Corners—Curl to out responsibility

Safeties—Deep half of the field.

53 Cover 3

This is the base coverage package of the 5-3 package.

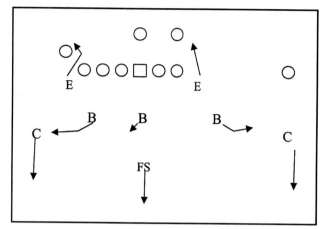

Figure 7-47

Ends—They are responsible for the flat behind the line of scrimmage (i.e., screens, swings, etc.). The end on the split side has hard rush responsibility. His aiming point will be the outside shoulder of the nearback. This will allow him to adjust to this back if he were to release into a pattern. If he does release, the end should jam him as hard as possible delaying his release

Outside Backers—Curl to out responsibility

Middle Backer—Hook to curl. His drop will be to the tight end side of the formation. If there are two tight ends, his initial drop will be seven yards straight back.

Corners—Deep one-third of the field

Free Safeties—Deep one-third of the field.

This is the lock adjustment of the 5-3 package. This is an excellent adjustment that can be made by the players on the field or called with the original play.

Ends and Backers–Same as base cover 3

Corners–The corner that is on the two receiver side of the field is responsible for the deep one-fourth of the field on his side. The one receiver side corner will lock on that receiver. This means that he will play man-to-man coverage on this player while he is on his one-third of the field. This means that he will release him to the free safety if he were to run any type of deep crossing pattern. In that case, he will still drop to his deep one-third looking to help in any way. He should be on the one-third dividing line helping with the deep middle of the field unless someone attempts to cross over to his deep one-third.

Free safety–Responsible for the deep half of the field.

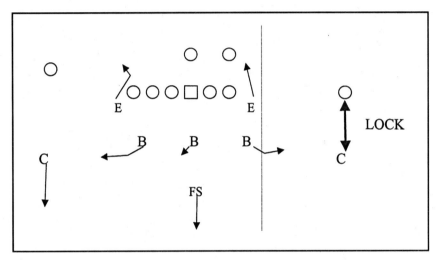

Figure 7-48

52 Adjustment to Twins

This is a recommended coverage adjustment to a twins formation. This is a cover 3 package for the 5-2. Someone will yell, "Twins right/left," and the defense will automatically adjust to cover 3.

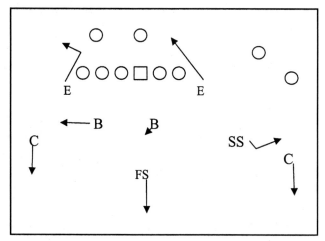

Figure 7-49

Ends–The end on the twins side has pass rush responsibility while the other end will maintain his regular rush/flat responsibilities.

Backers–They should adjust their alignment to the side opposite the twins. The furthest backer will align in a 50 technique and be responsible for the curl to out zone. The other backer will adjust to a 10 Technique and will have hitch to curl toward the tight end side. His drop should start straight back reading the tight end side first.

Corners–Deep one-third of the field. They should align five to seven yards off the widest split receiver on their side.

Strong Safety–The strong safety will align himself five yards off the line of scrimmage while splitting the difference between the widest receiver and the end man on the line of scrimmage. He has out/flat responsibility.

Free Safety–Deep one-third of the field.

53 Adjustment to Twins

This is a recommended coverage adjustment to a twins formation. Someone will yell, "Twins right/left," and the defense will automatically adjust to cover 3.

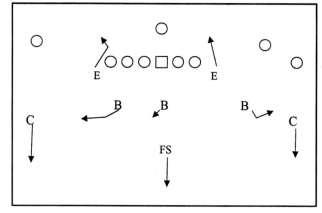

Figure 7-50

Ends–The end on the twins side has pass rush responsibility while the other end will maintain his regular rush/flat responsibilities.

Outside Backers–Curl to out responsibility. The backer on the twins side will align himself five yards off the line of scrimmage, splitting the difference between the widest receiver and the end man on the line of scrimmage.

Middle Backer–Hook to curl. His drop will be to the tight end side of the formation.

Corners–Deep one-third.

Free Safety–He is responsible for the deep one-third of the field.

52 Adjustment to Trips (Cover 5)

This is a recommended coverage adjustment to a trips formation. This is a cover 5 package for the 5-2. Someone will yell, "Trips right/left," and the defense will automatically adjust to cover 5.

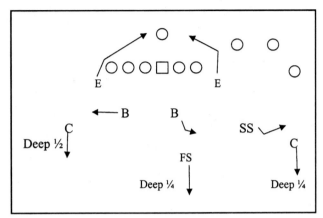

Figure 7-51

Ends–The end on the trips side will align on the line of scrimmage one yard inside the closest man in trips. He will step straight across the line to read quick screen, then rush the passer. The other end will pass rush without letting the back release to his side.

Backers–They should adjust to tight opposite the trips. The furthest backer will align in a 50 technique and be responsible for the curl to out zone, keying the TE. The other backer will adjust to a 20 Technique and will have hitch to curl toward the trips side.

Corners–Trips side corner has the deep one-fourth of the field on his side while the other corner has deep half responsibility.

Strong Safety–The strong safety will align himself five yards off the line of scrimmage while splitting the difference between the widest receiver and the end man on the line of scrimmage. He has out/flat responsibility.

Free Safety–He should align one yard outside the end man on the line of scrimmage. His zone is the deep one-fourth of the field between the two corners.

53 Adjustment to trips (Cover 5)

This is a recommended coverage adjustment to a trips formation. This is a cover 5 package for the 5-2. Someone will yell, "Trips right/left," and the defense will automatically adjust to cover 5.

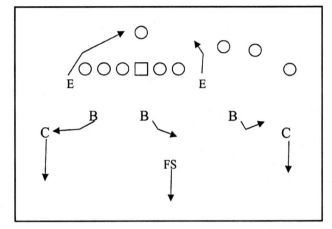

Figure 7-52

Ends–The end on the trips side will align on the line of scrimmage one yard inside the closest man in trips. He will step straight across the line to read quick screen, then rush the passer. The other end will pass rush without letting the back release to his side.

Outside Backers–Curl to out responsibility. The backer on the trips side will align himself five yards off the line of scrimmage, splitting the difference between the widest receiver and the end man on the line of scrimmage.

Middle Backer–Hook to curl. His drop will be to the trips side of the formation.

Corners–Trips side corner has the deep one-fourth of the field on his side while the other corner has deep half responsibilities.

Free Safety–He should align one yard outside the end man on the line of scrimmage. His zone is the deep one-fourth of the field between the two corners.

52 Cover 1 and Cover 1 Free

This is the man-to-man coverage for the 5-2 Package. Always number the receivers from the outside inward. Cover 1 free is man coverage without using the free safety allowing him to help where needed. Cover 1 requires the free safety to take the #3 man when a team aligns three or more receivers on one side of the field.

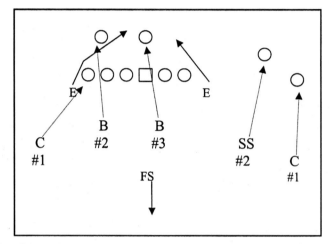

Figure 7-53

Ends—All-out pass rush.

Backers—They will always be responsible for a back. They should align four yards off the ball and, at the snap, take one lateral step, read their man and attack him. If he stays home to block, you will be rushing.

Corners—Number 1 to their side

Strong Safety—Number 2 on the two receiver side

Free Safety—He will key the quarterback; if the QB rolls out, he will attack him; if the QB drops back, he will drop to the deep one-third of the field.

52 Cover 1

Cover 1 requires the free safety to take the #3 man when a team aligns three or more receivers on one side of the field or aligns in a spread formation with two receivers on each side of the field.

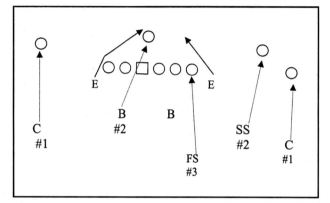

Figure 7-54

Ends—All-out pass rush.

Backers—They will always be responsible for a back. They should align four yards off the ball and, at the snap, take one lateral step, read their man, and attack him. If the QB stays home to block, he will be rushing. He should key the quarterback; if the QB rolls, he will attack him. If the QB hands off, he plays the run; if the QB drops back, he will drop into coverage on a 45-degree angle toward the side the quarterback is looking.

Corners—Number 1 to their side.

Strong Safety—Number 2 on the two receiver side.

Free Safety—Either has the #3 man on the three receiver side of formation or the #2 man versus a spread formation with two receivers on each side.

53 Cover 1 and Cover 1 Free

This is the man-to-man coverages for the 5-3 Package. As always, number the receivers from the outside inward. Cover 1 free is man coverage without using the free safety allowing him to help where needed. Cover 1 requires the free safety to take the #3 man when a team aligns three or more receivers on one side of the field.

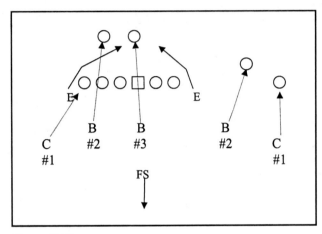

Figure 7-55

Ends—All-out pass rush.

Backers—The outside backer will always have the #2 man on their side while the middle backer has the #3 man. If his man is aligned in the backfield, he should align four yards off the ball and, at the snap, take a lateral step, read his man, and attack him. If the QB stays home to block, he will be rushing.

Corners—Number 1 to their side.

Free Safety—He will key the quarterback; if the QB rolls out, he will attack him; if the QB drops back, he will drop to the deep one-third of the field.

53 Cover 1

Cover 1 requires the free safety to take the #3 man when a team aligns three or more receivers on one side of the field.

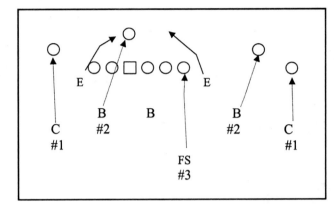

Figure 7-56

Ends—All-out pass rush.

Backers—The outside backer will always have the #2 man on their side. If his man is aligned in the backfield, he should align four yards off the ball and, at the snap, take a lateral step, read his man, and attack him. If the QB stays home to block, he will be rushing. The middle backer will key the quarterback; if the QB rolls, he will attack him. If the QB hands off, he plays the run; if the QB drops back, he will drop into coverage on a 45-degree angle toward the side the quarterback is looking.

Corners—Number 1 to their side.

Free Safety—Number 3 receiver on the three receiver side of the field.

CHAPTER 8

Special Teams

Special teams are one of the most overlooked segments in football. Most teams spend little or no time working on them in the preseason. When they do start working on them, it is usually with the kickers and long snappers. They will put in the teamwork when they are beginning to prepare for their first game.

That is not to say that you need to spend as much time on special teams as you do on your offense or defense. However, you need to spend a proportionate amount of your time developing them.

Consider the following scenario: A high school football game is played and the final score is 21-13. For the sake of this example, we will assume that each team had possession of the ball an equal number of times. Each team had possession of the ball seven times in the course of the game. This means that they had seven offensive and seven defensive possessions for a total of 14 possessions. We will say that they averaged six plays per drive (42 total plays per team). This means that there were 84 total plays in the game. There were five touchdowns scored out of 14 possessions. In this case, let's break down the special teams plays:

- Seven kickoffs—one to begin each half and five after touchdowns.

- Seven received kickoffs—one for every kickoff.

- Five extra point attempts—one after each touchdown.

- Five extra point defenses—one for every extra point attempt.

- Seven punts—from 14 possessions, minus five touchdowns, minus two turnovers.

- Seven punt returns—one for every punt.

- 38 total special teams plays.

- 19 special teams plays per team.

Staying with this example, you know that each team had 84 total plays in the game. We have to reduce this amount by the number of punts in the game, which was seven. This brings the total number of offensive and defensive plays down to 77 per team. Each team had 19 special teams plays in the game. That means there were 96 total plays per team in this game including offensive, defensive, and special teams plays. This means that 20% of your plays were special teams plays. This number will shock most people.

To break this down even further, each team in this scenario had 40% of their plays on offense and 40% on defense. This means that these teams spent 50% of their time on special teams compared to either just their offense or just their defense.

When you think of it these terms, the numbers are staggering. Would you have thought that you would run one special teams play for every two offensive plays in a game? To spend a proportionate amount of practice time on special teams as you do on offense, you would be spending approximately 20-25 minutes every practice on special teams.

Again, that is not to say you must spend 25 minutes of every practice on special teams. In fact, a good portion of special teams comes down to blocking and tackling. These are the two elements that should be worked on the most in practice anyway.

Another point to make is that you should use your best blockers and tacklers on your special teams. You will still have to set aside a percentage of your practice time to work on special teams as a unit. A good average is that you spend 8 to 12% of your practice time for special teams work as a unit. If you have four practices a week that are two hours long, you will spend eight hours practicing. This means you should spend approximately 45 minutes a week working on your special teams as a unit. During the preseason, you will get more practice hours in; this should increase the amount of time you spend on special teams per week.

Special teams can be fit into your practice week in many ways. You can work on them 10 to 12 minutes a day or 45 minutes all in one day. If you are going to work on a majority of your team work in one day, you should make it the last practice before game day. These practices usually have significantly less or no contact involved. Special teams work as a unit can be done with little contact. Work on the concepts and strategies of your special teams. Alignment and assignment are key elements the key element to work on. Work on extra points and field goals (depending on your level) every day for about five minutes. The worst way to lose any game is by a missed extra point. If your kicking game is perfected, you could end up being the winning team in a game decided by an extra point.

Potential special teams situations need to be stressed in practice. Your players need to be prepared for any situation that arises. Many variables apply to special teams play. On game day your team must be prepared for the following possibilities in special team situations:

- A fake punt, field goal attempt, or extra point attempt could happen any time the opposing team lines up in punt or kick formation on a fourth down.
- Your kickoff receiving team should be ready for an onside kick at any time in the game.
- The receiving team must also be ready for a pooched or botched kick that rolls around untouched for a period of time.
- Your kickoff team must be ready for all types of returns, including reverses.
- Your kicking team must be ready for bad snaps or holds during extra point attempts, field goal attempts and punts. They should have a back-up plan if a kick is no longer feasible in these situations.

The other things you must consider are the specialists. These are the kickers, punters, long snappers and holders. They must get repetitions every day. They should work on their skills every day for 10 to 15 minutes before the practice officially starts.

Special teams situations lend themselves to big plays. Close games are often won by a team that had a big play. If a game were to be determined by a punt or kickoff return for a touchdown, you would certainly want to come out the victor in those games. Many times special teams play is the difference between evenly matched teams. There is no excuse for poor special teams play.

Special teams plays and formations will vary greatly from team to team. This next section covers a few ways to do things. Remember, the methods outlined are not the only way to do things.

Punting Team

A team can do three things from a punt formation: punt the ball, fake the punt and run the ball, or fake the punt and throw a pass. Your punt team should be able to do all three. Your punting team is an important element on game day. This part of the game may determine field position. Low scoring games are often won by the team with the best field position.

The Punter

Obviously, the punter will be the backbone of your punting team. Identify your punters early so they can begin honing their skills. Whenever your punter has any downtime in practice, he should be using it to practice his punts. The ideal candidate for a punter would be a player that did not have another starting position on the team. Although this is the ideal situation, it is usually unrealistic. You should choose more than one punter for your team. Some young punters will improve at different rates. If you have a few players working on punting, one of them may excel beyond the others at any point and he would be positioned as the teams starting punter.

Balance is probably the most important attribute of a punter. Of course, there are other quality attributes you would like for him to possess. Coordination and good timing will be essential ingredients. He needs to have the ability to concentrate on what he is doing without being affected by distractions. He must be good under pressure and have the ability to think clearly when things do not go as anticipated.

Pre-punt Fundamentals

The first thing the punter must know before the snap is where he is going to punt the ball. Does he punt it as deep down the middle as possible, or toward one of the sidelines away from the return man? He must take field position into consideration before he punts the ball.

The next thing the punter will do is get in his stance and be ready to receive the snap. This may vary from team to team but this section covers the most common way it is taught. To simplify the steps, assume that the kicker is right-handed making his right foot his dominant foot. He will get in his stance with his kicking foot (right) slightly forward. The toes of his back foot (left) will line up slightly past the middle of his kicking foot. The toes of the back foot may line up as far back as the heel of the kicking foot if this is more comfortable for the punter. The distance should never be greater than heel to toe. The punter must be balanced. His feet can be no further than shoulder width apart. Figure 8-1 is an example of the positioning of the feet in the punter's stance. The dotted line shows the appropriate range to line up the back foot in the stance.

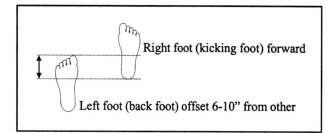

Right foot (kicking foot) forward

Left foot (back foot) offset 6-10" from other

Figure 8-1

The depth with which the punter will set up behind the center will vary. It will change depending on the punt formation your team uses. At the high school level, this would be anywhere from 9 to 14 yards back. This distance will vary at the youth level depending on the size and experience of your players. The kicking foot of the punter should be aligned with the center of the ball as shown in Figure 8-2.

When a punter's feet are properly aligned in his stance, he must get his body into a balanced position. He must maintain balance all the way through the kicking motion. His knees should be slightly bent. He should also be bent slightly forward at the waist. He should not stand erect waiting for the snap, nor should he bend over too much. He should find a nice, comfortable position.

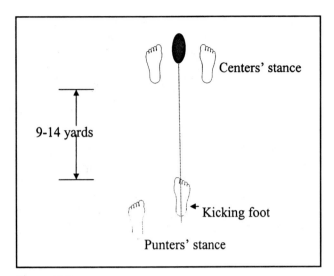

9-14 yards

Centers' stance

Kicking foot

Punters' stance

Figure 8-2

The punter must give a target with his hands for the center to aim for with the snap. He should always hold his target hands in the position he will hold the ball to kick it. The target area should be at the top inside of the punter's leg. This is where the punter will align his hands. They will be out in front of his body with his elbows slightly bent. Keep in mind that a low target is better than a high target. If the snap goes over the punter's head, it can roll a great distance. It will also be unlikely that he will be able to get to it and get off any type of punt. If the ball is too low, the punter has a greater chance of getting a hold of the ball and salvaging some type of punt.

Once the punter is ready to receive the snap, he must keep his eyes on the ball at all times. He should focus only on the ball throughout the entire punting procedure. As soon as the punter's feet are set, he must immediately focus on the ball. There are times when the center may snap the ball sooner than the punter expected. The punter should be ready for the snap at any time.

Now that the punter is ready to receive the snap, he must give a signal to the center telling him that it is time to snap the ball. Some teams will use a predetermined cadence while others will use silent hand signals by the punter. You can also use a combination of both methods. There can be a cadence that gets every player set and ready for the

punt, and then the punter will call for the snap with a silent hand signal once he knows his entire team is set and ready. You should always use some type of cadence. There will be situations where you may want to use a hard cadence to try and draw the defense offside. Before any cadence begins, someone must evaluate the defense to see if any blocking adjustments are needed before the snap. Although some teams use a back to call out the cadence, it is advisable to use the punter. He should be in control of the process. Whatever you do, be consistent. Every punt situation should look and sound the same to the defense. This will give you the ability to execute fake punts without tipping off the defense.

Post-snap Fundamentals

The punter must know how to receive the snap, execute his steps, drop the ball, and kick the ball properly. The following fundamental details are described as if your punter is right-footed.

The first thing the punter needs to do after the snap is catch the ball. As simple as this may sound, this is extremely important. If there is an errant snap, the most important thing on the punter's mind should be catching the ball. Inexperienced kickers will try to catch the ball with their hands in order to keep their feet consistent. This is a big mistake. If the snap is errant, they should be encouraged to move their entire body to get to the ball. They can readjust their footwork and get off a punt even if it is not as perfect as desired. If they don't catch the snap, there is a good chance there will never be a punt, which could be devastating to your team.

The most desirable way for your punter to catch the ball would be on the front of his body around the height of his belly button. When he catches the ball, he should not pull the ball into his body. This is wasted motion since he will have to extend his arms again to complete the punt.

Once he catches the ball, he must position it in his hands. He should position it as he steps. If he positions it first and then steps, he will lose valuable time. It will be a natural instinct for the punter to adjust the ball before stepping. He must be taught to adjust as he steps. Teach him this technique from the very beginning. If given enough repetitions, this technique will become natural to the punter.

Opinions vary as to where the player should place his hands on the ball. The player needs to be comfortable, but he also needs to bring the ball to his foot in a consistent fashion. A right-handed kicker will drop the ball with his right hand and guide the ball with his left hand. He should hold onto the ball as long as possible before dropping it by cupping the front side and bottom of the ball with his left hand. The right hand is on the back top of the ball. The thumb will be well over the centerline of the ball and the index finger will be on the other side of the center of the ball. The rest of the fingers will be comfortably spread. The player should be able to hold the ball in the air with only his right hand over it. If he can do this, he will have great control of the ball. The drop is extremely important. A bad drop means a bad punt; a good drop can be accomplished with different grips.

The number of steps a punter takes is critical; 1.5 steps are ideal. This is called the 'step and a half' method. Although other methods are taught, this is the most common and the most effective for getting off an effective punt quickly. This will not be a natural way for a new punter to step. You must watch him closely to be sure he never takes two steps.

The step and a half method is shown in Figure 8-3. The first thing that every punter must do is take the initial step in the direction they are going to punt the ball. From there, the footwork is in a direct line. From his pre-kick stance, he takes the half-step of 10 to 12 inches in the direction he is going to kick. He then takes a full and natural step with his back foot that will land 10 to 15 inches in front of the kicking foot. This is the plant foot in the kick. After the right foot makes the kick, he should naturally step forward landing his foot in a pre-snap relationship with the other. If this occurs, you will know that the kicker has achieved balance, which is an extremely important element of the kick.

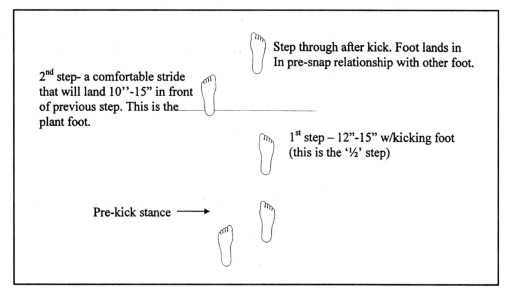

Figure 8-3

The punter should be ready to drop or place the ball onto the kicking foot. The ball will be kicked with the center of the foot. When the ball hits the foot, it should be tilted slightly downward and slightly inward. The left hand, or the guide hand, releases off to the side of the ball as the right hand holds onto the ball as long as possible before hitting the foot. It is very important to hold onto the ball as long as possible. The greater distance the ball has to travel without guidance from the hand, the greater the chance for an error. When you are talking about placement onto the foot, inches can dramatically affect the quality of the punt.

Once the ball drops, the leg will swing through to punt it. The leg must swing like a pendulum. The knee will be slightly bent but not stiff. As soon as the punter's plant foot is down, his kicking leg will whip through the ball. The kicking leg should continue right through the ball as far as it can naturally go.

When the ball hits the foot, the middle bottom of the ball will meet the thickest part of the foot, which is the center axis shown in Figure 8-4. The ball should be angled slightly inward and downward. The ball turns slightly inward and downward when it impacts the foot.

After the kick and follow through of the leg, the kicking foot should come back down naturally landing in a position that is relatively close to the pre-snap stance. He should end with the same amount of balance that he began with. His momentum should not take him forward or backward.

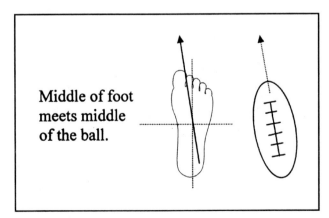

Middle of foot meets middle of the ball.

Figure 8-4

The ideal punt will have a spiral to it. This will be accomplished if all of the previous kicking elements are adhered to. The swing of the leg combined with the proper positioning of the ball will give you the desired results. Many coaches will have the punter kick the ball slightly to the side of the ball. You will get a desired spiral by slicing the ball, but you will lose power and accuracy. To achieve the maximum power out of the kick, the meat of the ball must contact the meat of the foot during a powerful pendulum-like motion.

Certainly, different ways exist to achieve similar results. The ways listed previously have been successful for many years. Keep in mind that some players may accomplish the same result with less orthodox methods. Allow a little leeway when you are working with your punters. Use this section as a guideline to get you started.

The Long Snapper

The long snapper is the man who snaps the ball to the punter. This does not necessarily have to be your regular center. In fact, many teams have a long snapping specialist. You want the best and the quickest snap to get back to your punter. The quicker it gets there, the quicker it gets downfield. The center must pass the ball to the punter. That is the element that you have to emphasize; the center is passing the ball through his legs. If he were to stand up out of his stance with the ball over his head and face the punter, he would still pass it the same exact way.

Note: Fundamentals of the snap are covered in 'The Snap' section later in this chapter. See Figure 8-19.

Punt Protection

Now that you're able to execute a punt, you need to protect the punter until he kicks the ball. Although there are numerous ways to protect the punt, one constant exists on every punt: the punter will have a punting lane to kick in. This lane goes in whichever direction he initially steps. We know that he is going to take 1.5 steps out of his stance. The area in front of the kicker is the most vulnerable to a blocked punt.

Figure 8-5 is an example of a punting lane. The triangle shows the most vulnerable area for a blocked punt. If a defender is able to quickly penetrate the A or B gap, he will be in an excellent position to block the punt. If the player is coming from the side to block the punt, he must be cut off before he can get to the front of the kicker. If you are able to protect an area that covers two yards on each side of the punter along with the middle of the lane, you will be able to successfully execute a punt.

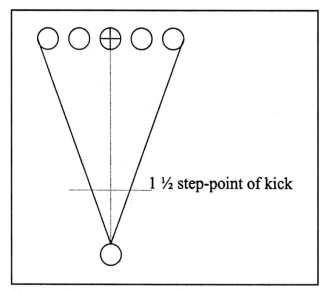

Figure 8-5

Figure 8-5 only shows the line of scrimmage from tackle to tackle. In most situations, the ends will be used to attack the punt returner. The backs will be responsible for blocking any penetration from outside the tackles.

Punt Formations

Although many different formations can be used to execute a punt, the most common formation is the tight formation. The tight formation is used by teams that are looking to get the greatest amount of protection to the punter. Figure 8-6 is one example of a tight punt formation. The interior linemen are

separated with a one-foot spread. They are each responsible for their inside gaps. They will always block down, even with a man lined up over them. The punter does not need to be aligned as deep in this formation. The average depth is 8 to 12 yards. Many teams will align the punter only eight to nine yards deep in this formation. Youth teams may use a shorter distance.

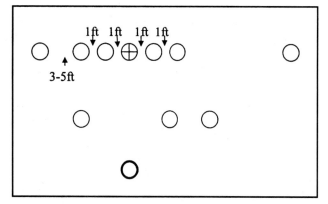

Figure 8-6

In Figure 8-6, the split end on the right will be the main threat to tackle the returner. He will attack the area of the punt return from the outside. He will go directly toward the returner without looping. This man should be within three yards of the ball when it is caught by the returner or when it hits the ground if the returner does not catch it. He must know where the punt is going before the snap so that he knows the path he needs to take down the field. Even though he knows the general area the ball is going, he needs to try and locate the ball as he heads down the field. He will key the reactions of the returner to try and locate the ball. He should not be looking back as he runs down the field.

The tight end on the left side is the next immediate threat to returner. He is aligned three to five feet outside the tackle. If there is a defender aligned inside him, he must first block him before releasing down the field. He would only need to make a one-second block if it became necessary. The punt should take less than two seconds, depending on your level. This man must get down the field quickly. He too must pursue the ballcarrier from the outside.

The spread formation is another widely used formation. This formation is used for maximum punt coverage. Teams will use this in situations where it is less likely for the defense to be attempting a block. Figure 8-7 shows an example of two different spread formations. The split between the center and guard is slightly shorter than the split between the guard and the tackle. The linemen in the spread formation will likely be rule blocking. This means they will know the particular man they are responsible to block.

The punter in this situation must be aligned deeper than usual. He will usually align from 10 to 14 yards. This will be affected by the level and ability of the teams' players. The punter will be deeper to allow him to get the punt off even if there is some penetration. Teams will put the punter very deep so that they are assured that their coverage guys will get to the spot of the kick swiftly. These punts are hard to return for this reason. Some teams will use this method when they are trying to pin a team back for field position purposes. Other teams will employ this when they fear a particular punt returner. The best way to stop a punt return is to not let it get started.

The split ends in this case are extremely important. They must be within two to three yards of the ball when it is caught. The objective would be to have the returner call for a fair catch. If the split ends have proper positioning, they will deny the returner an opportunity to run the ball. If the ball hits the ground, the split ends would allow it to roll to the most advantageous point. Once it starts to roll backwards, they will down it. If it is rolling toward the end zone they will down it before it gets there. They must position themselves so that no opponent has the opportunity to pick the ball up.

The combination formation is also widely used. This is a combination of the spread and tight formations. The alignment would resemble the spread formation while the assignment would more closely resemble the tight formation. This formation will allow you to move your punter closer if you want to get a little more distance on your punt. You can also leave him further back if you are trying to get better coverage on the punt. Figure 8-8 shows an example of the line spreads of the combination formation.

Figure 8-9 is an example showing the blocking assignment in the combination formation. The guards and tackles are responsible to block their

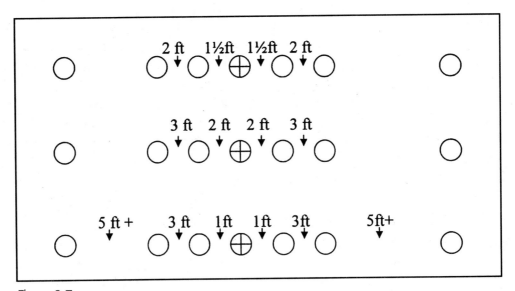

Figure 8-7

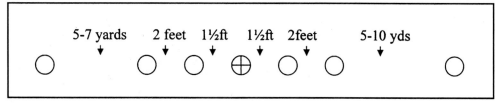

Figure 8-8

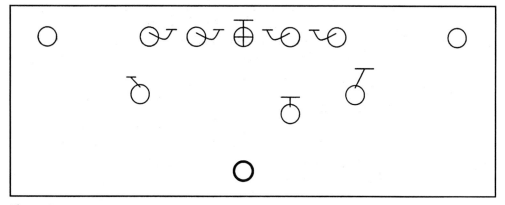

Figure 8-9

inside gaps. They are not responsible for any one particular man. They will take a quick inside step when the ball is snapped. This will put them almost shoulder-to-shoulder. The backs will be responsible for any outside penetration. Split ends are responsible for the punt returner. They must get themselves down the field quickly so they are in a position to stop any return immediately.

The backs can be aligned in different fashions. In Figure 8-10, there are three backs aligned to protect the punter. The two halfbacks have outside blocking responsibility while the fullback has inside responsibility. The fullback will first check to make sure there is no interior penetration, and then he will look to help out on the outside. If there are two immediate outside threats on his side, the fullback will help the halfback on that side pick them up. All backs have one-second block responsibility, then they must release down the field to attack the returner.

Figure 8-11 shows other possible backfield alignments. The blocking assignment will vary from formation to formation and from team to team. In every formation, there must be a back on each side

that is responsible for outside penetration. The middle blocking back can be used in different ways. Some teams will not align him in the middle and will use him to free up another player to get down the field immediately for the returner.

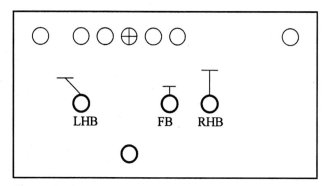

Figure 8-10

Punt Coverage

Punt coverage will be similar for most teams. Even teams that use different formations will use similar ways to cover the punt. Figure 8-12 shows a very common and effective way to cover a punt using a combination formation. The line spreads are not

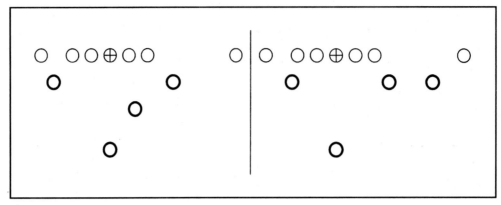

Figure 8-11

quite as far as spread punt formation, nor are they as close as the tight punt formation. This formation will give good protection to the punter as well as good coverage on the return of the punt.

Every player must first block and then release down the field in coverage. The block will consist of a solid chest-to-chest block before the release. A forearm or hand chuck is not acceptable. Every player has a section of the field they will release to and a lane they are responsible to protect. When it is clear where the return man is heading, they will adjust their paths accordingly.

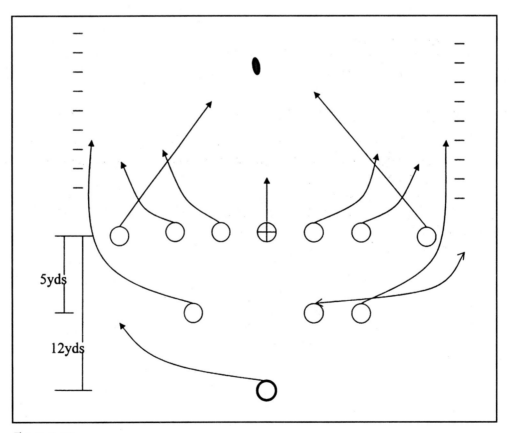

5yds

12yds

Figure 8-12

Punt Coverage Rules

Stance: Every player is in a two-point stance.

Line Splits: Two-foot line splits for everyone on the line. All line splits are closed to one foot inside the 10 yard line.

Line Rules: Inside gap, on, outside gap. Block from the inside gap. Close gap to one foot if inside gap is being threatened. Communicate with other linemen. Make solid contact with the defender then release downfield in coverage.

Cadence: "Set, ready, hit"

Alignment and Assignment:

- Center—Make a perfect snap, block area, then release upfield; stay in the lane in the middle of the hash marks.

- Guards—Rule block and then release upfield in lane three to five yards inside the hash marks.

- Tackles—Rule block and then release upfield in lane along hash marks.

- Halfbacks—Align five yards behind the tackle on the fullback side and five yards behind the guard on the other side. Block any immediate threat to the punter. Block from the inside out. If no interior threat exists, they will block the outside threat. After solid contact, release outside as contain men on the return. Release up the field after two seconds. They will not attempt a block after two seconds.

- Fullback—Aligned five yards behind the guard. He is responsible for the cadence. He will read the defensive formation and look for overload situations. He must never step backwards. He is responsible for any threat from guard to guard. After the punt he will be the safety on the right hash mark.

- Punter—Align 12 yards from the center. He will get off the punt in two to three seconds—less than two seconds is the goal. After the punt he becomes the safety on the left hash mark.

Punt Fakes

Numerous ways exist to fake a punt and every team will do it differently. Every team should have a fake punt that is a running play and a fake punt that is a passing play. The important thing to any type of fake is consistency. To pull off a quality fake, it must look and sound just like your punts. The same personnel must align in the same formation as if you were going to punt the ball. If you change you personnel, you will raise suspicion among the defenders. The same thing will happen if you change your alignment. If your ends are usually aligned tight when you punt, what do you think your opponent would think if one of them aligned wide?

The best time to use fake punts are when they are least likely. A fake punt will have a greater chance for success if the other team is not expecting it. Remember, if the play fails, your opponent will take possession of the ball at the spot at the end of the play. Can you afford to put your opponent in this field position? How much time is left on the clock? If you were inside your opponent's 50-yard line with less than 30 seconds to go, it may not be that risky to take the chance. If you were successful, you may be in position for a field goal or better. If you are unsuccessful, your opponent will have 20 seconds or so to gain 25 or more yards just to be in a position to attempt a field goal. You must consider these scenarios. Try to think of the worst-case scenario for every situation. If you can live with the results, it may be a good opportunity to fake the punt.

This section will cover two examples of fake punts. The first example is a running play; the second example is a passing play. You should not attempt to use these plays. Your fakes should be based on your offensive strengths. You should use blocking schemes that you use in your regular offense. The fake punts should not be dramatic changes.

In the pass play fake, you must have a punter who is capable of completing a pass. There would be no sense in attempting this play if you don't have confidence in your punter's ability to throw the ball.

The other thing you have to consider is your ends' ability to catch the ball. Chances are these players are not your starting receivers. They are in these positions because of their ability to make openfield tackles. Unless you are going to run a screen play or a swing pass, the pass will likely be thrown to one of the ends.

Since this play is usually run as a fourth down, the receiver should be in first down territory when he makes the catch. Always use the assumption that he will be tackled as soon as he catches the pass.

Figure 8-13 is an example of a pass play thrown from a punt formation. In this particular play, the pass is a roll out. There are some advantages to doing this. The first thing it will do is shorten any pass the punter will throw. The other advantage to this play is the clear read of the target receivers. If the primary receiver is not open, the secondary receiver is in an easy position to spot.

By rolling the punter out, you will be able to provide better protection. It is easier to block for him if he is isolated to one side. He is also moving in the same direction of his receivers. This will make the pass that much simpler.

If this play breaks down, the punter can continue running down the field with the ball in hopes of getting the first down. In fact, he should be instructed to keep the ball if the side is open as he rolls out. His first thought should be to run the ball. If the side is open, this is the safest option. Remember the saying: "When you throw the ball three things can happen and two of them are bad." Take the sure thing if it presents itself.

You should choose a play that you are comfortable with as your fake. The important thing is to perfect the play. As we know, the only way to perfect anything is to practice it.

The other type of fake you should have in place is a running fake. The best advice I can give you is to use a blocking scheme that is already familiar to your team. As with any fake, it must look like a punt play for it to be successful. This means that you can't change personnel in order to run the fake.

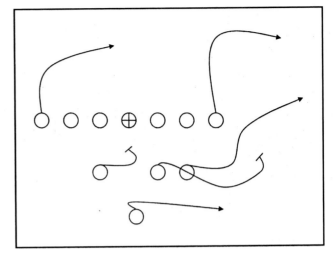

Figure 8-13

In most situations, it would be unwise for you to use the punter as the ballcarrier. The defense is already focused on him and will likely pick up the fake quickly. This means that the ball will go to one of the up backs. Although there are several ways to get him the ball, the most common way to get the ball to an up back is to have him intercept the snap. For him to do this he would need to be lined up relatively close to the midline. He should be aligned no further than the outside shoulder of the guard. Keep in mind that this must be the up back's regular alignment for your punts. If he aligns there only when you are faking the punt, it will easily be read by the defense.

The punter will be the man that sells these fakes. He will simulate an actual punt. He can do this one of two ways: one, he can act as if he is punting the ball; two, he can act as if it is an errant snap and he is going back to pick up the loose ball. He must sell it either way. He will go through all the movements that would be involved in an actual punt or errant snap situation.

Figure 8-14 is an example of a fake punt that is a running play. The punter will fake an errant snap. The # 3 back will intercept the snap and follow the block of the #2 back. The #2 back will read the block of the #1 back and decide whether to cut inside or outside of him. The #1 back will block the first man outside the tackle. He will try to seal one side of him as the running lane. The end will release down the field for at least five yards before looking to block. This will force the defensive backs off the line of scrimmage.

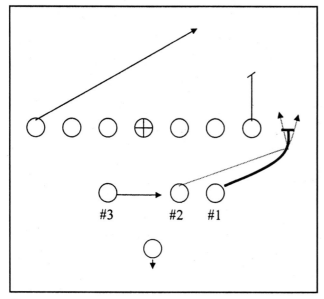

Figure 8-14

Punt Returns

Punt returns are an extremely important element in football. How much time do you spend practicing punt returns in practice? If you are like most teams then you are not practicing them enough. These are the types of plays that can break a game wide open. If executed properly, this may be your teams' best opportunity for a big play during a game. Field position is the deciding factor in many low scoring games. Win the field position battle and you will have a better opportunity to win the close games.

Punt returns don't just happen—they are well planned. Many teams put the burden of the return on the punt return man. In actuality, every man on the field is equally responsible for the proper execution of a punt return. The best thing you can do for your return man is to give him a clear running lane to choose. The quicker he heads up the field, the greater the chances are that he will be successful.

Strategy will be a major element in your return game. Make sure you are aware of all of the game situations before making any return decisions. Field position will play a major roll in your decisions. For example, you should not line up a return man inside your own 10 yard line. He would be instructed to let the ball roll if it were heading inside the goal line. Of course, he should be aware of the punt coverage first. If he has a clear running lane, I could take the chance on a return. He must be positive in these situations. He should never allow a ball to roll outside of the 10 yard line. This is where he needs to make a fair catch or a return.

The objective of a good punt return is to gain yardage. This is why your return men should always start straight up the field as they gain possession of the ball. They can then read the blocking scheme and choose the proper running lane. The more time your runner spends running toward a sideline, the greater the chances are for the punt team to react to the play. His mentality should be to gain as many yards as possible. If he is always looking for the big play, he may cost you field position. If he stays with the integrity of the return that was set up, he will increase his chances for a big play.

Use the field in your favor. If you are going to set up an outside return, try it to the wide side of the field if it is distinct. Consider returning the punt right up the middle of the field. This method is rarely utilized. Players have an outside mentality on punt returns. Sometimes the best choice is straight ahead.

The punt return will start with the punt return man. This person should be your best openfield runner. Speed may be the most important factor, but it is not the only factor. He must have good hands to catch the ball. Make sure that this person is confident and can handle pressure situations. He will be called on to make quick decisions that may affect the outcome of the game. You must weigh out all of the pros and cons before choosing your return man.

Figure 8-15 is an example of a punt return to the right against a tight punt formation. In this return there are two men back to receive the punt. Whichever man catches the ball will become the runner. Whenever possible the return man should not run to catch the ball in the opposite direction of the return. For example, if the ball is kicked between the return men and the return is set up to the right, the return man on the left should catch the ball since he will be heading to the right already to catch the ball. The return men are labeled as the free safety and strong safety. The offensive linemen are numbered to give a blocking reference to the return team. To run the return to the left, reverse the responsibilities shown previously.

Following is a list of rules for a punt return right or left. Figure 8-15 is an example of a punt return right. Use that diagram as a reference to understand the following rules:

Left End–Align yourself just outside the EMLOS. Rush the punter trying to block the punt from the outside in. if you don't block the punt, continue to the opposite side where you will be the safety blocker in the case that the return man is breaking loose. You are responsible for backside leakage.

Left Tackle–Align inside shade of #2. On the snap, attack #3 blocking him until the ball is kicked and then release down the line of scrimmage and set up in the wall five yards from the noseguard. Use your upfield shoulder to block any defender coming into the wall.

Noseguard–Align inside shade of the center to the return side. On the snap, attack #3 on the return side blocking him until the ball is punted, and then release down the line and set up in the wall five yards from the right tackle. Use your upfield shoulder to block any defender coming into the wall.

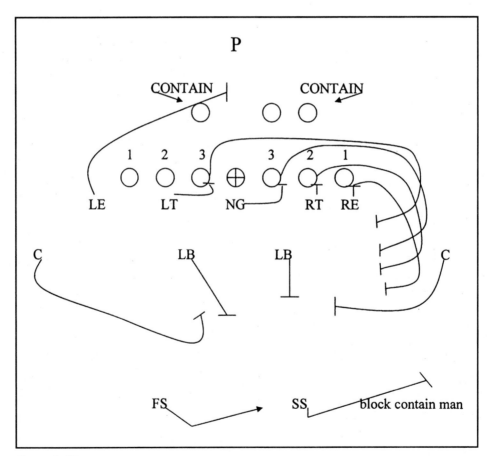

Figure 8-15

Right Tackle–Align outside shade of #2 blocking him until the ball is punted, and then release down the line and set up in the wall five yards from the right end. Use your upfield shoulder to block any defender coming into the wall.

Right End–Align outside shade of EMLOS blocking him until the ball is punted, and then release down the line and set up in the wall in an 8 x 8 relationship with the returner. Ideally, you will set up on the hash marks or numbers. Use your upfield shoulder to block any defender coming into the wall. You are the outside contain man on a fake punt so you must first read for the fake before releasing down the field.

Corner (away from the return side)–Align 3 x 5 outside the EMLOS. Check for fakes, defend against the pass. Release to within three yards of the LB; block the most dangerous outside threat with the upfield shoulder.

Corner (on the return side)–Same as the other C; you will go to the end of the wall and pick off the most dangerous threat to the return man getting to the wall.

Linebackers–Align head-up on #2 three to five yards off. Check for fakes, defend the pass and then sprint to 10 yards from the return man and block the most dangerous threat with your upfield shoulder.

Safeties–Align on the hash marks. Fair catch any short punts. Do not let the ball bounce on the ground. The C closest to the ball will call, "mine," and yell, "go" after catching it. The other corner will lead through the wall to block the punting teams' contain man. Do not catch the ball inside the 10 yard line but signal for a fair catch. If you are not going to catch the ball, continue to yell a word that notifies your entire team that the ball is on the ground and to get away from it.

Punt Block

Thoughts on blocking punts vary widely. Some teams will gamble everything to go after the punt, while others will take a more conservative approach. Figure 8-16 is an example of a more conservative approach: one side is going after the block while the other is setting up blocking for the

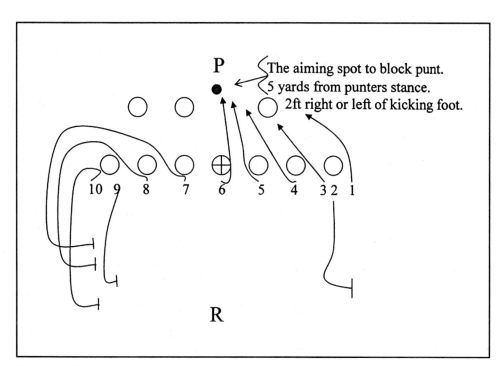

Figure 8-16

return man in case the punt is not blocked. In this example, the players are numbered instead of labeled in positions.

- 1, 3, and 4–Rush the spot; try to block punt; don't hit the kicker.

- 4, 5, and 6–Take the inside lane from the backfield blocker. Do not go into or outside him.

- 7, 8, and 10–Block the man you are on for three seconds and release down line to form wall.

- 9 and 2–Pull out early and check for fakes; defend the pass; defend the first threat outside you if there is a return.

- The return side is always opposite the block call. In this case, you are blocking right and returning left.

Field Goals and Extra Point Kicks

Field goals and extra kicks are very important aspects of the game. Many close games have been won or lost because of an extra point or a field goal. This is true at every level. Many professional football games have been decided by an extra point. Youth football teams are usually awarded two points for kicking an extra point and only one if they run or pass it. Children as young as 10 years old can be taught to convert extra-point kicks, and yet few of these teams practice this element enough.

Teams at every level should spend significant time on their kicking game. Three specialists are involved in the kicking game: the kicker, the center, and the holder. The offensive linemen are usually the same personnel that are already on the field. These players are already getting plenty of blocking repetitions in practice, although they must still practice as a unit every day to work on the nuances of blocking for a kick.

The kicker, the snapper, and the holder need to get a significant number of repetitions every day. These players should arrive at least 15 minutes before the official practice. They should stretch the relative muscle groups for their position and then practice their skills. They can work separately or as a group. They can also work in subgroups. For instance, the center can be snapping to the holder while the kicker is kicking off a tee or with a substitute holder.

These players should also get individual repetitions during practice. If there is ever a time when they are not involved in something else, they should be working on their techniques. During games, they should be practicing on the sideline whenever possible. Get a portable kicking net so that your kicker can warm-up just before you need him. These portable nets are useful and inexpensive.

The Kicker

The most important aspect of kicking field goals and extra points is accuracy. Don't make the mistake of looking for the player with the strongest foot and then stopping there. It would be better to have a player that can convert his kick consistently, even if he does not cover the distance that a less consistent kicker is able to cover. Many teams will have a specialist that only kicks the ball on their roster. High school teams are routinely using soccer player to fill the role of kicker. In the state of Delaware, one state championship team used a female soccer player as their place kicker.

Before we talk about the fundamental requirements of a place kicker, let's focus on the mental aspect. The kicker must be mentally tough. He can't falter under pressure. Remember, many times a kick will be the deciding factor in close games. You want your kicker to enter the field very confident in his abilities in these situations.

The fundamentals described in this section are based on a right-footed straightaway kicker. This is the easiest technique to teach and can be very accurate if done properly. If you prefer a soccer-style kicker, it would be advisable to seek assistance from someone who specializes in these types of kicks. The approaches to both are very similar, even though the kicking mechanics differ.

The kicker's steps will be very similar to those of the punter. The one and a half step approach should be used. To do this, the kicker's stance will have his kicking foot set as much as six inches in front of his plant foot. Figure 8-17 shows two different types of stances. One has more stagger than the other. Both of these stances are acceptable; the kicker should use the one he is most comfortable with. The first step will be a half step taken with the kicking foot; this is why the six-inch stagger is more common. The player does not feel as though he is taking as small a stride because his feet are already separated somewhat.

After the feet are set, the kicker must prepare his body. He must be balanced yet leaning slightly forward—ready to explode through the ball. His shoulders should be square with the crossbar of the goal post with his arms hanging comfortably by his side. His head must be down with his eyes focused on the tee. His head must stay down with his eyes focused on the tee throughout the kick. This is by far the most important thing you will teach any kicker.

The steps to the ball are similar to the steps of the punter. Figure 8-18 is an example of a one and a half step approach. This approach is a safe and effective way to get a kick off quickly. The kicker starts from the staggered stance as previously outlined. The first step he takes is with his kicking foot, which is the right foot in Figure 8-18. This step is the half step portion of the one and a half step approach. This step should only be a 12- to 15-inch step. The next step is with the plant foot, which is the left foot in our example. By this time, the ball should be on the tee and ready to be kicked. This stride should be a full and natural stride that will land on a 3 x 3 inch relationship with the tee. This means that the toes of the plant foot will be three inches to the left of the tee and three inches back behind the tee.

The kicking leg will swing like a pendulum through the ball. The foot will contact the ball just above the middle of the bottom half of the ball. On a high school size football this would be 4.5 to 5 inches from the bottom tip of the ball, assuming that the ball is approximately 14 inches in total length. After the leg swing, the kicking foot should land naturally in front of the tee. The body motion should be forward. Some young kickers have a tendency to lean back when they kick. Look for this movement and correct it.

Differing opinions exist on what the plant foot should do after the kick. Some coaches feel that it should naturally come off the ground after the kick, while others feel it should remain planted. Either method is acceptable. Your kicker should do whichever makes him most comfortable.

The head must stay down throughout the follow-through portion of the kick. The kicker should never be allowed to look up at the kick until after his kicking foot has firmly landed on the ground. If he looks up too soon he will surely slice his kicks.

Do not stress distance when teaching your kickers. Stress the importance of accuracy, which will be achieved through consistency. The distance will come with practice. There are no extra points awarded for the length of a kick; it must go through the uprights to be awarded points.

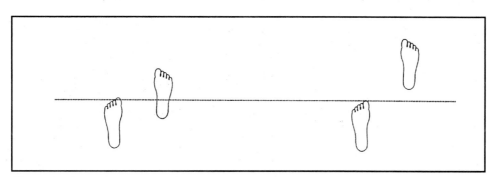

Figure 8-17

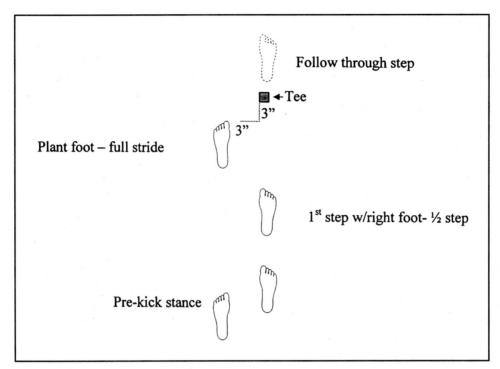

Follow through step

←Tee

3"

3"

Plant foot – full stride

1ˢᵗ step w/right foot- ½ step

Pre-kick stance

Figure 8-18

The Snap

The first thing the snapper must do is get into a proper stance. He should be relaxed and comfortable. His knees should be flexed and his back close to parallel with the ground. His toes can be aligned with a toe-to-instep relationship all the way up to a toe-to-toe relationship. His stance should be no more than a toe-to-instep stagger. Many coaches use a toe-to-instep relationship. The center should use the most comfortable and stable stance.

He will align the ball on the ground before he grasps it. Of course, he is not allowed to pick the ball up off the ground to adjust it. He should adjust the ball so that his fingers are across the laces with his dominant (snapping) hand. He will grip the ball as if he were going to throw an overhead pass. He will place the other hand on the outside of the ball for guidance. The guide hand should be placed on the side of the ball wherever the snapper feels most comfortable. Some will have it closer to the front of the ball, while others will have it closer to the back.

When he snaps the ball, it must be one continuous motion with both hands. The ball should snap back and through. The snapper will break his wrist as he passes the ball just as he would if he were passing it overhead. His hands must follow through after the release of the ball. The only way to perfect the snap is with practice. There should never be a day that the long snapper doesn't practice his snaps.

Remind the center that his main objective is to get off a quality snap—blocking is secondary. With the new rules that are in place, no one will be allowed to hit the center until his head is back up and in a position to defend himself. Once he snaps the ball, he should bring his head up and wait for any defenders that come toward him. The guards will always be blocking down to close off the A gaps. He will most likely assist one of the guards when he blocks.

The depth with which the holder will set up behind the center will vary at different levels. At the high school level, this would be anywhere from six to eight yards back. This distance will vary at the youth level depending on the size and experience of your players. The tee should be aligned with the center of the ball as shown in Figure 8-19.

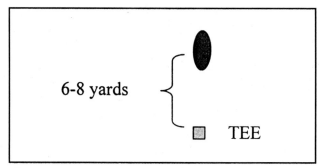

Figure 8-19

The Holder

The holder will be set up just to the right of the tee with a right-footed kicker and to the left with a left-footed kicker. If he is on the right, his left knee will be on the ground just behind and to the side of the tee. His right foot will be comfortably and naturally in front and him. He should be in a position that will allow him to spring to his feet quickly.

His arms should be extended out naturally in front of the tee. He will give the center a target to hit with his hands. His thumbs and index fingers will be facing each other yet slightly spread apart. The rest of his fingers should be naturally spread apart. He should receive a spiral snap right between both hands. The momentum of the catch should bring the hands and the ball back just over the tee where he will set the ball quickly with the laces facing out where possible

The ball should be held lightly in place with the index finger on the top of the ball. Some holders will use two or three fingers to hold the ball. This is OK as long as they do not apply too much pressure down on the top of the ball. The ball should have a slight lean backwards on the tee.

The holder must concentrate on getting the ball on the tee and holding it there correctly. He cannot think of anything else. It is illegal for any defender to contact him so he should never have to worry about defending himself.

Field Goal Formation

Blocking for the kick is very similar to blocking for a punt, only it is simpler. The blockers will concentrate solely on stopping defensive penetration. Figure 8-20 is a common example of a kicking formation. The line spreads are one foot or less all the way down the line of scrimmage. The blockers responsibility is his inside gap. He cannot allow any inside penetration. When he blocks a man coming inside, he will try to block across the defender's body. This will delay him long enough to allow the kick to get off. Do not worry about devastating blocks in this situation. The line just needs to get their entire body out in front of the defender.

The center needs to concentrate only on snapping the ball. It is illegal to hit the center until his head is up and he is in a position to defend himself. When he is up, he should assist one of the guards blocking the inside penetration of the defenders.

The halfbacks are aligned three feet behind the ends. The inside foot of the halfbacks' stance should split the crotch of the end three feet behind him. The outside foot will be offset back, which will align the halfback on a small angle. His blocking responsibilities are from the inside out. As the ball is snapped, he will block the innermost penetration outside the end.

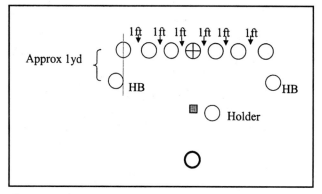

Figure 8-20

There should be a contingency plan in affect in the case of an errant snap. The snapper will repeatedly yell out a word that his teammates will recognize as the signal to execute the contingency plan. For the sake of this example, the word "fire" is used as the signal. If the snap were bad and a proper kick would be unlikely, the holder would begin yelling, "fire," along with the kicker.

When the team hears the "fire" call, they will immediately institute the alternative plan. Figure 8-21 is an example of such a plan. It is a run or pass option by the holder. The kicker will become the lead blocker for the holder. Depending on where he picks up the ball, the holder will sprint to the easiest side of the line. If he has the room, he will just keep the ball and run for daylight. If he is pressured, he will throw a pass to the end or the halfback on that side. The ends will do a seven to eight yard out pattern while the halfbacks will release into the flat at a two- to three-yard depth.

Your team should have a fake field goal and extra point attempt. They should be devised to fool the defense into thinking your team is kicking the ball. Many teams put so much emphasis on rushing the kick but they have coverage weaknesses that can be exploited. Take the time to develop well-structured fakes and practice them often.

Field Goal Defense

Field goal defense is very similar to defending against a punt. You must be concerned with the fake. The difference is that there will not be a return, which will allow many of your defenders to concentrate on stopping the kick. Figure 8-22 and Figure 8-23 are examples of rushes used against a kick. The first one is the field goal block. This one is designed to put maximum pressure in an attempt to block the kick. Nine players will align on the line of scrimmage and eight men will rush. One of the outside men will peel back to protect against any possible fakes. He must look as if he is rushing the kicker to disrupt the blocking scheme of the offense.

All players that are going for the block should aim for a spot right in front of the tee. Their hands should be up as he kicks the ball. They must be sure to take a path that will allow them to block the kick without hitting the kicker or the holder. Keep in mind, your team will receive a penalty if anyone roughs the kicker or the holder. Your players also have to be aware that they cannot strike the center until he is in a position to defend himself. These penalties can be devastating to a team so stress these points often.

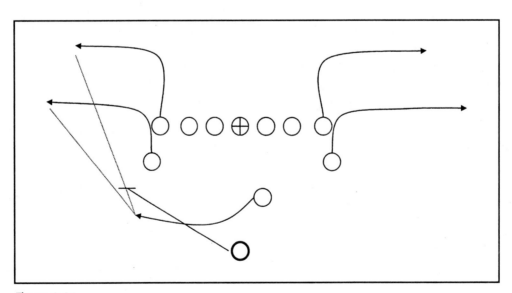

Figure 8-21

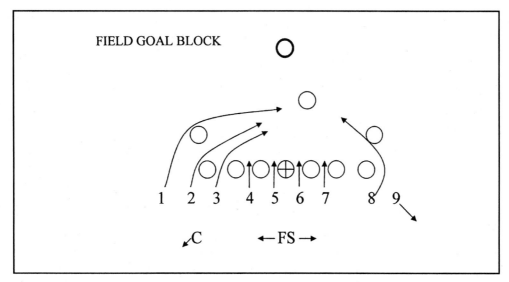

Figure 8-22

Figure 8-23 is an example of a more conservative way to defend the kick. For the sake of this example, we will call this play 'field goal safe.' On this play there are four defenders that will not rush the kicker. The rest of the team will still attempt to rush and block the kick.

The four defenders that will not rush the kick are labeled as linebackers and corners. They will be responsible to stop any fake whether it is a pass or run play. They will accomplish this by covering the four biggest pass threats in man-to-man coverage. These four players are the key to the success of any fake. If your opponent throws a pass, these players will be the intended receivers. If your opponent runs the ball, these players are the lead blockers of the play.

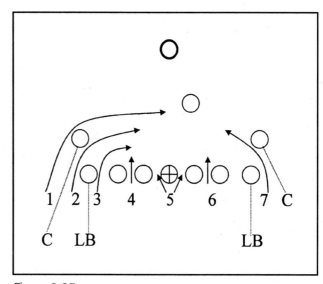

Figure 8-23

In Figure 8-23, the defenders are keying the halfbacks and ends. Any type of fake will involve these players. The defender will watch their first move. If they set up to block, the defender will attack them looking for a run fake. If they release down the field, the defenders will cover them wherever they go.

Kickoffs

Kickoff coverage is one of the more basic aspects of football. The players learn their base responsibilities and then just react to the ball. This is where sheer will and determination are the requirements for success. The best players on kickoff coverage are those with great instincts. Some players just have a 'nose' for the ball. These players are the ones that should be on your kickoff coverage teams.

Other important qualities go into choosing players for kickoff coverage such as speed and tackling ability. The most important quality these players must possess is the ability to make tackles in the openfield. Not all good tacklers are good openfield tacklers. Some players make great fundamental tackles in controlled areas but don't fare as well when it comes to openfield tackling. Good openfield tacklers usually possess quickness and balance. They have the ability to change directions without losing speed. They have good instincts and most of all, they never hesitate. They know where they have to be and they get there.

Speed is another factor to consider when choosing these players. They don't all have to be lightning fast, but they must possess average or better speed. It is important to get to the ball quickly as well as have the ability to catch up with the runner.

Defensive backs and linebackers are the players that usually possess the qualities you are looking for in a coverage man. Your backup strong safety would be much more qualified than your noseguard or defensive tackles to play these positions. If you use your 10 best openfield tacklers on your team for kickoff coverage, you should be in good shape.

Since there are countless ways to cover a kickoff and many different thoughts on kickoff coverage, you will need to develop your own style. This section demonstrates four different ways: two deep kicks and two onside kicks.

The two deep kicks are the wedge breaker and the lane method of kicking. The wedge breaker is used against teams that use wedge blocking in their return scheme. The lane method is an all-around basic way to cover kicks. The two types of onside kicks that are demonstrated are the basic onside kick and a loaded onside kick where all the players readjust their pre-kick position to the side the ball is being kicked.

For simplicity, the players are numbered in all of the following diagrams. Details and player responsibilities are listed at the bottom of every diagram. Read the rules and follow the players in the diagram to familiarize yourself with their responsibility.

Kickoff versus Wedge Return

Alignment–Seven yards from the ball.

Stance–Hands on knees facing kicker.

Start–As the kicker passes, you turn and jog, picking up speed; never pass the kicker; sprint as ball is kicked; carry out your assignment.

Assignments:

- 1 and 4–Sprint directly to the ball, avoiding blockers and make the tackle.

- 2–Contain men.

- 3 and 5–Wedge breakers; break through wedge to get the ball

- Kicker–Make a good kick and then you become safety; stay 20 yards in front of the ball.

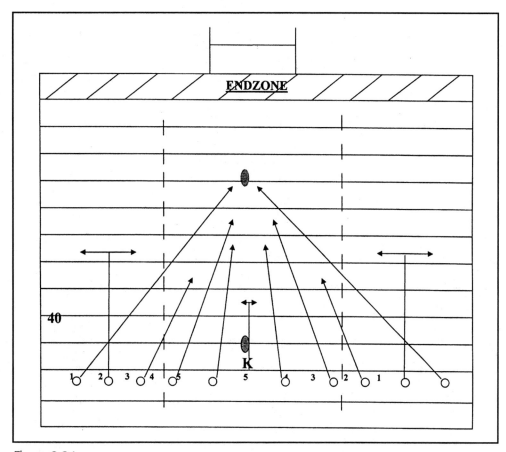

Figure 8-24

Kickoffs with Lane Responsibility

Alignment–All seven yards from the ball.

Stance–Hands on knees facing the kicker.

Start–As the kicker passes, you turn and jog picking up speed; never pass the kicker; sprint as the ball is kicked; carry out your assignment.

Lane Assignments–The lane is 10 to 15 yards directly forward and then sprint for the ballcarrier. The further from the ball, the shorter the distance in the lane. The player with the more direct route to the ball will stay in the lanes longer.

- 2, 3, 4, and 5–Stay in the lane. If the ball is kicked to the sideline, players on the opposite side break the lane.

- 1–Contain men.

- Kicker–Make a good kick and then you become safety; stay 20 yards in front of the ball.

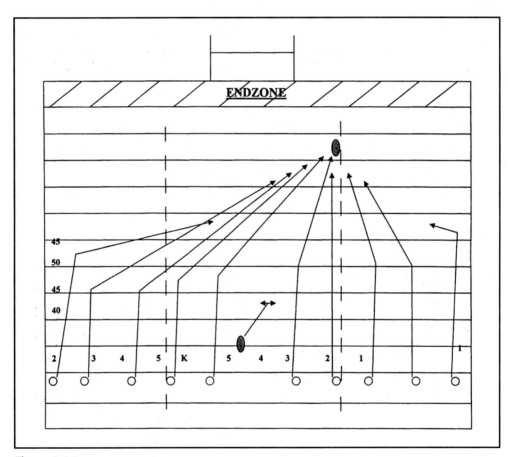

Figure 8-25

Onside Kick

Alignment–Seven yards from the ball.

Stance–Hands on knees facing kicker.

Start–As the kicker passes, you turn and jog picking up speed; never pass kicker; time yourself to be as close to the ball when kicked and close to full speed.

Assignments:

- Kicker and Offside #1–Contain men
- Remainder of Players–Sprint directly to the ball

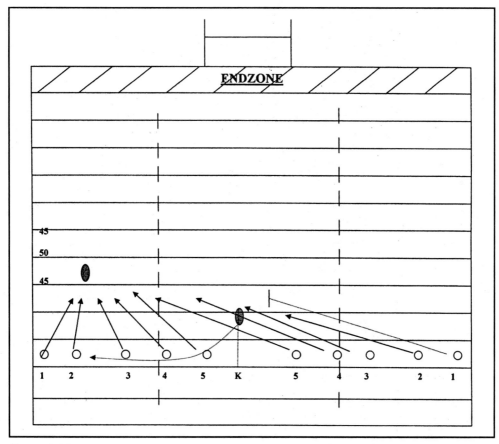

Figure 8-26

Onside Kick-Loaded

Alignment–Seven yards from the ball.

Stance–Hands on knees facing kicker.

Start–The kicker yells, "load" and the offside players will sprint to the positions shown before; just as they reach their positions, the kicker will start. As the kicker passes, the offside players turn and jog, picking up speed, never passing the kicker. They should time themselves to be as close to the ball when kicked and close to full speed. The kicker will align himself in the best position to execute the kick after he yells "load."

Assignments:

- Kicker and Offside #1
- Remainder of players–Sprint directly to the ball from reset positions shown before.

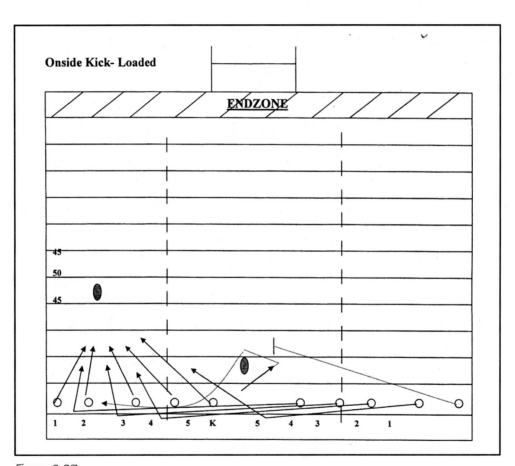

Figure 8-27

Kickoff Returns

Kickoff returns are formed with offensive-minded personnel. Blocking is the most important element involved with the return teams. Keep this in mind when choosing your personnel. The type of blocking becomes openfield blocking which can be different than controlled blocking on the line of scrimmage. Tight ends, wide receivers, and backs are usually the better openfield blockers. Quick linemen are excellent choices to play the line in this situation, but they must possess better than average speed. Do not use slower linemen in these situations.

This section outlines three types of returns: a middle wedge return, a lane return toward the sideline, and the coverage of an expected onside kick. Blocking assignments are based on the alignment of the kicking team's personnel. These players are numbered for identification purposes. Figure 8-28 is an example of the formations used as examples. The kicking team is numbered on the left and right side while the receiving team is labeled by position.

Kicking Team

L = Left   R = Right

Receiving Team

LT = Left Tackle   RT = Right

Tackle

RG = Right Guard   LG = Left Guard

C = Center   B = Back

R = Return Man

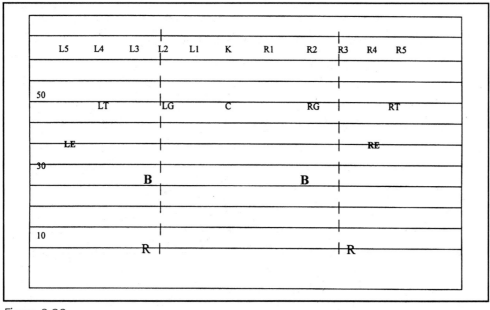

Figure 8-28

Middle Wedge Return

Note: The diagram shown in Figure 8-29 is based on the high school level and should be adjusted to suit the younger levels.

Rules:

- *LT*–sprint 20 yards from the ball, get butt to ball aligned and block L3.
- *LG*–sprint 20 yards from the ball, get butt to ball aligned and block L2.
- *C*–sprint 20 yards from the ball, get butt to ball aligned and block L1.
- *RG*–sprint 20 yards from the ball, block R3, push to right sideline.
- *RT*–sprint 20 yards from the ball, block R4, push to right sideline.
- *LE*–shuffle in and back 10yds, align butt to ball, insure L4.
- *RE*–shuffle back to 25 yard line, block R1 to left.
- *B*–set up wedge 10 yards in front of reception, on 'go' call attack middle of wedge and double-team remaining defender.
- *R*–if he is the returner he will follow the backs through the wedge and break off their double-team block; the other one is the blocker who will insure the catch, and then get three to five yards in front following the backs wedge and blocking any leakage that occurs.

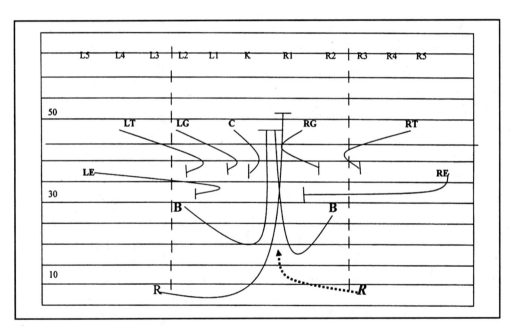

Figure 8-29

292

Lane Return Right

Note: The diagram shown in Figure 8-30 is based on the high school level and should be adjusted to suit the younger levels.

[Insert Diagram 8-30]

Rules:

- *RG and RT*–turn and face each other on the 30 yard line, execute block on R3 at the 35 yard line.

- *C*–go back 12 yards, turn and block L1 to outside.

- *LG*–go back 12 yards, turn and block L2 to outside.

- *LT*- go back 15 yards to hash, turn and block L3-5, whichever is the most immediate threat to lane.

- *LE*- go to far hash mark, turn and block R1

- *RE*–shuffle back five yards, and then head toward hash mark; look to block R2

- *B*–get to hash mark on return side and double-team R4 or first immediate threat

- *R*–the return man on the right is the intended receiver. He will catch any ball from the left hash mark all the way to his sideline (two-thirds of the field), make a clear call that you are going to catch the ball; if return man on the left receives the ball, they just switch responsibilities. The returner who is the blocker will insure the reception and then get to the outside of the lane to block the contain man.

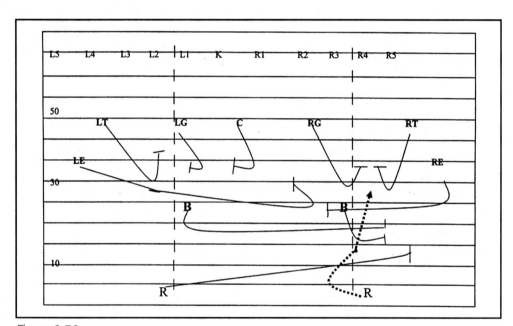

Figure 8-30

The onside kick reception is set up when there is a high likelihood that your opponent will attempt it. If your opponent is down late in the game, this is where it may be attempted.

The personnel in these situations must be changed. This is when you will put in your hands team. These players have the surest hands on the team. Possession of the ball is the most important aspect in these situations. Even if they kick the ball deep, it is OK to sacrifice return yards for possession of the ball.

The alignment of your players will also be important. You want to fill any potential pockets for the ball to get to. Try and create triangles with the man in the back getting the ball and being protected by the front men. No matter who gets the ball, they must know that position is the most important thing. They should try to cover and protect the ball at all cost.

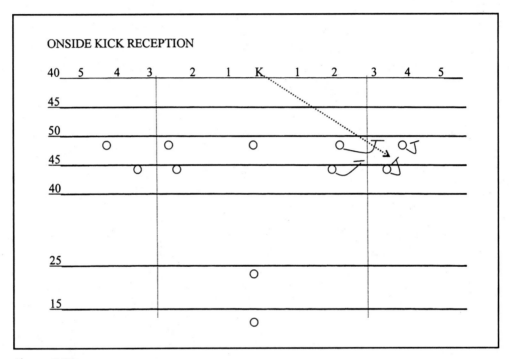

Figure 8-31

CHAPTER 9

Practice

"If you don't do it in practice, you won't be able to do it games."

-Unknown

This is a very prolific quote. The importance of this quote comes down to the word 'it.' Fill in any word or phrase for the word 'it' and the quote still holds true. One of the most suitable substitutes for the word 'it' would be 'execution.' If you can't execute it perfectly in practice you won't be able to execute it perfectly in games.

If you notice, I added the word 'perfectly' to the latter statement because the meaning of practice is perfection. The purpose of practice is to *perfect* everything about your team from the skills you teach to the game plan you prepare. When you put in a new play for your offense, you need to perfect it before you use it in a game. This is one of the most common mistakes young coaches make. They want to create new plays, and then they try using them in game situations before they are ready. They will even take it a step further; they will scrap the play if it is unsuccessful instead of going back to practice and perfecting that play before trying it again.

Simple and perfect is a much better combination than fancy and average. Vince Lombardi had a legendary career by combining basic football with flawless execution. Arguably, he had one of the greatest impacts on football coaching in the history of the game. His theory was that to win you only had to outexecute your opponent. He believed that football came down to only two things: blocking and tackling; if you were to outblock and outtackle your opponent, you will win the game.

This is perhaps the most important section in this manual. Practice is where it all begins. If you want to be truly successful, you need to have a quality practice plan and you need to perfect it.

Practice Schedule Overview

This section covers an overview of the practice schedule that your team will use during a season. This is something that can and should be planned months in advance. A practice overview is a plan with an outline.

You need to plan all of the things you will teach your players, from the fundamentals to the playbook. You will then want to set up a time frame to accomplish these things. After you have a plan, you should set up an outline of every practice. This outline will give you a timed guideline to follow when you set up your actual practice plan for that day.

The difference between a practice plan and a practice outline is in the details. For instance, a practice outline will say that your team will be working on defensive skill broken down by position. The practice plan for the same day would give detailed instructions broken down by position. Not only would the exact skill you are working on be outlined in the practice plan, the exact drills you will use to teach them will also be detailed.

The practice plan is much easier to produce if you first outline your goals in an outline. This is extremely important for the preseason. It will insure that you implement everything you will need to be ready for the season in a timely fashion.

The practice schedule is based on a four-week preseason with five practices per week (20 practices). The first week of the season usually has five practices, while the rest of the weeks in the season are reduced to three to four practices depending on your level. This is just for example purposes. You will base your overview and outline on the amount of practice time you will have available.

It is important to remember that position coaches have the freedom to create and perform their own drills that they feel will teach the fundamental techniques you are trying to accomplish. When you convert your practice outline into a practice plan you will need the input of your entire staff.

Schedule Agenda

Week #1

The first week is perhaps the most important week of the season. The coaches will outline your expectations and, at the same time, try to gain the respect of the players. This is when you will establish the basic practice routines that will be followed throughout the course of the year. A parents meeting should be held on the first day. Lay out your expectations for them and for their child. Be very clear about your playtime policy. Do not sugarcoat anything. Explain your policies clearly and concisely.

The main emphasis of this week will be conditioning. Your warm-up routine will be taught as well as most agility drills that will be used throughout the season. All players should be evaluated and timed. A motivational chant such as "pride," "eam," or "eagles" should be introduced. The chant would then be used throughout your entire practice regimen. This chant will be used in flex counts as well as the breakdown chant, huddle breaks, and the end of every practice. You can use any chant you like but it should be something the team will rally around.

Basic fundamentals will also be introduced during this week. Stances and starts will be emphasized. Positions and formations will be introduced. Offensive and defensive side numbering will be introduced.

Positions will be established during this week. After the second practice, the coaches will meet to break the players down by position. Although the players will be put into positions, they will still be able to change positions throughout the season. If a player prefers to be in a different group than he is placed, he will be allowed to move and you will evaluate his performance and review his progress.

Find your specialists (kickers, punters, and long snappers) and have them start working on their skills before and after every practice. They should be arriving a minimum of 15 minutes early every day to work on these skills.

Hitting techniques will be introduced in walk-through stages. Blocking and tackling skills will be broken down step by step. If full equipment is worn at the end of the week, hit dummies and bags at full speed.

Week #2

Although this week will be an intensive fundamentals week, players will be broken up by position and will be taught the fundamental skills and drills for their position. They will establish their practice routines for the position and the warm-up segment that will be a part of every practice.

Perfection should be the theme of this week. Your players will be drilled in the fundamental skills that are relative to their position. This is where you need to use your time wisely. Keep your drills short in length. It is better to perform five drills that highlight a skill rather than one or two drills for extended periods. If you have 15 minutes to work on a positional skill, it would be better to perform five different drills at three minutes per drill than to work on one ore two things for the entire 15 minutes. Not only is this a more effective method, but it is also more fun for your players; they are exposed to different things and they are moving at a rapid pace.

The pace of your practice is important. Keep it moving and keep it organized. This is where the practice outline and the practice plan will help you stay organized. Teams that practice without a plan will always spend too much time on one are and be forced to neglect another area.

Your offensive and defensive systems will be introduced this week. You should teach all of your teams base formations. You will also have the opportunity to introduce plays from your playbook. You can introduce anywhere from four to six plays during this week. Do not try to overwhelm them with your entire offense. Pick a few of your base plays and perfect them. You should not be introducing new plays without perfecting the ones you already have. Remember the saying, "Practice doesn't make perfect; perfect practice makes perfect."

This is the week that you will introduce full contact. Basic hitting fundamentals will be emphasized throughout every practice. It is best if you match-up players with equal skill ability during this week. It can be very intimidating for a new player to get whipped by your toughest tackler. Let them build their confidence in the beginning. It is more important at this stage to be fundamentally sound when your players are hitting. As time goes on you will start to emphasize the importance of making devastating type hits.

Do not use too many full-contact tackling drills. Make optimum use of your tackling dummies and tackling sleds if you have them. Teach the tackling drills in progression. Use drills that don't have the tackler take the ballcarrier to the ground. Remember, the emphasis should be on the fundamentals. Many high-profile programs rarely perform full-contact tackling drills during their practices. At whatever level you coach, the fundamentals are the most important thing you will teach your players. Sneak in an intense tackling drill near the end of the practice and use it as a team motivator.

This is also the week that you should pick up the intensity level. Teach them that they can improve their skill by the way they mentally approach everything they do on a football field. Keep them fired up at all times. The first time they make a devastating block or tackle with intensity they will understand the value that intensity brings them. Make a big deal of it when you see a good hit. If you begin whooping and hollering in a positive way, they will become hungry for more. They will step up their intensity level to try to achieve more. This will also fire up the rest of the players around them. It will have a snowball effect that can help your team immensely.

Intrasquad scrimmaging will begin this week. This is the time to see how well you are executing the plays that you have implemented. Thud tackling should be used during these scrimmages. This means that the defense will be at full speed all the way up to and including contact with the ballcarrier. The play will stop after the initial impact with the ballcarrier. The tackle will not be completed. Again, the emphasis is on execution and fundamentals.

Scrimmaging is where coaches make their biggest mistakes in practice structure. Many teams will spend 75% or more of their practice time scrimmaging at full contact. As the season wears on this becomes more and more prevalent. It seems as if coaches run out of things to teach and the only thing they can think to do is scrimmage. This is a huge mistake because it creates a lot of downtime and it doesn't help every player improve his skills.

That is not to say that scrimmaging doesn't play an extremely important role in practice. However, you have to be smart about the way you approach it. You should regulate the amount of time you spend scrimmaging. You also need to have an agenda for your scrimmage time. Use this time to work on a particular play or series of plays. Use the scrimmage to find out where a play has strengths and weaknesses, and then fix them during the other parts of your practice.

Some coaches say they need the scrimmage time to work on the timing of their plays and that is justifiable. However, just manage the time your team spends on full-contact scrimmaging. Your players should be working on the timing of their plays when they are in their individual stations. When you are taking the time to correct a mistake by one of your running backs, the rest of the backs will benefit from the correction because they will end up in similar situations. If you are making those running back corrections during scrimmage time, then you are giving a lot of irrelevant information to the rest of your players. This is time they can work on their own skills.

Another thing coaches say is that they want to work on the timing of the plays as a team. One way to do this, other than full-contact scrimmaging is by setting up an opponent's defense using blocking dummies. Then you can run through your plays rapidly and still work on relevant blocking assignments. When you do this you can involve more offensive players. Have your entire first and second team offenses running in succession. As soon as the first team has executed a play, the second team immediately lines up to run a play of their own while the first team is in a huddle calling their next play. Then, of course, your second team will be huddling while the first team is executing its play. It is all about time management. Make the best out of the time you have available.

Week #3

Week three is merely an extension of the second week of practice. The emphasis is still on fundamentals and execution. This is the time that you should begin to perfect the things that you introduced the prior week.

Your starting players should be established at this time. This is the time when you can teach the advantages of working hard and improving skills. Let them know that they can move right into a starting spot if they prove themselves. Do not lock into any starting players at this time. Everyone should feel that they have to continually prove themselves to earn a starting position. If players are close in ability at this time, I would not make a starting distinction between them. Rotate them in the starting rotation and make sure they are aware that one of them will earn the starting spot and that the other will have an opportunity to move up into that spot by proving himself in practice.

This will be the week that you should work on your team defensive schemes. You have already spent significant time working on positional skills and the fundamentals of playing defense. Spend this time working on the team concept. You should be working on all of your stunts and fronts packages. Teach them how to make the standard adjustments for different offensive formations they will encounter.

Your offense will introduce two to four new plays depending on the progress they have made with the plays you have already instituted. Continue to work on and perfect the other plays. Make sure that you are putting in new plays that complement existing plays. For instance, if you are going to put in a bootleg play, you should already have put in the play that it boots off of. You may even want to put those two plays in together.

Week #4

During the last week of practice in the pre-season, execution, execution and execution will be the three most important things you will try to accomplish. You should have at least seven or eight plays perfected and working on a total of 10 to 14 total plays. Your defensive system should be entirely in place at this time.

This is the week that you will put in your special teams. The individual skills have been worked on for a couple of weeks; it is now time to put it together as a team. By the end of the week your team should know the basic formations and concepts for all of your special teams.

Game Weeks

Practice times will vary during game weeks depending on your level. Many high school teams will have 10 to 12 hours of practice time in a game week. Youth teams are usually limited to six hours or less of game-week practice time during the season. Practices will obviously have to be adjusted accordingly. This is where you need to be organized and intelligent. Prioritize the importance of the things you want to work on. Do not waste time working on things in practice that don't improve your team. Work smart, not hard.

This brings up another important element of coaching: leadership. Specifically, I am talking about schoolwork. No matter what level you coach, your players are attending school throughout the season. You cannot emphasize the importance of schoolwork enough to your players. Make an effort to mention it every day in practice. When you have your team huddles before or after practice you can simply mention that you expect them to not only do

their schoolwork, but also to apply the same effort at school as they do on the field. Coaches are mentors to young boys. They believe in you, so you should use that gift to make them better students and better people.

At the youth level, you will assume that you will get in three practices a week before a game while high school teams are getting four or five practices in per week. Use your time wisely. The first practice of the week should be used to review the previous week's game and to plan for the upcoming game. High school teams should use the first day for film review and an in-season weight training program. Use the first hour and a half to review an edited version of your last game and an edited version of your upcoming opponent. The coaches should edit the films down to pertinent material. This is not movie time with popcorn and candy. After films, the team should spend a well-organized hour in the weight room working on strength training. The JV team should work on strength training while the varsity watches films. They will then go out on the field and work on the upcoming game plan.

The practices in the middle of the week should emphasize the execution of your game plan against your upcoming opponent. Every drill that is performed should emphasize your opponent. If you are tackling bags, then tell your players they should imagine they are tackling the opponent. Create excitement during these practices. Get your team fired up. The intensity levels should be very high during these practices.

As the season moves on your practices will start to fall into a routine. Do not become complacent. Spice it up. Come up with new drills to use throughout the practice. Do not reduce the amount of time you spend in your individual station. As the season moves on, coaches tend to spend increasingly more time scrimmaging as a team. Keep the emphasis on perfecting the fundamentals.

Practice Outline

The following outline is part of the practice overview for the season. This is something that should be done months before the season begins. These outlines should be adjusted to the amount of time and the number of days you have available. They are all two-hour practices. If you have two and a halfhour long practices you will be able to introduce things at a more rapid pace. If you have 'two a day' or even 'three a day' practices in the beginning of the season, you can adjust it by sessions. The second session of a 'three a day' practice would be considered practice #2 in the outline and so on.

Practice #1

5:45: Staff introductions and player orientation

6:00: Warm-up lap (2x2)

> Flexes–set up lines–teach chants

6:20: Form running

6:25: Speed lap–water break

6:30: Stance and starts–as a team

6:40: Stations–approx. 10 min. per station

> Timed 40's (two times each)
>
> Pass and catch
>
> Stance and start individual

7:05: Speed lap–water break

7:10: Agility Stations–approx. two minutes per station

> Push ups/sit ups–10 per set alternating
>
> Up-downs
>
> Figure 8's

7:20: Speed lap–water break

7:25: Introduction to positions

7:35: Agility stations repeated

7:45: High hurdle laps and gassers

7:55: Team meeting

Practice #2

6:00: Warm-up lap (2x2)

> Flexes
>
> Form running

6:25: Stations–approx. 10 min. per station

> Timed shuttles 10 yards x 4 reps (two times each)
>
> Pass and catch
>
> Stance and starts 45- and 90-degree starts

6:55: Speed lap–water break

7:00: Stance and starts–first steps of bird dog–freezing after every step

7:10: Agility stations–approx. two minutes per station

> Push ups/sit ups–10 per set alternating
>
> Up-downs
>
> Figure 8's

7:20: Speed lap – water break

7:25: Introduction to hitting positions and power angles

7:35: Bag jams with hands. Four lines teaching hitting position and power angle w/bags

7:45: Agility stations–approx. two minutes per station

> Box drill
>
> Grass drills
>
> Shuffle around bags

7:55: High hurdle laps and gassers

8:00: Team meeting

Practices #3 and #4

6:00: Warm-up lap (2x2)

> Flexes

> Form running

6:20: Bird Dog Intro—Refer to Linemen Warm-up Drills section in Chapter 3, Figure 3-89.

6:35: Speed lap—water break

6:40: Positional Stations—teach all daily warm-ups at each station. Daily warm-ups for each position are listed later in this chapter.

> Station 1. Backs and receivers

> Station 2. Quarterbacks

> Station 3. Linemen

Note: This is the point where you will separate the players into their projected positions; changes can be made later.

7:25: Speed lap—water break

7:30: Agility stations—approx. two minutes per station

> Push ups/sit ups—10 per set alternating

> Up-downs

> Figure 8's

7:40: Georgia Southern review-team

7:45: Tackling intro—Man-on-man carry drill

8:00: High hurdle laps (2)—Lay down position

Practice #5

Note: This should be the first full pads practice. If it is not, repeat practice #4.

6:00: Warm-up lap (2x2)

> Flexes

> Form running

6:25: Tackling—walk-through drills

6:30: Bag tackling drills—Refer to the Bag Tackling Drills section in Chapter 5.

6:45: Speed lap—water break

6:50: Stations

> Backs

> 1. Daily warm-ups

> 2. Formation review

> 3. Introduce two plays—23/47 dive—33/37 belly

> Linemen

> 1. Daily warm-ups

> 2. Complete Georgia Southerns

> 3. Teach all blocks—Refer to the Linemen Skills Section in Chapter 3.

7:30: Speed lap—water break

7:35: Live Hitting Drills—Refer to the Tackling Drills section in Chapter 5. Use the controlled tackling and drills that use thud tackling

7:55: High hurdle laps

Note: Potential centers should be chosen and try some snap exchanges after practice.

QB'S and Centers will be asked to show up 10 minutes early to practice exchanges.

Practice #6

6:00: Warm-up lap (2x2)

    Flexes

    Form running

6:20: Bag tackling drills

6:30: Speed lap–water break

6:35: Stations

    Backs

    1. Daily warm-ups

    2. Play skelly

    3. Intro two plays–dive–belly

    4. Drill intro–pick from drills in the running back section

    Linemen

    1. Daily warm-ups

    2. Bag drills

    3. Play intro two plays–use LOS markers

    4. Drill intro–pick from drills in the linemen section

7:30: Speed lap–water break

7:35: Controlled scrimmaging–two stations separated by experience–five-yard boundaries set. two offensive linemen versus one defensive lineman and one linebacker–back takes handoff through one of three holes–positional coaches should be instructing their position throughout.

7:50: Tackling circle–Refer to the Team Circle drill in Chapter 5, Figure 5-44.

7:55: High hurdle laps

Practice #7

6:00-7:20: Same as practice #6–Add one new play

7:20: Introduce defensive techniques and gaps

7:25: Defensive stations

    Defensive line

    Linebackers

    Defensive backs

Each station should teach stance–starts–alignment–Use a few different drills from each positions drill section

7:50: Team gauntlet drill

8:00: High hurdle laps

Practices #8 and #9

6:00-7:20: Same as practice # 7–Add a new play

7:25: Scrimmage–first team offense

7:50: Team tackling drill

8:00: High hurdle laps

Practices #10 through #15

6:00: Lap–flexes–form running

6:15: Bag tackling drills

6:25: Offensive stations

Backs

1. Daily warm-up routine

2. Run skelly

3. Play intro

4. Drills

Quarterbacks

1. Daily warm-up

2. Join backs

Linemen

1. Daily warm-up routine

2. Run skelly

3. Play intro

4. Drills

7:05: Defensive skill stations–skills and drills by position

Defensive linemen

Defensive backs

Linebackers

7:15: Team defense–game plan

Defensive linemen and linebackers–front and stunt packages

Defensive backs–Coverage packages–join rest of team

7:25: Team offense–scrimmage

7:55: High hurdles and laps

Practices #16 through #20

6:00: Lap–flexes–form running

6:15: Bag tackling drills

6:25: Offensive stations

Backs

1. Daily warm-up routine

2. Run skelly

3. Play intro

4. Drills

Quarterbacks

1. Daily warm-up

2. Join backs

Linemen

1. Daily warm-up routine

2. Run skelly

3. Play intro

4. Drills

7:05: Defensive skill stations–skills and drills by position

Defensive linemen

Defensive backs

Linebackers

*See Note.

7:15: Team defense–game plan

Defensive linemen and linebackers–front and stunt packages

Defensive backs–coverage packages–join rest of team

7:25: Team offense–scrimmage

7:55: High hurdles and laps

Note: Practice #17 and #18, at 7:05-7:25 substitute special teams

Work on special teams as a unit. Put in kicking and receiving and punting and receiving. Skill players should be working every day.

Game Week Practices

The following practice outline was developed to give you an idea of what a typical practice week may look like at the high school level. Keep in mind that it will just be a general overview. The actual practice schedule will be much more detailed. Adjust your game week schedule according to your level.

Scouting reports will play a significant role when developing a practice plan for a specific week. Before each week of practice, every coach will be given that weeks practice plan, which will be a general overview of that weeks practice. Every day each coach will be given a daily practice agenda. Everything you do that day should be detailed down to the minute.

This plan is based on a practice week from Monday through Thursday, with a game on Friday night. If allowed, meet every Saturday morning during the season for a one and a half hour weight lifting program. If you are unable to meet on Saturdays, execute your weight lifting program on Monday along with your team film study sessions.

The coaching staff will meet at some time during the weekend, for an extended period of time to review films of your games as well as your next opponent's films. Films will be edited to contain only player relevant material. This edited version will be the one reviewed by the entire team on Monday.

Monday

☐ Skills, Film day—Helmet, shoulder pads only.

One hour skills session, followed by one and a half hours of film and scouting report review

- Line—*Positional pulling drills, the following drills will be extensively worked versus bags: pull wall-off, pull trap(kick), pull hook, pull lead.

  *Play skelly versus opponent.
- QB's—Passing warm-up (footwork and loosen arm) w/center versus bag
- RB's—Handoff drills, running game skills and agilities

- WR's, TE's—Catch work
- Skill Positions—Come together for pass skelly
- Film study—our game review, opponent film review

Tuesday

☐ Skill Reps/Game Plan Reps versus Opponent

Based on two and a half hour practice

Note: The phrase three-quarter contact refers to the tackling progression. The defender will drive through the ballcarrier at full speed but will not bring him down to the ground; an early whistle will be applied. This is run at full speed and all other aspects of the drill other than tackling are 100% full contact.

3:15: Specials—QB's take snaps from centers with ghost footwork, long snappers and holder reps, punter/kicker reps, receivers handwork at 10 yards, running back handoff drills, line bird dog

3:30: Warm-up lap, flexes, form running, chants lead by captains throughout, end with fire-up sequence.

3:50: Offense—stations—skills and drills

- Backs—daily regimen—42/28 drill with blaster and combo footwork stations, belly drill with defender three-quarter contact, toss drill with defender
- Line/TE's—daily regimen, Georgia Southerns, sled and chute work
- QB's—daily warm-up, join backs
- WR's—stalk block drills

4:00: Offense—Play skelly—new play intro where applicable, first and second team

- RB/QB—play skelly—running game
- Line, TE's—positional breakdown, technique work, run skelly vs opponent defense
- WR—route work, pass catch drills

4:15: Offense–Pass skelly first and second team

- RB,QB,WR,TE–Pass skelly versus opponent secondary
- Line–pass skelly versus opponent with potential stunt package

4:25: Offense–Team three-quarter contact live versus opponent as per scout report, first and second teams

4:45: Defense- stations skills and drill eight-min

- LB's , DB's, D-Line

4:58: Tackling stations one and a half minutes per station

1. Popsicle tackling
2. Three-quarter tackling triangle
   - Form tackling lifts
   - Variable tackling drill, live

5:05: Fronts and Stunts seven and a half minutes

- Line and LB's–rep stunt packages
- DB's–pass coverage versus opponent as per scout report

5:12: Team defense–skelly opponent offense –recognition and reaction

5:20: Special teams–run through all–first and second teams

- Punt, Punt return, Kickoff and return

5:30: Extra point and field goal practice

5:37: Conditioning

5:45: End

Wednesday

- □ Skills With Major Emphasis on Game Plan versus Opponent

3:15: Specials–QB's take snaps from centers with ghost footwork, long snappers and holder reps,

punter/ kicker reps, receivers handwork at 10 yards, running back handoff drills, line bird dog

3:30: Warm-up lap, flexes, form running, chants lead by captains throughout, end with fire-up sequence.

3:45: Offense–stations–skills and drills–five min

- Backs–daily regimen–42/28 drill with blaster and combo footwork stations, belly drill with defender three-quarter contact
- Line/TE's–daily regimen, Georgia Southerns
- QB's–daily warm-up, join backs
- WR's–stalk block drills

3:50: Offense–Play skelly–first and second team

- RB/QB- play skelly–running game
- Line, TE's–complete Georgia Southerns run skelly versus opponent defense
- WR- route work, pass catch drills

4:00: Offense–Pass skelly first and second team

- RB,QB,WR,TE–Pass skelly versus opponent secondary
- Line–pass skelly versus opponent with potential stunt package

4:10: Offense–three-quarter contact live versus opponent as per scout report, first and second

4:55: Tackling stations one and a half minutes per station

- Popsicle tackling
- Three-quarter tackling triangle
- Form tackling lifts
- Variable tackling drill

5:03: Fronts and Stunts seven and a half minutes

- Line and LB's–rep stunt packages
- DB's–pass coverage versus opponent as per scout report

5:13: Team Defense–skelly opponent offense–recognition and reaction versus scout team

5:30: Extra point and field goal practice

5:37: Conditioning

5:45: End

Thursday

☐ Extensive Game Preparation

Helmet and shoulder pads only.

3:15: Flexes and form running

3:30: Team offense. first team then second team in quick rotation

- Complete offensive game plan run versus bags (opponent's defense)
- 15-play script will be emphasized.

Note: The 15-play script is a culmination of the 15 plays most likely to succeed versus an opponent, based on the scouting report.

4:10: Defense–Stunts and fronts

- D-line and LB's–stunts and fronts–reads and recognition
- DB's–pass skelly versus opponent passing game and potential passing plays

4:20: Team Defense

- Complete game plan versus scout team offense at half speed–no significant contact
- Scout team will run opponent's offense as per scouting report.

4:35: Kickoff game plan–all scenarios first and second teams

4:45: Kickoff receiving–all scenarios first and second teams

4:52: Punt team–first and second teams

4:57: Punt block team–first and second teams

5:00: Punt return–first and second teams

5:05: End

7:00 pm: Pasta dinner

Note: I like to have a pasta dinner as a team the night before every game. We suggest that a different players family host it every other week. This is a great way to bring together the players and the families that support the program. The pasta dinner may be replaced by a team breakfast in certain game situations.

Friday

☐ Game Day

- All players will be required to arrive one and a half hours before home games.
- We will enter the field one hour before the game. We will enter the field in a consistent and regimented manner that will be practiced in the preseason. Every player will participate in all chants and "fire up regimens."
- A pregame flex program will be performed following our specific pre-game warm-ups. A detailed pregame regimen will follow. We will leave the field approximately 30 minutes before the game to go to the locker room for a pregame meeting.
- We will reenter the field in a consistent manner 10 minutes before the game. When we enter the field, we will perform our pregame "fire-up drills." Emotions will be high!
- Game day decorum will be reviewed with all players before the season begins. Our emphasis will be on teamwork and sportsmanship. We will develop a camaraderie that will be apparent on game days.

Saturday

Weight Lifting Day–one to one and a half hours

Parents Meeting

The worst thing you can do when you have your parents meeting is to sugarcoat what their children will be doing. You will have a large group of parents who have never been involved with football and have no idea what to expect. They need to know that this will be one of the most demanding things their child has ever done. It is a physically and mentally demanding sport. They will certainly have to make sacrifices as a family. If you don't lay it out at this point, you will be sorry later.

Make sure you also point out all of the positive things that their child will get out of football. Following are some of the things I tell the parents during my meeting. These are not verbatim:

- Practice times for the year are ……….

- Practice is mandatory and strictly enforced.

- If players are late for practice they will be penalized.

- Football is taught at practice not at the game.

- Every child will be taught the fundamentals of football.

- Every kid will be given a chance to prove themselves.

- Not every kid will get significant play time in every game.

- Many kids will play both offensively and defensively.

- The best player will start. If the score is close he will play most of the game.

- Our goal is to win every game. This doesn't mean win at all cost.

- Your children will be taught how to be winners.

- You will not agree with everything we do as coaches.

- We will always do what we believe is in your child's and the teams best interest.

- There will be no favoritism shown to any player.

- Nothing will ever be "taken out" on a player.

- This will probably be one of the hardest things your child has ever done.

- This is a physical sport. Your child will get bumps and bruises.

- He will be physically tired after practice especially in the beginning of the year.

- Football is not for everyone.

- It won't make your son a quitter if he doesn't want to play football.

- Your sons' chances of injury are greater if he doesn't want to be here.

- Your child will be taught a lot of positive lessons

- He will learn about teamwork, commitment, goals, desire and motivation.

- If he is not a starter he will be given an opportunity to win a starting position.

- If he is a starter he will have to continue to earn his position.

- We ask that you do not talk to you child during practice.

- Feel free to discuss any problems or concerns, the coaches are available to talk after practice.

- You can ask me any question, just remember you may not like the answer.

Positional Warm-up Routines

These are the warm-up schedules that will be used every day. They are broken down by position. All drills are detailed in the corresponding section of this manual. For example you will find running back drills detailed in the drills portion of the running back section of this manual and so on.

You can vary these warm-up routines to suit your needs and preferences. The important thing is to make sure that the things they do are specific to the skill required to accentuate their position.

Running Backs

- Handoff drill

- Bird Dog

- 42/28 Drill–'ultimate combination drill' varying the footwork portion

- Belly drill

- Toss dill
- Long ball

Quarterbacks—Make five passes in each drill then move on to the next drill

- Follow-through drill
- Load shoulders drill
- Shoulders and hips drill
- Three-step drop drill
- Four corners drill
- Sprint out drill

Linemen

- Circle up drill
- Bird Dog
- Georgia Southerns
- Chute drills
- Sled drills

Team Conditioning

The first thing every player must do is warm up their muscles, and then stretch them out before beginning any strenuous practicing. Go through the warm-up program as a team. It is extremely important that these are done to perfection as a team. Your warm-up routine will set the tone for your practice. It should be performed with enthusiasm. Every player must equally participate. All chants should be spoken loudly and concisely by every player. Make sure that every player takes this portion of practice seriously.

Warm-up lap-this is done at a slow pace to warm the muscles before stretching.

Note: Commands are given by captains, and replies are given by the entire team.

Clap and Break

- Command–"clap it out" (slap thighs 2x's then clap. Repeat)

- Command–"ready, breakdown" (everyone in breakdown position and holding)
- Command–"rest"
- Reply–"pride" (snap up, feet together seven clap hands 3 x's)

Jumping Jacks

- Command–"10 4-count jumping jacks, are you ready?"
- Reply–"Yes sir"
- Command–"begin"
- Command–"1,2,3" reply "1"–Command–"1,2,3" reply "2" and so on to 10

Leg stretch

- Command–"right over left, stretch"(with legs straight players put right keg over their left and put their helmet to their knees).
- Command–"rest"
- Reply–"Pride" (slap thigh pads twice and clap as saying pride)
- Command–"left over right, stretch"(with legs straight players put left leg over their right and put their helmet to their knees).
- Command–"rest"
- Reply–"Pride" (slap thigh pads twice and clap as saying pride)

Quad stretch

- Command–"Ready, front" (everyone drops to the ground chest first)
- Command–"Right hand left ankle"(grab outside ankle and pull)
- Command–"Rest"
- Reply–"Pride'
- Command–"Left hand right ankle"(grab outside ankle and pull)
- Command–"rest"
- Reply–"Pride"

Hamstring and Hip Stretch

- Command—"ready, sit through" (move to sitting position by swing legs around in front of you)
- Command—"right into left, long leg, stretch" (place right foot into knee, work helmet down to knee of long leg, grabbing the ankle).
- Command—"rest"
- Reply—"pride"
- Command—"short leg stretch" (work helmet down to bent knee)
- Command—"rest"
- Reply—"pride"
- Command—"lay back" (stay in same position but lay back on ground)
- Repeat drill with left leg into the right knee.

Butterflies

- Command—"butterflies, pull them in" (pull both feet in with both heels in crotch)
- Command—"stretch" (hold ankles and push knees toward the ground with elbows)
- Command—"rest"
- Reply—"pride"
- Command—"ready. On your feet" (everyone snaps up to their feet)

Up Downs

- Command—"20 up downs are you ready?"
- Reply—"yes sir" (start jogging in place)
- Command—"hit it" repeat 20 times (hit chest on ground, bounce back to feet)

Clap and Break

- Command—"clap it out" (slap thighs 2x's then clap. Repeat)
- Command—"ready, breakdown" (everyone in breakdown position and holding)
- Command—"rest"

- Reply—"pride" (snap up, feet together seven clap hands 3 x's)
- Command—"collapse the lines" everyone will fall in line behind the captains line ready for form running drills.

Form Running Drills

These are performed from the lines formed after stretching. Form is the emphasis that is placed on all of these drills. The elbows of your players should be bent at a 90-degree angle and held closely to the body throughout the drills. The arms will move in a pendulum-like motion when they run, maintaining the 90-degree angle bend of the arms.

All drills are 10 yards long. Each drill will be repeated back in the opposite direction.

High Knees

- The knees should pump high, getting the thighs parallel to the ground with every step. It should take 25-30 steps to reach 10 yards. If they are not getting that many steps in, then they are traveling too far between steps. Make the corrections.

Butt Kickers

- With every stride your heel will strike the back of your butt. Again, it should take 25-30 steps to reach 10 yards.

Backwards

- Maintain balance.

Carioca

- This is a sideways run. The right foot crosses in front of the left, and then they step out with the left foot and the right foot crosses behind the left foot until they reach 10 yards.
- Repeat in the opposite direction on second repetition.

Sprint

- Full-speed 10-yard sprint.

High Hurdles

Objective: To improve conditioning; to work on the explosiveness of the lower body.

Description: All of your players will be lined up on all fours on one sideline of the field, equally spread apart from the back of one end zone to the other. There should be a minimum of three yards between each player. It is OK to turn down the back end zone lines if you need the room to fit the number of players on your team. On the coach's whistle the last player will hurdle over every teammate, and then he will set back up at the beginning of the other sideline on all fours. The coach will continue to blow the whistle for the next player in line to repeat the hurdle procedure. Each one will set up next to the last player they hurdle. The drill will continue until the team has lapped the field one to three times.

Coaching Points: Make sure that every player goes over the top of every other player. If one player cheats, the entire team is penalized by having to do another repetition. They should pump their knees high, never allowing their feet to drag. It is good to run this drill at the end of practice.

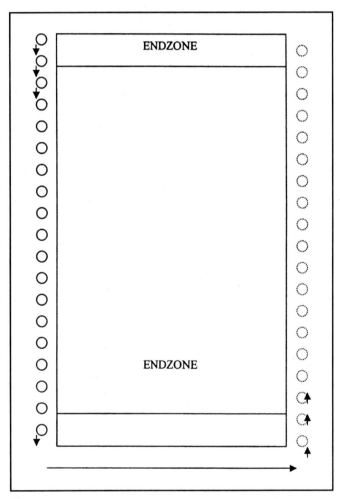

Figure 9-1

Practice Plan

Following is a copy of a practice plan. The plan consists of the detailed list that will be followed for one specific practice. The difference between the practice plan and the practice outline is in the details. The plan is based on the outline. Where a practice plan may call for drills at an individual station, the plan will list the actual drills to be performed. A practice outline will mention when to put in new plays for the offense. The practice plan will specify exactly what plays will be put in.

Typical Practice Schedule

3:15: Specials—QB's take snaps from centers with ghost footwork, long snappers and holder reps, punter/kicker reps, receivers handwork at 10 yards, running back handoff drills, line bird dog

3:30: Warm-up lap, flexes, form running, chants lead by captains throughout, end with fire-up sequence.

3:50: Offense—stations—skills and drills

- Backs—daily regime—42/28 drill with blaster and combo footwork stations, belly drill with defender three-quarter contact, toss drill with defender
- Line/TE's—daily regime, Georgia Southerns, sled and chute work
- QB's—daily warm-up, join backs
- WR,s—stalk block drills

4:00: Offense—Play skelly—new play intro 121/929 buck sweep, first and second team

- RB/QB—play skelly—running game
- Line, TE's—positional breakdown, technique work, run skelly versus opponent defense
- WR—route work, pass catch drills

4:15: Offense—Pass skelly first and second team

- RB,QB,WR,TE—Pass skelly versus opponent secondary

- Line—pass skelly versus opponent with potential stunt package

4:25: Offense—Team versus bags or three-quarter contact live versus opponent as per scout report,first and second teams

4:45: Defense- stations skills and drill, eight minutes

- LB's—read and recognition drills, pick any three
- DB's—angle pursuit drills pick two, interception drill
- D-Line—pass rush drill, anti-reach drill, anti-trap drill

4:58: Tackling stations one and a half minutes per station

1. Popsicle tackling
2. Three-quarter tackling triangle
3. Form tackling lifts
4. Variable tackling drill.

5:05: Fronts and Stunts seven and a half minutes

- Line & LB's—rep stunt packages
- DB's—pass coverages versus opponent as per scout report

5:12: Team Defense—skelly opponent offense —recognition and reaction

5:20: Special Teams—run through all first and second team

- Punt, punt return, kickoff and return

5:30: Extra point practice

5:37: Conditioning

5:45: End

> "Four things cannot come back: the spoken word, the spent arrow, the past life, and a neglected opportunity."
>
> -Arabian Proverb

CHAPTER 10

Game Preparation

This is where you can set yourself apart from other teams. Be organized; be prepared for anything. You should spend the whole week preparing for your upcoming opponent.

Scouting

The ideal scenario is that you have seen your opponent play before you play them. When that isn't possible, talk to other coaches who have played your opponent. Most coaches will help you because they want to show you how smart they are. When you are scouting an opponent you want to know the following questions:

• What type of offense do they primarily run?

• What type of defenses?

• Do they have any tendencies?

• Who are the best players offensively and defensively?

• Do the players have tendencies (i.e., one back always goes outside when he gets the ball)?

• Special team tendencies?

• Can the quarterback throw?

• Is there one main receiver he throws to?

• Do they stunt a lot and who stunts the most?

• What are there defensive line alignments and techniques? Backers?

Obviously, you want to get as much information as possible. It is very important to scout your opponent. Whenever it is possible, the coaching staff should go to see the other teams in person. Another thing you want to do is have film of your opponent. The film will come in handy for picking up details you may miss when you are at the game.

The first thing you want to do is familiarize yourself with the players on the other team. Most high school games will have a program that will give you all the information you will need.

The next thing you want to do is watch the other teams' pregame warm-up. Many times the team will run though all of the plays on their game plan when they are warming up. This is why you should chart your plays when they run through them before the game. This is also a good time to take notes on who is playing what positions. You should make note of the jersey numbers of the starting players. Their formations should also be charted both offensively and defensively. You can make notations about the skills of individual players (i.e., the quarterback's arm strength, players with good hands, the kicker's foot strength).

Once the game begins you need to chart every formation your opponent lines up in, including offense, defense, and all special teams formations. You should chart every play they run, making sure to include as many details as you can. Make sure you identify who carries the ball on every running play. You also must chart the play information. The play information you need is the down-and-distance to go for a first down, the yard line they are on, the play number in the series since they have taken possession and any clock information that is available. If there are special circumstances that affect a play, chart them also. Chart as much defensive information as possible. Chart the alignments of the defensive players.

After the game you need to sit down with all of the information you have accumulated and decipher it. If you have film, you should review the film play by play and rechart everything. You will be able to accumulate much more detailed information on film. You may watch the same play three times if needed. You are looking for patterns or tendencies. Fill in a stats sheet for the team as if you were doing it for your own team. A stats sheet will list individual accomplishments such as rushes, passes caught, tackles and so on. By doing this you may find out some information you overlooked.

The next thing you want to do is break down a down-and-distance chart. Start with first-and-ten and list every play they run. Then list second-and-long, second-and-short, third-and-long, third-and-short, and any fourth down plays they didn't punt or kick.

Next, you want to break out groups of plays. Make a separate chart of every passing play (diagram every play). Then you want to do the same thing with long yardage situation plays and then short yardage plays.

You will do the same thing with their defense. The important thing here is alignment and

assignment of every player especially the defensive linemen. Many defensive linemen will fall into habits where they do the same thing every time they align themselves in a certain way. Diagram coverage packages as well as stunt packages that you pick up.

Diagram all special teams situations. Make sure to chart the alignment and assignment of every player. Do not underestimate the importance of charting special teams. The most likely area of the game to pick up tendencies will be on special teams. If you know exactly what your opponent is going to do, it will make things a whole lot easier on your team in those situations.

At this point, you will have collected an enormous amount of information. Much of it is already separated into categories that will give you an overview of that portion of their game. You will now decipher the rest of the information you have and you will find more trends and tendencies. The deeper you dig the more you will discover.

Game Plan

After you have scouted your opponent, it is time to make up a game plan. Your game plan will vary from week to week based on your opponent. However, this does not mean you will make dramatic changes every week. Stay within your base schemes when you develop your plan. It would be a huge mistake to put in entirely new offenses for an opponent. That would be throwing away everything you have worked on up to that point. You don't have to dazzle your opponent with brilliance; all you have to do is outexecute them. Instead of wasting time changing the things you do, take that same amount of time and work on perfecting the things you do.

Your game plan should consist of things that you already have within your system. This does not mean that you cannot add a new wrinkle or two. Find the things that you already do well and find out where you think they will work against your opponent. Find your opponent's weaknesses and exploit them.

Whenever you make up a game plan, be thorough. You should have a detailed plan for offense, defense, and every aspect of special teams. Your plan should be in writing. It should have an overview of what you wish to accomplish. The next thing it should include is a scouting report. Every coach should have a detailed copy of the entire scouting report. You should also make a scaled down version for your players. The report should have the opponent's plays charted out. The players should become as familiar with their opponent as possible. You can go as far as testing your players at the end of the week. Give them a chart of their offensive plays and, for homework, have them list their base responsibility for each of the plays.

They should have the written game plan at the beginning of the week so they can study it immediately. This will help them understand the things you will review in practice during the week since your practice time should be geared toward your opponent. Make sure that you walk through your opponent's offense, defense, and special teams. It is always better for them to see these things on the field. Whenever you run offensive plays versus a defense, make sure you are running them against your opponent's defense. Even if you are running your offense against bags, the bags should be aligned to simulate your opponent's defense.

Play Script/Chart

You should create a chart that details the plays that you will call based on current game situations. You should also script plays that you feel will be effective against your opponent. The play script will represent the plays that you want run in the beginning of the

game to see how affective they will be against your opponent. It is a good idea to have a ten-play script that you will run early in the first half. Game situations may alter the order you execute these plays, but you want to see these plays executed as early as you can in the game.

Chart your plays for every situation. You should include the following categories when you make your chart:

• Short yardage plays

• Long yardage plays

• Two-minute plays

• Extra point plays

• Fourth down plays

• Specialty or trick plays

Break down the down-and-distance plays in one to three yards, four to six yards, 7 to 10 yards, and 11 plus yards. Chart what you would run on second down and those distances, and then chart third down at each distance. Even if you don't look at the chart much during the game you will be in good shape. You will have already geared your mind to think about what you will do in most situations. It is great mental preparation for coaches.

The following chart is an example of a charted game plan for the offense. It has categories for most game situations you will encounter. Following that is a blank game plan that you can copy and use to prepare for your games. Put a lot of thought into the chart and be sure to fill out every section thoroughly. Even if you never glance at it during a game, you will have helped yourself immensely just by preparing it.

FALLSTON GAME #1

Figure 10-1

Long Yardage Plays
141 WAGGLE KEEPER
929 WAGGLE REVERSE
SLOT 171 CURL TRAIL
134 TRAP "X"
STRONG SLOT 128 NAKED
928 CRISS CROSS

Short Yardage Plays
5 WEDGE
SLOT 137 BELLY RICE (RUN ICE)
TIGHT I 147 RICE
SLOT 147 DIVE
141 WAGGLE KEEPER

Fourth Down Plays
5 WEDGE
SLOT 137 BELLY RICE (RUN ICE)
TIGHT I 147 RICE
928 CRISS CROSS
929 WAGGLE REVERSE
141 WAGGLE KEEPER
SLOT 171 CURL TRAIL
STRONG SLOT 942 NAKED RUN

Extra Point Plays
141 WAGGLE KEEPER
141 WAGGLE REVERSE
STRONG SLOT 142 NAKED
929 WAGGLE REVERSE

Scripted Plays
1. SLOT 147 DIVE
2. SLOT 137 BELLY RICE (RUN ICE)
3. STRONG 949 TOSS
4. 929 BUCK SWEEP
5. TIGHT I 943 RICE
6. SLOT 923 DIVE
7. 134 TRAP
8. 142
9. 141 WAGGLE KEEPER
10. STRONG SLOT 142 NAKED
11. SLOT 933 BELLY RICE
12. 144 COUNTER "X"
13. 141 WAGGLE REVERSE
14. STRONG TWINS 171 UNDER PASS
15. SLOT 171 CURL TRAIL

NOTES:
Watch for crashing ends

Middle backer will stunt frequently.

See which gap tackles are shooting

Pass deep when they are in cover 2

2 Minute Plays
STRONG TWINS 171 UNI
STRONG SLOT 142 NAKI
141 WAGGLE KEEPER
141 WAGGLE REVERSE
SLOT 171 CURL TRAIL
BLUE 11 SPRINT PASS
STRONG 949 TOSS

Pass Plays
STRONG SLOT 942 NAKI
BLUE 11 SPRINT PASS
STRONG TWINS 171 UNI
SLOT 171 CURL TRAIL
141 WAGGLE PASS

2nd Down

Dist	Run	2nd Down	Pass
1 - 3	STRONG 949 TOSS 929 BUCK SWEEP 144 COUNTER "X" 141 WAGGLE KEEPER	142 CRISSCROSS 134 TRAP SLOT 923 DIVE SLOT 933 BELLY RICE	STRONG SLOT 942 NAKED 141 WAGGLE PASS BLUE 11 SPRINT PASS SLOT 171 CURL TRAIL
4 - 6	SLOT 137 BELLY RICE (RUN TIGHT I 147 RICE 142 STRONG 949 TOSS	929 BUCK SWEEP 929 WAGGLE REVERSE 134 TRAP 926 COUNTER "X"	STRONG SLOT 128 NAKED STRONG SLOT 942 NAKED BLUE 11 SPRINT PASS 141 WAGGLE PASS
7 - 12	STRONG 949 TOSS 929 BUCK SWEEP 134 TRAP 142	141 WAGGLE KEEPER TIGHT I 147 RICE 144 COUNTER "X" 142 CRISSCROSS	STRONG SLOT 942 NAKED STRONG TWINS 171 UNDEF STRONG SLOT 128 NAKED BLUE 11 SPRINT PASS
13 +	134 TRAP 141 WAGGLE REVERSE STRONG 949 TOSS 928 CRISS CROSS	141 WAGGLE KEEPER	STRONG SLOT 128 NAKED STRONG TWINS 171 UNDEF BLUE 11 SPRINT PASS STRONG SLOT 942 NAKED

3rd Down

Dist	Run	3rd Down	Pass
1 - 3	TIGHT I 147 RICE 5 WEDGE SLOT 137 BELLY RICE (RUN) SLOT 923 DIVE	142 141 WAGGLE KEEPER 141 BUCK SWEEP 929 BUCK SWEEP	STRONG SLOT 942 N/ STRONG SLOT 128 N/ BLUE 11 SPRINT PAS:
4 - 6	STRONG 949 TOSS SLOT 137 BELLY RICE (RUN) 141 BUCK SWEEP TIGHT I 147 RICE	141 WAGGLE REVERSE 929 WAGGLE REVERSE 141 WAGGLE KEEPER	STRONG SLOT 942 N/ STRONG SLOT 128 N/ STRONG TWINS 171 L BLUE 11 SPRINT PAS:
7 - 10	141 WAGGLE REVERSE 141 WAGGLE KEEPER 142 CRISS CROSS 929 WAGGLE REVERSE	928 CRISS CROSS 134 TRAP 144 COUNTER "X"	STRONG SLOT 942 N/ SLOT 171 CURL TRAIL STRONG SLOT 128 N/ 141 WAGGLE PASS
11 +	142 CRISS CROSS 929 WAGGLE REVERSE 141 WAGGLE KEEPER 928 CRISS CROSS	141 WAGGLE REVERSE 134 TRAP "X" STRONG 949 TOSS	SLOT 171 CURL TRAIL STRONG TWINS 171 L STRONG SLOT 942 N/ STRONG SLOT 128 N/

| | Long yardage Plays | Fourth Down Plays | Scripted Plays 1. 2. 3. 4. 5. 6. 7. 8. 9. 10. 11. 12. 13. 14. | Gadget Plays | 2 Minute Plays |
| | Short Yardage Plays | Extra Point Plays | | | Pass Plays |

	Run Plays	2nd DOWN	Pass Plays		Run Plays	3rd DOWN	Pass Plays
1-3				1-3			
4-6				4-6			
7-12				7-12			
13+				13+			

Figure 10-2

Depth Charts

Make sure you make a list of players for offense, defense and special teams. The best thing you can do is make a depth chart for every position including special teams. If a player needs to come out of the game, the next player on the list needs to know he is the sub before the game starts. This will save you a lot of aggravation on the sideline. Every player needs to know his position on the depth chart.

Have all your wholesale changes ready ahead of time. We like to use the term "A" team and "B" team instead of 1st or 2nd string. You could also use colors like white and blue teams.

Make sure you have a complete first and second string for every phase of the game, including special teams. Each player must know what team he is on before the game. If you call out "blue kicking team" then those 11 players should run out on the field and be lined up correctly. Diagrams 10-3 and 10-4 are examples of blank depth charts.

LEFT END	LEFT TACKLE	NOSEGUARD	RIGHT TACKLE	RIGHT END
1	1	1	1	1
2	2	2	2	2
3	3	3	3	3

	LINEBACKER		LINEBACKER	
	1		1	
	2		2	
	3		3	

CORNER				CORNER
1				1
2				2
3				3

	SAFETY		SAFETY	
	1		1	
	2		2	
	3		3	

Figure 10-3. Blank depth chart 52 defense

LEFT GUARD	CENTER	RIGHT GUARD
1	1	1
2	2	2
3	3	3

	LEFT TACKLE	RIGHT TACKLE	
	1	1	
	2	2	
	3	3	

WIDE RECEIVER		TIGHT END
1		1
2	QUARTERBACK	2
3	1	3
	2	
	3	

LEFT HALFBACK	FULLBACK	RIGHT HALFBACK
1	1	1
2	2	2
3	3	3

Figure 10-4. Offensive depth chart

Game Day

One thing that will separate most teams is how organized they are on game day. If you've done all your pregame preparation, then you are halfway there.

Decorum

Make sure every player and coach knows how you expect him to act throughout the day. They need to know that you will never accept them mouthing off to anyone including referees or other players. The best policy is to not allow them to say anything to the opponent no matter what they say or do to him.

You will never win an argument with a referee! Referees rarely reverse their calls. At the youth level the officials are not always very experienced. There is nothing you can do about it so use it to your advantage. Be seen as the responsible coach. Before the game starts let him know that you may want to know what a player did when he makes a call. Make it clear to him that you only want this information so you can teach the players.

Coaching Responsibility

Each coach should have scout responsibilities during the game. Every coach should be looking at a different aspect of the game on every play. For instance, if your team is on offense, there should be a coach responsible to watch the defensive line to scout their alignments and tendencies. Another coach would watch their backers and so on. You also want a coach watching your own lineman to see if they are executing their assignments. No one man

can see everything. Make sure every coach is watching his keys. Make the adjustments throughout the game. Use your play script and charts.

Chart your plays during the game. Have a coach chart every play that is called. He should also be charting the results of the play. The following chart is an example of a blank play chart for games. You can copy it and use it or simply create your own.

Motivation

Players need to get fired up before games. Although motivational techniques will vary, you should always keep it positive. Enthusiasm is contagious—be enthusiastic. If you display positive energy and intensity your players will feel that energy and it will transfer to them. Positive leadership is a must.

Motivation should not only be left to the coaches. The players should be encouraged to motivate each other. They should always acknowledge the positive things they see their teammates do during a game. If someone makes a great block, every player that saw it should make a big deal of it. Encourage them to give each other hugs or high-fives. There is nothing wrong with everyone sharing their emotions, especially when they are positive emotions.

Again, the emphasis should be on the positive. This doesn't mean that you shouldn't point out the negatives; you need to turn the negative into a positive. Point out what the player did wrong and then tell him how confident you are that he will turn the same situation around in his favor the next time it occurs.

DOWN AND DISTANCE	YARDLINE	PLAY CALLED	PLAYER	RESULTS & NOTES

Figure 10-5. Play chart

CHAPTER 11

Scouting Report

Offensive Team

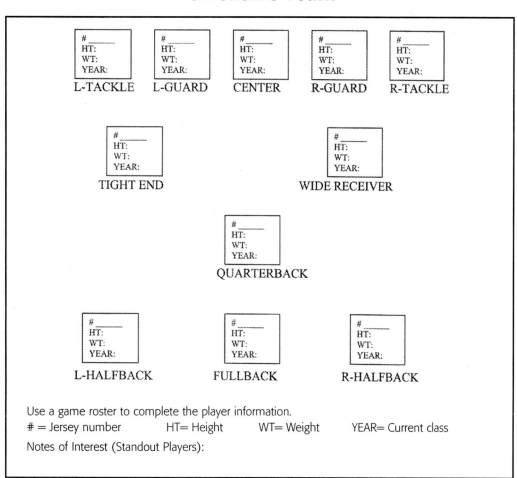

Use a game roster to complete the player information.

\# = Jersey number   HT= Height   WT= Weight   YEAR= Current class

Notes of Interest (Standout Players):

Defensive Team

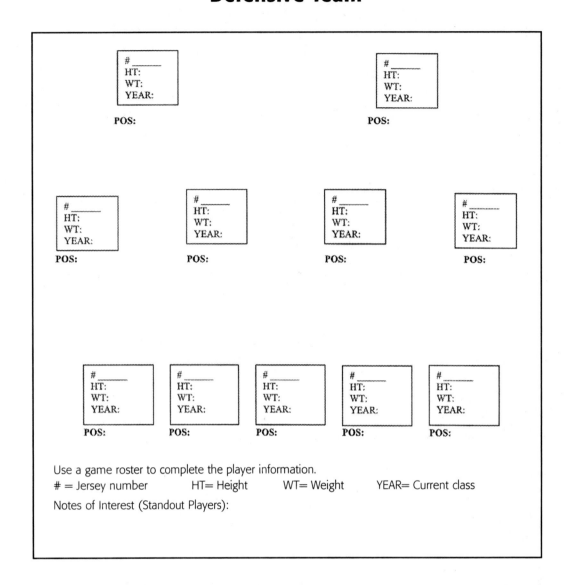

Use a game roster to complete the player information.

\# = Jersey number   HT= Height   WT= Weight   YEAR= Current class

Notes of Interest (Standout Players):

Pregame Scratch Sheet Warm-up Plays

O O □ O O   O O □ O O

O O □ O O   O O □ O O

O O □ O O   O O □ O O

O O □ O O   O O □ O O

O O □ O O   O O □ O O

Diagram plays run in pregame warm-ups.

Kickoff

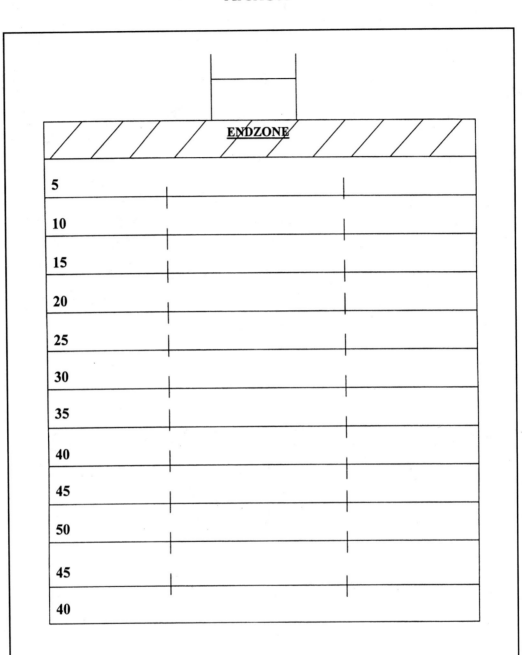

Diagram every kickoff. Use a dotted line to show the path of the ball. Make note of the height of the kick. Number the players on the kickoff team at their start position. Chart the path of every player, where possible.

Receiving

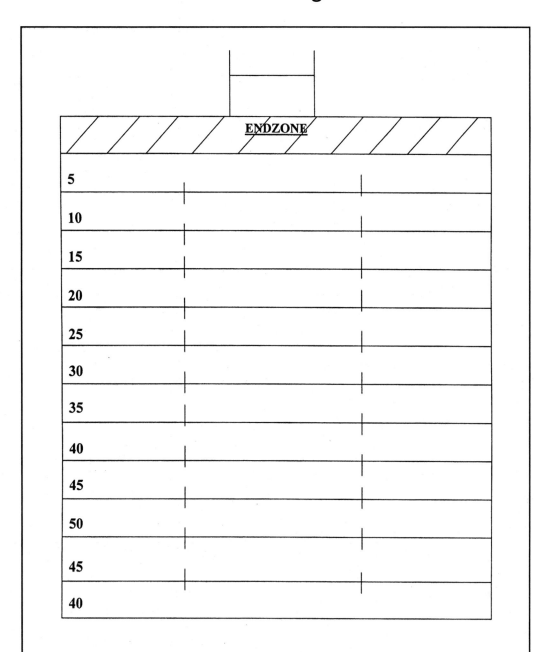

Diagram every kickoff. Use a dotted line to show the path of the ball. Make note of the height of the kick. Mark the position of each player on the receiving team. Chart the path of every player where possible. Diagram the receiving team's blocking schemes. Circle standout return men. Chart any tendencies.

Scout Sheet Offense

TEAM_____   DATE_____

○ ○ ☐ ○ ○

Series #_____ Play #_____
Down_____
Distance_____
Yardline_____
Result of play Gain/Loss_____

○ ○ ☐ ○ ○

Series #_____ Play #_____
Down_____
Distance_____
Yardline_____
Result of play Gain/Loss_____

○ ○ ☐ ○ ○

Series #_____ Play #_____
Down_____
Distance_____
Yardline_____
Result of play Gain/Loss_____

○ ○ ☐ ○ ○

Series #_____ Play #_____
Down_____
Distance_____
Yardline_____
Result of play Gain/Loss_____

○ ○ ☐ ○ ○

Series #_____ Play #_____
Down_____
Distance_____
Yardline_____
Result of play Gain/Loss_____

Defensive Scout Sheet

Diagram all defensive alignments. Make new chart for every different formation defense aligns.

○ ○ □ ○ ○

○ ○ □ ○ ○

Defensive Tendencies: Alignment, base assignment, stunt tendencies

Base defense:

Base coverage and DB tendencies:

Linebacker tendencies:

Defensive end tendencies:

Interior line tendencies:

Punt Team

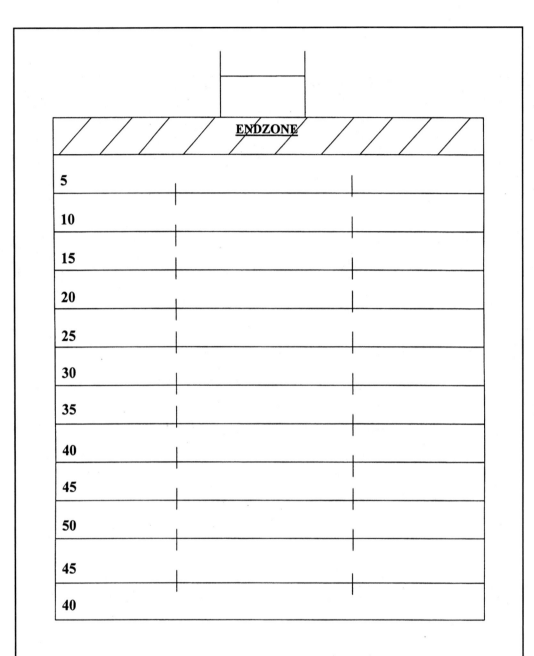

Diagram every punt. Use a dotted line to show the path of the ball. Make note of the height of the kick. Number the players on the punt team and show their alignment. Chart the path of every player, where possible. Diagram all fake punts.

Punt Return

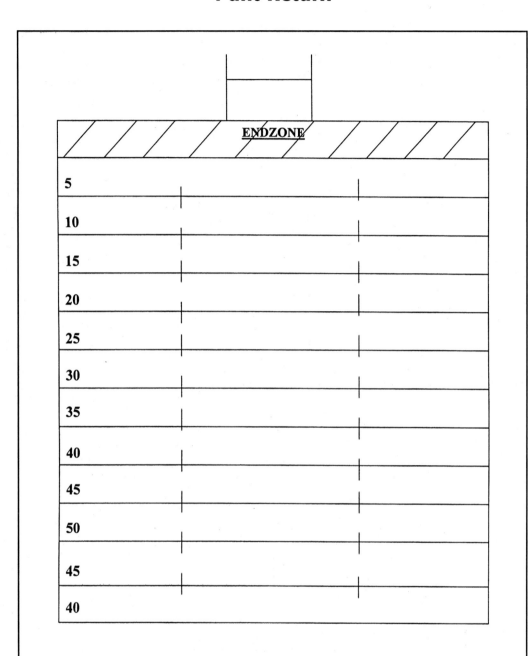

ENDZONE

5
10
15
20
25
30
35
40
45
50
45
40

Diagram every punt. Use a dotted line to show the path of the ball. Make note of the height of the kick. Mark the position of each player on the receiving team. Chart the path of every player where possible. Diagram the receiving team's blocking schemes. Circle standout return men. Chart any tendencies.

Offensive Scratch Sheet (Running Plays)

O O □ O O   O O □ O O

O O □ O O   O O □ O O

O O □ O O   O O □ O O

O O □ O O   O O □ O O

O O □ O O   O O □ O O

Offensive Scratch Sheet (Passing Plays)

○ ○ □ ○ ○

_____

○ ○ □ ○ ○

_____

○ ○ □ ○ ○

_____

○ ○ □ ○ ○

Tendency Chart (Running Plays)

Play frequency   Five most frequently used running plays

O O □ O O

Total # times used____
down____distance____   down____distance____
down____distance____   down____distance____
down____distance____   down____distance____
down____distance____   down____distance____
Does this play set up: counter, boot or reverse?

NOTES:

O O □ O O

Total # times used____
down____distance____   down____distance____
down____distance____   down____distance____
down____distance____   down____distance____
down____distance____   down____distance____
Does this play set up: counter, boot or reverse?

NOTES:

O O □ O O

Total # times used____
down____distance____   down____distance____
down____distance____   down____distance____
down____distance____   down____distance____
down____distance____   down____distance____
Does this play set up: counter, boot or reverse?

NOTES:

O O □ O O

Total # times used____
down____distance____   down____distance____
down____distance____   down____distance____
down____distance____   down____distance____
down____distance____   down____distance____
Does this play set up: counter, boot or reverse?

NOTES:

O O □ O O

Total # times used____
down____distance____   down____distance____
down____distance____   down____distance____
down____distance____   down____distance____
down____distance____   down____distance____
Does this play set up: counter, boot or reverse?

NOTES:

Note: Use jersey numbers for all skill position players when diagramming plays.

Tendency Chart (Passing Plays)

Play frequency   Five most frequently used running plays

○ ○ □ ○ ○

Total # times used____
Down_____ Distance_____
Down_____ Distance_____
Down_____ Distance_____
Down_____ Distance_____
NOTES:

○ ○ □ ○ ○

Total # times used____
Down_____ Distance_____
Down_____ Distance_____
Down_____ Distance_____
Down_____ Distance_____
NOTES:

○ ○ □ ○ ○

Total # times used____
Down_____ Distance_____
Down_____ Distance_____
Down_____ Distance_____
Down_____ Distance_____
NOTES:

○ ○ □ ○ ○

Total # times used____
Down_____ Distance_____
Down_____ Distance_____
Down_____ Distance_____
Down_____ Distance_____
NOTES:

○ ○ □ ○ ○

Total # times used____
Down_____ Distance_____
Down_____ Distance_____
Down_____ Distance_____
Down_____ Distance_____
NOTES:

Note: Use jersey numbers for all skill position players when diagramming plays.

Tendency Chart (Short Yardage Plays)

Top two short yardage plays–three yards or less to go for the first down

O O □ O O

Total # times used____
Down_____ Distance_____
Down_____ Distance_____
Down_____ Distance_____
Down_____ Distance_____
NOTES:

O O □ O O

Total # times used____
Down_____ Distance_____
Down_____ Distance_____
Down_____ Distance_____
Down_____ Distance_____
NOTES:

Tendency Chart (Long Yardage Plays)

Top two long yardage plays – second down and more than 12 yards, or third and more than eight yards to go for the first down

O O □ O O

Total # times used____
Down_____ Distance_____
Down_____ Distance_____
Down_____ Distance_____
Down_____ Distance_____
NOTES:

O O □ O O

Total # times used____
Down_____ Distance_____
Down_____ Distance_____
Down_____ Distance_____
Down_____ Distance_____
NOTES:

Note: Use jersey numbers for all skill position players when diagramming plays.

Tendency Chart (Fourth Down Plays)

○ ○ □ ○ ○

Down_____ Distance_____ Yardline_____
Down_____ Distance_____ Yardline_____

NOTES:

○ ○ □ ○ ○

Down_____ Distance_____ Yardline_____
Down_____ Distance_____ Yardline_____

NOTES:

Tendency Chart (Extra Point Plays/Alignment)

○ ○ □ ○ ○

Total # times used_____
NOTES:

○ ○ □ ○ ○

Total # times used_____
NOTES:

Note: Use jersey numbers for all skill position players when diagramming plays.

ABOUT THE AUTHOR

Mike Aruanno is the head football coach at Caravel Academy High School in Bear, Delaware. He previously worked as an assistant coach at Caravel Academy and at Washington Township High School in Sewell, New Jersey.

Aruanno spent the majority of the last 20 years coaching youth football in his community. As a head coach at the youth level, Aruanno amassed a record of 95-9 and led his teams to six championship games in eight seasons. He has never lost more than one regular season game in his entire career as a head coach.

Aruanno currently resides in Middletown, Delaware, with his wife, Susan, and his son, Michael Jr. His daughter, Shari, his son-in-law, Kevin, and his granddaughter, Taylor, reside in Hawaii, where Shari is serving in the Navy.